P9-BIM-033

THE

FRENCH COOK.

BY

LOUIS EUSTACHE UDE,

CI-DEVANT COOK TO LOUIS XVI. AND THE EARL OF SEFTON,

AND STEWARD TO HIS LATE

ROYAL HIGHNESS THE DUKE OF YORK.

Arco Publishing Company, Inc.
New York

Published 1978 by Arco Publishing Company, Inc.
219 Park Avenue South, New York, N.Y. 10003

Introduction © 1978 by Arco Publishing Company, Inc.

Library of Congress Cataloging in Publication Data

Ude, Louis Eustache.
  The French cook.

  Includes index.
  Photoreprint of the 1828 ed. published by Carey, Lea
and Carey, Philadelphia; with new introd.
  1. Cookery, French. I. Title.
TX719.U3   1978   641.5'944   77-22145
ISBN 0-668-04381-4

Printed in the United States of America

ADVERTISEMENT.

It was intended that the present edition of this work should have been dedicated to his late Royal Highness the Duke of York,—permission to this effect having been given to the Author, who was then in the household of that illustrious and lamented Prince. The public character of his late Royal Highness is best attested by his public services, and the sense entertained of his loss by the nation at large. But it may be permitted to those whom circumstances placed about his person to give their humble testimony to the private qualities of that illustrious individual, to the condescending kindness by which he made himself loved and honoured, to the consideration for the interests and feelings of all, and the unfailing benevolence and generosity of his nature in the whole circle of those dependent on his will. No man in extending assistance more laid aside the consideration of the distance at which his rank placed him. In his Royal Highness the unprotected and unfortunate have lost a great protector; and those who had the good fortune to be placed in his service, a master, whom they remember with equal respect, admiration and gratitude.

PREFACE.

WERE the number of works published on a given subject conclusive to prove the superfluity of any addition, this volume would not have been again offered to the world. The present author would not have increased the existing mass of works on his science, had it not appeared to him that no preceding one resembled his own in design, and that even the subjects to which former writers have directed their attention, have not, in their hands, been treated with any thing of the *tact* which, in Cookery, perhaps more than in any other art, is requisite.

It is the intent of this work to convey, by rules, deduced from a combination of theoretical science and practical experience, a knowledge of the science of FRENCH COOKERY; a science which claims the name as distinguished from the system of other nations. To say that it stands apart from these in elegance, delicacy, and refinement; in uniting, with taste and judgment, ingredients which lose their value when used without discriminating intermixture; by the exercise of which, the highest gratification is conveyed to the palate of which the organ is susceptible; in every thing, in short, which distinguishes a science, founded on principle, and reduced to a system, from a mere mechanical art.

Of the qualifications which the Author has brought to his task, it becomes him to say little; but it may be presumed, that upwards of forty years practice and assiduous application to the study of his profession, have gone far to give him a thorough knowledge of it, and it will probably be conceded that to conquer all the difficulties attached to it, is not a trifling task. The patronage and encouragement he has received in this country, at the hands of one of the best masters that man ever served, co-operating with experience, enabled him to succeed in all his undertakings. His gratitude can cease only with his existence.

The Author is convinced of his accuracy when he says, that Cookery is an art appreciated by only a very few individuals, an art which requires, in addition to a most diligent and studious application, no small share of intellect, and the strictest sobriety and punctuality: without the latter, the very best Cook is unavoidably deficient in the delicacies of his profession: there are cooks, and cooks, as there are painters, and painters: the difficulty lies in finding the perfect one; nor does the Author fear the charge of extravagance when affirming that, to an individual ranking in the higher circles, the acquisition of a *good* cook ought to be a subject of as much satisfaction as the possession of any other of the means by which gratification is conveyed to the tasteful or luxurious.

In England the few assistants allowed to a head cook, and the number of dishes he has to prepare, often deprive him of an opportunity of displaying his abilities; and after many years of the utmost exertion to bring his art to perfection, he has the mortification of ranking no higher than an humble domestic.

As several noblemen and ladies of distinction have remarked that his book contained too many French terms, the Author has endeavoured in this edition to meet their wishes (as their goodness and liberality towards him imperatively demand) by giving translations of such names as were translatable. But he must still observe, as he did in the preceding editions, that Cookery, like any other art, which is of foreign origin, its nomenclature is, like theirs, in the language of the people who first cultivated it; added to which, different languages do not often possess synonymous terms, and hence the impossibility of transferring, by an equivalent, certain terms into English, so as to convey any intelligible meaning. In cases when these circumstances operate, French terms have been unavoidably retained; but care has been taken to give, at the bottom of the respective pages where the expressions occur, such elucidations as may be fully explanatory of their import to the practitioner.

As the manner of dressing *entrées* is explained hereafter, it may be proper for the author to observe here, that the word *entrée* has no equivalent in English. It is the name of any dish of meat, fowl, game, or fish, dressed and cooked for the first course; all vegetable dishes, jellies, pastries, salad, prawns, lobsters, and in general every thing that appears in the second course, except the roasts, are termed *entremets*.

The following is an explanatory translation of such words as are of most constant occurrence:—

French.					English.
Potages,	-	-	-	-	Soups.
Entrées,	-	-	-	-	Made dishes. 1st course.
Entremets,	-	-	-	Made dishes. 2d course.
Jelées,	-	-	-	-	Jellies and Fromage,
Marquez,	-	-	-	-	Mark, put or prepare.
Masqué,*	-	-	-	-	Covered with, &c.
Sauté,†	-	-	-	-	Fry lightly on the stove.
Reduire,	-	-	-	-	To reduce, or boil down.
Relevé,	-	-	-	-	Remove.

Most of the dishes retain their original name. In a former edition, the articles in season were enumerated; but the author has found it useless in the present one, because, when in London, the markets and shop-keepers are always provided according to the season; the price of the various articles is always the thermometer to be consulted: when in the country, the Cook must use in preference the produce of the farm and gardens. The futile search after novelty in Cookery is a running after the philosopher's stone. Every thing is equally good when done in perfection.

* *Masqué* signifies covered. The meaning of this dish is, that you should cover all the part specified with sauce; when you meet with this word, it is always accompanied with thick sauce; *masqué* signifies *covéré* with the sauce.

† *Sauté* is another term of art; *fried* is not the proper expression, because *sauté* means, as soon as the contents of the *sauté*-pan are affected by the great heat, you should with great celerity turn over the fillets, of whatever kind. The beauty of a *sauté* is the perfection of its nicety, and you can never attain that point if you are not extremely particular; you should touch every fillet lightly with your finger; if you find it firm and give way a little, it is done properly. A shade too hard or too soft in the fillet will at once condemn it.

The sweet dishes which conclude this work, will no more bear translating than *"plum-pudding"* will in Paris; which bears the same name there that it does in London: so *Suédoise*, *Charlotte* of apples, or *Charlotte* of apricot, rice, and apples, *Chartreuse* of fruits, apple *fritures* glazed, *soufflées*, *miroton* of apples, *croquettes* of rice, *farcie d'abricots*, *croquettes* of potatoe, *panequet*, are at once French and English: however, no difficulty can result from a dish bearing a foreign name, as the way of making it is explained in English, and the learner will be easily familiarized with their names. The various articles will be treated of in their respective classes as usual; of which there are seven, viz. *soups*, *fish*, removes of either fishes and soups; *entrées*, *entremets*, roasts for the second course; in the first course there are always removes; then the removes of roasts, called *soufflées*, or *biscuits à la crême*, or *fondus*, &c. &c. It is necessary to remember all these observations, as they teach the learner to serve with order. By taking a dish from the different classes, a dinner may be composed without further assistance than is afforded by this book. Suppose you have eight persons at dinner, you can not send up less than four *entrées*, a *soup*, and a *fish;* you must have two removes, viz. for the second course, two dishes of roast, next four *entremets;* and if you think proper, two removes of the roast, or one roast, and a dish opposite that, which will answer the remove, and, at the same time, fill the place and save trouble and expense. Multiplicity of dishes does not constitute a good dinner; a judicious selection of them is always preferred by the man of taste.

Make the bill of fare, by choosing out of each

chapter whatever you may want, namely: *soup* (under the head *soup*); *fish* (under the head *fish*), from the corresponding title in the article under *entrée*, *entremets*.

From this it may be inferred that a single article is to be taken out. For the second course you should act on the same principle, the roasts must likewise not bear any resemblance to each other. In summertime you will select two dishes from among the vegetables, one from among the jellies, and one out of the chapter of pastry; as for instance:

Bill of Fare for a Dinner of Four Entrées.

Soupe printannière, or spring soup.
Crimp cod and oyster sauce.

Two Removes.

Fowl à la Montmorenci, garnished with a ragout à l'Allemande.
Ham glazed with *Espagnole*, sauce under it.

Four Entrées.

Fricassée of chicken mushrooms.
Lamb chops sauté, with asparagus, peas, &c.
Fillets of fat chicken, *sauté au suprême.*
Petits pâtés of fillet of fowl à la béchamelle.

Second Course.

Fowls roasted, garnished with water cresses.
Six quails.

Four Entremets.

Asparagus with plain butter.
Orange jellies in *mosaiques.*
Cauliflower with *velouté* sauce.
Petit gateaux à la Manon.

Two Removes of the Roast.

Soufflée with lemon-peel.
Ramequin à la Sefton.

From the above statement it will be easy to make
a bill of fare of four, six, eight, twelve, or sixteen
entrées, and the other courses in proportion. The
author has inserted a bill of fare for a dinner of twenty *entrées.* The second course is in the same proportion, as it requires the same number of dishes
for the second that have been served in the first.
Observe, that whenever there are more than four
entrées, symmetry must always be attended to: the
two flanks for a dinner of six *entrées* must be parallel,
that is to say, if you place *petits pâtés* on one side,
you must have *croquettes* on the other; if you have
a *vol au vent* on one side, you must place a *pâté
chaud* opposite, and so on; a judicious arrangement
of dishes gives additional merit to a dinner, and the
entrées of any appearance should be always parallel,
it adds wonderfully to the effect.

The second course requires also a different arrangement when you have more than four *entrées.* At
the two flanks you must have two dishes of vegetables, if approved of; and at the four corners, a jelly,
a pastry, a lobster salad, and a cream jelly, &c.; if
you have a different instruction, you may put two

sweets in the flanks, two vegetables at each opposite corner, and an Italian salad, and a dish of prawns at the two other corners.

Bill of Fare of Six Entrées.

Dinner for Twelve or Fourteen Persons.

Two Potages.

Good woman's soup, *dite flamande*, white and thick.
Soup *à la bauveau*, brown and clear.

Two Fishes.

Turbot, with lobster sauce.
Slices of crimped salmon boiled, with caper sauce over it.

Two Removes.

Turkey *à la perigueux*, with a *purée* of chesnut under it.
A Westmorland ham glazed, and garnished with green.

Six Entrées.

Cutlets of mutton braized, with *soub se* sauce.
Salmi of young partridges *à l' Espagnole*.
Vol au vent of salt fish *à la maître d'hôtel.*
Casserole of rice, with a *purée* of game.
Sauté of fillets of fowl *à la Lucullus*, with truffles.
Fillets of young rabbits *à la orlies*, white *poivrade* sauce.

Second Course.

Two Roasts.

Three partridges roasted.
Three woodcocks.

Six Entremets.

Spinach with *consommé*, garnished with fried bread.
Whole truffles *au vin de champagne.* *
Lobster salad *à l'Italienne.*
Jelly of *marasquino.*
Buisson of *gâteau à la Polonoise.*†.
Charlotte of apples with apricot.

Two Removes of the Roasts.

Biscuit à la cream.
Fondus.

Dinner for Sixteen or Twenty Persons.

Two Potages.

Soup *à la Reine.*
Brunoise, clear.

Two Fishes.

Turbot, garnished with fried smelts, lobster sauce.
Slices of salmon, with *Genévoise* sauce.

Four Removes.

Fowls *à la Condé, ragoût à l'Allemande.* Westphalia ham glazed, and *Espagnole* under it.	Remove the soup.
A rump of beef braised, glazed, and garnished with green cabbages. A loin of veal roasted *à la béchamelle.*	Remove the fish.

* Whole truffles are cooked or braised with the cham, but as they are drained before they come to table, they should not be put with cham, but braised with champagne.

† Buisson means a dish of pastry dressed thus:

Eight Entrées.

Fillets of young partridges *à la Lucullus*, with truffles.

Small *timballe* with a *salpicon.* Twelve, at least, will be required to fill the dish.

Croquettes of fowls *au velouté.*

Small fillets of fowl *à la Pompadour.*

Three small partridges *à la Barbarie*, with truffles.

Two small chickens *poëlé*, with tarragon sauce.

Cutlets of pork *à la mirapoix*, brown sharp sauce, or *sauce Robert.*

Cutlets of mutton *à l'Italienne.*

Second Course.

Four Roasts.

Eight snipes.

A hare roasted.

Two wild ducks.

A capon, garnished with cresses.

Eight Entremets.

Salsafis à la sauce blanche.

Macaroni *à l'Italienne.*

Poached eggs, with gravy of veal clarified.

Brocoli *au velouté.*

Jelly *de noyau rouge.*

Italian cheese *à l'orange.**

Gateaux à la Madeleine farcie, de crême à la vanille.

Little *bouchées*, garnished with marmalade.

---

* *Fromage à l'Italienne, à la fleur d'orange.*

Four Removes of the Roasts.

Soufflé à l'essence de citron.
Ramequin, with parmesan cheese.
Biscuit *à la* cream.
Petits choux pralinier.

Dinner for Twenty or Twenty-four Persons.

Four Potages.

Soup of rabbits *à la Reine.*
Soup Julienne.
Soup *à la Carmélite.*
Soup *à la Clermont.*

Four Fishes.

Turbot and lobster sauce.
Pike baked, Dutch sauce.
Three slices of crimped cod, oyster sauce.
Matelotte of carp.

Four Removes.

Rump of beef glazed *à la flamande.*
Leg of pork, garnished with green.
Boiled turkey, celery sauce.
A fillet of beef *puqui à la sauercroutte.*

Twelve Entrées.

Small *casserolettes* of rice, mince of fowl.
Scollops of fillets of fowls, with truffles.
Turban of fillets of rabbits.
Petits pâtés à la nelle.   Au fumet de gibier.
Cutlets of fillets of partridges.
Chartreuse of palates of beef.

Fillets of soles *à la ravigotte*.
Small cases of sweetbread *à la Vénitenne*.
Grenade of small fillets of fowls *à l'essence*.
Attelets of sweetbread, *Italienne* sauce.
Petits pâtés of oysters *à la* Sefton.
Partridges and cabbages dressed, with Spanish sauce.

Second Course.

Four Roasts.

Two fowls with cresses.
Five woodcocks.
Two ducklings.
Two young rabbits.

Twelve Entremets.

Spinach *à la* cream.
Asparagus with butter.
Cream *au caffé*, white.
Sultane with a *vol au vent*.
Small *lozenges garnies*, of apricot.
Meringues à la Chantilly.
Cauliflower *au velouté*.
Salsifis à l'Espagnole.
Jelly of Madeira.
Fromage Bavarois au chocolate.
Gateau praliné, garnished.
Jelly of *marasquino rose*.

Four Removes.

Two dishes of *fondus*.
One of *talmouse*, or cheese-cake.
One of *choux en biscuit*.

Here the plain Roasted Meat should come in (a leg of mutton or other joint.)

The Author has here given only a specimen of the form and general arrangement of a bill of fare; the selection of the articles rests with the Cook, or the person who orders the dinner. You may serve a good dinner without adhering to the identical dishes which he has selected, or rather mentioned as it were at random. He thinks it would be useless to go beyond sixteen *entrées;* for a multiplicity of dishes is easily made out. He will only observe that with twenty *entrées,* the counter-flanks should exhibit copious *entrées;* and that for the second course there should be introduced what we call *moyens d'entremets,* or ornamental dishes, or *brioches*; or *biscuits,* or *babas,* either in the counter-flanks, or at the top and bottom of the table.

Eight large pieces of ornaments are not exactly wanted with twenty *entrées;* but when you have thirty-two *entrées,* you must put large pieces at the top and bottom, and the two flanks; and four smaller ones in the four counter-flanks.

Whenever a dinner consists of more than eight *entrées,* those huge pieces are indispensable; but it is then impossible for any Cook to dress them without assistants; by himself, he would be able to send up to table nothing but common dishes, to either of the courses.

The second course for the dinner of twenty *entrées,* has not been mentioned, as it is known that there ought to be the same number of dishes as in the first course; there should be also the same number of roasts in the room of removes, or of large *entrées;* two at the top and bottom, two at the flanks, and four at the counter-flanks. If you have assistants enough to make the ornamental pieces, then remove the four roasts of the counter-flanks with *soufflés, biscuit, fondus, &c.;* and put four large pieces at the top and bottom, and on the two flanks.

The Author has added two cold pies, which are likewise served at a large dinner. He likes them to be sent to table with the first course; and to remain there between the two courses. By this means the epicure and dainty eater will always have something before them. They are not at all in the way, but improve the look of the table.

N. B.—The pies may be either of game or poultry.

It only remains to add, that the Author has spared no pains to render this edition worthy of the praises which he gratefully remembers have been bestowed on the preceding one. The encouragement he has met with has added, where nothing was before wanting, to his desire to render this Work as perfect, both in design and execution, as individual knowledge and assiduity could render it.

ADVICE TO COOKS.

THE Author trusts that he will not be accused of vanity, in seeking to enforce good precepts, as well as by giving good examples. Cookery is an art which requires much time, intelligence, and activity, to be acquired in its perfection. Every man is not born with the qualifications necessary to constitute a good Cook. The difficulty of attaining to perfection in the art, will be best demonstrated by offering a few observations on some others. Music, dancing, fencing, painting, and mechanics in general, possess professors under twenty years of age, whereas, in the first line of cooking, pre-eminence never occurs under thirty. We see daily at Concerts, and Academies, young men and women who display the greatest abilities; but in our line, nothing *but the most consummate* experience can elevate a man to the rank of Chief Professor. It must be admitted, that there are few good Cooks, though there are many who advance themselves as such. This disproportion of talent among them is the cause of the little respect in which they are held; if they were *all* provided with the necessary qualities, they would certainly be considered as artists.

What science demands more study than **Cookery?**
You have not only, as in other arts, to satisfy the
general eye, but also the individual taste of the persons who employ you; you have to attend to economy, which every one demands; to suit the taste of
different persons at the same table; to surmount the
difficulty of procuring things which are necessary to
your work; to undergo the want of unanimity among
the servants of the house; and the mortification of
seeing unlimited confidence sometimes reposed in
persons who are unqualified to give orders in the
kitchen; without assuming a consequence, and giving
themselves airs which are almost out of reason, and
which frequently discourage the Cook.

In fact, a thousand particulars, too tedious to detail,
render this employment at once laborious and unhon-
oured. Nevertheless, if you are extremely clean,
if you are very sober, and have, above all, a great
deal of activity and intelligence, you will succeed one
day or other, in acquiring that confidence which these
qualities always inspire. You have not the power
which other artists and mechanics have, of putting
off for another day what can not be done in this; the
hour imperiously commands, and the work must be
done at the appointed time. Be ever careful then to
have all things ready for your work by the time it is
required, and proceed without noise or confusion.

If you possess a thorough knowledge of your profession, or enjoy the entire confidence of your employer, do not be so inconsiderately proud of it, as to
treat any one with disdain, a practice too common
among persons in place. Do not take any other advantage of your superiority, than to be serviceable to
the utmost of your power; although you ought not to

be regarded merely as a servant, yet forget not that you have still a duty to fulfil; you are obliged to serve at the precise hour, to anticipate all that can give pleasure to your employer; to have every thing ready which he has ordered, and what he frequently will forget to order; and to watch strictly over those in your department.

If you confide any thing to persons under your control, be careful always to have it done under your own eye; that you may be able to answer for the fault, if there is any. It often happens that the company who dine together, have not the same taste: try as much as possible to furnish them with what they like; and, above all, never object to change any dish which is not approved of. Were you even the best Cook in the world, if you are obstinate in pursuing your old routine, without seeking to please those who employ you, you will merely exist, without acquiring either consideration, reputation, or fortune.

Great cleanliness is requisite in the utensils you make use of: entrust to no one but yourself the examination of the copper utensils of the kitchen, which are very dangerous. Every time you use a stew-pan or other utensil, see that it has been well scoured and cleaned. The scullery-maids scour the outside of their coppers, and scarcely ever give themselves the trouble to clean the inside; from which circumstance it will happen that the taste will be entirely spoiled, and the persons who eat what has been cooked in dirty vessels, are often exposed to colics and other maladies, without knowing the cause of them. It is on a good first broth, and good sauce that you must depend for good Cookery; if you have entrusted this part to persons who are negligent, and if your broth has not been well skimmed, you can make but indifferent work; the broth is never clear, and when you are obliged to clarify it, it loses its goodness and savour. The Author elsewhere remarked, that any thing clarified requires high seasoning, and consequently is not so healthy. A stock-pot well managed, saves a great deal of trouble, for it would be ridiculous in a small dinner to make several broths. When you have put into the stock-pot the articles and ingredients as directed in the Chapter on that subject, the same broth will serve you to make the soup, and white or brown sauce, &c. Economy should be the order of the day, seeing the dearness of every thing used in the kitchen. You should be very careful to take off the fat, and skim the soups and sauces; it is an operation which must be repeated again and again: the smallest drop of fat or grease is insufferable; it characterises bad cookery, and a Cook without method. The different classes of cookery, viz. the soup, the *entrées*, the fish, the *entremets*, the roasts, the jellies, the decorated *entremets*, the pastry, &c. all require the greatest attention. The theory of the kitchen appears trifling; but its practice is extensive: many persons talk of it, yet know nothing of it beyond a mutton-chop or a beef-steak.

Cooks in this country have not the opportunity of instructing their pupils that we have in France, except at the Royal Palace, where every thing is, and must be, done in perfection, as neither hands nor expense are objects of consideration. The chief Cook should be particular in instructing his apprentices in all the branches before-mentioned; and that they may be certain of teaching them properly, not the slightest particularity of the art must be omitted. The difficulties to be conquered are a national prejudice which exists against French Cookery; and the circumstance of a young man coming to this employment from school, with his taste settled, and remaining a long time in a kitchen, before he will attempt to taste any thing that he has not been accustomed to; if he does not like Cookery himself, he never can be a good Cook. Cookery can not be done like pharmacy; the Pharmacist is obliged to weigh every ingredient that he employs, as he does not like to taste it; the Cook, on the contrary, must taste often, as the reduction increases the flavour. It would be blind work indeed without tasting; the very best soups or *entrées* in which you have omitted to put salt, are entirely without flavour: seasoning is in Cookery what chords are in music; the best instrument, in the hand of the best professor, without its being in tune, is insipid. I shall recommend particularly to a cook, to bestow great attention to the sauces, which are the soul of Cookery. One great difficulty in cooking is the names of the dishes; Cooks seldom agree upon this point: some names owe their origin either to the Cook who invented them, or to the first Epicure who gives them a reputation. Cookery possesses few innovators. * The Author has himself invented several dishes, but has been shy in giving them his name, from a fear of being accused of vanity. He confesses there are some ridiculous names; for instance, *soup au clair de lune, soup à la jambe de bois, la poularde en bas de soie, les pets*

* In this edition the Author has given his name to several dishes which have originated in himself. He has been induced to do this from the marked approbation with which those dishes have been received at table, and from the circumstance of their being almost universally recognised by the titles thus given.

de nonne, &c. &c. with many others equally ludicrous.

As Cookery originated in France, it is not astonishing to find most of the names of French extraction—*soup à la Reine, à la Condé, à la bonne Femme,* &c. *entrées à la Richelieu, à la Villeroi, à la Dauphine, à la du Barri.* Why should we not see in this book the names of those true Epicures who have honoured good Cookery by their approbation, and have by their good taste and liberality elevated it to a great superiority in this country, over what it is now in France? The Author ventures to affirm, that Cookery in England, when well done, is superior to that of any country in the world. *Béchamelle* owes its name to a rich *financier* who was a great Epicure. He is surprised not to find in Cookery the names of those who have given a celebrity to that science, such as *Apicius, Lucullus, Octavius,* and others of a later day, who patronized it under the reign of Louis the Fourteenth. Voltaire exclaims,

" Qu'un Cuisinier est un mortel divin:"

Why should we not be proud of our knowledge in Cookery? It is the soul of festivity at all times, and to all ages. How many marriages have been the consequence of meeting at dinner? How much good fortune has been the result of a good supper? At what moment of our existence are we happier than at table? There hatred and animosity are lulled to sleep, and pleasure alone reigns. It is at table that an amiable lady or gentlemen shines in sallies of wit, where they display the ease and graceful manners with which they perform the honours of the table. Here the Cook, by his skill and attention, anticipates their wishes, in the happiest selection of the

best dishes and decorations: here their wants are sat-
isfied, their minds and bodies invigorated, and themselves qualified for the high delights of love, music,
poetry, dancing, and other pleasures; and is he whose
talents have produced these happy effects, to rank
no higher in the scale of man than a common servant? Yes, if you adopt and attend to the rules that
I have laid down, the self-love of mankind will con-
sent, at last, that Cookery shall rank in the class of
the Sciences, and its Professors deserve the name of
Artists.

The Philosophers of the world are divided into
two classes, the true and the false. Of the latter, is
every dogma which undervalues innocent enjoyment of whatever nature. Many people rail against
attributing much importance to the pleasures of the
table; but it is not observable that these moralists are
more averse than others to gratifications of the palate
when opportunity occurs. It is a poor philosophy
whose object is to decrease the means of pleasure and
enjoyment. And if Cookery is productive of these,
why deny to it the merit which is accorded to every
other invention and science which tends to the same
end?

If you follow my precepts, you will never have
any ill luck. Never be afraid of doing too much
for your employer: the idle very seldom succeed.
Take great care of the company you keep; a bad
companionship is of the worst consequences to a man
cook; it makes him take the habit of going out frequently, and returning home again too late to attend
to his business: these bad principles will be always
highly prejudicial to a Cook, and will prevent him
from attaining the perfection required.

ON COOKERY,

AND ITS IMPUTED ILL EFFECTS ON HEALTH.

MANY persons, but particularly Medical Practitioners, have, from time immemorial, been the declared enemies of Cooks and Cookery. The determination of the latter to keep mankind under their despotic dominion, has engaged them in a perpetual warfare against whatever might oppose their peculiar interests. But the author will dare to affirm that good Cookery, so far from possessing any deleterious tendency, is, on the contrary, highly conducive to the preservation of health, inasmuch as it protects the appetite against the disadvantageous monotony of plain food. He will not, however, pretend to deny, that, like every thing else, it should be used with discretion; but on what enjoyment, or even ordinary function of life, he would ask, is not discretion an indispensable attendant? The mischief then lies only in the abuse. A skilful and well-directed Cookery abounds in chemical preparations, highly salutary to weak stomachs. There exists a salubrity of aliment suited to every age. Infancy, youth, maturity, and old age—each has its peculiarly adapted food, and that not merely applicable to digestive powers in full vigour, but to stomachs feebly organized by nature, or to those debilitated by excess.

He is greatly concerned at being obliged to combat a still more powerful, though amiable enemy to Cookery. The Ladies of England are unfavourably disposed towards our art; yet he finds no difficulty in assigning the cause of it. It is particularly the case with them (and indeed it is so in some measure with our own sex) that they are not introduced to their parents' table till their palates have been completely benumbed by the strict diet observed in the Nursery and Boarding-Schools. Here then are two antagonists to Cookery—the Ladies and the Doctors, whose empire is as extensive as the universe, and who divide the world between them. However, in spite of the envious, the Ladies will still wield the sceptre of pleasure; while the dispensations of the Doctors will be sought for by us only when under the influence of pain.

Nature affords a simple remedy against the abuse of good cheer—ABSTINENCE. If you have eaten too much, doubtless you will feel inconvenienced. In that case, have immediate recourse to some weak tea,* which will speedily liberate your stomach from the superfluities which encumber and oppress it, without leaving those intestinal pains which are rather the result of the medicine than the effect of the disorder. Numbers of persons attribute the gout to the frequent use of dishes dressed in the French way. Many years experience and observation have proved to me, that this disorder has not its origin in good cheer, but in excesses of other kinds. Have we not

* Galen and Hippocrates said, that they left behind them two still greater Doctors than themselves—WATER and ABSTINENCE.

seen, in years past, numberless individuals who have lived entirely on French Cookery, to very advanced ages, without being afflicted with that disorder? and do we not see daily, that the greater number of those who suffer the acute agonies of it, derive it from their predecessors, rather than from their own habits of life? A copious and sustained exercise is the surest preventive. It is true, the gout more frequently attacks the wealthy than the indigent: hence it has been attributed to their way of living; but this is an error. It is exercise only which they need; not an airing on horseback, or in a carriage, but that bodily activity which, occasioning fatigue, would enable them to enjoy the sweets of repose. The Author does not attempt then, as empirics do, to prescribe ineffectually a remedy to *cure* the gout; but he has this advantage over them, that he affords a positive preventive against it; and thus withholds many a sufferer from falling under their dominion. If the Art of Cookery had been held in a little more estimation, there can be no doubt, but that among its professors many might have been found of sufficient information and sufficiently devoted to the interests of the human race, to give prescriptions in Cookery as Doctors give them in medicine. *We* have this advantage, however, over *them,* that our compositions are always *agreeable to the palate,* while theirs are *horribly disgusting.* The Author could therefore recommend a skilfully dressed dish, as in all respects more salubrious than simple fare. He does not mean to deny that a plainly roasted joint, well done, is food of easy digestion; but he peremptorily proscribes all salted and underdone provisions. Pork, in whatever way it may be dressed, is always unwholesome; yet if dressed in the French fashion, the stimulant of a sauce makes it aperient, and it of course is less indigestive than when dressed plainly. Our manner of dressing vegetables is more various and extensive than in England, a circumstance which embraces the double advantage of flattering the palate and being of easier digestion.

The Author would recommend as a certain preventive against disorder, great bodily exercise—as hunting, billiards, tennis, shuttlecock, fencing, &c. for gentlemen; and for ladies, dancing, and such lively exercises as are suited to their sex: walking also, but not the grave and deliberate movements of a magistrate, but an active and accelerated pace, such as may occasion fatigue. Thus you may find health and appetite, which afford the pleasure of self-government, by keeping you from the power of Doctors and Doctors' stuff.

One more remark, and that on the disproportion of talent which exists among Cooks. A person who has never tasted made dishes, sits down for the first time, perhaps, to indifferenly dressed ones: hence arises, at first setting out, an impression, which the Author confesses it is hardly ever possible to overcome. He himself prefers a thousand times plain dishes to a made dish that is badly seasoned, badly trimmed, and, above all, dressed in an uncleanly manner, and served up with a disagreeable appearance. But the wealthy are able to vanquish these disadvantages, by engaging in their service persons properly qualified to be placed in the rank of ARTISTS.

First Course

Plate 1.

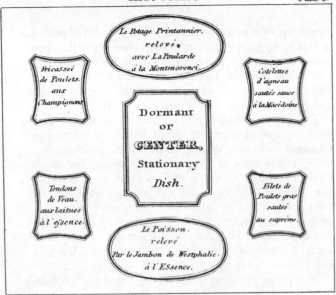

Le Potage Printannier.
relevé*
avec La Poularde
á la Montmorenci.

Fricasseé
de Poulets.
aux
Champignons

Cotelettes
d'agneau
sautés sauce
á la Macédoine.

Dormant
or
CENTER.
Stationary
Dish.

Tendons
de Veau.
aux laitues
á l'essence.

Filets de
Poulets gras
sautés
au suprême.

Le Poisson.
relevé
Par le Jambon de Westphalie.
á l'Essence.

Second Course.

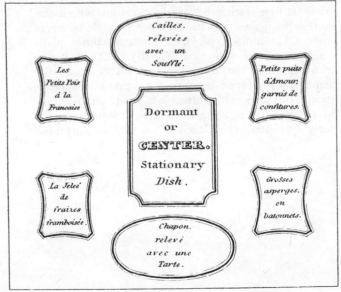

Cailles.
relevées
avec un
Soufflé.

Les
Petits Pois
á la
Francaise

Petits puits
d'Amour:
garnis de
confitures.

Dormant
or
CENTER.
Stationary
Dish.

La Jeleé
de
fraixes
framboisée.

Grosses
asperges.
en
batonnets.

Chapon.
relevé
avec une
Tarte.

* relevé avec means removed by.

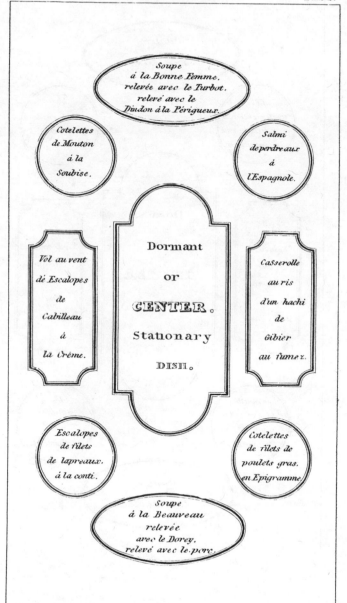

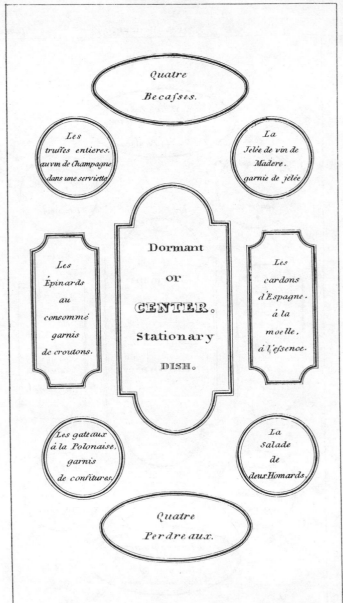

Quatre
Becasses.

Les
truffes entieres.
au vin de Champagne
dans une serviette

La
Jelée de vin de
Madere.
garnie de jelée

Les
Épinards
au
consommé
garnis
de croutons.

Dormant
or
CENTER.
Stationary
DISH.

Les
cardons
d'Espagne.
à la
moelle.
à l'essence.

Les gateaux
à la Polonaise.
garnis
de confitures.

La
Salade
de
deux Homards.

Quatre
Perdreaux.

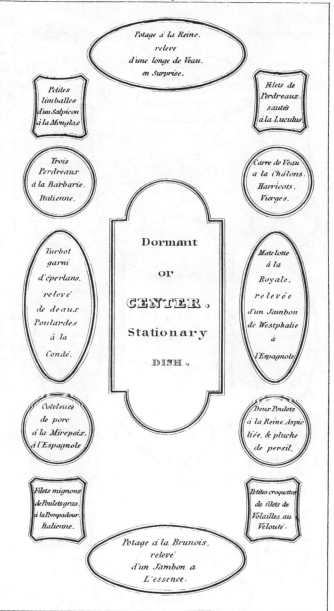

Potage à la Reine.
releve
d'une longe de Veau.
en Surprise.

Petites
limballes
d'un Salpicon
à la Menglas

Filets de
Perdreaux.
sautés
à la Luculus

Trois
Perdreaux
à la Barbarie.
Italienne.

Carre de Veau
a la Châlons.
Harricots.
Vierges.

Turbot
garni
d'éperlans.
relevé
de deux
Poulardes
à la
Condé.

Dormant
or
CENTER,
Stationary
DISH.

Matelotte
à la
Royale.
relevée
d'un Jambon
de Westphalie
à
l'Espagnole

Cotelettes
de porc
à la Mirepoix.
à l'Espagnole

Deux Poulets
à la Reine. Aspic
liée, & pluche
de persil.

Filets mignons
de Poulets gras.
à la Pompadour.
Italienne.

Petites croquettes
de filets de
Volailles au
Velouté.

Potage à la Brunois.
relevé
d'un Jambon a
L'essence.

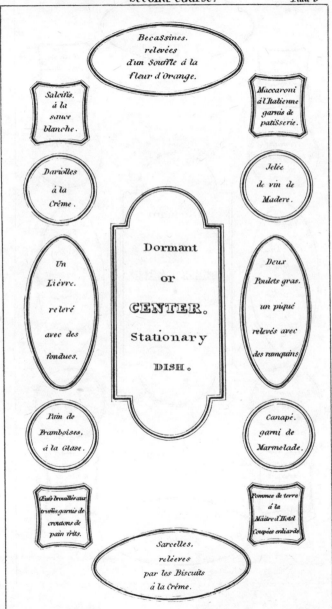

Becassines.
relevées
d'un Soufflé á la
fleur d'Orange.

Salcifis.
á la
sauce
blanche.

Maccaroni
á l'Italienne
garnis de
patisserie.

Dariolles
á la
Crème.

Jelée
de vin de
Madere.

Un
Lièvre.
relevé
avec des
fondues.

Dormant

or

CENTER.

Stationary

DISH.

Deux
Poulets gras.
un piqué
relevés avec
des ranquins

Pain de
Framboises.
à la Glase.

Canapé.
garni de
Marmelade.

Œufs brouillés aux
truffes garnis de
croutons de
pain trits.

Pommes de terre
á la
Maitre d'Hotel
Coupées enliardes

Sarcelles.
reléeves
par les Biscuits
á la Crème.

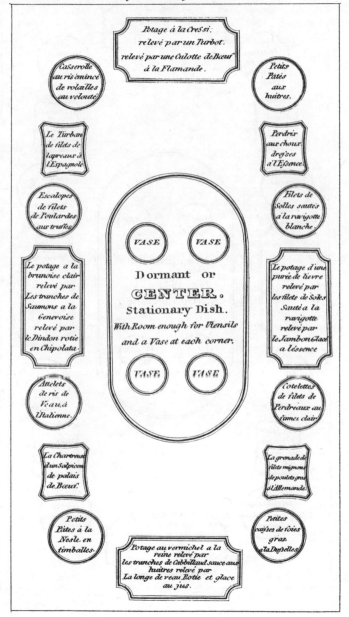

Potage à la Cressi:
relevé par un Turbot.
relevé par une Culotte de Bœuf
à la Flamande.

Casserolle
au ris émincé
de volailles
au velouté

Petits
Pâtés
aux
huîtres.

Le Turban
de filets de
lapreaux à
l'Espagnole

Perdrix
aux chour
dressées
à l'Essence

Escalopes
de filets
de Poulardes
aux truffes

Filets de
Solles sautés
à la ravigotte
blanche

VASE   VASE

Dormant or
CENTER.
Stationary Dish.
With Room enough for Utensils
and a Vase at each corner.

VASE   VASE

Le potage a la
brunoise clair
relevé par
Les tranches de
Saumons a la
Genevoise
relevé par
le Dindon rotie
en Chipolata.

Le potage d'une
purée de lievre
relevé par
les filets de Soles
Sauté a la
ravigotte
relevé par
le Jambon Glacé
a l'essence

Attelets
de ris de
Veau, à
l'Italienne.

Cotelettes
de filets de
Perdreaux au
fumez clair

La Chartreuse
d'un Salpicon
de palais
de Bœuf.

La grenade de
filets mignons
de poulats gras
à l'Allemande.

Petits
Pâtes à la
Nesle. en
timballes.

Petites
caisses de foies
gras.
à la Dusselles.

Potage au vermichel a la
reine relevé par
les tranches de Cabbillaud sauce aux
huîtres relevé par
La longe de veau Rotie et glace
au jus.

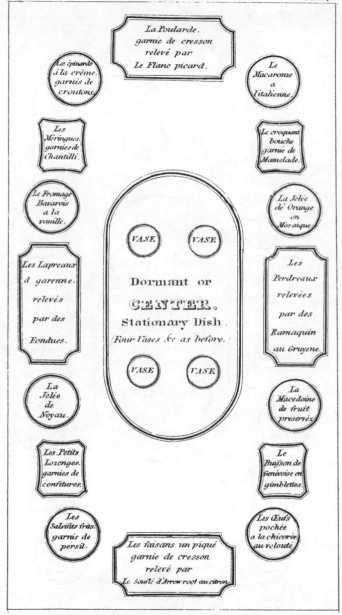

La Poularde.
garnie de cresson
relevé par
Le Flanc picard.

Les épinards
à la crême.
garnis de
croutons.

Le
Macaronie
a
l'italienne.

Les
Méringues.
garnies de
Chantilli.

Le croquant
bouche
garnie de
Mamelade.

Le Fromage
Bavarois
a la
vanille.

La Jelée
de' Orange
en
Mos aique

Les Lapreaux
d' garenne.
relevés
par des
Fondues.

VASE   VASE

Dormant or
CENTER.
Stationary Dish.
(Four Vases &c as before.

VASE   VASE

Les
Perdreaux
relevées
par des
Ramaquin
au Gruyene.

La
Jelée
de
Noyau.

La
Macedoine
de fruit
preservés

Les Petits
Lozenges.
garnies de
confitures.

Le
Buisson de
Genévoise en
gimblettes.

Les
Salsifas frits.
garnis de
persil.

Les Œufs
pochée
a la chicorée
au velouté

Les faisans un piqué
garnie de cresson
relevé par
Le soufflé d'Arrow root au citron

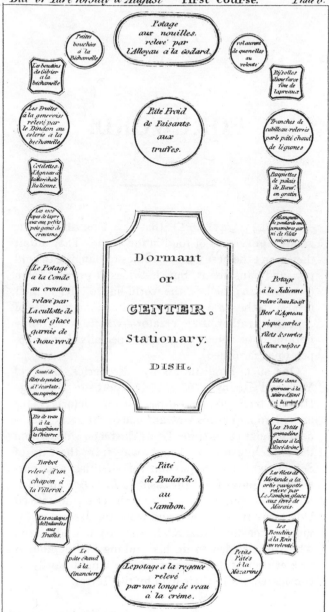

Potage
aux nouilles.
relevé par
l'Alloyau à la Godard.

Petites
bouchées
à la
Béchamelle

vol au vent
de quenelles
au
velouté

Les boudins
de Gibier
à la
bechamelle

Rissolles
d'une farce
fine de
Lapreaux

Les Fruites
à la genevoise
relevé par
le Dindon au
celerie à la
bechamelle

Pâté Froid
de Faisants.
aux
truffes.

Tranches de
cabilleau relevés
par le pâté chaud
de légumes

Cotelettes.
d'Agneau à
la Maréchale
Italienne.

Paupiettes
de palais
de Bœuf.
en gratin

Les esca-
lopes de lapre
aux une petits
pois garni de
croutons.

Blanquet
te poulards aux
concombres gar
ni de filets
mignons.

Le Potage
à la Condé
au crouton
relevé par
La cuisotte de
bœuf glacé
garnie de
choux verd.

Dormant
or
CENTER.
Stationary.
DISH.

Potage
à la Julienne
relevé d'un Roast
Beef d'Agneau
pique sur les
filets & sur les
deux cuisses

Sauté de
filets de poulets
à l'écarlate
au suprème

Filets dans
queroux à la
Maitre d'Hotel
et la grand

Ris de veau
à la
Dauphines
la Chicorée

Les Petits
grenadins
glacés à la
Macédoine

Turbot
relevé d'un
chapon à
la Villeroi.

Pâté
de Poularde.
au
Jambon.

Les filets de
Merlande à la
ortie ravigotte
relevé par
Le Jambon glacé
aux têtes de
Marais.

Les escalopes
de Poulardes
aux
Truffes.

Les
Boudins
à la Rein
au velouté.

Le
pâté chaud
à la
financiere

Petits
Pâtés
à la
Mazarine

Le potage à la régence
relevé
par une longe de veau
à la crème.

The Potages at the extremeties & on the flanks & the Poissons on the counter flanks.

FOREWORD.

I HAVE ALWAYS FELT that the English are the greatest purveyors of food in the world. They admit they aren't the best when it comes to banging the old pots and pans about, but that doesn't prevent them from bringing the best the world has to offer to their tables. In this area their importance is in the role of consumer rather than creator—which is certainly nothing to be defensive about, especially if you happen to be famished.

One such Englishman was Frederick Duke of York and Albany (1763-1827), second son of George III and uncle to the future Queen Victoria. This lucky lord had as his steward one of the great Continental cooks of his time, Louis Eustache Ude, whom the Duke presumably lured away from the Earl of Sefton (who had a passion for shellfish and partridge, to judge from the dishes *à la Sefton* in Ude's repertoire). Sefton apparently is the one who enticed Ude away from France and from the service of his unlucky master, Louis XVI. It is easy to understand why Ude decided to do his cooking in England: A former chef of the King of France would hardly be considered one of their own by the Terror.

Ude makes no bones about his contribution to the level of civilization in England. "The Author ventures to affirm," he says, "that Cookery in England, when well done, is superior to that of any country in the world." Cooking in France after the revolution must have been really terrible to move a Frenchman to say that.

You are holding in your hands a facsimile edition of a cookbook that Ude brought out in England and America. It went through several editions and this is the 1828 edition printed in Philadelphia. Today, when the writing and publishing of cookbooks has descended to its lowest level—what with stolen or doctored recipes, phony categories, promotion of applicance rather than food, and downright silly or insulting titles—it is refreshing to come across a volume that not only takes the art and science of cookery seriously, but takes just as seriously the art of *writing* about cookery. If you are one of those persons who likes to curl up with a good cookbook the way other people curl up with novels, then you have a rare treat in store.

Now that people are getting fed up—literally and figuratively—with low-fat, low-cholesterol, low-salt, low-everything cooking, they are beginning to look back to a time when people's main concern about food was how it tasted. It seems that these people, despite their high–everything diet, lived healthier, happier, longer lives than we do. As a result of this interest—spurred on by such books as John and Karen Hess's *The Taste of America* and Calvin Trillin's *American Fried*—many reprints and facsimiles of early cookbooks are appearing in the bookstores and people are slowly being converted back to the basics. Kind things are even beginning to be said about lard.

As a practical cookbook, *The French Cook* is not as out of date as it might appear. Of course, some of the ingredients are now not readily available and large joints of meat are virtually unheard of, but any experienced cook can adapt most of these recipes or even follow the original method. I have always felt that any cookbook from which you can learn even a single good dish is worthwhile—and good dishes are here in abundance.

So here's to Louis Eustache Ude. Like most chefs, he was touchy as hell—grousing about the lack of respect given him, complaining about the number and quality of his assistants, even grumbling about the manners of his employers, and always, *always* giving the back of his hand to other cooks and writers. But he never wavers from his line that cooking is an exalted profession. "Cookery is an art appreciated by only a very few individuals," he writes, "an art which requires, in addition to a most diligent and studious application, no small share of intellect." That shaft may have been directed at early 19th-century English nobility, but today it would mow down a whole row of "food writers."

MILTON GLADSTONE

FRENCH COOK.

CHAPTER I.

SAUCES, BROTH, AND CONSOMMES.

I SHALL commence with BROTH, as the foundation of Cookery. By the 1st broth, any trimming of meat will answer, provided you are cautious in taking off all the scum and fat, otherwise your broth will be too much coloured to settle your sauce; but if you are cautious in this respect, this broth will do to moisten all your sauces. The next is, when you have only a small dinner; but in a good kitchen, broth should be always in the larder; otherwise you must settle your stock-pot according to the dinner that you have to give, or make; for four entrées, twenty pounds of beef, for broth only, without the roast, for it should be observed, that any joint roasted in the kitchen is entirely wasted for the cooking. Many families complain of the expence of kitchens, never taking into consideration the immense weight of a large joint, particularly before they have trimmed it properly, and made it fit to come before company.

No. 1.—*First Broth.*

Take part of a breast, or of a rump of beef, with some of the *parures*, or trimmings. Put the meat into a stock-pot with cold water. Set it on the fire, and watch the proper moment to skim it well. If this broth is not clear and bright, the other broths and sauces will also be spoiled. Be particular in taking off the black scum; pour a little cold water into the above, to raise up the white scum. When all the scum has been removed, put in a few carrots, turnips, heads of celery, and leeks, four large onions, one of which is to be stuck with five cloves; then throw a handful of salt into the stock-pot, and let the whole simmer for five hours. Skim away all the fat, then strain the broth through a double silk sieve. Lay the piece of beef in a braziere pan; pour over some of the broth, to keep it hot, till the moment that you serve up. You make your broth in this manner, when you want to use the beef for one of your removes; otherwise you cut the beef smaller, to be sooner done. This first broth serves to moisten all the other broths, of which the different names are as follows:—

No. 2.—*First Consommé.*

Mark* in a stock-pot a large piece of buttock of beef, or other part with a knuckle of veal, and the trimming of meat or fowls, according to the quantity of sauce you may wish to make. This broth will admit all sorts of veal or poultry. Let the meat stew on a gentle fire. Moisten with about two large ladles-full of the first broth; put no vegetables into this broth, except a bunch of parsley and green onions. Let them sweat thoroughly; then thrust your knife

---

* *Mark* is a French term, which signifies, that all the ingredients requisite are to be put into the stock-pot.

into the meat: if no blood issue, it is a sign that it is
heated through. Then moisten it with boiling broth
to the top, and let it boil gently for about four hours;
after which, use this *consommé* to make the sauces,
or the *consommés* of either poultry or game. Take
off the fat and scum of all the various broths, and
keep the pots full, in order that the broth be not too
high in colour. When the broth remains too long on
the fire, it loses its flavour, acquires too brown a colour, and tastes strong and disagreeable.

No. 3.—*Consommé of Poultry.*

BEEF is no longer required in the *consommés*
either of poultry or of game. Put a few slices of ham
in the bottom of a stew-pan, or of any other vessel,
with some veal, take the knuckle in preference.*
Lay over the veal the loins of fowl and trimmings.
Then moisten about two inches deep with the first
consommé, and let it sweat on a fire, so confined, that
the blaze may not colour the side of the vessel.
When the meat is heated through, (which you ascertain by thrusting your knife into it, as above,) cover
it with the first *consommé;* seasoned with mushrooms, a bunch of parsley and green onions, taking
especial care to keep the vessel very full; and let the
meat boil till it be done properly. The broths are
more savoury and mellow when the meat is not over-
done. Skim away the fat when the broth is boiled,
and strain the *consommé* through a silken sieve, and
use when wanted.

No. 4.—*Consommé of Game.*

If you are to send up *entrées* of partridges, you
must have ready, a *consommé* of partridges. Put
into a stew-pan a few bits of veal, the backs, &c. of
partridges to be laid over them; to these may be add-

* The leg of veal is divided into three different fleshed parts,
noix, sounoix, and *contre noix,* and three bones, the knuckle,
the casis, and the marrow-bone.

ed, if you think proper, a few carcases of rabbits if you have any. If you moisten with a *consommé* containing ham, there is no occasion to put in any more; if not, a few slices of ham will not be amiss. If your *entrées* are with *truffles,* add the parings of your *truffles* and a few mushrooms. When the *consommé* is sufficiently done, strain it through a cloth, or silk sieve, and use it when you have an opportunity. Do not omit a bundle seasoned.

No. 5.—*Consommé of Rabbits.*

MARK* the various *consommés* with the bones and trimmings of rabbits. Do the same as for a *consommé* of partridges; put in truffles, if your *entrées* are to be with truffles. Do not omit the bundle.†

No. 6.—*Blond of Veal, or Gravy of Veal.*

Put a few slices of Westmoreland ham (the lean only) into a pretty thick stew-pan. Lay over them some fleshy pieces of veal. You may use rump of veal. Pour into the stew-pan, a sufficient quantity of first *consommé* to cover about half the thickness of the meat. Let it sweat on a stove, over a brisk fire. Watch the stew-pan and the contents, for fear of burning. When the broth is reduced, thrust a knife into the meat, that all the gravy may run out; then stew the glaze more gently. When the whole is absolutely *à glace*, of a good colour, you must let it stew till brown,, but take care it does not burn, to prevent which, put it on red-hot ashes. Keep stirring your stew-pan over the fire, in order that the glaze may be all of the same colour. Turn the meat upside down, that it may not stick. When your

---

* *Mark* means, to make each *consommé* with the trimmings either of game or fowls.

† *Bundle* or *Bunch,* is made with parsley and green onions; when seasoned, you must put to it some bay-leaves, or two bunches of thyme, a bit of sweet basil, two cloves, and six leaves of mace.

glaze is of a dark red colour, moisten with some hot broth; let the glaze detach before you put the stew-pan on the fire, for it might still burn. Season with mushrooms and a bunch of parsley and green onions. When the gravy has boiled for an hour, it is done enough. Take off the fat, and strain it through a silken sieve.

No. 7.—*Gravy of Beef.*

Trim, with layers of fat bacon, the bottom of a thick stew-pan; cut four large onions by halves, lay the flat part over the bacon; take a few slices of beef, put them in the same manner as in the gravy of veal, moisten with the first broth only. Let this sweat, in order to get all the gravy out of the beef, and when the broth is reduced, thrust a knife into the meat; let it stew gently on a slow fire, till the gravy be of a light brown colour.* Next moisten with some first broth, throw in a large bunch of parsley and of green onions, a little salt and a pepper corn. Let the whole boil for one hour; take the fat off, and drain it through a silk sieve, to use it when wanted.

No. 8.—*L'Aspic.*

Take a handful of aromatic herbs, such as burnet, chervil, and tarragon. Boil them in white vinegar; when the vinegar is well scented, pour into your stew-pan some *consommé* of fowl reduced; season well before you clarify. When the *aspic* is highly seasoned, break the white of four eggs into an earthen pan, and beat them with an osier rod; throw the *aspic* into those whites of eggs, and put the whole on the fire in a stew-pan; keep beating or stirring till your jelly gets white, it is then very near boiling. Put it on the corner of the stove, with a cover over it, and a little fire on the top of it. When quite clear

---

* The browner the glaze is, the better; but care must be taken not to burn it, as it will then be bitter.

and bright, strain it through a bag, or sieve, to be used when wanted.

N. B. If you should want to use it for a *mayonaise*, or as a jelly in moulds, you must make sure of its being stiff enough. Then put a knuckle of veal in a small stock-pot, a small part of a knuckle of ham, some trimming of fowl, or game. Season this with onions, carrots, a bunch of herbs well seasoned; pour into it half a bottle of white wine, and moisten with good broth; let it boil gently for four hours, then skim away all the fat, drain it through a silk sieve; put that in a stew-pan, with two spoonfuls of tarragon vinegar, and four whites of eggs, salt and pepper to clarify; and keep stirring on the fire till the whole becomes very white, then put this on the side with a little fire over the cover; when you find it clear, drain it in a cloth or jelly bag, and use it for *aspic;* if not, do not put in any vinegar, *jelée,* for pie or galentine does not require acid.

No. 9.—*Jelée of Meat, for Pies.*

The *jelée* of meat for pies, is not to be prepared in the same manner as the *aspic.* Neither aromatic herbs nor vinegar are to be used. The *jelée* is to be made as follows: Put into a stew-pan a good piece of beef, two calves' feet, a knuckle of veal, remnants of fowl, or game, according to the contents of your pies, two onions stuck with cloves, two carrots, four shalots, a bunch of parsley and green onions, some thyme, bay-leaves, spices, &c., and a small piece of ham. Sweat the whole over a very slow fire, then moisten with some good broth, let the stew-pan be covered close, and those ingredients stew for four hours, but very gently. When done, taste and season it well, and clarify it as you do the *aspic.* In order that it may keep the better, put it into ice.

No. 10.—*Le Suage, or l'Empotage.* *

MARK† in a *marmite* twenty pounds of beef, a knuckle of veal, a hen, and if you have any remnants of fowl or of veal, you may put them in likewise. Moisten this stock-pot with two large ladles full of broth. Sweat it over a large fire. Let it boil to *glaze* without its getting too high in colour. Next fill it up with some first broth that is quite boiling. Put some vegetables into this pot, which is intended for making soup only. But you must put very few into the *consommés* which are to be reduced, and would have a bitter taste if they were to retain that of the roots, and accordingly not be fit to be used in delicate cookery. *L'empotage* requires no more than five hours to be done; strain it through a silk sieve, and use it when you have occasion for it, to moisten any thing for soup, only clear or pure.

No. 11.—*Clarified Consommé,*

Is to be clarified as specified for the *aspic* and *jelée* of meat. You must not forget, that such articles as are to be clarified, require to be more highly seasoned than others, as the clarifying takes away some of the flavour.

No. 12.—*Clarified Gravy.*

Gravy of veal, or beef, is to be clarified with whites of eggs. The gravy of veal is best suited for the table of the great. The gravy of beef may do for private families of the middle class.

No. 13.—*Le Bouillon de Santé.*

Mark or put into an earthen pot‡ or stock-pot, six

* Remark, that this broth is to be made for a very large dinner only.

† *Mark* must be understood as a term to express the putting in of all the requisite articles.

‡ In France, these broths are generally made in an earthen pot, but such pots can not be found in England.

pounds of beef, one-half of a hen, and a knuckle of veal. Moisten with cold water. Let it boil so that the scum rises only by degrees; skim it well, that it may be quite clear and limpid. When skimmed. throw into it two carrots, two leeks, a head of celery, two onions stuck with three cloves, and three turnips. Let the whole simmer gently for four hours. Then put a little salt to it, and skim off the grease or fat before you use it.

No. 14.—*White Roux.**

Put a good lump of butter into a stew-pan, let it melt over a slow fire; when melted, drain the butter, and squeeze out the butter-milk, then powder it over with flour, enough to make a thin paste; keep it on the fire for a quarter of an hour, take care not to let it colour, and pour it into an earthen pan to use it when wanted.

No. 15.—*Brown Roux.*

Put into a stew-pan a piece of butter proportionate to the quantity of *roux* you want to prepare. Melt it gently, squeeze out the buttermilk, then put flour enough to make a paste; you must fry it on a slow fire, and then put it again over very red ashes, till it be of a nice colour; but mind this is to be obtained only by slow degrees. When of a light brown, you pour it into an earthen pan, and keep it for use. It keeps a long while.

No. 16.—*The Coulis.*

Make the *coulis* in the same manner as the gravy of veal, with slices of ham, and slices of veal, &c.

---

* We are unable to find an equivalent in English for the French term *roux*. It is an indispensable article in cookery, it serves to thicken sauces; the brown is for sauces of the same colour; and the colour must be obtained by slow degrees, otherwise the flour will burn and give a bitter taste, and the sauces become spotted with black.

When the *glaze* is of a nice colour, moisten it, and let it stew entirely. You must season it with a bunch of parsley and green onions, mushrooms, &c. Then mix some brown *roux* with the gravy of veal, but do not make it too thick, as you could not get the fat out of your sauce, and a sauce with fat neither has a pleasing appearance nor a good flavour. Let it stew for an hour on the corner of the stove, skim off the fat, and strain it through a tammy, &c.

No. 17.—*Grand Espagnole.*

Besides some slices of ham, put into a stew-pan some slices of veal. Moisten the same as for the *coulis;* sweat them in the like manner; let all the *glaze* go to the bottom, and when of a nice red colour, moisten with a few spoonsful of first *consommé,* to detach the *glaze:* then pour in the *coulis.* Let the whole boil for half an hour, that you may be enabled to remove all the fat. Strain it through a clean tammy. Remember always to put into your sauces some mushrooms, with a bunch of parsley and green onions. It is time to observe to the professors of cookery, that the flavour comes from the seasoning: if you neglect to put into your dish the necessary articles to a nicety, the flavour will be deficient. Mind that the sauce or broth, when kept too long on the fire, loses the proper taste, and takes, instead of it, a strong and disagreeable one.

No. 18.—*Espagnole of Game.*

The same operation as above, except that in this you introduce the loins and trimmings of either young or old partridges, in order that this sauce may taste of game. Put them to sweat. Remember that such sauces, if kept too long on the fire, lose their savour, and *fumet* of the game.—This method may be thus abbreviated: *mark* a good *consommé* of game; when done, reduce it to glaze, then by putting a small bit of that glaze in either sauce, it will save you time and expense, and will answer much better.

No. 19.—*Sauce tournée.* *

Take some white *roux*, dilute it with some *consommé* of fowl; neither too thin nor too thick. I must repeat what I have already said, a sauce when too thick will never admit of the fat being removed. Let it boil on the corner of the stove. Throw in a few mushrooms, with a bunch of parsley and green onions. Skim it well, and when there is no grease left, strain it through a tammy, to use it when wanted.

No. 20.—*Sauce à l'Allemande.*

This is merely a *sauce tournée* as above reduced, into which is introduced a thickening† well seasoned. This sauce is always used for the following sauces or ragouts, viz. *blanquette* of all descriptions, of veal, of fowl, of game, or palates, ragout, *à-la-toulouse*, loin of veal, *à-la-béchamel*, white *financière royale*, &c. &c .

No. 21.—*The Veloutée.*

Take much about the same quantity of *consommé* and of *sauce tournée*, and reduce them over a large fire. When this sauce is very thick, you should have some thick cream boiling and reduced, which you pour into the sauce, and give it a couple of boilings; season with a little salt, and strain through a tammy. If the ham should be too salt, put in a little sugar. Observe, that this sauce is not to be so thick as the *béchamel.*

No. 22.—*White Italian Sauce.*

After having turned some mushrooms, throw them into a little water and lemon-juice to keep them white. Formerly it was customary to use oil for

* *Sauce tourneé* is the sauce that the modern cooks call *velonté,* but *velonté* will be found hereafter.

†Thickening, is what is called, in French, *liaison;* the yolk of two or four eggs.

these sauces, as on account of its being much lighter, it would rise always to the top, whereas in thick sauces, butter does not. Put into a stew-pan two-thirds of *sauce tournée*, and one-third of *consommé;* and two spoonsful of mushrooms chopped very fine, and especially of a white colour, half a spoonful of shalots likewise chopped, and well washed in the corner of a clean towel. Reduce this sauce, season it well, and send it up.

No. 23.—*Brown Italian Sauce.*

It is requisite in a kitchen to have what is commonly called an *assiette,* which is a dish with four partitions, intended for the reception of fine herbs. You must always have ready some parsley chopped very fine, some shalots the same; if the mushrooms were chopped before-hand they would become black; therefore, only chop them when you have occasion for them; the fourth partition is intended for the reception of bunches of parsley and green onions. The chopping and mincing of the above is the business of the apprentice, if there be one under the head cook; if not, of the junior kitchen maid.

Take two spoonsful of chopped mushrooms, one spoonful of shalots, one ditto of parsley.* Throw the whole into a stew pan, with two-thirds of *Espagnole* sauce, and one-third of *consommé.* Some people add white wine to the sauce. In France, where there is a choice of light wines, it might be done easily, but in England, where Champaign is the only wine that can be used, it would be too dear; besides, the sauce may be made very good without any wine whatever, if you know how to work it well, to its proper degree, with a little salt, and still less pepper. Brown sauces are not to be made thick. When the sauce is done enough, you must shift it

---

* This sauce will have a better taste, if you fry the finer herbs in a little butter, and moisten them after with the *Espagnole* and *consommé.*

into another stew-pan, and put it *au bain marie.* If you were not to skim this sauce with particular care, you might skim off all the parsley, which must remain in it. Italienne that are preferred by all the epicureans, chop some of the mushrooms, after they have been in butter to preserve them very white; observe, they must be very fine; put them in a small stew-pan, with a small ladle of blonde doreal, the same quantity of *Espagnole* sauce, let that sauce boil gently in the side of the stove, to scum all the fat; seasoned with salt and pepper, and put it *au bain marie* for any thing wanted.

No. 24.—*The Sauce Hachée.*

This sauce, although seldom or ever used in good cookery, is frequently to be met with at taverns and inns on the road. Such as it is, it is to be made in the following way. Chop some girkins, mushrooms, capers, and anchovies, which throw into a brown *Italienne,* and that is what is called a *sauce hachée.* Why have I called this a tavern or common inn sauce? Because it is not requisite to have an *Italienne* well prepared. A common browning made with butter and flour, moistened with a little broth, or gravy, and some fine herbs in it, will answer the purpose of those who know no better.

No. 25.—*White sharp Sauce.*

Pour into a stew-pan four spoonsful of white vinegar, to which add some tarragon, (if you have no tarragon, use tarragon vinegar,) and about twenty pepper-corns; reduce the vinegar to one-fourth of its original quantity, pour into the stew-pan, six spoonsful of *sauce tournée,* and two spoonsful of *consommé;* then reduce this sauce over a large fire. Strain it through a tammy, and then put it again on the fire. When it boils, thicken it with the yolks of two eggs, work it with a small bit of butter. In case it should happen to be brown, pour a spoonful of cream into it, to restore the white colour, and put a little cayenne and salt. This sort of sauce is used for all the palaces.

No. 26.—*The Brown sharp Sauce, or Poivrêê.*

In a small stew-pan, put a small bit of butter, a small carrot cut into dice, a few shalots the same, same parsley roots, some parsley, a few slices of ham, a clove, a little thyme, the half of a bay-leaf, a few grains of pepper-corn and allspice, with a little mace. Let the stew-pan now be put on a slow fire, till it begins to be of a fine brown all round; then keep stirring with a wooden spoon; pour into the stew-pan four spoonsful of white vinegar, and a small bit of sugar. Let this reduce nearly *à glace*. Then moisten with some *Espagnole* and a little *consommé*, that you may be enabled to take the fat off from the sauce; season with cayenne and a little salt. Taste whether there be salt enough, but mind it is not to be too acid, skim off the fat, and strain the sauce through a tammy, and serve up.

No. 27.—*The Aspic Lié.*

Put in a stew pan such herbs as are called *ravigottes*, namely, burnet, chervil, and tarragon. Add two or three spoonsful of white vinegar, and let the herbs infuse on a slow fire for half an hour. Then moisten with eight spoonsful of *Espagnole;* let the whole stew for ten minutes or a quarter of an hour. Season it well, and strain it through a tammy, to use when wanted.

No. 28.—*White Ravigotte.*

The same as above, except that, instead of *Espagnole*, you use *sauce tournée*. Let it boil for half an hour, then strain this sauce through a tammy. Have the same herbs as above, chopped very fine, blanch them in a little salted water, lay them in a sieve to drain, and pour the *ravigotte* into the sauce. Work it with a small lump of butter, season with salt and pepper, and send up. Never omit to taste the sauce, for occasionally, according to the palate of the host, some ingredients may be wanted, others too plentiful, which may be easily remedied: when too salt, a small bit of sugar corrects the briny taste.

No. 29.—*Ravigotte â-la-Ude.*

Take a tea-spoonful of catsup, ditto of cavice, ditto of Chili vinegar, ditto of Reading sauce, a lump of butter of the size of an egg, three spoonsful of thick *béchamel*, a little new cream, salt and pepper, and a little parsley chopped fine, and blanch very green; this sauce is in high request, and entirely the composition of the Author.

No. 30.—*The Maître d'Hôtel.*

Take four spoonsful of *Allemande:* work this sauce over a stove with a small lump of fresh butter. Take some parsley chopped very fine, throw it into the sauce with a little salt and pepper, and the juice of a lemon. Let this sauce be thick, if intended to *mask** any *entrée* whatever. At any rate it is easy to thin a sauce; but if too thin, it is a hard matter to thicken it, except with a lump of butter and flour, yet, let it be ever so well managed, it is but a sad contrivance.

No. 31.—*Maître d'Hôtel maigre*

Is nothing more than plain butter sauce with a little chopped parsley, salt, pepper, and lemon-juice. If shalots are acceptable, a few may be added, the same as to the *maître d'hôtel* above.

No. 32.—*Tarragon Sauce, or Pluche.*

See No. 25, *White sharp Sauce.* Blanch some tarragon, either in fillets, squares, or any other shape you may think proper, and put it into the sauce. It

---

* Mask, means to cover over with the sauce.

is then called Tarragon Sauce. In other *pluches*, tarragon must always prevail. You may make *pluches* of parsley, chervil, &c. with the sauce called white sharp sauce.

No. 33.—*The Bourguignotte.*

Cut some truffles into balls of the size of a nutmeg: take some small round mushrooms, and put about twenty of each into a small stew-pan; pour over them a pint of red wine, with a small lump of sugar. Let the wine be reduced to a glaze. Then throw into the stew-pan six spoonsful of *Espagnole*, and two of *consommé.* Let the whole boil for half an hour, taste it, and if well seasoned, serve it up.

No. 34.—*The bon Beurre.*

Take some *Allemande*, (Vide No. 20) rather thick, into which put a bit of buttter. Work the sauce well, season it, and serve up with the juice of half a lemon salt, and cayenne pepper.

No. 35.—*The Béchamel.*

Take about half a quarter of a pound of butter, about three pounds of veal, cut into small slices, a quarter of a pound of ham, some trimmings of mushrooms, two small white onions, a bunch of parsley and green onions; put the whole into a stew-pan, and lay it on the fire till the meat be made firm. Then put three spoonsful of flour; moisten with some boiling hot thin cream. Keep this sauce rather thin, so that whilst you reduce it, the ingredient may have time to be stewed thoroughly. Season it with a little salt, and strain it through a tammy, when it retains no taste of flour, and the sauce is very palatable.

No. 36.—*The Béchamel maigre,**

Is prepared as above, with the exception of the

---

* This sauce is intended chiefly for those who conform to the Roman Catholic religion.

meat, which is to be omitted. If you have made any sauces from fish, put a little of the juice or gravy of the fish with the cream. When done, strain it through a tammy, and serve up.

No. 37.—*The Genoese Sauce.*

This sauce is made by stewing fish, yet it is natural enough that it should find its place among the other sauces. Make some *marinade* of various roots, such as carrots, roots of parsley, onions, and a few mushrooms, with a bay leaf, some thyme, a blade of mace, a few cloves, and some branches of sweet basil—fry the whole slowly over a mitigated fire, in a stew-pan, with some butter, till the onions are quite melted. Pour in some Madeira or other white wine, according to the size of the fish you have to dress, let the vegetables stew. When done enough, use it to stew your fish in, when done take some of the liquor to make the sauce. Take a little brown *roux*, and mix it with some of the *marinade*, to which add two or three spoonsful of gravy of veal. Now let these stew gently on the corner of the stove; skim off all the grease, and season well, pour the sauce through a tammy. Then put to it two spoonsful of essence of anchovies, and a quarter of a pound of butter kneaded with flour, and throw them into the sauce. When this is done, squeeze into it the juice of a lemon, work the sauce over the stove to make it very smooth, and cover the fish with the sauce, which must accordingly be made thick and mellow.

No. 38.—*Sauce à Matelotte for Fish.*

Melt some brown *roux*, into which throw a few onions cut into slices: keep it stirring over the fire till the onions be dissolved in the *roux*. Then moisten with the wine in which your fish has been stewed, and which, by the bye, must be red wine. Add some *parures*, or trimmings of mushrooms, with a bunch of parsley and green onions, well seasoned with spices; bay leaves, thyme, sweet basil, cloves, all-spices, &c. Let the flour be well done. Remember to throw in a few spoonsful of gravy of veal. Now taste whether the sauce be properly seasoned, and strain it through a tammy. Then take a few small glazed onions and mushrooms, ready done, likewise a few small *quenelles*, and put into it some of the sauce, and keep this little ragout, to put over the fish when your *matelotte* is in the dish. When you are ready to serve up, you must add the juice of a lemon, and two spoonsful of essence of anchovies. Work the sauce well, that it may be quite mellow. Cover your fish with the sauce, and then pour the ragout over.

No. 39.—*Sauce à Matelotte for Entrées.*

See *Sauce Chambord.* It being the same which is used for the *matelottes* of brains, &c. The *matelotte* when not of fish, is made with a *ragout à la financière*, into which you introduce essence of anchovies and some crawfish, when you can procure them: this sauce must be highly seasoned with salt, cayenne, and lemon-juice.

No. 40.—*Apple Sauce for Geese and Roast Pork.*

Peel some apples and cut them into quarters, put them into a stew-pan, with a little brown sugar, and a little water. When they are melted, stir them well with a wooden spoon, add a little butter to it, and send up.

No. 41.—*Purée of Sorrel.*

Wash and pick some sorrel, and then put it into a stew-pan with a little water: keep stirring with your spoon to prevent its burning; when melted, lay it in a hair sieve to drain, then put it on the table and chop it well with some trimmings of mushrooms. When chopped fine, put it into a stew-pan with a little butter and a few small pieces of good ham; let it fry a long time on the fire, in order to drain the water it contains. When it becomes quite dry, mix it with four spoonsful of *Espagnole*, or more, if you have any occasion for a large quantity; and let it stew for a long while over a small stove. After it has been continually boiling for an hour, rub it through a tammy. If it should happen to be too thick, dilute it with a little *consommé* or *Espagnole*. If too acid, put a little glaze and sugar. You must always put some cabbage-lettuce with the sorrel, to correct its acidity. When you make *purée* of sorrel, if you have no sauce to put to it, put a spoonful of flour to thicken the sauce, and dilute with gravy of veal, and proceed then as before. If you have no gravy of veal or of beef, two spoonsful of broth, and a small bit of glaze, will answer the same purpose.

No. 42.—*Sorrel en maigre.*

Pick your sorrel, let it melt, drain it, and lay it on the table, as above. Mind that the table be very clean. Then chop the sorrel for a long time, and very fine, fry it gently in a stew-pan with a little butter. When it has been kept for about half an hour on a slow fire, to drain all the humidity, throw in a spoonful of flour: moisten with boiling hot cream, and let it stew on a slow fire for an hour. Then season it with a little salt. If your sorrel should be too acid, put a little sugar to it. Then thicken it with the yolks of four eggs, and serve up.

If you should prefer making a *Béarnoise*, you make a kind of pap with flour and cream, or milk, and let it boil. When the sorrel is done enough, pour the *Béarnoise* into it, and let it boil ten minutes, then put the yolks of four eggs immediately after to thicken it. In this manner the cream will never curdle, whereas, if you follow the other method, it most frequently will. If it be with broth that you wish to prepare your sorrel, instead of cream or milk, you mix some with it, and use the yolks of eggs in the like manner, and that is what we call *farce.**

* A dish much used by the Roman Catholics; Eggs *à la farce.*

No. 43.—*Purée of Céleri.*

Cut the whitest part of several heads of celery, which blanch in water, to take off the bitter taste, then drain it and put them in cold water. Let it cool, and drain all the water off. Then put it into a stew-pan with a little *consommé* and sugar. Let it stew for an hour and a half, and be reduced till there be no kind of moisture. Then mix it with four spoonsful of *béchamel* or *velouté*, strain the whole through a tammy, and put it *au bain marie.** When ready to send up, refine the sauce with a little thick cream, to make it white.

No. 44.—*Purée of Onion, or Soubise.*

Take a dozen of white onions. After having peeled and washed them, cut them into halves, take off the tops and bottoms, mince them as fine as possible, and blanch them to make them taste sweeter and take off the green colour of the onions. Then set them melting on a small stove, with a little butter. When they are thoroughly done, and no kind of moisture left, mix four spoonsful of *béchamel*. Season them well, rub the *purée* through a tammy, and keep this sauce hot, but without boiling. You must also put a small lump of sugar with the sauce if ne-

---

* *Bain marie* is a flat vessel containing boiling water; you put all your stew-pans into the water, and keep that water always very hot, but it must not boil. The effect of this *bain marie*, is to keep every thing warm, without either altering the quantity or the quality, particularly the quality. When I had the honour of serving a nobleman in this country, who kept a very extensive hunting establishment, and the hour of dinner was consequently uncertain, I was in the habit of using *bain marie*, as a certain means of preserving the flavour of all my dishes. If you keep your sauces, or broth, or soup, by the fire-side, the soup reduces and becomes strong, and the sauce thickens as well as reduces.

It is necessary to observe, that this is the best manner of warming turtle soup, as the thick part is always at the bottom of the stew-pan; this method prevents it from burning, and keeps it always good.

cessary. When you have the oven hot, put the onions hermetically closed in a small stew-pan well covered, and let them simmer for one hour, with a small bit of ham, bit of mace, half a bay leaf, and this method gives a better flavour.

No. 45.—*Purée of Onions, Brown, and Lyonaise.*

Peel and wash twelve onions clean, then mince them, and fry them in a stew-pan with a little butter, till very brown. Then moisten with some *Espagnole*, if you have any; if not, *singez** with two spoonsful of flour, mixed with some gravy of veal or beef. Now scum the fat, and season well with salt, pepper, and then strain the *purée* through an old tammy, for these sort of *purées* would destroy new ones, and will always leave the taste of onions.

For the *Lyonaise* make a *purée* of onions likewise, but then keep the sauce a little more liquid. Take some very small white onions, cut them into rings, and fry them till they be of a light brown, then lay them on a clean towel to drain, and throw them into the sauce. Give them one single boiling, that the fat, getting at the top, may easily be skimmed off; and serve up.

No. 46.—*Bretonne.*

The same as above, some denominate it *Bretonne,* some *Lyonaise.*

No. 47.—*Purée of White Beans.*

New white beans are the best suited for making a *purée.* Put them into boiling water if they be fresh, and in cold water if they be dry, with a little butter in either case, which makes the skin more mellow. When they are done, throw in a handful of salt, to give them a seasoning. Fry a few slices of onion in a little butter; when they are of a nice

* *Singez* is putting some flour into the stew-pan.

brown colour, *singez* them with half a spoonful of flour; moisten with gravy of veal, and season with a little salt and pepper, and skim off the grease. When the flour is done, mix it well with the beans, let them boil fifteen minutes, squeeze them well before you rub them through the tammy. Let your *purée* be rather liquid, as it gets thick when on the fire. A short time before it is sent up, mix with your *purée* of beans a small bit of butter, and then serve up.

The *purée en maigre* is prepared in the same manner; cut instead of *sauce grasse*, you use *jus maigre*, or milk. If you wish to make it white, you must sweat the onions gently and slowly, that they may not get brown.

No. 48.—*Purée of Mushrooms, White and Brown.*

If you wish to make a white *purée* of mushrooms, you must turn the mushrooms white in a little water and lemon-juice: chop them; then put them into a stew-pan, with a very small bit of butter. When the mushrooms are what we call melted, moisten them with four or six spoonsful of *velouté* or *béchamel*. Do not let them boil long, for fear they should lose their taste and colour. Then rub them through a tammy. It is no easy matter, indeed, with regard to mushrooms, yet this sauce is called *purée* of mushrooms.

It is almost useless to observe, that for the brown *purée*, it is enough to moisten with some *Espagnole* only. If you were to fry the mushrooms brown, they then would turn black, and make the sauce of the like colour. Skim your sauce. Put a little sugar into both. All such sauces as are called *purée*, must be made thicker than others.

No. 49.—*Purée of Green Peas, new and dry.*

The *purée* of green peas for an *entrée*, is prepared in the same manner as that described for *potage* or soup. You must only keep it thicker, and richer, which is done by mixing a little glaze with it. But if you were to put too much, the *purée* then would no longer retain its green colour; neither must you let it boil, for it will lose its green colour.

The *purée* of dry peas is made as follows. Stew the peas with a large piece of bacon, the breast part, a few carrots and onions, a bunch of parsley and green onions, a little thyme, and bay-leaves, and some cold water. Let them boil four hours. When quite done, pound them in a mortar, and then rub them through a tammy, with the liquor they have been boiling in. Let it be properly seasoned, and a short time before you send up, pour in a *verd de persil*, or *verd d'épinards*, to make it green.

No. 50.—*Purée of Chestnuts.*

Take some fine new chestnuts; slit the peel with your knife, and put a little butter into a frying-pan. Fry the chestnuts till the peel comes off, then boil them in a little *consommé* and sugar. When done, add four or six spoonsful of *Espagnole*, and rub the whole through a tammy. Keep this sauce rather liquid, as it is liable to get thick.

No. 50. (*a*)—*Purée of Asparagus.*

Take a bunch of green asparagus, break them in the tender part, and wash them well, then blanch them in boiling water, with salt to make them very green; when they begin to be tender, drain them and put them in cold water; when they are cold, drain them on a perfectly clean towel, put a small bit of fresh butter in a stew pan, with the asparagus, some branches of green parsley, a few green onions, and fry them quickly on a sharp stove to keep them as green as possible. Add to this a little salt, a large lump of sugar, with three or four spoonsful of *sauce tournée*. If you have no sauce, *singez* with a spoonful of fine flour, moisten with good broth. Cook quick, and rub this *purée* through a clean tammy, and add to it a little of the green of spinach, to render it very green. This *purée* should taste rather sweet.

No. 51.—*Les Nouilles.*

Nouilles are noting but a French paste, which the cooks prepare themselves. Lay flat on your table, or dresser, half a dozen spoonsful of flour; make a hole in the middle, and put in a small pinch of salt, a little water to melt the salt, the yolks of three eggs; a lump of butter of the size of a walnut; mix the whole well, flatten the paste with a roller, about one line thick, cut it into slices of about an inch broad, and next cut your *nouilles* nearly as thick. Blanch them in boiling water to take off the flour that sticks around, and when they are blanched, drain them and let them cool, that they may not stick together. Put them to boil in some good *consommé*. When sufficiently done, drain and put them into whatever sauce you may fancy, either a *blanquette*, an *Allemande*, or a *velouté*. If they are to be served with a fowl, use *velouté;* and Parmesan cheese, if served for an *entremêt;* but if for soup, serve them in the broth in which they were boiled. This soup is very good with Parmesan cheese; have the cheese scraped, and serve it separately in a plate.

No. 52.—*The Macédoine.*

This sauce can never be good but in the spring season, as green peas, asparagus, French beans, and artichoke bottoms, are indispensably requisite, besides carrots, turnips, heads of cellery, and small cauliflower sprouts. As it is very difficult to procure all these vegetables and roots at the same time of the year, you must do the best you can, and put in as many as you are able to procure. Cut some carrots in the shape either of olives, of balls, or small thin corks. Blanch them in a little water, then set them to stew with a little sugar and a few spoonsful of *consommé*, over a sharp fire, that they may glaze without breaking. Stew the turnips in the like manner, but separately. Mind that the glaze of your roots be not made too high in colour. The other vegetables are to be boiled in salt and water. Lay them on a clean towel to drain, mix them with the carrots and turnips, and three spoonsful of *béchamel.* Toss them gently, so as not to destroy the shape of the ingredients. If you are short of other vegetables, you may use cucumbers and mushrooms; cautious however in using them, as they will make the sauce too thin, if you do not pay particular attention. When the vegetables are done separately, and you put in a brown *Espagnole* sauce instead of *béchamel,* this mixture of vegetables has been termed *Lyonoise;* that however is a winter sauce; the *macédoine* is a summer sauce.

No. 53.—*Sauce d'Attelets.* *

Take a spoonful of fine herbs, such as mushrooms, parsley, shalots, and a little butter, which fry slightly in a stew-pan. When the herbs begin to fry, without however being too dry, *singez* with a little flour, and moisten with broth or *consommé.* Reduce over a large fire, without skimming off the fat. Season with pepper, salt, and small spices. When the sauce begins to thicken, take it off the fire. Then throw in the yolks of two or three eggs, well beaten: keep stirring, and pour the sauce over whatever it may be intended for.

No. 54.—*Sauce for Sturgeon.*

We call *sauce d'esturgeon* a *marinade,* that which has served either to baste the sturgeon whilst roasting, or serves as a sauce when baked. When the sturgeon is done either in the oven or on the spit,

---

* This sauce is generally used to stick the crumbs of bread round whatever you may wish to put in crumbs, instead of butter. It is made use of for *attelets* of palates of beef, sweetbreads, fillets of rabbits, &c. &c.

(the author prefers the spit, as the fish is more firm than when done in the oven; only it requires to be basted often with the *marinade*, and not to be too near the fire, otherwise it will get dry and take too much colour;) take part of this *marinade*, which reduce with some other sauces, either brown or white; and when it begins to get thick, put in a good lump of butter kneaded with flour, a little *glaze*, some essence of anchovies, and the juice of a lemon. Mind not to put too much salt, as a very little is required when you use anchovies. Besides, you are always able to add salt if requisite.

No. 55.—*Red Sauce Cardinal.*

Reduce some *sauce tournée* with a few spoonsful of *consommé* of fowls. When the sauce is sufficiently done, take some butter of craw-fish,* which throw in. Work it well, with a small lump of fresh butter, to prevent the other butter from turning to oil. Give it a good seasoning, and add to it the juice of a lemon. The spawn of lobster is better, gives less trouble, and has a finer flavour.

No. 56.—*Lobster Sauce.*

A hen lobster is indispensable for this sauce. Put some of the spawn of the fish into a mortar, to be pounded very fine; add to it a small bit of butter. When very fine, rub it through a hair sieve, and cover till wanted. Break the lobster with great care, cut all the flesh into dice, but not too small; dilute some of the red spawn in melted butter, with two spoonsful of essence of anchovies, a little salt and Cayenne pepper, two spoonsful of double cream, and mix it all well before the meat is put to it, as the meat must retain its dice-like form. Do not let this sauce boil. It must be very red. Add to it a teaspoonful of *carice*, and observe, the *carice* should be

---

* Butter of craw-fish:—In England the spawn of lobster is used; it should be well pounded.

very old; two or three years age renders that sauce excellent.

No. 57.—*Sauce à la Lucullus.*

Lucullus was one of the most renowned of antiquarian gourmands; it is therefore natural to assign the name of a man who has brought the art of cookery into so high a repute, to a sauce requiring so much pains, attention and science to perfect; a sauce which can only be sent up to the table of the wealthy and true connoisseur. After having worked the fillets, as indicated at the *entrées*, you have the legs and loins left to make the sauce, which is to be proceeded in as follows. Put into a small stew-pan a few slices of ham, one or two pounds of veal, and the legs and rump of a partridge on the top of the former, moisten with a wine-glass of good *consommé*, and put the whole on a slow fire, in order to sweat it through; thrust your knife into the partridge, if no blood comes, moisten with boiling *consommé*, enough to cover the meat; season with a bundle of parsley and green onions, a few blades of mace, one clove, a little thyme, half a bay-leaf, four or five allspice, the trimmings of truffles and mushrooms; let your *consommé* boil till the partridge is well done, then strain through a silk sieve, and reduce the *consommé* to a very light glaze. Then take a sufficient quantity of *béchamel*, and mix a spoonful of glaze of game with it; but as this glaze would make the sauce of a brown colour, you must have a few spoonsful of cream to mix with it. You must have for your *sauté*, some truffles cut into the size of a penny. Put them separately into clarified butter, with a little salt.

When you are going to send up the dinner, *sautez* or fry gently the truffles, and when done drain the butter off: put them separately into a small stew-pan, with a little essence of game and truffles. As you are to *mask* those parts only which are not decorated, take up the fillets and dip them into the sauce, but no deeper than the part which you have glazed slightly, in order to render the truffles blacker. When you have dished a large fillet and a small one alternately, you *mask* the *filets mignons* with the remainder of the sauce, and put in the middle the truffles, cut to the size of a penny, which have been lying in a sauce like that which has been used for the fillets. *

No. 58.—*Velouté, or Béchamel, a new method.*

As it is not customary in England, to allow a principal cook six assistants or deputies, for half a dozen or even ten *entrées*, I have thought it incumbent on me to abridge, to the best of my abilities, the various preparations of sauces, &c. Put into a stew-pan, a knuckle of veal, some slices of ham, four or five pounds of beef, the legs and loin of a fowl, all the trimmings of meat or game that you have, and moisten with boiled water, sufficient to cover half the meat, make it sweat gently on a slow fire, till the meat is done through; this you can ascertain by thrusting your knife into it; if no blood flows, it is then time to moisten with boiled water, sufficient to cover all the meat; then season with a bundle of parsley and green onions, a clove, half a bay-leaf, some thyme, a little salt, and some trimmings of mushrooms. When the sauce has boiled long enough to let the knuckle be well done, skim off all the fat, strain it through a silk sieve, and *reduce*† this *consommé* till it is nearly a glaze; next take four spoonsful of very fine flour, dilute it with three pints of very good cream, in a stew-pan big enough to contain the cream, *consommé*, flour, &c.; boil the flour and cream on a slow fire. When it boils, pour to it the *consommé*, and continue to boil it on a slow fire if the sauce be thick, but on a quick fire if the sauce be thin, in order to thicken it. Season with salt, but put no pepper. No white sauce admits pepper, except when you in-

---

* When this sauce is made with great care, it is undoubtedly the *ne plus ultra* of the art.

† *Reduce* means to boil down till reduced.

troduce into it something chopped fine, pepper appearing like dust should therefore be avoided; this sauce should be very thick. Put it into a white basin through a tammy, and keep it in the larder out of the dust.

This sauce is the foundation, if I may use the expression, of all sorts of little sauces; especially in England, where white sauces are preferred. On this account I have relinquished the former method. In summer I was unable to procure any butter fit for use. I accordingly was forced to do without, and discovered that my sauce was the better for it. You must always keep this sauce very thick, as you may thin it whenever you please, either with *consommé* or with cream. If it were too thin, it could not be used for so many purposes.

No. 59.—*Common Rémoulade, and Green Rémoulade.*

Take two or four eggs, boil them hard, then pound the yolks in a mortar, add a spoonful of mustard, pepper, and salt, three spoonsful of oil, one spoonful of vinegar, and break the yolk of a raw egg into it: if you have good sauce in your larder, in preference to the raw egg, put in one spoonful of it to prevent the *rémoulade* from curdling; rub it through a hair sieve, and serve it up.

The *rémoulade verte* is the same as the other, only you have a *ravigotte*, composed of chervil, burnet, tarragon, and parsley. Pound all these, and rub the *rémoulade* and *ravigotte*, in the state of a *purée*, through a tammy. Throw a little *verd de persil* into the *rémoulade*, to make it look quite green. Add likewise a little Cayenne pepper. If approved of, you may put a few chopped shalots. Should you want more sauce, double the quantity of your ingredients. N.B. If you can not procure all these herbs, a little parsley will do, provided you put into the sauce, half a tea-spoonful of each of the following sauces, Chili vinegar, tarragon, Harvey's sauce, carice, and elder vinegar, all which ingredients give exquisite flavour to the *ravigotte.*

No. 60.—*Mayonnaise.*

Take three spoonsful of *Allemande,* six of *aspic,* and two of oil. Add a little tarragon vinegar that has not boiled, some pepper and salt, and chopped *ravigotte,* or some chopped parsley only. Set the whole over some ice, and when the *mayonnaise* begins to freeze, then put in the members of fowl, or fillets of soles, &c. The *mayonnaise* must be put into ice: but the members must not be put into the sauce till it begins to freeze. Dish up the meat or fish, cover it with the sauce before it be quite frozen, and garnish the dish with whatever you think proper, as beet-root, jelly, nasturtiums, &c.

No. 61.—*Egg Sauce.*

Chop two hard eggs, throw them into melted butter, and serve up.

No. 62.—*Verd d'Epinards, or Green Extract of Spinach.*

Pick and wash two large handsful of spinach; pound them in a mortar to extract all the juice. Then squeeze the spinach through a tammy, and pour your juice into a small stew-pan, which put *au bain marie,* * that it may not boil. Watch it close, as soon as it is poached lay it in a silk sieve to drain, and when all the water is drained, use the *verd,* to green whatever may be required. Observe, that the *verd d'epinards* made according to his receipt is far superior to the boiled.

No. 63.—*Verd de Persil.*

The same operation as above. Parsley is a necessary ingredient in many sauces, it gives them an

* See *Bain marie,* page 19.

agreeable flavour. The *verd d'épinards* is without savour, so that it may be used for *entremtês;* but the *verd de persil* is intended for *entrées* and sauces only.

No. 64.—*Sauce à la Pompadour.*

Fry or sweat white a few chopped mushrooms and shalots in a little butter. When well melted, add to them six spoonsful of *sauce tournée,* and two spoonsful of *consommé.* Stew them for three quarters of an hour, on the corner of the stove, and skim off the fat: you must keep your sauce rather thin; then throw in a thickening made of the yolks of three eggs. Moisten with a spoonful or two of cream; add a little pepper and salt, and work your sauce well. When it is done, have a little parsley chopped very fine, blanch it, drain it, and let it cool, that it may look quite green; mix it with the sauce, and serve up. A little lemon-juice may not be amiss, but be aware that acids will always alter the taste of good sauces to their disadvantage, except when highly seasoned.

No. 65.—*La Dusselle.*

This sauce is only used for *panures** broilings, and papillottes, what are called in England the *cotelettes à la Maintenon.* Put a little butter into a stew-pan with an equal quantity of rasped bacon, together with some fine herbs, parsley, shalots, mushrooms, pepper and salt, and a little rasped ham; and stew them on a slow fire. When the fine herbs are done, beat the yolks of four eggs, moisten with the juice of a lemon, and pour that thickening into the *dusselle.* Mind your fine herbs must not be too much done, for in that case the eggs would not thicken the sauce. The *dusselle* is generally used for *cotelettes à la Maintenon,* sweetbreads, and fat liver *caisses,* fillets of rabbits, *fillets mignons à la Pompadour,* mutton tongues, *les papillottes,* &c. &c.

---

* I call *panures* every thing that has crumbs of bread over it.

No. 66.—*Les Pointes d' Asperges.*

Pick some nice asparagus, not however of the finest, but all of an equal size. Cut off the tops only, about an inch long, and blanch them in water with a little salt, but do not boil them too much. Then put them with whatever you choose, but only at the last moment, and that for two different resasons; the first, because they are liable to turn yellow; the other, because they would give a bitter taste to the sauce. If you wish to serve any thing up with asparagus tops, you must put them into a little *velouté* or *Allemande.* They do not look well in a brown sauce. For this reason they are seen in *Macédoines, Chartreuses, pâtés de legumes, vol au vents,* &c. If intended for soups, never put them in but at the moment you send up.

No. 66 (*a*).—*Les Petits Pointes d'Asperge.*

Have some small asparagus, well cleaned, then cut them all equally of the size of small peas, wash and blanch them in boiling water with salt; when they become tender, drain, and put them in cold water. Dry in a clean towel, and put them in a stew-pan with a small bit of butter, a little bunch of green parsley and green onions, letting them simmer quickly on the stove; add a good lump of sugar, a little salt, two or three spoonsful of *sauce tournée,* if you have any, if not, a spoonful of flour, moistened with a spoonful of good *consommé;* let this boil to keep the asparagus very green, put the thickening of two or more eggs, according to the quantity, two eggs for a pint of asparagus—peas, and so in proportion. This method, when well done, has precisely the taste of peas, and is excellent for *entremêts* as well as for sauce; for *entremêts* you must use water only, but for sauce they should be made tasty.

No. 67.—L'Haricot Brun.

Cut some turnips into the shape of heads of garlic, wash them clean, and stew them with a nice *Espagnole*, without frying them in butter, as many persons do. If your sauce be of a fine brown colour, the turnips will acquire the same. Add a little sugar. With regard to salt, it is needless to say, that not a single dish, or sauce, can be prepared without it. When you have no *Espagnole sauce*, take the trimmings of the chops of which you intend to make your *haricot*, and put them into a stew-pan with carrots, turnips, an onion, a little thyme, and a bay-leaf; moisten with a ladle of broth, let it all sweat till the broth is reduced to a glaze of a good colour; then moisten with some boiling water; season with a bunch of parsley and green onions; let it boil for an hour, and strain it through a sieve. Fry the turnips of a good colour, dust them with a spoonful of flour, and moisten with the liquor; skim off all the fat, and cover the chops with the sauce.

No. 68.—L'Haricot vierge.

Cut small turnips into the shape either of corks, or olives, or into any other shape according to your fancy. Blanch them with one single boil in water; drain them; next stew them with a little sugar, and two spoonsful of good *consommé*. Mind they must stew over a sharp fire, that they may be reduced speedily, for otherwise they would be too much done. When they are *à glace*, or reduced, take them off the fire. Pour in three or four spoonsful of *velouté*, according to the new method. If the sauce be too thick, put to it a spoonful of thick cream; do not forget a little salt. This sauce must always be white, and is generally required with glazed articles, which have a sufficient degree of substance.

No. 69.—Hollandoise verte, or Green Dutch Sauce.

Take a couple, or four spoonsful of *sauce tournée*, reduced with a little *consommé*. Give a good seasoning to it; add a *verd de persil*, and work the sauce well. When you send up (and not before,) add a little lemon-juice, for otherwise the sauce would turn yellow.

No. 70.—*Dutch Sauce.*

Put into a stew-pan a tea-spoonful of flour, four spoonsful of elder vinegar, a quarter of a pound of fresh butter, the yolks of five eggs, and a little salt. Put it on the fire, and keep continually stirring it. When it has acquired thickness enough, work it well, that you may refine it. If it should not be curdled, you have no occasion to strain it through a tammy; season well, and serve up. Some people do not like elder vinegar, in that case use tarragon, or plain vinegar. But odorous vinegar is far preferable.

No. 71.—*Sauce Blanche, or French melted Butter.*

Put into a stew-pan a quarter of a pound of fresh butter, a spoonful of flour, a little salt, half a gill or glass of water, half a spoonful of white vinegar, and a little grated nutmeg. Put it on the fire: let it thicken, but do not allow it to boil, for fear it should taste of the flour. Serve up.

No. 71 (*a*).—*Melted Butter. English manner.*

Put into a stew-pan a little flour, a small quantity of water, and a little butter: when the butter is melted, and the sauce quite thick, without having boiled, serve up.

No. 72.—*Ragoût à la Financière.*

You must procure cock's combs, cock's kidneys, fat livers, and a few fowls' eggs. The combs are to be scalded in the following manner. Put the whole of them into a towel, with a handful of salt that has not been pounded. Then lay hold of the four corners of the towel, and dip the part containing the cock's comb into boiling water. Leave it in for a minute, and then take it out, and rub the whole well together, to take off the first skin that is about the combs, and open your towel; if the combs be not skinned sufficiently, dip them into the boiling water a second time; but mind they do not get too firm, because that prevents them from whitening. When they are well skinned, or scalded, pare the little black points that the blood may be extracted. Next put them into a stew-pan of water, and lay them on the corner of your stove for two hours; in which there must be but a very little fire. (Put your hand very frequently into the water, and if you find it too hot for your hand, the combs have spoiled; you put them in the water to extract the blood, and to do this must have it of the same heat as the blood was when the bird was living. If you make the water too hot the blood becomes hardened, and will never come out, which is the cause of the combs so often turning black.) Next blanch them, and put them into a little *blanc*, by which is meant butter, salt, water, and a slice of lemon. Try them frequently, lest they be too much done. The kidneys are not to boil, for then they would break. The eggs are to boil a little, in order that the first skin may come off. This being done, throw the whole into *blanc*. As soon as the combs are done, have ready a nice *Espagnole* reduced, with large mushrooms turned, and some small *quenelles*, which have been poached separately. Mix together, and drain the *ragoût*, the combs, the kidneys, and the eggs. Put the whole into the sauce with the *quenelles;* stir gently, not to break the latter; season well, and use it as occasion may require.

No. 73.—*La Godard.*

This is the same *ragoût* as the *financière*, only it serves to garnish a sirloin of beef. You then add *pigeons gautiers*, and larded sweetbreads; keep your sauce thin, as you have nothing to mask.* This sauce

* *Mask* signifies to cover; when you do not mean to mask, the sauce must be thinner.

must be of a very peculiar flavour; *reduce* two glasses of good Madeira, with a very small bit of sugar, and when almost brought to glaze, put your sauce and *ragoût* to it, which addition constitutes the difference between this and the *financière*.

No. 74.—*La Chambord.*

This is a *ragoût* like the *financière*, with this difference, that you must first reduce a pint of Madeira wine, and mix it with *Espagnole.** Add to the above garnish, soft roes of carp, some good sized craw-fish; mind to take off the small claw of the craw-fish, and to cut the nose very short; and two spoonsful of essence of anchovies. The *quenelles* are to be poached in a spoon. This, to be performed properly, requires two spoons: fill one with the *farce*, which has been levelled all round, with a knife dipped into boiling water. With the other spoon, which is laying also in boiling water, take the *quenelle* out, and put it into a buttered stew-pan. When you have thus *marked* your *quenelles*, pour some boiling water into the stew-pan, and boil them for a quarter of an hour. A small quantity of salt is required in the water. Some people poach the *quenelles* in broth. In my opinion it is wasting the broth.

No. 75.—*Salmi Sauce à l'Espagnole.*

Cut four shalots, and a carrot into large dice, some parsley-roots, a few bits of ham, a clove, two or three leaves of mace, the quarter of a bay-leaf, a little thyme, and get a small bit of butter, with a few mushrooms. Put the whole into a stew-pan over a gentle fire; let it fry till you perceive the stew-pan is coloured all round. Then moisten with half a pint

* This sauce only serves for fish, either salmon, or carp, if you have boiled your fish with *marinade* made with wine, reduce the liquor to put to the *ragoût;* but if it is salmon, use only part of the *marinade,* as that fish gives an oily taste to the sauce; carp and jack give a very good flavour.

of Madeira wine, and a very small lump of sugar. Let it reduce to one-half. Put in six spoonsful of *Espagnole* and the trimmings of your partridges. Let them stew for an hour on the corner of the stove. Skim the fat off, taste whether your sauce be seasoned enough; strain it over the members, make it hot without boiling; dish the *salmi*, and reduce the sauce, which strain through a tammy. Then cover the *salmi* with the sauce.

No. 76.—*Butter of Crawfish.*

Pound the shells and lesser claws, &c. in a mortar with a good lump of fresh butter, till made into a paste. Put this into a small stew-pan *au bain marie.* When it is quite hot, strain it through a tammy over a tureen, or earthen pan, containing cold water. The butter will rise on the surface. Take it when entirely cold, and use it as occasion may require.

No. 77.—*Butter of Anchovies.*

To make this butter, you must have young anchovies. Take them out of the pickle and wash them weel. Take off the bones and head; then pound them in a mortar with fresh butter, till very fine; rub this through a hair sieve. Put this butter, when made, into a pot well covered, to use when wanted; observe, however, that it soon becomes rank.

No. 78.—*Glaze.*

Glaze is very seldom made on purpose, except on particular occasions. Lay on the fire a stock-pot, with plenty of veal, and a small quantity of beef and ham; moisten with broth; when stewed for a proper time, skim it well. The glaze of sweated broth is not so bright. Season the broth with carrots and onions, a large bunch of parsley and green onions; but no turnips or celery, for they give a bitter taste. If you should have a grand dinner, and wish to glaze of a nice colour, put more veal into your *Espagnole*. The moment it comes to a glaze, put part of it into a small stew-pan, for the purpose of glazing only. The most common glaze is made of remnants of broth, the liquor of *braize*, or *fricandeaux*, &c., which are to be reduced on a brisk fire. If you keep your reduction too long, it will become black and bitter. Always warm your glaze *au bain marie*, that it may not get too brown.*

No. 79.—*La Sauce Robert.*

Cut some onions into small dice, fry them of a fine brown, moisten them with some *Espagnole* or *singez*,† and moisten with some gravy of veal. Skim it, that the sauce may look bright; put in a little pepper and salt, and just before you send up, mix a spoonful of mustard.

No. 80.—*La Livernoise.*

Is a *Macédoine*, which you make with some *Espagnole*, instead of *béchamelle*. Reduce some carrots and turnips *à glace*, then put them into the *Espagnole*, which must not boil. Mind that the sauce does not taste of the roots.

No. 81.—*Le Hochepot.*

Turn some carrots, and in winter time blanch them. When they are young, that operation may be dispensed with. Boil them in a little broth and sugar; when done, reduce the broth, and put the whole into a good *Espagnole*. Give them a good seasoning, skim the fat off and serve up.

No. 82.—*La Polonoise.* ‡

Take some of the liquor in which a pike has been boiling. Make a little white *roux*, moisten with the

---

* *Bain marie.*—See note to No. 43.

† *Singez* means, put flour to it with the dredging-box.

‡ This sauce is only made for pike; take the liquor which the fish has been boiled in, and make your sauce of it.

liquor, and reduce it over a large fire. Take a pint of thick cream, boil it, and whilst boiling keep turning it constantly, to prevent a kind of skim from rising. Mix the whole with the sauce, which is to be kept. Have ready some small turnips cut into corks or sticks, that have been boiled in a little water with salt and sugar; drain them well; add them to the sauce; taste whether it be duly seasoned, and *mask*, or cover the fish.

No. 83.—*Cucumbers for Blanquette.*

Cucumbers are good only when quite young; you must take care, however, that they have not a bitter taste. Those are the best that have a rough shaggy coat. Cucumbers are cooked in various ways, either for sauces or for *entremêts*. It is useless to fry them in white clarified butter, (as practised in France.) As soon as they have been pared, stew them in a little *sauce tournée* and sugar, but do not let them stew too long. Lay them in a hair sieve to drain, reduce the liquor in which they have been stewing, and thicken it with the yolks of four eggs. Do not put the cucumbers into the sauce till you are going to send up, for the sauce would get too thin.

No. 84.—*Essence of Cucumbers.*

Peel the cucumbers as above, and keep the *parings*, which are to be made into a *purée* with a little butter. When entirely melted, drain the butter, and moisten with the *sauce tournée*, in which you have stewed the cucumbers, and which have been drained upon a hair sieve, and covered with a round of paper. Reduce this *purée* to a state of absolute consistency, and mix with it four large spoonsful of *béchamelle*. You must also put a little sugar when you stew the cucumbers in the *sauce tournée*. After having thrown in the *béchamelle*, and reduced it, strain the *purée* through a tammy. Put in the scollops of fowls, and toss them in the sauce. If the sauce should happen not to be white enough, pour one or two spoonsful

of thick cream into it. A short time before you send
up, throw the cucumbers into the sauce. Serve hot,
and well seasoned.

This *entrée* is in high estimation amongst the *bons
vivans*, but it requires the greatest attention, or it
will turn out to be but a very indifferent dish.

No. 85.—*Green Peas in White Sauce.*

You must procure some very young peas. Do not
take those which have a kind of kernel, for they are
liable to break, and thicken the sauce. Put the peas
into an earthen pan, with a small bit of butter, and
plenty of fresh water. Handle and shake the peas
well in the water, and then drain and put them to
sweat in a stew-pan, on a little stove, with a small
bunch of parsley and green onions. When they are
nearly done, pour in four or six spoonsful of *sauce
tournée;* reduce it over a large fire, thicken it with
the yolks of two eggs, a little sugar, and send it up.
If the sauce be intended to *mask* or cover the *entrées,*
it must be kept thicker.

No. 86.—*Green Peas l' Espagnole.*

Prepare as above; the only difference lies in using
Espagnole instead of *sauce tournée.* Be particular
in skimming the fat before you reduce the sauce.
Whenever there are peas in a sauce, you must always
put a little sugar.

No. 87.—*Les Pois au Lard, or Peas and Bacon.*

Cut about a pound of bacon (the breast part,) fat
and lean, into square pieces of about an inch; which
boil in water for about half an hour to take off the
salt, drain them, and fry them till they are quite brown.
Then throw them among the peas, that you have previously handled in butter as above. Let them sweat
with a bunch of parsley and green onions. When
well sweated, take the parsley out, and put in a spoonful of *Espagnole,* with a little sugar and salt. There

must be little or no sauce, if intended for *pois au lard* only; but if intended for sauce, it must be thinner.

No. 88.—*La Sauce au pauvre Homme, or Poor Man's Sauce.*

This sauce is generally sent up with young roasted turkeys. Chop a few shalots very fine, and mix them with a little pepper, salt, vinegar and water, and serve it in a boat.

No. 89.—*Love-Apple Sauce.*

Melt in a stew-pan a dozen or two of love-apples; (which before putting in the stew-pan, cut in two, and squeeze the juice and the seeds out,) then put two shalots, one onion, with a few bits of ham, a clove, a little thyme, a bay-leaf, a few leaves of mace, and when *melted*, rub them through a tammy. With this *purée* mix a few spoonsful of good *Espagnole*, a little salt and pepper. Boil it for twenty minutes, and serve up.

No. 90.—*Sauce à la Bigarade, or Bitter Orange Sauce.*

Cut off the thin rind only, and quite equally, of two bitter oranges. Blanch it. Have ready a rich *Espagnole* reduced, and throw the rind, with a small bit of sugar, into it, and season it well. When you are going to send up, add the juice of one of the oranges and a little lemon. The sauce must be made strong, on account of the acids.

No. 91.—*La Sauce au Céleri.*

Cut off the stalks of a dozen heads of celery. Pare all the heads, and let them be well washed. Blanch them. Stew them in a *blanc*, with some beef-suet, some fat of bacon, a small bit of butter, a little salt, and some lemon-juice. When they are done, drain them well, cut them about an inch in length, and put them into some *béchamelle.* This sauce is not to be too highly seasoned, but kept thick for the purpose of *masking.*

No. 92.—*The Pascaline.*

This sauce is most particularly sent up with lamb or mutton trotters. Make a white *Italienne* (Vide No. 22.), keep it rather thin. Thicken it with the yolks of two eggs, mixed with the juice of a lemon. A short time before you send it up, throw in a little chopped parsley that has been blanched.

No. 93.—*Sauce à l'Aurore.*

Pound the spawn of a lobster with a little butter, and strain it through a hair sieve. Take the straining, and mix it with a *sauce tourné* reduced, and the juice of a lemon. This sauce must be highly seasoned with pepper and salt, &c. It is generally sent up with fillets of trout, or fillets of soles.

No. 94.—*The Toulouse.*

Have an *Allemande* ready (Vide No. 20.), and rather thick. Throw into it a *ragoût* of cocks' combs, kidneys, fat livers, the choicest mushrooms, small *quenelles,* &c. It should be observed, that in cookery there are two kinds of white *ragoûts,* the one with the *béchamelle,* is called the *Ragoût à la Royal;* the other with the *Allemande,* is called the *Toulouse,* which, however, is the same as the *Allemande.*

No. 95.—*La Wasterfisch.*

When you have boiled the perch with roots of parsley, a few slices of onions, as many shreds of parsley, and some pepper and salt, drain through a silk sieve, part of the seasoning which has been reduced, with four spoonsful of *velouté* or *béchamelle.* Then take some roots of parsley and some carrots, cut in the same manner as for the *julienne*, and let them stew with a little pepper and salt, and water. Drain them and throw them into the sauce. You must mix a few heads of parsley that have been blanched very green with this sauce, and a small bit of butter, some pepper and salt, and a very little lemon. Mask the perch, or fillets of soles with it.

No. 96.—*Oyster Sauce.*

Be careful in opening the oysters to preserve the liquor. Put them into a stew-pan over a stove on a sharp fire. When they are quite white and firm, take them out of the water with a spoon, and drain them on a hair sieve; then pour off the liquor gently into another vessel, in order to have it quite clear. Put a small bit of fresh butter into a stew-pan, with a spoonful of flour, fry it over a small fire for a few minutes; dilute it with the oyster-liquor; add to it two spoonsful of cream; let it boil till the flour is quite done, then add the oysters, after having taken off the beards. Season with a little salt, and one spoonful of essence of anchovies. If the oyster sauce is to serve with fowl, do not put anchovies in it, but add three or four spoonsful of good *béchamelle*.

No. 97.—*L'Italienne with Truffles.*

Chop some nice black truffles. Sweat them in a little *consommé*, and mix them with the *Brown Italian Sauce* (Vide No. 23.) If you happen to have no *Italienne* ready, stew them for half an hour in an *Espagnole* only. Let this sauce be kept thin and highly seasoned.

No. 98.—*La Manselle.**

Make a *salmi* as indicated above, with this difference, that you pound all the parings and bones, &c.

---

* This sort of *salmi* is generally used for woodcocks or partridges, if requisite.

which you put into the sauce when it is done. **Rub**
this *purée* through a tammy, and pour it over the
members of game or fowls. This sauce is to be kept
hot, without boiling, otherwise it will curdle.*

No. 99.—*Sauce à la Maréchalle.*

Take a handful of green tarragon, and boil it for
ten minutes in four spoonsful of white vinegar. Put
in a very small lump of sugar with a little salt. When
the vinegar is half reduced, pour in four large spoonsful of *sauce tournée* reduced, and give it one single
boil, then thicken with two yolks of eggs. Strain the
sauce through a tammy, and add to it a quarter of a
pound of fresh butter. Work your sauce well, and
pour it over the meat or fish, quite hot. This sauce
is to be kept rather thick, that it may adhere either
to the meat or fish. N. B. If you have no tarragon,
use tarragon or elder vinegar reduced, and proceed
as above directed.

Observations relative to the Sauces.

Amongst the number of sauces that have been
mentioned, many may be found that are not to be
used. The author, however, thought it incumbent
upon him to introduce them all, from a fear of incur-
ring censure. If four *entrées* only are to be sent up
to table, it would be ridiculous to make preparations
that would answer the purpose of a grand dinner.
Instead then of using a great many sorts of *broth*,
suage, coulis, &c. merely prepare a stock-pot the
preceding day, if you have leisure, with twenty
pounds of beef, a knuckle of veal, and a hen; do not
season with too much vegetable. As this is to be
used for sauces, the vegetable would give a disagreeable taste to some of them when reduced.

When you are to send up a dinner of six or eight
entrées, with a view of not carrying the expense to

* This sauce is called by the modern cooks, *salmi à l'ancienne;*
the ancients, however, knew what they were about.

an extreme, take a nice rump of beef, and about twelve pounds of buttock, a leg and knuckle of veal, and as there must be no waste, the rump is used to make a remove; make *grenadins*, or *fricandeau*, or *quenelles* with the *noix* of veal. By this means the expense is reduced. On the preceding evening put into a stock-pot twelve pounds of beef, with the bones and trimmings of the rump, a knuckle of veal, and a few other parings, if you have any. Set the pot to skim, and season it with two large onions, one of which is to be stuck with four cloves, three carrots, four large leeks, as many turnips, a head of celery, a little salt, and leave the whole to stew on a slow fire for five hours. Strain the broth through a silk sieve, and skim the fat; for if the broth of any description be not thus skimmed, it will turn sour in the course of the night, particularly in hot weather. On the next day mark your sauces with this broth; and the day on which you are to serve the dinner, make another stock-pot with the rump, a knuckle of veal, and a hen, seasoned in the same manner as above. This broth is used for *potages*, and to moisten the *braizes*.

Mark* in a stew-pan some thin slices of ham, and a few slices of veal, moistened with some of the broth, which reduce to a glaze. When it begins to thicken, so as to stick, put the stew-pan on a very slow fire, in order that the glaze may get a good colour without burning; then moisten with the broth, to which you add a bunch of parsley and green onions, and a few mushrooms; let them stew for an hour. Next make a *roux*, and moisten it with part of the gravy of veal; and keep some of it for the gravy of the roasts; skim all the grease off, and use it when occasion may require.

For the white sauces, put some slices of ham in the stew-pan with a few pieces of veal, the bones and remnants of fowl, which moisten with the same broth you have used for the *coulis* or *Espagnole*. When

* Mark, or prepare.

the meat is sweated through, cover it entirely with boiling hot broth, season with a bunch of parsley and green onions and a few mushrooms, and stew the whole for an hour and a half; skim off the fat. This *consommé* is used to make either the *velouté*, or *béchamelle*, No. 58, or *la sauce tournée*, which is the key to all other thick sauces, &c.

The stock-pot must be put on the fire at an early hour. The rump of beef must be kept hot. Reduce to glaze the broth that you have left after having made every article. This glaze may serve either to strengthen or to glaze. If you are frequently set to work, you must always have a little glaze ready. By this means you have no occasion to reduce your liquor till the following day, and it will serve for the morrow.

CHAPTER II.

POTAGES AND SOUPS.

No. 1.—*Soupe de Santé*, or *au Naturel*.

TAKE some broth well skimmed, and the fat taken off. Take thin slices of crust of bread, cut round, of the size of a shilling. Soak them separately in a little broth. As you are going to serve up, put the whole into a tureen without shaking, for fear of crumbling the bread, which would spoil the look of the broth, and make it thick; add some of the vegetables that have been boiled in the broth, and trimmed nicely.

No. 2.—*Potage consommé of Fowl*.

Take some *consommé* of fowl, and clarify it, after having mixed with it some veal gravy, to give it a good colour. Prepare the bread as above. N. B. This will not serve for a large dinner.

No 3.—*Potage à la Clermont*.

Take some good broth, mixed with a little gravy of veal, in order to give a nice brown colour to the broth. Take a dozen of small white onions; cut them into rings, and fry them in clarified butter. When they are of a fine colour drain them on a sieve, throw them into a little broth made hot, to rid them of the butter that might remain; then mix them with the clarified broth, and let them boil for half an hour. Put in thin bits of bread, as in No. 1, and some salt. Remember that the bread would spoil the look of the broth, if put in whilst the latter is boiling.

No. 4.—*Potage à la Julienne.*

Take some carrots and turnips, and turn them ribband like, a few heads of celery, some leeks and onions, and cut them all into fillets thus: ▬▬▬▬ Then take about two ounces of butter and lay it at the bottom of a stew-pan, and the roots over the butter. Fry them on a slow fire, and keep stirring gently; moisten them with broth and gravy of veal, let them boil on the corner of the stove; skim all the fat off, put in a little sugar to take off the bitter taste of the vegetables: you may in summer time add green peas, asparagus-tops, French beans, some lettuce, or sorrel. In winter time the taste of the vegetables being too strong, you must blanch them, and immediately after stew them in the broth: if they were fried in butter, their taste would also be too strong. Bread as above.

No. 5.—*The Julienne with consommé of Fowl.*

The same as above, only you moisten it with *consommé* of fowl, and put in the back of a roasted chicken, which stew with the roots, and send up with the bread as above.

No. 6.—*Cressi Soup.*

Take the red part of eight carrots, two turnips, the white of four leeks, two onions, three heads of celery, all washed very clean. Mince the whole small, put a bit of fresh butter at the bottom of a stew-pan, and the roots over it; put it on a slow fire. Let it sweat a long while, and stir it frequently; when fried enough to be rubbed through a tammy, add a small crust of bread, moistened with some broth; let the whole boil gently. When done, skim all the fat off, and rub the whole through a tammy. Put it to boil on the corner of the stove in order to skim off all the grease, and the oil of the vegetables; then cut some crumbs of bread into dice, fry it in butter till of a good colour, and put it into the soup when you serve up. This *purée* may be used with rice, vermicelli, Italian paste, small macaroni, &c.

No. 7.—*Soupe à l'Aurore.*

Take some carrots, the reddest that are to be met with, scrape them well; wash them clean; then take off the outside till you come to the middle part. Sweat it in about a quarter of a pound of fresh butter, on a very slow fire. When the carrots are soft enough, put in a crust of bread well rasped, and moistened with some good broth. Let the whole boil for about an hour, and rub it through a tammy, then pour a little more broth in, that it may boil again. Skim it; when you have taken off the fat, it will be of a reddish colour. Put in some bits of soft bread cut into dice, that have been fried in butter till they are of a light brown. Observe, that *purée* is in perfection only when the carrots are new, old carrots will not answer: this *purée* may be used as above with rice paste, &c.

No. 8.—*La Brunoise.**

Take some carrots, turnips, &c. cut them into dice, and in summer time fry them in butter; but in the winter season blanch them. When fried without having lost their original colour, moisten them with rich broth, seasoned with salt and a little sugar, and let the whole boil for about an hour. You may add green peas, asparagus-tops, &c. Skim off the fat, and put bits of crust of bread, the same as No. I. soaked separately in broth. These you put in only at the moment of serving up, that the bread may not crumble.

* This soup has the same flavour as the *Julienne*, the only difference is in the shape of the vegetables.

No. 9.—*Soupe à l'Allemande.*

Make a *pâte à nouilles* (see *pâte à nouilles*), cut into dice, blanch and drain it, and then let it cool. Boil them in rich broth. When thoroughly done, take them out of the broth, and throw them into a good rich *consommé* of fowl well clarified. When you take them out of the liquor in which they have boiled, you must use a skimmer, and drain them in a clean napkin, then put them into the *consommé*, and serve up. If you do not use these precautions, the broth will be muddy, and not so well flavoured.

No. 10.—*Soupe à la Condé.*

Take about a pint of red beans, well washed, let them soak in soft water for about a couple of hours: then put them into a small pan with a pound of the breast part of bacon, a knuckle of veal, and the legs and back of a roasted fowl, if you have any such thing by you. Put the whole together with an onion stuck with two cloves, a carrot, and a couple of leeks, a bunch of parsley, green onions, thyme, bay-leaves, and a little salt and pepper. Moisten with soft cold water, and let the beans boil till they are quite soft. Then take the beans, pound them, and rub them through a sieve; moisten with the liquor sufficiently thin to admit the fat being skimmed off. Then boil the soup in the corner of the stove till all the white scum is entirely gone, then the soup must be very red. Slices of bread fry and prepare as in No. 6. If you have good *consommé* in the larder, you may dispense with putting any beef, veal, or fowl in the beans; bacon only, or the knuckle of a ham, if you have one. The fat of the ham will be better than bacon.

No. 11.—*Soupe à la Faubonne.*

Prepare the vegetables and roots, as in No. 6. Mince some cabbage lettuce and sorrel, and sweat them separately; throw them into the soup when you have skimmed off the fat. Slices of bread as above. This soup is almost the same as the *Cressi* No. 6, the lettuce and sorrel give an additional flavou⁻, and vary it slightly.

No. 12.—*Soupe à la Carmelite.*

Take some lentils *à la reine*, which prepare as the beans above: when stewed, rub them through a tammy; moisten the *purée* with a little gravy of veal, and rich broth. When well skimmed throw in the bread. Send up rather thin, as it is liable to thicken when getting cold.* If you have a couple of rumps of fowl from the *sautée*, make a *purée* of it the same as that for the *soup à la reine*, which will make the soup more delicate.

No. 13.—*Purée of Green Peas.*

Take three pints of large peas of a nice green colour, sweat them with a quarter of a pound of butter, and a handful of parsley and green onions, over a slow fire, till they be thoroughly stewed, then put them into the mortar with the parsley and green onions; when they are well pounded, rub them through a *tammy*, and moisten this *purée* with the best *consommé*. Leave it on the corner of the stove; for if it were to boil, the peas would lose their green colour. Just at the moment of sending up, put in square slices of bread nicely fried.

No. 14.—*The same made very green.*

Take three pints of large green peas, fresh gathered, boil them with a handful of parsley and green onions in salt and water, very quickly; when they become tender, drain and put them in the mortar, pound them well; and when you rub the *purée* through the *tammy*, moisten with good broth, season with

---

* This soup is very good to make when you have *soupe à la reine* left; mixed with it, it is excellent.

salt and sugar; let it be very hot, but mind it do not boil, it will lose its green colour: the bread cut and fry as above. When the peas are not very green, you may use the green of spinage. See page 33, or elsewhere green extract of spinage or parsley.

No. 15.—*Macaroni with consommé.*

Take a quarter of a pound of Naples macaroni, and boil it in water, till it is nearly done. Strain well, and put it into a rich *consommé* to boil. Let it be well done; rasp some Parmesan cheese, which send up separately in a plate.

No. 16.—*Lazagnes au consommé, or Flat Macaroni.*

Take Naples *Lazagnes;* boil them as the macaroni (Vide No. 15), and serve up in the same manner, with cheese in a separate plate.

No. 17.—*Rice Soup.*

Take half a quarter of a pound of Carolina rice, picked clean, and washed in two or three different waters, till no smell or dirt remain. Blanch it in boiling water, and drain it. Then take some rich broth, season it well, throw the rice in and let it boil, but not so as to be too much done, for then it breaks and does not look well.

No. 18.—*Rice with different sorts of purée.*

The rice is to be prepared as above: only mix it with the *purée* you have chosen one hour before you send up, in order that the rice may retain the taste and colour of the vegetables. The *purées* intended for soups are not to be so thick as those that are intended for sauces. Those that are most generally used, are *purée* of carrots, turnips, celery, white beans, red ditto, lentils, green peas, the *cressi*, &c. The mode of proceeding is the same with all the various kinds of *purée;* they only differ in the taste and colour of the particular vegetable used. All the various vegetables being mixed together, take the name of *cressi.* When used separately, each retains its own respective appellation, and is made as at No. 6. p. 47.

No. 19.— *Vermicelli Soup.*

For eight people take a quarter of a pound of *vermicelli,* which blanch in boiling water to take off the taste of dust. Strain it and throw it into some broth that is boiling, otherwise the *vermicelli* would stick together, and could not be diluted unless crumbled into a thousand pieces. All *pureés* used as above. Mind, the *vermicelli* must be boiled in broth before you mix it with any of the *purée,* and take care to break the *vermicelli* before you blanch it in the water, otherwise it will be in long pieces and unpleasant to serve up.

No. 20.— *Italian Pastes.*

Take Italian pastes, and prepare them as above (Vide No. 19,) and as follows (Vide No. 21.) Italian pastes are made of various shapes, but are always alike in flavour: they mix well with all sorts of *purée.*

No. 21— *Vermicelli à la Reine.*

Blanch the *Vermicelli* in boiling water, drain it, and throw it into some rich *consommé* well seasoned. When done, a short time before you send it up, thicken it with the yolks of eight eggs, mixed with cream, and pour the vermicelli into the tureen for fear the thickening should get too much done, which would be the case if it remained on the corner of the stove.

No. 22.— *Turnip Broth.*

Is made with about a dozen turnips, peeled and

cut into slices. Blanch them for a sort time in water; drain them, and put them with a knuckle of veal, a small piece of beef, and the half of a hen, into a stew-pan; and pour some rich boiling broth over the whole. Let the whole stew for about two hours. Then strain it through a double silk sieve, and use it with rice, vermicelli, &c. &c.

No. 22.—*Potage à la Reine: a new Method.*

For twelve people take three fat chickens or pullets, which are generally cheaper and better than fowls: skin them, take out the lungs, wash them clean, and *mark* them in a pan with a bunch of parsley only; moisten the whole with good boiling broth: let it stew for an hour, then take out the chickens: soak the crumb of two penny loaves in the broth; take off the flesh of the chickens, and pound it with the yolks of three or four eggs boiled hard, and the crumb of bread which has been sufficiently soaked in the broth. Rub the whole through a tammy; then put a quart of cream on the fire, and keep it stirring continually till it boils. Pour it into the soup. It is not liable to curdle as when the other method is used, and it tastes more of the chickens. If you think proper to add either barley, rice, or vermicelli, let it be stewed in broth beforehand, and pour it into the soup only when quite done. When you have a great dinner, and fowls are very dear, you must use the fillets for *entrées*, and make the soup with the legs only; the soup is as good, but not quite so white, as when made with the fillets.

No. 24.—*Semolina with consommé.*

Boil some *consommé* and throw the *semolina* into it. If you are inclined to mix a *purée* with it, keep the *semolina* thinner. You may use any *purée* you please, the same as with rice, No. 18.

No. 25.—*Cream of Rice.*

This is flour of rice, which you make yourself in the following manner. Take a pound of rice, well washed, in different waters, and drained and wiped with a clean towel. Let it get quite dry; then pound and shake it through a sieve. Take one or two spoonsful of this flour, and dilute it with broth, rather cold than hot. All this time you have some broth on the fire; throw the flour of rice thus diluted into the broth, and keep stirring till you find the soup is not too thick and may boil without the rice burning. This same kind of rice flour may serve for *soufflés* of the second course.

No. 26.—*The Garbure with Brown Bread.*

Take a knuckle of ham, perfectly sweet, a knuckle of veal, and about six pounds of flank of beef, which put into a pan, with an onion stuck with two cloves, a few carrots, &c.; pour over the above two ladles of broth, and let the whole sweat over a slow fire. When the meat is done through the middle, cover it entirely with boiling broth, and let the whole stew for three hours. Then take one or more cabbages, which are to be washed clean and blanched. *Braize* them between layers of bacon, and moisten them with the liquor in which the sweating has been made, strained through a silk sieve. You must observe, that if the cabbages are not made rich and mellow, they are good for nothing. Add to the above, either sausages, bacon, or stewed legs of geese, if you have any: mind above all things, that the cabbage be not too briny, for the soup then would not be eatable. When the cabbage and broth are stewed enough, cut very thin slices of rye-bread: drain the cabbage in a cloth, so that there be no fat left, then take a large deep silver dish, lay a bed of bread, and over that, one of cabbage, and moisten them with a little broth; let them *gratiner* on a slow fire. When the cabbage and bread are sufficiently moistened, lay on six or eight beds more of each, and let it simmer on the stove. Send up with the ham on the middle; the bacon, the legs of geese, and sausages on the borders, and some broth separately. This soup is never seen in this country, it requires a very deep and very large dish.

No. 27.—*Potage with Cabbage.*

Take four cabbages, with curling leaves; wash them clean, blanch and *braize* them with a little seasoning; observing, however, that for a soup they are not to be so highly seasoned, as for an *entrée*. Your soup may be prepared as in No. 1. Cut the cabbages into quarters, and put them into the soup when the latter is in the tureen. This broth is to be prepared plain, and kept clear, as the cabbages, being *braized*, are very tasty; cut them nicely, and put them on the top of the soup.

No. 28.—*German Cabbage Soup.*

Take a white cabbage, mince and wash it well, and let it sweat on a slow fire in a little butter. When it begins to get tender and to be a little reduced, moisten it with half broth and half gravy of veal very clear; skim off the fat, and when the soup gets of a fine brown colour, throw in slices of bread cut to the size of a penny thus (), and send up.

No. 29.—*Soupe à la Bonne-Femme; or good Lady's Soup.*

Take two handsful of sorrel; after having taken off the stalks, put the leaves one above another and mince them. Take the hearts of two or three cabbage-lettuces, which mince likewise. Wash the whole well, then take about two ounces of fresh butter, and put the herbs to melt in a small stock-pot. When so, moisten with broth,* and let it boil for an hour. Skim

* If you have in the larder, the back and legs of a roast fowl, put them into a stew-pan with a few carrots, turnips, and celery;

off the fat, and throw in a little sugar, to take off the acidity of the sorrel. Then thicken the soup with the yolks of eight eggs, mixed with a little cream. Remember to keep a little broth to soak the bread in. If you were to put the bread in, you would not be able to stir the soup. When you put the thickening in, the bread will all break into crumbs.

No. 30.—*Potage aux Nouilles.*

Take a handful or two of flour, with which mix a little salt, the yolks of three eggs, a little water, and a small bit of butter. Let this paste be as compact as possible. Spread it very thin on the table, next cut it in small slices as a *Julienne;* then blanch it in water, drain it, and let it cool, in order to get rid of the flour, which might spoil the appearance of the soup. Throw the paste into some rich broth, and let it stew till it is mellow. You may introduce either turnip broth, or *purée* as above.

No. 31.—*Soupe à la Borgosse.*

This soup, although a *potage de desserte,* has some admirers even amongst the first epicures. If you should have left in your larder a small quantity of rice soup, or peas soup, or good lady's soup, mix and make them hot, but without boiling, as the thickening would most undoubtedly curdle. Rub the whole through a tammy, and put it into a stew-pan *au bain marie.* Then boil some green Windsor beans; when done, skin them, andthrow the kernels into the soup: when you are going to send up, put in some bits of bread cut into dice, fried in butter, and well drained of the butter.

No. 32.—*Milk Soup, with Almond Laurel.*

Boil in a quart of milk, a leaf of almond laurel,

a little parsley and chervil, &c.; moisten with some good broth; let the whole boil till thoroughly done; skim it well, strain it, and moisten the sorrel with this.

some sugar, and a little salt. Thicken it with the
yolks of six eggs just as you are going to send up.
Have a tin-cutter, and cut some slices of bread of
the size of a penny, (as the bread crumb only must
be used.) Cut as many pieces, and put them on a
baking sheet over one another; then pour over them
some fine pounded sugar, and place them in the oven.
Then put the salamander over, to give them a good
colour. Just as you are going to serve up, throw
two pieces of bread into the soup tureen, and pour
the soup over them. Serve quick.

No. 33.—*Potage au Lait d'Amande.*

Boil a quart of milk as above, seasoned with a little
salt. The bread as in No. 32. Put a quarter of a
pound of sweet almonds, and a dozen of bitter ones,
into hot water, peel and pound them in a mortar;
moisten with a little milk to prevent their turning
into oil. When sufficiently fine, rub them through
a tammy, and throw them into the soup instead of a
thickening. They must not boil. *

No. 34.—*La Tortue. Turtle Soup.*

If you wish to make turtle soup with less difficulty,
cut off the head the preceding day. In the morning
open the turtle: this is done by leaning heavy with
your knife on the shell of the animal's back, whilst
you cut it off all round. Turn it upright on its end,
that all the water, &c. may run out. Then cut the
flesh off along the spine, with your knife sloped towards the bones, for fear of touching the gall, which
sometimes might escape your eye. When you have
obtained all the flesh that is about the members, wash
them clean, and let them drain. Have ready a large
vessel full of boiling water on the fire, put in the
shells, and when you perceive that they come off
easily, take them out of the water, and prick all the

---

* This soup and the above are intended for Lent, when the
Catholics eat neither meat nor butter.

shells of the back, belly, fins, head, &c. Boil the back and belly in water till you can take off the bones, without, however, allowing the softer parts to be sufficiently done, as they will boil again in the sauce. When these latter come off easily, lay them on earthen dishes singly, for fear they should stick together, and put them to cool. Keep the liquor in which you have blanched the softer parts, and let the bones stew thoroughly in it, as this liquor must be used to moisten all the sauces.

All the flesh of the interior parts, the four legs and head must be sweated in the following manner. Lay a few slices of ham on the bottom of a very large stew-pan. Lay over the ham two or three knuckles of veal, according to the size of the turtle, and over the veal, the inside flesh of the turtle, and the members over the whole. Then partly moisten it with the water in which you are boiling the shell, and sweat it thoroughly. You may ascertain if the meat be thoroughly done, by thrusting your knife into the fleshy part of the meat. If no blood issue, it is time to moisten it again with the liquor in which the bones, &c. have been boiling: put in a large bunch of all such sweet herbs as are used in the cooking of a turtle: sweet basil, sweet marjoram, lemon thyme, winter savory, two or three bay-leaves, common thyme, a handful of parsley and green onions, and a large onion stuck with six cloves. Let the whole be thoroughly done. With respect to the members, probe them, to see whether they are done, and when done, drain and send them to the larder, as they are to make their appearance only when the sauce is absolutely completed. When the flesh is also completely done, drain it through a silk sieve; make a white *roux* very thin, for turtle soup must not be much thickened; when the flour is sufficiently done on a slow fire, and has a good colour, moisten it with the liquor, and turn this sauce over the fire till it boils. Ascertain that the sauce is neither too thick nor too thin, then put the stew-pan on the side of the stove, to skim off all the white scum, and all the fat and oil, that rises on the surface of the sauce. By this time all the softer parts will be cold enough; cut them about an inch or two square, without waste, throw the whole into the sauce, which must simmer gently. Then try them again, for if done enough, they are not to be kept on the fire any longer. Skim off all the fat and froth. Take all the leaves of the herbs from the stock, sweet basil, sweet marjoram, lemon thyme, winter savory, two or three bay-leaves, common thyme, a handful of parsley and green onions, and a large onion cut in four pieces, with a few leaves of mace, put them in a stew-pan, with about a quarter of a pound of fresh butter. Let this simmer on a slow fire, till they are quite melted, then pour in one bottle of good Madeira wine, adding a small bit of sugar, and let this boil gently for one hour. When done, rub this through a tammy, and put it into the sauce. Let this boil, till no white scum rises: then take with a skimmer, all the bits of turtle, out of the sauce, and put them in a clean stew-pan; when you have all out, pour the sauce over the bits of turtle, through a tammy, and proceed as follows. Make some *quenelles à tortue*, which being substitutes for eggs, do not require to be very delicate. They are made in the following manner: take out the fleshy part of a leg of veal, about one pound, scrape off all the meat, without leaving any sinews or fat, and soak in milk about the same quantity of crumbs of bread. When the bread is well soaked, squeeze it, and put it into a mortar, with the veal, a small quantity of calves' udder, a little butter, the yolks of four eggs, boiled hard, a little Cayenne pepper, salt, and spices, and pound the whole very fine. Then thicken the mixture with two whole eggs, and the yolk of another. Next try the *farce* in boiling hot water, to ascertain its consistency; if you find it too thin, add the yolk of an egg. When the *farce* is perfected, take half of it, and put into it some chopped parsley. Let the whole cool, in order to roll it of the size of the yolk of an egg; poach it in salt and boiling water, and when very hard drain on a sieve, and put it into the turtle. Before you send up, squeeze the juice of two or three lemons, with a little Cayenne pepper, and pour that into the soup. The fins may be served as a *plat d'entrée* with a little turtle sauce; if not, on the following day you may warm the turtle *au bain marie*, and serve the members entire, with a *matelotte* sauce, garnished with mushrooms, cocks' combs, *quenelles*, &c. When either lemon-juice or Cayenne pepper have been introduced, no boiling must take place. It is necessary to observe, that the turtle prepared a day before it is used, is generally preferable, the flavour being more uniform. Be particular, when you dress a very large turtle, to preserve the green fat* in a separate stew-pan, and likewise when the turtle is entirely done, to have as many tureens as you mean to serve each time. You can not put the whole in a large vessel, for many reasons: first, it will be long in cooling; secondly, when you take some out, it will break all the rest into rags. If you warm in a *bain marie*, the turtle will always retain the same taste, but if you boil it often, it becomes strong, and loses the delicacy of its flavour.

N. B. It is not the fashion to serve eggs with turtle, but it may be necessary to inquire whether they are preferred.

Some people require besides *fricandeaux*, *blanquettes*, &c. all of which are prepared in the same manner as veal. (See *fricandeaux, blanquettes.*)

No. 35.—*Spring Soup.*

Take carrots, turnips, heads of celery, and small onions, cut into the shape of olives, blanch them, in winter; but in summer, fry them with a little butter, and put them to boil in clear broth, with a little sugar. Put the soup in the corner of the stove to skim

---

* Be cautious not to study a very brown colour, the natural green of the fish is preferred by every epicure and true connoisseur.

away all the butter. Have ready the green tops of asparagus, and French beans cut into lozenges, which have been boiled separately in water very green, put them into the soup, when you send up, with slices of crust of bread cut of the size of a penny, and soaked separately in a little broth; if you have any peas, you may put in some likewise, to boil with the soup.

No. 36.—*Potage à la Jardinière, or Gardener's Soup.*

This is like all other Spring soups, only add leaves of sorrel and lettuce, without the stalks. Vegetable soups are in general very wholesome, and have always the same taste. The cutting of the vegetables forms the only variety.

No. 37.—*Mutton Cutlet Soup, or ScotchBroth.*

Take some of the worst cutlets of the neck, according to the number of persons you expect at dinner; trim them, but not too finely, put them by, and with the trimmings make the soup in the following manner: put in a stew-pan the mutton trimmings, some scragg ditto, and a knuckle of veal, moisten this with good boiling broth; then season the broth with a bunch of celery, leeks, parsley, one large onion, with two cloves, the trimmings of the turnips, cut in dice, and one or two carrots. Let this boil gently three hours, season it with salt, and skim off the fat; when it becomes of a good flavour, drain it over the chop, that you must put in a small stew-pan, large enough, however, to contain the *potage*, have some barley that has been boiled a long time. In general, I have my barley from the nursery or the storekeeper, when they throw it out, it is then quite in season for the soup; wash it very well, and put it with the turnips and chop to boil one hour. Skim again before you serve up. No bread is used to this soup. Celery cut into dice, with the turnips give additional flavour: sometimes the author adds, just at dinner time, a little parsley chopped very fine, just as you serve up.

No. 38.—*Hochepot Soup.*

Cut some carrots, turnips, and a few heads of celery, into the shape of small corks or otherwise. Blanch them, and put them into some nice brown clear broth. Let them boil for about an hour or more. You must have a few mutton chops done separately, that they may not make the broth look white. Throw them into the soup, with the bread as in No. 1. Serve up hot and without any fat. The same is done with ox tails or some of the cheek of the beef; but take care to boil the cheeks for some time separately in water, and to pour the water away, otherwise the soup will taste like tripe. When you make the soup with the cheek, and serve it up along with the broth, it is a great treat in a country house.

No. 39.—*Mock Turtle, English Fashion.*

Take a calf's head very white and very fresh, bone the nose part of it; put the head into some warm water to discharge the blood. Squeeze the flesh with your hand to ascertain that it is all out. Mind the water should never be too hot for you to bear your hand in it; as long as you can bear it, the blood will come out, but if you suffer it to be too hot, it will turn the head black. When well disgorged, blanch the head in boiling water; when firm, put it into cold water, prepared *blanc* in the following way to boil it in: cut half a pound of fat bacon, a pound of beef suet, an onion stuck with a clove, and two slices of lemon; add to these slices of carrot, a bunch of parsley, green onions, thyme, bay-leaves, sweet basil, salt and pepper; put all these into a vessel, with water enough to contain the head; boil the head in this, and take care to put it in a cloth when done, and observe that it be not over-done; let it cool in the liquor, then make the sauce in the following manner.

Put into a stew-pan, a pound of ham cut in slices, put over the ham two knuckles of veal; a large onion, and two carrots, moisten with some of the broth, in which you have boiled the head, to half the depth of the meat only: cover the stew-pan, and put it over the fire to sweat through, let the broth reduce to a very good colour, turn up the meat, for fear of burning. When you have a very good colour, and you find that the glaze is very brown, moisten with the whole broth from the head, season with a large bundle of sweet herbs, viz. sweet basil, sweet marjoram, lemon thyme, common thyme, two cloves, a bay-leaf, a few allspice, parsley, green onions, and a few mushrooms; let this boil together for one hour, then drain it. Put into a stew-pan a quarter of a pound of very fresh butter, let it melt over a slow fire; put to this butter as much flour as it can receive; let it go gently over a slow fire, till the flour has acquired a very good brown colour; moisten this gradually with the broth, that you put through a silk sieve, till you have employed it all; add half a bottle of Madeira; let the sauce boil, that the flour may be well done; take off all the scum and fat; cut the calf's-head into square pieces of about an inch each; put them to boil in the sauce; season with salt and Cayenne pepper, and lemon-juice, and add some *quenelles.*—(See *farce à quenelle*), the bit of calf's head should always have the skin on one side; but you should leave none of the meat on that does not adhere to the skin, otherwise the meat will break in the soup and look unseemly. It is out of fashion now to use eggs, but on this head consult the taste of your principal.

Observe, that you must not have the *quenelles* too delicate, for they would break in the soup, and spoil the look of it; the calf's head must not be too much done; thrust your knife into the skin, and if the knife enters and detaches itself easily the meat is done enough. Some gentlemen will have their mock turtle green; in that case, you must do as follows; put into a stew-pan a quarter of a pound of fresh butter, mince one or two onions, add a handful of each of the herbs described above, and some parsley, and sweat it all gently over a slow fire. When the herbs are well done, moisten with some of the sauce, and rub it through a tammy. Lastly, mix this with the sauce, and the turtle will be green, without any alteration in the flavour.

No. 40.—*Potage à la Bouveau.*

Take some turnips, peel them, and use a cutter with which you cut out a few balls as round as possible, but very small. Blanch them, and boil them in some *consommé* well clarified, with a little sugar. Serve up with bits of bread as in No. 1. It must appear very bright; put to it two spoonsful of gravy veal.

No. 41.—*Potage à la Regenca.*

This potage can only be in perfection when you have game, and is not very expensive, as it usually is made with unused bones and legs of pheasants, proceed as follows:

Take the back, the leg, and other bones of one or two roasted pheasants, which place in a stew-pan, with slices of carrot, onions, celery, turnips, and a little chervil, moisten with good boiling broth, and let it boil gently for two hours. Skim all the fat, and drain the broth through a silk sieve; have some pearl barley, which has been well washed and boiled in water several times. Boil it in some of the broth. When the barley is done, take out with a skimmer several spoonsful; put what is in the broth in the sieve, and pound it in the mortar, with the yolks of six eggs: when you have finished pounding it, rub it through a clean tammy, adding to the broth half a pint of cream boiled, and salt of good taste; serve as hot as possible, with the barley in it that you took out first.

ENTRÉES THAT ARE TO BE SERVED AS SOUPS, OR
WHICH WANT MUCH SAUCE, AND ARE CONSEQUENT-
LY TO BE SERVED IN DEEP DISHES.

No. 1.—*Macaroni with Parmesan cheese.*

BOIL some Naples macaroni in water, salt and butter. When it is done, put into a stew-pan a quarter
of a pound of butter, some rasped Parmesan cheese,
some *Gruyère* or Swiss cheese, likewise a little pepper, and a spoonful of cream. Then drain the macaroni, and toss it till the cheese be well mixed with it;
then pour it into a dish; sprinkle some rasped cheese
over it, baste it with a little butter; and use the salamander to make it brown, for the butter would turn
to oil if you were to bake it in the oven.

No. 2.—*Breast of Mutton à la Bourgoise.*

Take some breast and scrag of mutton, cut in square
bits, of two or three inches each in size. Let it have
as little fat as possible, put the mutton in a stew-pan,
with a little fat or butter. Fry the mutton till it is
of a very good colour, and very brown, then throw
the fat out, *singez* with a little flour, salt, pepper,
one onion, a bunch of parsley and green onions, seasoned with a few bay-leaves, thyme, &c. Moisten
with water only, and let this boil gently till the mutton is nearly done; then take all the fat out, by putting the sauce in a small vessel. Let the fat rise to
the top, then put the sauce again, and add to it two
quarts of young peas; let them boil gently, till done.
Take out the bunch and onion, season of a good taste,
and serve up. This is an excellent means of cooking
the lower part of mutton for servants, as the author
has done always in the summer. When you have

any bacon to spare, add some to it, it gives additional flavour.

No. 2.—*Breast of Lamb with Green Peas, brown.*

Braize the whole breast; when it is done take out
the small bones, flatten it between two dishes, and let
it cool. Next cut it into the size of small chops, and
warm it in some of the liquor in which the breast
has been braized: lastly, drain, and glaze it, and cover it with the peas in the following manner.

Take some very fine peas, which you handle in
water with a little fresh butter; drain them; then
sweat them over a very slow fire, with a small slice
of ham, and a bunch of parsley and green onions.
When they are nearly done, take out the ham, and
the parsley and onions; reduce them with two spoonsful of *Espagnole* and a little sugar. They are used
to mask the meat. If you have no *Espagnole*, put
a tea-spoonful of flour with the peas, moisten with
some of the liquor which has braized the breast of
lamb or mutton; reduce it, and season with salt and
pepper; mind that the sauce must be very short.

No. 4.—*Breast of Lamb with Peas, white.*

Take a breast of lamb, which braize as above.
Stew the peas also in the same manner; but instead
of using the *Espagnole* you must use the *sauce
tournée.* When you have no *sauce tournée* a small
bit of butter and a tea-spoonful of flour, will answer
the same purpose; moisten with broth only. Thick-
en the sauce with the yolks of two eggs, that it may
look whiter. (See *Sauces.*)

No. 5.—*Tendons of Veal with Peas.*

(See *entrées de Veau.*) I mention them here, only
because they are sent up in deep dishes. The peas
are prepared as above. (See *Sauces.*)

No. 6.—*Tendons of Veal, en Haricots Vierges.*

Braize them as indicated *(entrées of Veal,)* and mask them with an *haricot vierge.* (See *Sauces.)*

No. 7.—*Tendons of Veal en Chipolata.*

Braize the *tendons* as above. The *chipolata* is made in the following manner. Have some chestnuts ready peeled and boiled: take a few small sausages, which twist to make them very short, prick them with a fork, and put them in a *sauty-pan* in the oven; when done, drain the fat, and add some small onions stewed very white, likewise bits of bacon, the breast part, cut into the shape of corks, which also should be stewed white, and some mushrooms, which you stew with some *sauce tournée.* When the sauce is in a proper state of forwardness, skim all the fat, and thicken it; put in all the ingredients, and after having dished the *tendons* in the shape of a *miroton,* or one upon another round the dish, put the *chipolata* into the middle, but keep some of the sauce to mask the *tendons.* You may add some cocks'-combs, &c. It is almost unnecessary to observe that all the ingredients of the *chipolata* should be done separately, and put into the sauce when ready to serve up. When you want to serve the *chipolata* white, you should use white sauce instead of brown; the reason for having two colours is, that sometimes in spite of your endeavours to keep the tendons, as well as all the other ingredients, white, you can only succeed in obtaining a darkish colour. In that case, you should make the *chipolata* brown. This is an excellent dish, but has not a very prepossessing appearance, as the *tendons* do not dress well. If it be well done, it never looks well, but if it be ill-done, it is absolutely uneatable.

No. 8.—*Green Peas with Bacon, French Fashion.*

These may be served without any other meat; but they may also serve as a sauce for *tendons,* either of veal, or of lamb, members of fowl, and giblets of turkey. It is to be observed, however, that those articles which are served in a deep dish, should be cut up, as you could not carve them in so much liquid. Take about a pound of bacon from the breast, cut it in bits of an inch square, boil it in water to extract the salt, then fry it in a little butter till it becomes of a fine brown. Next handle some fine peas, and a little fresh butter in cold water. After having drained them, put them into a stew-pan with the bacon, a bunch of parsley and green onions. Let the whole sweat over a slow fire. When nearly done, moisten with two or three spoonsful of *Espagnole* and a little bit of sugar. Boil them a few minutes. Send up either with or without other meat. Do not neglect seasoning with a little salt and pepper, but be cautious of the brine of the bacon.

No. 9.—*Breast of Mutton en Haricot.*

Braize the breast of mutton as you would do any other meat; when done, take out the small bones and let the breast cool. Then have the meat cut into hearts; warm them again separately in a little of the liquor, and after having drained them, mask them with the haricot. (See *Sauces.*)

No. 10. (*a*)—*Haricot of Mutton à la Burgeoise.*

Cut the breast, neck, and scrag of mutton in pieces of about three inches each; put them into a stew-pan with a little fat of any kind. Let the meat fry a nice colour in a stew-pan, or fry-pan; when the mutton becomes of a good colour, shake the flour box over, and add some salt and pepper. Moisten this with boiling water, adding a large onion, with two cloves stuck in it, a bunch of parsley and green onions well spiced. Let this boil till the meat be nearly done; skim all the fat, and then add some turnips that you have trimmed without much loss, and have fried with a little sugar to give them a good colour. Put the turnips to the mutton, skim away all the fat, and take out the onions and the bunch, and serve up. This is a useful and agreeable family dish. Sometimes you put potatoes in lieu of the turnips, but take care they do not break.

No. 11.—*Breast of Mutton en Hochepot.*

Braize* it as above, and mask it with a *hochepot.* (See *Sauces.*)

No. 12.—*Lamb's Pluck à la Pascaline.*

Take the head, trotters, liver, lights, &c.; bone the head and trotters as well as you can. Set them to disgorge, and blanch them. Then boil them in a *blanc* as you would do a calf's head. When thoroughly done, drain them and cover them with the *pascaline*, which is nothing more than a white *Italienne*, that you have thickened. (See *Sauces.*)

No. 13.—*The Civet of Hare*

Is introduced here, to imply that it is sent up in a deep dish. See *entrées of Game*, and *Hare Soup.*)

No. 14.—*Duck, with Sour-Crout.*

Sour-crout is sold ready pickled. Drain some,

---

* *Braizes in general.*—It is necessary to observe, that every thing which has the name of BRAIZE, must be done thoroughly, and must likewise be seasoned with vegetables, spices, sweet herbs, &c. BRAIZES belong rather to a common style of cookery, but to be made in perfection require the utmost nicety of the art. They require so much care, and such constant attention, as to be frequently neglected in a gentleman's kitchen. I shall name the things in most common use, which belong to the class of braizes, viz. fricandeaux, sweet-breads, mutton, *à la soubise*, tendons of veal in all their styles, *galentines, cotelettes à la dreux,* ditto *à la chalon,* partridges with cabbage, pheasants ditto, rump of beef, breast of ditto, leg of mutton, &c. &c. are all braized. Every thing that is termed *poële* must have its proper time to be done; and as the *poële* should preserve the colour of the fowl, and sometimes even whiten it, it is not an easy matter to make it in perfection.

and put it into a braizing-pan with a piece of bacon (the breast part,) a bunch of parsley and green onions, spices, bay-leaves, thyme, and mace; put also a little whole pepper. Next place the duck in the middle of the sour-crout, cover the whole with layers of bacon, and moisten with some liquor of *braize*, or top-pot,* strained through a silk sieve. If you happen to have a knuckle of ham, you may put it in after having blanched it. You may add a German sausage, together with some English sausages, observing that the small sausages must not be added till half an hour before serving up, otherwise they would be too much done. Three hours are required for the above to be done over a slow fire. When the sour-crout is done, put it into a large hair sieve to drain; then dish it, that is, put it into a deep dish with the duck in the middle, the sausages and bacon, &c. being put round it. The duck will be better if cut into four, as it is difficult to carve any thing that has so many other things with it.

No. 15.—*Members of Duck with French Sour-crout.*

Braize the duck, in the same manner as that with the *purée* of green peas, and mask it with the sour-crout, which is made as follows:—Take off the stock of a white cabbage, mince the whole nearly as is done for sour-crout; cut some bacon (the breast part) into small squares of about an inch in size; fry them a little, and then take them out to put the cabbages into the grease, in which they are to sweat. When nearly done, put the bacon in again, and moisten with some thin *sauce tournée*, because if it were thick you could not get the fat off. Skim off all the fat, reduce the cabbage, and use it to mask the duck. You may also put in some sausages that have been braized with the duck.

* Top-pot, is the fat that rises over the broth.

No. 16.—*Haricot of Turkey Giblets.*

We call giblets of turkey, the pinions, the neck, the liver, the gizzard, &c. When all those parts have been washed clean, and scalded, to disgorge all the blood, blanch them, and simmer them over a sharp fire, then wipe them very clean, and place them in a stew-pan. Wrap them up in layers of bacon; moisten with good broth, a little salt and pepper, and a bunch of parsley seasoned. When done, drain them, and after having placed them in the dish, cover them with the *haricot.* (See *Haricot.*)

No. 17.—*Haricot of Turkey Pinions.*

Take the pinions of half a dozen turkeys; bone them as far as the middle joint, and let them disgorge in warm water; next blanch and singe them, mark them well wrapt up in layers of bacon, and moisten with a *braize*, if you have any: if not, with a small bit of butter, a little broth and salt, an onion and two cloves, and a bunch of parsley and green onions. When done, drain them and mask with the *haricot.*

No. 18.—*Legs of Fowls with Nouilles.*

When you have a large dinner to send up, you necessarily have a vast quantity of fillets of fowl, and as many legs. You must use them in preference for a deep dish. Bone the thighs, season well inside, and sew them up so as to give them a good shape. Next braize them as white as possible, and sauce them with the *nouilles.* This dish is excellent. For a family dinner, the day after company, you may make a soup of it; instead of sauce put broth, and let there be less *nouilles.* This dish has a very bad appearance, but is very cheap, and wholesome from the simplicity of materials. After a great dinner, you must, of course, have some legs of fowl remaining; (breast of fowl is not so good in this way; see *nouilles* to make them.

No. 19.—*Eggs à la Tripe.*

Take a dozen of eggs boiled hard, cut them into thick round slices, and put them into the sauce, which follows. Cut three large white onions into dice; fry them white in butter; when they are nearly done, powder them well over with flour, and moisten with some good milk, and a few spoonsful of cream. Keep stirring with a wooden spoon to prevent their burning. When the sauce is done, grate a little nutmeg into it, and season it with a little salt and pepper, &c. then throw the eggs in and send up. Take care that the sauce is well done before you add the eggs to it, and that you do not break the eggs in it.

No. 20.—*Eggs à la Crême en Surprise.*

Take a dozen of eggs boiled hard, and cut them in two. Then take out the yolks, and rub them through a hair sieve. Chop the whites very fine, and make a *sauce à la crême,* which is marked the same as melted butter, except that you moisten it with cream. When the sauce is well done, add to it a lump of butter, throw the chopped whites into the sauce, and season it well. Lastly, pour the sauce and whites into the dish, and cover the whole with the yolks, which you baste with a little butter, and make them brown with a red hot shovel or salamander. This dish is only served at the tables of the rigid adherents to the Catholic faith. It is not a great curiosity, but when you have to serve a large dinner *tout en maugre,* it is desirable to know sufficient dishes to fill out the table.

No. 21.—*Hochepot of Ox's Tail.*

Beef tail is very good eating, but in general it is seldom set up as an *entrée,* although *en hochepot et en haricot* (see *Sauces*) they may be served in a deep dish. The beef tail is to be cut in the joints, and left to disgorge in water. It must next be blanched. You then let it cool, and put it between layers of bacon, to prevent its getting black. Moisten and season it with carrots, onions, &c. When done, drain it, and serve up with the sauces abovementioned. Observe, that this dish must be well done, as the meat should detach itself freely from the bones. Be particular in seasoning this braize. You should have onions, and a bundle seasoned.

No. 22.—*The same, en Haricot brun.*

Braize as above, and cover with *haricot brun.* (See *Sauces.*)

No. 23.—*The same, with Green Peas.*

The same as above; mask with green peas, No 7. page 67 *

* Tureens are out of fashion, but the dish must be served at a family dinner, or in the steward's room. Deep dishes are very well adapted to these *entrées.*

CHAPTER III.

REMOVES OF THE SOUPS AND FISH.

No. 1.—*Rump of Beef glazed.*

THE rump is undoubtedly the best part of the beef,
and particularly for French cookery; it is necessary
to select for this dish, that which is most covered with
fat; eut out the small fillet first; then take out the
bone, and tie it round of a good shape; put it into the
stock-pot in which you make the broth. When done,
drain it a quarter of an hour before dinner-time, that
you may trim it well and glaze it several times. Dish
it with green parsley all round. It is necessary to
observe, that as the best eating part is that which is
most covered with fat, the cook must be particular
in trimming the fat, and leaving only what is necessary to receive the glaze. The manner of cutting the
meat is a great advantage to the savour; the cook
should mark the place with chopped parsley, as was
the constant practice of the author, when he had occasion to serve the rump of beef.

Several people *braize* the rump of beef, a practice
of which the author does not approve, as it gets too
highly seasoned for people who have so many other
things to eat. The sauces and *garnitures* that are
served at the same time are sufficiently seasoned,
without the beef being so likewise. Besides, the first
method is the most economical, as the braized rump
furnishes too rich a liquor to be used in delicate cook-

ery. Moreover, when boiled in the common way, the rump is more wholesome, makes more broth, and therefore deserves the preference. However, not to disappoint such as might like it, he will proceed to treat of

No. 2.—*Rump of Beef Braized.*

Take a rump of beef well covered with fat: bone it, tie it up with packthread. Then put layers of bacon at the bottom of a braizing-pan; lay the rump of beef with its top part upwards on the bacon: next cut into slices a large quantity of veal, which serves to wrap up the beef; then cover the whole with layers of bacon, put in some carrots, onions, parsley, green onions, thyme, bay-leaves, mace, cloves, spice, salt, and pepper. Moisten with a little broth; then close the braizing-pan as hermetically as possible, and let the meat stew on a slow-fire for four hours; when done, reduce some of the liquor, and glaze it with the same. Then take some carrots that have been braized with the beef, and trim them of a nice shape. They must be served up glazed. Add likewise some glazed onions, and braized lettuce, all which roots and vegetables put round the rump in small heaps, then send up with some of the liquor that you have thickened with brown sauce; if you have no sauce, put half a quarter of a pound of butter into a small stew-pan, mix with it a tea-spoonful of flour, moisten with some of the liquor; add a little gravy to give it a good colour, and when well done, put it over the rump.

No. 3.—*Breast of Beef, à la Flamande.*

Take that part of a breast of beef which contains the gristle, and season it the same as the rump. Let it boil gently for four hours, and then drain the liquor through a silk sieve. Reduce it to *glaze*, with which you must *glaze* the breast of beef. Then garnish the dish with carrots, turnips braized, and cabbage done separately, and sauce with a very good

Espagnole; when you have it, put a little of the reduction of the braize. This is an excellent dish when
done with care. This beef may be garnished sometimes with cucumber *farcée,* sometimes with glazed
Spanish onions, and at others with artichoke bottoms,
&c. In France, they put *petits patés* round it, a
custom the author does not approve of.

No. 4.—*Sirloin of Beef Roasted.*

The principal observation and direction required
with regard to this article, is, that it is of all the parts
the most delicate; and when the piece is very big,
the fire must be more moderate, as it is a long time
before the middle can be warm. If your fire is sharp
the meat will be burnt on the outside, and quite raw
in the middle. Another necessary observation is,
that when you put the spit too low, the meat loses a
great deal of the heat, receiving it only from the top:
to keep down the colour, it is better to cover it with a
few sheets of white paper, and uncover it only when
the meat is nearly done. Take care, however, not to
cover the meat too hermetically, merely paper the
part that faces the fire, otherwise the beef will not be
roasted, but boiled.

No. 5.—*Leg of mutton roasted.*

This joint is with reason the especial favourite of
an English epicure, and the dish that makes its appearance oftener than any other at his table. Welsh
mutton is in very great repute; but I have frequently dressed Leicestershire, equal to any mutton in the
world. This joint does not admit of being covered
with paper. It must be cut in the joint, that it may
be bent round when placed on the spit. This operation makes the meat carve better, as the sinews have
been cut, they will not shrink, and the gravy remains
longer in the meat. A leg of mutton shows its ex-
cellence when the sinews are very small, and the
back appears very brown; it is never in that state
till it has attained three or four years of age, and it

should have that age to be in perfection. The leg should be roasted by a pretty sharp fire to keep the gravy round it.

No. 6.—*Saddle of Mutton roasted.*

This joint is likewise a great favourite, and possesses very delicate meat, particularly if carved in the proper way; the only objection is the great weight of the joint, and the disproportionate quantity of meat that can be cut from it. You must procure for this joint a proper skewer, give a little nick with the chopper to separate the bone near the tail, and put the skewer through; then tie the saddle on the spit, and roast it the same way as the leg, before a sharp fire, otherwise it will not be so tasty.

To carve it well, you should make an incision about three inches along the bone, cutting it sideways as a cutlet; in this way the meat is better. Those persons who dislike the fat, may leave it on their plates. By this mode of carving, you may serve twelve people instead of six.

No. 7.—*Braized Leg of Mutton, otherwise Gigot de Sept Heures.*

Put the leg of mutton into a braizing pan; trim it with a little veal, a few carrots, onions, and a bunch of parsley and green onions, properly seasoned. Cover the whole with thin slices of bacon, to prevent its being burnt. (Observe, if the bacon has been cured with saltpetre, it will turn the mutton red.) Let it stew for about four hours; then strain the liquor through a silken sieve; reduce it to glaze; and then glaze the leg of mutton which you send up, with glazed onions or white beans *à la maître d'hôtel*, or *à la Lyonaise.*

No. 8.—*Loin of Veal roasted.*

Take a fine loin of veal, which cut quite square. Introduce *attelets*, or skewers, in the flank which

you have rolled up. Then fix it on the spit, and cover it with buttered paper. Take the paper off about
a quarter of an hour before you send the joint up,
that it may be of a nice brown colour. Gravy alone
is requisite under the joint.

No. 9.—*Loin of Veal à la béchamel.*

When you have served a loin of veal, and very
little has been eaten of it, take off the fillet, cover the
whole with some buttered paper, and put it to warm
in the oven; when well warmed, make a *blanquette*
with what you have taken out; replace it in the fillet,
and serve up very hot. This is as good as a new dish
and looks as well. Observe, that these removes are
to be served only with the dessert, by which is
meant, whatever is left in the parlour; the following
remove is of the same kind.

No. 10.—*Loin of Veal à la Crême.*

The same as the first, No. 8. As soon as it is done,
take off the fillet and cut it in scollops, which throw
into the *sauce à blanquette*.) See *Sauce à blanquette*.) Put this *blanquette* into the aperture, and
send up with the same sauce under it.

No. 11.—*Calf's Head plain.*

Take a nice calf's head and bone it, that is to say,
take off the bones of the lower jaw, and of the nose,
which you cut off as close to the eyes as possible.
Then put all this into a large vessel with warm water,
to wash and disgorge off the blood, or otherwise the
head would look reddish. Then blanch it thoroughly and let it cool. Now make a *blanc* in the following manner: one pound of beef suet, cut into dice,
one pound of fat bacon, also cut into dice, half a pound
of butter, the juice of a lemon, salt and pepper, one
or two onions, a bunch of parsley, seasoned with
thyme, bay leaves, cloves, mace, allspice, and water
enough to cover the calf's head. When the *blanc*

has boiled for an hour, fold the head up in a clean towel, let it boil in that *blanc* for about three hours. When done, drain it. Take out the tongue, flay it, and then replace it. A calf's head must be served up quite hot, with a sauce called *au pauvre homme*, namely, minced shalots, parsley ditto, vinegar, salt and pepper, and the brains well minced.

No. 12.—*Calf's Head, with Love-Apple-Sauce.*

The same as in No. 11; with this difference only, that it is to be covered with love-apple sauce, *masked*, with the sauce.

No. 13.—*Calf's Head bigarrée.*

Take a nice calf's head, which prepare as in No. 11; drain it whilst hot, that you may be able to give it a good shape; then divide it into two parts, which squeeze hard between two dishes, placing a heavy weight over, and let them cool. When quite cold, dip one half into the yolks of four eggs well beaten up with butter, and a little salt and pepper, then into crumbs of bread. This is to be repeated twice. Do the same with the other half, only add plenty of chopped parsley to the crumbs of bread, that it may be made quite green. (Have some butter melted, and dipping a paste-brush into the butter, shake it over the crumbs of the bread, otherwise the bread will burn in the oven; this method preserves the colour. Do not forget a little salt and pepper in the crumbs of bread.) Next put both halves of the head into an oven till they are of a nice brown colour, and serve up with either a sharp sauce, an *Italienne*, or a love-apple sauce. When you have no other sauce by you but a little glaze, make some good melted butter, and put to it some blanched and chopped parsley, some salt and Cayenne pepper, and the brains chopped. Add a small bit of glaze or portable soup, and you will find this sauce as good as many others.

No. 14.—*Calf's Head du Puits certain.*

Bone a calf's head. Make a *farce* or force meat with veal, fat bacon, and sweet herbs, chopped fine and highly seasoned. Add to it two or three yolks of eggs. When made, stuff the calf's head with it, and sew it up all round, to prevent the stuffing from falling out, then wrap it up in a cloth, and stew it *à la braize;* that is to say, put it into a braizing-pan with an abundance of slices of veal and layers of bacon, seasoned with carrots, a bunch of parsley, thyme, bay-leaf, and spice; moisten with a glass of white wine, and a ladle-full of broth. Let it stew for four hours, and serve up with a *financière.* You must reduce a glass of Madeira to put in the sauce, as it should be highly seasoned.

No. 15.—*Calf's Head à la Chambord.*

Dress it as indicated at No. 13. When finished and drained, take pieces of pickled cucumbers and truffles cut into the shape of nails, with which symmetrically stick the head; then sauce it with a *financière,* garnished larded sweetbreads, large *quenelles,* pigeons *à la gautier,* and some craw-fish, which you have trimmed, by picking the tail, and cutting the point of the claws, and taking off the smaller claws.

No. 16.—*Farm-Yard Turkey à la Montmorenci.*

Take a large fat farm-yard turkey; truss it up as if it were to be *poëlé;* dip the breast into boiling hot water to make it firm; which will enable you to lard it nicely; then *braize* it with a good fire on the cover of the pan, that the bacon may get dry and retain the glaze better when you glaze it. Take care not to do it too much; drain it, and serve up with a *financière* of a fine light brown colour and well seasoned. The turkey will be better if you put it on the spit to be roasted, covered with bacon and paper; it will not be equally white, but it will have a finer flavour.

No. 17.—*Turkey and Celery Sauce.*

Truss it nicely, wrap it up in layers of bacon; then boil it in plain water with a little salt, butter, and lemon-juice. Drain it, and *mask** it with celery sauce. (See *Sauces.*)

No. 18.—*Turkey à la Périgueux, with Truffles.*

Take a nice fat turkey the moment it has been killed; empty it, and put plenty of salt inside of the body, to draw the blood out. Then let it cool, and prepare some truffles in the following manner; take two or three pounds, peel them, and smell whether they are all of a good flavour, and not musked. Then pick out the smallest from amongst them, and chop them very fine. Take some fat white bacon, and rasp it so as to obtain the fat only, without any of the sinews. When you have thus rasped a sufficient quantity to fill the body of the turkey, put the chopped truffles into the mortar, pound them with the rasped bacon, season with salt, pepper, spices, &c. then mix this with the large truffles, and put all in the turkey. Let the turkey remain thus for two or three days, to acquire the flavour of the truffles; sew the bird up as soon as you have finished it, and when you want it roasted, put it on the spit covered with bacon on the breast, and a few sheets of white paper, and take great care when you open the paper that you do not loosen the truffles. Serve up with clear *Espagnole.*†

No. 19.—*Fowls à la Condé.*

Take a couple of fine white fowls, empty them, take off the bone of the breast, and the sinews of the legs, then truss them, and put a little butter into the

---

* *Mask*, means to cover it with the sauce.

† This dish is one of the best possible, if it is well seasoned and roasted. It is necessary to observe that the carver must serve the inside with the fillet, as that is one of the best parts of the dish.

body, seasoned with lemon juice and salt, which will make the fowls look better and whiter. Next *mark* them in a stew-pan, trimmed with layers of bacon, cover them well; and pour over them a *poëlé*, which is made in the following manner: take a pound of veal, a pound of fat bacon, and a little fat of ham all cut into dice. Fry the whole white in half a pound of butter. Moisten with boiling water; season with a bunch of parsley, salt, and pepper, a little thyme, half a bay leaf, and a clove, and when sufficiently stewed, strain it through a hair-sieve over the fowls, which stew for three quarters of an hour over a slow fire, keeping the fire, however, brisk on the cover of the stew-pan. When done, drain and dish them with a tongue *à l'écarlate* in the middle, and the sauce *à la financière* under it.

No. 20.—*Fowls à la Montmorenci*

Are prepared the same as fowls *à la Condé*, with this single exception. that the breast is to be larded and glazed of a fine colour: garnish with larded sweetbreads, *quenelles à la cuillière*, &c. and a *ragoût à l'Allemande* for sauce.*

No. 21.—*Capons à la Turque.*

Take two white capons, empty and put them into warm water that they may disgorge the blood, which would otherwise raise a great deal of scum. Have ready some rice which has boiled till soft in rich *consommé*, put this rice well seasoned into the body of capons; then truss them, cover them with layers of bacon, wrap them up in paper, and spit them. They should be an hour roasting. When done, dish them with a garnish of soft rice, and a *velouté* for sauce.

* Observe that the difference of ragouts is in their colour only; *financiére* is brown; *Allemande*, or *Royal*, or *Toulouse*, are white. In general, you must put white sauce with glazed *entree*, and brown with white.

No. 22.—*Westphalia Ham à l'Essence.*

Take a small Westphalia ham, and trim it well.
Be particular in sawing off the knuckle, in order not
to break the bone into splinters. Keep it one day in
water, to take out the brine, and boil it in plain water for four hours. When done, drain it, take off
the rind, and give it a nice round form. Then put it
in the oven for a few minutes to dry the fat, which
otherwise could not be glazed properly. When quite
dried, glaze it of a fine colour, and serve under it an
essence. (See *Sauces.*)

Receipt to make a Ham better than those of West-phalia.

As soon as the pig is cold enough to be cut up, take
the two hams, and cut out the round bone, so as to
have the ham not too thick; rub them well with common salt, and leave them in a large pan for three days;
when the salt has drawn out all the blood, throw the
brine away and proceed as follows; for two hams
of about eighteen pounds each, take one pound of
moist sugar, one pound of common salt, and two ounces of saltpetre, mix them together, and rub the hams
well with it, then put them into a vessel large enough
to contain them in the liquor, always keeping the
salt over them; after they have been in this state three
days, throw over them a bottle of good vinegar. One
month is requisite for the cure of them; during that
period they must be often turned in the brine; when
you take them out, drain them well, powder them
with some coarse flour, and hang them in a dry place.
The same brine can serve again, observing that you
must not put so much salt on the next hams that you
pickle. If the hams are smaller, put only three quarters of a pound of salt, but the salt will not do any
harm if you do not let them remain too long in the
brine; if you can get them smoked, they are then not
so subject to be infected by vermin; no insect what-

ever can bear the bitterness of the soot; the smoke of
lierre or wood is preferable to the smoke of coal. Be
particular that the hams are hung as far as possible
from the fire, otherwise the fat will melt, and they
will become dry and hard.

No. 22.—*Ham with Madeira.*

Take in preference a Westmoreland ham, which
prepare in the same manner as directed above; but
it need not be left so long in water, as it is not so
briny as the Westphalia hams are. Blanch it in water only during two hours. Then drain it, and put it
into a braizing-pan, trimmed with thin slices of veal
at the bottom, seasoned with carrots, onions, parsley,
bay-leaves, spices, &c. Pour over these two glasses
of rich *consommé* and a bottle of Madeira, let it boil
for about a couple of hours. When done, pour some
of the liquor, after having skimmed off the fat, to reduce to an *Espagnole*, which is the proper sauce.

N.B.—When the ham has boiled for two hours in
the water, you must trim it instantly, before you put
it with the wine, that you may send it up the moment you take it out of the braize. Reduce the liquor to make the glaze for it.

No. 24.—*Ham with Windsor Beans.*

Boil the ham as in No. 22, glaze it in the same
manner, and serve under it Windsor beans, dressed
as follows:

Take some very small Windsor beans, boil them
in water with a little salt; when boiled enough, take
a little *velouté*, into which throw a half quarter of a
pound of fresh butter, a little chopped parsley and
winter savory, toss the beans in that sauce after having drained them, and dish the ham over the beans.

No. 25.—*A Roast Beef of Lamb.* *

Take the saddle and the two legs of a lamb, cut on

* The appellation of " *roast beef of lamb,*" must sound very

the middle of each leg a small *rosette*, which is to be larded, as also the fillets. Roast the whole, and glaze the larded parts of a good colour. In France it is served up with *maître d'hôtel*, but in England with gravy under it, and mint sauce in a boat.

No. 26.—*Saddle of Mutton, or Roast Beef de Mouton.*

The same preparation as above. This is sent up in particular cases only; when large dishes are wanted to cover a table of extraordinary magnitude, or to display the magnificence of the host.

No. 27.—*Saddle of Fawn, or Chevreuil.*

The same as No. 26. When larded, put it into a very large vessel with salt, pepper, and onions cut into slices, parsley, vinegar, spices, &c. Leave it to pickle for two or three days, taking great care to turn it frequently on every side. Then roast it, and serve with a *poivrade* under it. Mind that the fillets and both legs must be larded.

No. 28.—*The Haunch of Venison.**

It was customary in France to cut off a small *rosette* from the leg, lard it, and then pickle it. In England it is customary to put it on the spit, then make some paste with flour and water only, and case the venison with it, securing it with a few sheets of paper. It can not be done thoroughly in less than four hours. It is

extraordinary to an English ear, but the singularity of the name is as nothing, when compared with the importance and necessity of the dish. At a very great dinner, it is essential to have some dish of magnitude. This has a very good appearance, and is truly excellent. I beg to recommend the trial of a *maître d'hôtel* under, as the butter, parsley, salt, pepper, and lemon-juice, agree well with the gravy of the meat; those who make the experiment will assuredly approve of it.

* The great point in roasting venison is to keep as much as possible the fat from melting; the paste put over it, is to prevent the heat of the fire from wasting it.

usually served up with red currant jelly made hot with a little port wine. The women cooks in this country, put the flour over the roast just before they remove it from the spit, a custom which is utterly absurd, and can not be sufficiently reprobated. I approve of the practice of flouring roasted meat, if it be done *early* enough to imbibe the gravy, and get nicely browned, when it becomes very tasty. In the other case, the froth of the flour and butter adhere to the palate, and have a most abominable taste.

No. 29.— *The Neck of Venison*

Is also to be roasted; but as it is not by far so thick as the haunch, the paste may be less thick, if you take great care to stop the spit in the under side of the neck.

No. 30.— *Leg of Pork.*

Take the leg of a porket, rub it over with salt, and put it well covered with salt also in a vessel, wherein it must be left for ten days. Then boil it in water, and send it up with green cabbage all round, and a peas pudding, which must be made as follows:

Take a quart of dry peas, wash them clean, wrap them up in a clean towel, and throw them into the same vessel as the leg. When the peas are done, strain them through a sieve, put in a good lump of butter, some salt, two yolks of egg, and poach the pudding wrapped up in a clean towel, to make the pudding of a good substance.

No. 31.— *Fowls à la Mirepoix.*

Take a couple of white fowls, which empty and truss with the legs bent down. Then make a *mire-poix* in the following manner: take a few slices of ham, some rasped bacon, butter, salt, bay-leaves, parsley, and lemon-juice; let the whole fry white on a very slow fire. When the rasped bacon and butter are well mixed together, put the fowls into an oval stew-pan trimmed with layers of bacon, which moisten with the *mirepoix* and a spoonful of broth, to prevent their frying. They must stew for an hour* on a very slow fire: then drain them well, and serve up an *Espagnole,* or a *ravigotte.*

N.B.—All voluminous *entrées* may be served as a *relevé* (remove;) as for instance, a large *noix* of veal *à la bourgeoise,* a large *carée* of veal garnished with vegetables, and, in short, whatever is of too great a magnitude for an *entrée.*

No. 32.—*Boiled Turkey with Oyster Sauce.*

This is to be boiled in the same manner as in No. 18. (See *Oyster Sauce,* No. 96, page 42)

Fish sent up with the Soups; or as a Remove of the Soup.

No. 1.—*Turbot and Lobster Sauce.*

Choose a very white and fine skinned turbot; three quarters of an hour before dinner, or an hour if the turbot is very large, put it into boiling water and salt, with lemon slices over it; start it very quick, when it begins to boil draw the pan on the side of the fire. If the turbot boils too fast, it will be woolly; when you have ascertained with your knife that it is quite done, serve with green parsley on the broken places; and put round the dish some horse-radish scraped fine; serve the lobster sauce separately in a boat. Observe that you must make an aperture on the back of the turbot; it will by that means be sooner done.

Lobster Sauce.

Take a hen lobster, cut the flesh into small dice,

---

* You must, however, proportion the time to the size of the fowl. A small one will of course require less time, as a very large one would demand more.

keep the eggs, which pound with a quarter of a pound of fresh butter, and strain through a hair sieve. You then make some melted butter: let it be rather thick; mix the eggs of the lobster with it, and throw into it a little essence of anchovies, a small quantity of cavice,* and a little cream. Take care that the sauce does not boil, for it would curdle, and lose its colour.

No. 2.—*Broiled Turbot.*

Marinade the turbot in sweet oil, salt, pepper, &c. and broil it on a slow fire: but it can not be sufficiently done in this way in less than an hour. You must accordingly put it on a slow fire in due time. Then, when you serve, cover it with caper-sauce, which is to be made as follows: make some melted butter with a little glaze in it; when melted, throw in some essence of anchovies, a few capers, and a drop of vinegar. Then give it a good seasoning, and *mask*, that is pour the sauce over the fish.

No. 3.—*Boiled Salmon with Lobster Sauce.*

Put the salmon into boiling water, the same as the turbot, with salt only. Serve up with lobster sauce, and never use vinegar with salmon, as it spoils the taste and colour of the fish.

No. 4.—*Slices of Salmon broiled with Caper Sauce.*

Marinade your slices of salmon in oil and salt, broil them on a slow fire, and cover them with caper sauce.

No. 5.—*Crimped Salmon*

The Thames salmon is undoubtedly the best, but its price is so high as to render it unattainable by any but the rich; the author has occasionally bought it at sixteen shillings per pound, which brings the price of one dish only to more than four pounds; it requires

---

* Mackay, in Piccadilly, sells the best, that is to say, the only genuine cavice.

to be boiled quickly in salt and water. Serve up with
lobster sauce. Fifteen minutes is sufficient to boil it.
If you leave it too long in the water, it loses all its
taste and colour.

No. 6.—*Salmon with Genévoise Sauce.*

Take a few shalots, some roots of parsley, a bunch
ditto, seasoned with spices, thyme, bay-leaves, and a
few carrots. Let the whole be lightly fried in a little
butter. Then moisten with white wine (Maderia in
preference.) Let it boil for three-quarters of an hour.
When the *marinade* is done, drain it through a tammy over the fish, which stew in that seasoning. As
soon as the fish is sufficiently stewed, drain it, pick
off all the scales, and return it into the vessel where it
has already boiled, with some of the liquor to keep it
hot, and mind to cover it, to prevent it from drying.
Now reduce some of the *marinade* with good *Espagnole*, skim off all the fat, throw in a good piece of fresh
butter, well kneaded with flour, a little essence of anchovies, the juice of a lemon, some Cayenne pepper,
and a little salt. When you have drained the fish,
dish it and cover it with the sauce, and send some likewise separately in a sauce-boat.

N. B.—Salmon is also served *au court bouillon.*
(See No. 27, page 96.)

No. 7.—*Cod with Oyster Sauce.*

Boil the fish in boiling water and plenty of salt;
mind that if the fish is very large, you must not boil
it too fast, as it then becomes woolly; be careful before sending up, to ascertain with your knife whether
it is well done. Serve with oyster sauce, as described No. 96, page 42. Observe, all white fish should
be boiled in hard water, pump water will make the
fish white and firm, while soft water will spoil it.

No. 8.—*Slices of Crimp Cod.*

Boil the slices in the same manner as the fish when

whole, and send them up with the same sauce; mind that ten or fifteen minutes are sufficient to boil them.

If you are obliged to wait after the fish is done, do not leave it in the water, but take it out and leave it over the boiled water, cover it with a clean cloth; and when you are to serve, dip it again into the hot water, by this method you preserve its flavour, and are able to serve it hot.

No. 9.—*Crimp Cod with Cream Sauce.*

The same as above. The sauce *à la Crême* is made in the following manner: take a quarter of a pound of butter, a little flour, some cream and a little salt, mix them together, and turn them on the fire, but do not let the sauce boil. Then cover the fish with it.

N.B.—It is not served up so in England.

No. 10.—*The John Dorey, with Lobster Sauce.*

Boil it in the same manner as you do turbot. (See No. 1.) Send it up with lobster sauce. (See *Lobster Sauce*, No. 1, page 87.)

No. 11.—*Ditto, broiled with Anchovy and Caper Sauce.*

Marinade in oil, and broil it in the same manner as you do turbot. The same sauce also, with capers; and, it should be observed, that but little oil is required, as it is only necessary to prevent the fish drying and adhering to the gridiron.

No. 12.—*Soles fried or boiled.* *

Boil the soles in boiling water with a little salt and vinegar. Fried soles are to be covered with crumbs

---

* *Observations on Fish in general.*—It is necessary to have the fish well purged of all the blood, as the least redness left in it is very prejudicial. When the soles or whitings are large, it is natural to conceive that they will be longer frying or boiling than when small. Pay proper attention to the following observation: fish not well done is uneatable; and served up in that state, it

of bread, which is done in the following manner: break two eggs, which beat with a little salt: dip the soles into this *omelette* first, then into crumbs of bread. Fry the fish till it is of a fine colour. Shrimp sauce is made as follows: make some melted butter, with which mix a little essence of anchovies: throw in the shrimps, some cavice, and send up in a sauce-boat.

No. 13.—*Broiled Soles.*

Dip them into beaten eggs and crumbs of bread as above, but twice, using melted butter the second time. Broil them till they are of a light brown, and send up with the shrimp sauce.

No. 14.—*Fried Whitings.*

Take very fresh whitings, empty them well, and flay them. Then fasten the tail in the mouth with a small skewer, and dip the fish into an *omelette*, the same as the soles, then into crumbs of bread, and fry them till they are of a light brown. (See *Shrimp Sauce*, No. 12, above.)

No. 15.—*Fried Whitings, French fashion.*

Let the whitings be very fresh, and of an equal size: empty and scrape them well all over; then wash them in different waters. When quite clean, slit them equally on the back, and dip them into flour only. Next fry them in very hot oil, and over a large fire, otherwise when you put them in, they might cool the dripping. When of a light brown, send them up with shrimp sauce in a sauce-boat. I have directed *oil* to be used in frying those fishes, as the Catholics do not use animal food, and are fond of what we term greasy fritter, on *maigre* days, oil is the best fritter therefore that can be adopted.

would prejudice the company against the rest of your dinner. By this want of attention, you lose all chance of pleasing your employer.

No. 16.—*Boiled Whitings.*

The author deems it useless to explain what is generally known, about boiling whitings, or fish of any other sort; and will, therefore, content himself with mentioning a particular or two which might have escaped the memory of some of his brethren, who are desirous of displaying variety. When you want to boil the whitings, it is better not to open the belly, as they have a better appearance on the table. Mind to keep the skins whole, otherwise they will look very bad.

No. 17.—*Boiled Mackarel.*

Boil the mackarel as you would any other fish, and make a fennel sauce. The fennel is to be boiled in boiling water with salt; then it is to be chopped very fine, and thrown into melted butter; and serve up. Mind if you boil the mackarel too much, they lose both skin and flavour, and have a wretched appearance on table.

N. B.—It is necessary to observe, that in England it is the custom to send up this fish with the fennel sauce, and garnished with fennel round.

No. 18.—*Broiled Mackarel.*

Pick out in preference mackarel, with soft roes, which are the most delicate. Gut them, open them at the back and *marinade* them in oil,* salt, and pepper. Next broil them, but unless they are done enough they are never good. The *maître d'hotel* sauce is to be made separately, and served in a boat. Those who wish to have the mackarel dressed in the French fashion, must have some parsley chopped very fine, mix it with some fresh butter, salt, pepper, and lemon-juice, put this into the aperture of the mackarel's back, when well broiled; and serve as hot as possible on a hot dish.

* The oil is to prevent the fish from drying, and sticking to the gridiron.

The fillets of mackarel are to be cut from the bone, and trimmed of a good shape; put them into a *sauté* pan with some clarified butter and a little salt over them till dinner time, then put them to do into the oven, or on the stove; drain them upon a clean sheet of paper; dress them on the dish, and cover them with the *maître d'hotêl* sauce.

N. B.—All other methods of dressing fish, will be found in the chapter of *entreés*.

No. 19.—*Boiled Haddocks.*

They are boiled in the same manner as soles, and served up with shrimp sauce. You may use haddocks for *quenelles*, or *filets*, as well as whitings.

No. 20.—*Skate with Shrimp Sauce.*

Skate must be boiled in water with a little salt and vinegar. The sauce is sent up separately in a boat. Skate may be served up also with caper sauce.

No. 21—*Boiled Pike with Dutch Sauce.*

Empty and scale the pike, wash it well after it has stood for an hour in cold water, to disgorge all the blood; then boil it like any other fish, and serve up with a Dutch sauce.

No. 22.—*Baked Pike.*

Scale and empty the pike, without injuring the skin of the belly, into which introduce a *farce*, which would drop out if not well secured. This *farce* is made of two handsful of crumbs of bread, one handful of chopped beef-suet, parsley ditto, salt, pepper, and spices, two whole eggs, and a little fresh butter. Mix the whole together, and pound it in a mortar: then stuff the pike with it, and turn the pike with its tail fastened in its mouth by means of a skewer; next dip it, first into an *omelette*, and then into crumbs of bread, and again into crumbs of bread; then baste it over with butter, before you put it into the oven. If you are to send up two, one of them is to be made of a green colour, by means of a quantity of chopped parsley being mixed with the crumbs of bread. Mind the oven must be well heated. When the pikes are of a fine brown, cover them with paper, and let them be well done through. Serve up with a Dutch sauce. (No. 70, page 33.)

No. 23.—*Pike à la Genévoise.*

Scale and wash the pike, and stew it in the same manner as the salmon, No. 6, page 89.

No. 24.—*Pike à la Polonoise.*

Wash the pike clean as above, then cut it into slices as if you wanted to make a *matelotte;* then fry in a quarter of a pound of butter the following herbs: a few carrots cut into dice, a few roots of parsley, a bunch of parsley and green onions, seasoned with mace, cloves, thyme, and bay-leaves, and a little ham. When fried, moisten the whole with a sufficient quantity of boiling water, and let it boil for one hour. When the *marinade* is well stewed, drain it through a silk sieve over the slices of pike, and let them stew, but not too long, for they would break. When the fish is done enough, take the liquor in which it has boiled, to moisten a *béchamelle maigre,* which you make in the following manner: take a few bits of ham, some mushrooms, a bunch of parsley, and green onions, a small white onion, which fry white in butter, then put to it a large handful of flour, let it fry a little, and moisten with the liquor in which the pike has been boiling. Stir this with a wooden spoon: let it boil till the flour is well done, throw in a pint of thick cream, that has already been boiled, and reduce the whole till the sauce is thick enough to cover the fish. Next take some turnips, cut into dice, stew them in a little broth and sugar; drain them and throw them into the sauce, after the latter have been drained through a tammy. Drain the pike also, and cover it with the sauce, and the turnips.

N. B.—This sauce requires a little sugar, on account of the turnips. Mind the sauce is well seasoned.

No. 25.—*Pike à la Chambord.*

Scale the pike, and let it disgorge in water for an hour or two. Then lard it in different places on one side of the back, and bake it in a *marinade au vin*, as you would do in the *marinade à la Genévoise*. That part which has been larded must stand uppermost, to prevent the part which is not larded from getting dry, cover this with layers of bacon, and be particular in basting frequently with the seasoning. When the fish is done, glaze the parts that have been larded, and *mask* the others with a *ragoût à la Chambord*. Observe that the *quenelles* must be made of fish. The garnish is generally composed of large *quenelles*, small pigeons (squab pigeons,) larded sweetbread of lamb, &c. Take a little of the *marinade*, skim off the fat, reduce it nearly to glaze, and mix it with the *Chambord*, which is no other thing than a *financière* with the addition of a little essence of anchovies, the juice of a lemon, and a little Cayenne.

No. 26.—*Pike au Cour Bouillon.*

Take a large pike, which empty, without scaling it. Then wash it clean, and drain it. Next boil some vinegar, and when boiling, pour it over the scales of the pike, which will turn blue, and the scales will curl up if the vinegar is hot enough. Wrap the pike up in a towel, and let it boil in the *cour bouillon*, which is prepared as follows:* (No. 27.)

* If you happen to be in the country, where pike is plentiful, you may make fillets of them, for they are as good as any other fish for that. They must be dressed in the same way as fillets of soles or whitings, *à la maître d'hôtel*, or *ravigotte*, or *à la orlies*.

No. 27.—*Cour Bouillon for Fish au bleu.*

Take two of each of the following roots: carrots, onions, roots of parsley, leaves of ditto, thyme, bay-leaves, mace, cloves, spices, which fry in butter without their getting too much colour. Then pour into it two bottles of white and a bottle of red wine with salt, &c. This *marinade* being stewed properly, will serve several times for stewing the fish, but remember each time you use it, it requires a little water; besides, it would become too strong in the course of time. Take some of that liquor to make the sauce *matelotte, Genévoise,* &c.

This manner of boiling the fish is too expensive in England, where wine is so dear; but a very good *cour bouillon* can not be made with vinegar. Besides, fish *au cour bouillon* is always eaten with oil and vinegar, which is not customary in England.

No. 28.—*Trout à la Genévoise.*

This fish is the most delicate that can be prepared *à la Genévoise.* The *marinade* to be made the same as in No. 6, for salmon, page 89; or above, No. 27.

No. 29.—*Roast Sturgeon.*

Spit the sturgeon: make a *marinade* with white wine, with which baste the sturgeon. Next take some of the *marinade* that you reduce with four large spoonsful of good *Espagnole* sauce. When the sauce is of a good consistency, put in it about half a pound of fresh butter kneaded with a little flour, salt, and Cayenne pepper, the juice of a lemon, and a spoonful of essence of anchovies. If you have no *Espagnole*, make a little *roux*, with flour and butter, and moisten with the *marinade;* add to it a little glaze, and proceed as above.

No. 30.—*Baked Sturgeon.*

Make a *marinade* the same as above, and bake the fish with that *marinade.* The sauce as above.

No. 31.—*Sturgeon plain boiled.*

Boil the sturgeon as you would any other fish. Send up with Dutch sauce; mind that the fish is very firm, and requires more time to boil.

No. 32.—*Carp au bleu, without Sauce.*

Take a fine carp, which empty without injuring the belly. Take off the gills, and after you have washed it clean, pour over it some boiled vinegar, by which means the scales will curl up, and the fish get a blue colour. Then wrap the carp up in a towel, and stew it in the *cour bouillon.* (See No. 27, page 96.)

No. 33.—*Carp farci, baked.*

Take a fine carp, scale and empty it. Then detach one side of the fillets, without injuring the head. Take this flesh, and that of another carp of a smaller size, and make a *farce* in the following manner: take the crumb of two penny loaves, soak it in cream or milk, then squeeze it, and put it into a mortar, with an equal quantity of the flesh of the carp, nearly as much fresh butter, with a little chopped parsley, a few mushrooms fried in a little butter, salt, pepper, and spice. When all these ingredients have been pounded in a mortar, add a couple of eggs, and continue pounding for a long time, then take a little, which throw into boiling water, and taste. If it be too *delicate*, which means too thin, add one egg more, pound it again, and then rub it through the sieve *à quenelles;* and fill up the cavities in the fillets of the carp, giving it the primitive shape of the carp. Take care however to give it a good shape. Next let it be done thoroughly in the oven, and serve it with caper sauce under it. This method is frequently adopted by Roman Catholics.

No. 34.—*Carp, Sauce à Matelotte.*

Take a fine carp, scale and empty it. Then let it

stew in wine enough to cover it. After having drained it well, take that wine to make the sauces, and send it up, covered with *sauce à matelotte*. (See *Sauces.*)

No. 35.—*Broiled Carp with Caper Sauce.*

Scale and empty the carp. Wash it, and wipe it quite dry. Then *marinade* it in oil, salt, and pepper; broil it, and send it up with caper sauce as follows:

No. 36.—*Caper Sauce for Fish.*

Take some melted butter, into which throw a small bit of glaze, and when the sauce is in a state of readiness, throw into it some choice capers, salt and pepper, and a spoonful of essence of anchovies.

No. 37.—*Tench.*

Tench, in England, are eaten boiled, with a Dutch sauce, yet they are far better *en matelotte.*

No. 38.—*Perch.*

These likewise are sent up boiled, with Dutch sauce; but you will find a different way to dress them in the following *entrée.*

No. 39.—*Perch au Water-Suchet.*

Scale and clean the perch as much as possible; put them to boil with some parsley tied up in a bundle, and some salt, in a quantity of water sufficient to boil the perch; then have some parsley roots cut in small fillets about one inch in length, and boil them in a little water. When the roots are done, put them with the perch; ten minutes are sufficient. Have some parsley leaves blanched very green in salt and water, drain the perch from all the liquid, and put it into a tureen; put the roots and parsley leaves to it, and throw the liquor over it through a silk sieve. Send up slices of bread and butter in a separate plate.

CHAPTER IV.

FARCES, OR FORCED MEAT.

No. 1.—*Quenelles of Veal.*

TAKE the fleshy part of veal, cut it into slices, and scrape it with the knife till you have got off all the meat without the sinews. About half a pound of this rasped meat is sufficient for an *entrée.* Boil either in your stock-pot, or in plain water, a calf's udder. When it is done and cold, trim all the upper part, cut it into small pieces, and pound it in a mortar till it can be rubbed through a sieve. All that part which has been thus strained through the sieve, you make into a ball, of the same size as the meat, which you have also rolled into a ball; you then make a *panade* in the following manner: you must have three balls, one of udder, one of meat, and one of *panada.*

Panadas for Farces in general.

Soak in milk the crumbs of two penny rolls for about half an hour, then take them out, and squeeze them to draw out all the milk: put the crumbs into a stew-pan with a little *béchamelle,* a spoonful of *consommé* and proceed as follows: put in a separate small stew-pan a litle butter, a small bit of ham, some parsley, a few small chalots, one bay-leaf, then one clove, a few leaves of mace, and some mushrooms; fry them gently over a slow fire. When done, moisten with a spoonful of broth. Let it boil for twenty minutes, and drain the broth over the *panada* through a sieve; then reduce the *panada* on the fire; mind to keep constantly stirring, and when quite dry, put in a small piece of butter and let it dry farther; then add the yolks of two eggs, and put the *panada* to cool on a clean plate, to use when wanted. Observe, the *panada* is wanted for all sorts of farces or false meats, you should be careful to give a good flavour to the *panada* as the farce receives no taste from any thing else. *Quenelles* are one of the articles which try the skill of a good cook, particularly those of game or fish. This dish is valuable to the poor as well as the rich, and the easiest of digestion imaginable, if rightly prepared. A medical man, familiar with light dishes of food, would cetainly recommend this to his patient.

When the *panada* is cold, roll it into balls, the same as the two other articles, but let the balls be all of a size. Pound the whole in a mortar as long as possible, for the more *quènelles* are pounded, the more delicate they are. Then break two eggs, whites and yolks together, which you pound likewise: now season with pepper, salt, and spices in powder; when the whole is well mixed together, try a small bit, which you roll with a little flour; then poach it in boiling water with a little salt. If it should not be firm enough, put another egg without beating the white, which only makes the *quenelles* puff, and hollow inside. When you have made the *farce*, rub it through a sieve. If you are in a hurry, you may use only crumb of bread soaked in milk without *panada*, but the *panada* is most tasty.

Many persons who use the same ingredients as the author, but not in the same way, will perhaps feel inclined to censure his method; yet such as will adhere to it, will derive great benefit from it; the materials are to be well pounded and seasoned.

No. 2.—*Quenelles of Fowl.*

The *quenelles* of fowl are made with the fillets only, all other parts being too full of sinews. Take the fillets of young chickens, for you must never use those of an old fowl, as they are tough and thready. Veal when very white is much better than tough fowl. Cut this meat into dice and pound it in a mortar, till it can be rubbed through a sieve. Next make three balls, as you have done for the *quenelles* of veal. Then pound, season, and try them in the same manner as directed above, as they must be made firm or soft, according to the use they arc intended for. *Quenelle au consommé clarifié*, for instance, must be very delicate and soft. If they are to be served in a *ragoût*, either white or brown, they must be made firmer, and so on. The *farce à quenelles* is much used in cookery. With it alone you may make various good *entrées;* and it serves besides to garnish *ragoûts, matelottes, godards, chambords, pâtes, chauds,* &c. &c. Observe particularly, that when you use the *quenelles* very small, the *farce* may be very delicate, but if you make any *boudin,* or *turban,* or any other different kind of *entrée,* in proportion to the size of it, you must keep the *quenelles* firm, which depends solely on ther having more eggs; this addition makes the *farce* softer when raw, but increases its firmness when poached.

The author can not sufficiently enlarge on the subject of *farces,* as they are of such general utility in large dinners, as well as extremely economical. It is useless to remind the practitioner of the necessity of using economy—the best cookery, where you omit salt and pepper, goes for nothing.

No. 3.—*Quenelles of Rabbits.*

The best *quenelles* are made with fillets only. If you are engaged by a nobleman who has game in abundance, take the fillets for the *quenelles;* with the legs and shoulders make a *giblotte,* or a pie English fashion for the servants, and with the remaining bony parts make the *consommé.* When you lift up the fillets, you must leave the sinews about the carcass. Pound the meat, and make a *panada* as for other *quenelles.*

Take a calf's udder likewise, which prepare as directed above. *Quenelles* differ in flavour and appellation,
only in consequence of the meat of which they are
made. Remember, that the *panada* and calf's udder are indispensable articles. Follow what is prescribed at No. 1, for the *quenelles* of veal, which have
been mentioned first, as being more frequently used
than all others. They are very good and likewise
very cheap, as veal is always requisite for sauces and
broth. Half, or three quarters of a pound of veal is
no great drawback, neither can it weaken the sauce,
although of service to make several good *entrées*, as
will be shown hereafter.

No. 4.—*Quenelles of Partridges.*

Take the fillets of three young partridges. Take off
the skin and the sinews; cut the meat into dice, and
pound it as directed above; rub this through a sieve.
Scrape the bottom of the sieve, and make a ball of the
same size as those of the *panada* and udder. When
you have mixed the three ingredients together, add
two whole eggs, and the yolk of a third. Then season with pepper, salt, and allspice. Try the *quenelle*
as directed above. This *farce* will serve for different
entrées, which are all to be found under their respective names in the article *partridges.*

No. 5.—*Farce of Fowl à la Cream.*

Make use of the *panada* and udder as mentioned above, but no herbs are required in the *panada,* instead of which put a little bechamel. Take the
white flesh of a fowl that has been roasted; take off the
skin and sinews, chop the meat very fine; then pound
it as you do for other *farces.* Put in the yolks of
four eggs, after the *farce* has been pounded and well
seasoned. Beat the whites of the eggs, and mix them
gently with the rest, stirring the whole with a wood-
en spoon. Use this *farce* when requisite. It is generally used for the fowl *à la cream;* if you have in
the larder a cold roast fowl, you may make that *en-*

rée with it; empty the fowl by cutting a square hole in the breast, the white flesh you make the *farce* with and then replace it in the cavity, as directed farther on.

This farce is the same which many cooks denominate *souflé* of fowl; only when you want to make a *souflé*, you must make the *farce* more delicate; but for the fowl *à la crême*, or any other bird, (for you may make either fowl, chicken, pheasant, partridge, or any bird whatever,) observing only when you make *farce* of game, introduce *consommé* of game in the *panada*, and *fumée* of the game with the sauce.

No. 6.—*Farce a Gratin of Partridges, Rabbits and Fowls.*

The *farce à gratin* is made in the same manner as the *farce à la crême*, with the only difference, that you must not beat the whites of the eggs, and that this *farce* is to be kept delicate and soft. Take the flesh of roasted chickens, or young rabbits, or young partridges, &c. The manner of using it is explained in its proper place. This *farce* is intended for the stuffing of such articles as are not to be put on the fire again, or very little; such as calf's ears, calf's feet, sheeps' trotters *en canelon*, and *rissolles*, as also quails, tongues, and larks *au gratin*. There are some *gratins* that are also *émincés*, and are treated of in their proper places. Observe, that this *farce* is indispensable in good cookery.

No. 7.—*Boudins à la Richelieu.*

As soon as you have rubbed the *farce quenelles* through a sieve, have some onions cut sideways into dices or *filets*, and that have been sweated white, which you must mix with the *farce* before it gets firm, to prevent the onion from breaking. The *boudins à la Richelieu*, are a *farce à quenelles* either of fowl or of veal; they are never made of game.* The au-

---

* The *boudins à la Richelieu* are most excellent eating. In France they are always recommended for delicate constitutions;

thor, however, is inclined to think that a *boudin à la Richelieu* of game might be attempted with success, though contrary to general usage. At some future period he proposes to make the expériment.

No. 8—*Boudins à la Sefton*

Are made with *quenelles* the same as those above, only instead of onions sliced sideways, put mushrooms, sliced in the same manner, and sweated white in butter. When you drain the mushrooms, preserve the liquor, which pour into the sauce that serves for the *boudins*. The flavour of mushrooms must prevail in these *boudins*, the same as that of onions prevails in the *boudins à la Richelieu*. This *entrée* is very preferable to that with onions.

No. 9.—*Quenelles of Whitings.*

Take the fillets of four whitings. If in a Roman Catholic family, on a fast-day, instead of an udder use butter. The *panada*, however, is far superior. In either case you must soak the crumb of bread in some good milk, and squeeze it well in a towel. Do not put the same quantity of butter as you would of udder, as the butter would not remain in. In every other respect these are made like other *quenelles*.

No. 10.—*Farce of Carp.*

Take the flesh of two carps, which you must chop, pound, and rub through a sieve. Soak some crumb of bread in some good milk; have a few mushrooms and a little parsley chopped very fine. Set the herbs to sweat in a little butter, over a very slow fire. Then let them cool in a hair sieve. Next put the bread, that has been soaked and squeezed properly, with the

the general observation, that French cookery is too rich, is here particularly out of place, for there is neither fat nor sinews, and very little seasoning in this dish, and it is of very easy digestion.

flesh of the carp that has been rubbed through a tammy, into a mortar, with a lump of butter of about the same bulk as the flesh of the carp, and season with pepper, salt, allspice, three or four eggs, whites and yolks together: *farces* with butter, require more eggs than those with udder. Yet before you put more than three, you must try to roll some of the *farce* in a little flour, and to poach it in boiling water. You then taste, and add to the seasoning if required. When completely done, rub it through a sieve, and let it cool in the larder, and use it when you have occasion. This *farce* is used for petty patties of carp. We also make *quenelles* for *matelottes*, and likewise for the *carp farces*.

No. 11.—*Farce de Godiveau, for the Pâtés à la Mazarines, &c.*

Take three-quarters of a pound of very white veal, a pound and a half of beef suet, which you strip of all the sinewy skins: chop the suet separately, and the veal the same. When you have chopped them both, take some herbs, such as parsley, shalots and mushrooms, which chop also very fine, and sweat in a little butter; mix the whole together, veal, suet, and herbs, and season with pepper and salt. Then chop them again. Break two eggs, yolks and whites, and if the *godiveau* appears to be well mixed, put a little piece into the oven in a small tart mould. If it rises well, and is properly seasoned, that is a sign of its being done; if not, put it into the mortar again with a little milk or water.

By dint of great practice, you acquire the facility of observing accidents which can not be properly explained. In the summer season, for instance, the suet being very soft, you find more difficulty in using it. If you have any clean ice, put some small pieces into the *godiveau*, to make the meat suet combine the better.

No. 12.—*Green Marbled Farce.*

Make a *farce à quenelles* as directed above. Take part of it, and mix it with a *verd de persil* (see *Sauces*) which you have drained, in order that the water may not make the *farce* thinner. If you wish to use it quite of a green colour, you mix it with the whole; but if you intend to *marble* either *galantines*, or fillets of soles, you put on slightly a part white, and another green. Then roll and poach them, and when they are cut they look like marble. It is easy to conceive, that if you wish to make it marble-like, you must alternate the green and white by laying on the green at occasional distances.

No. 13.—*Red Marbled Farce.*

This is much the same as the former. In France we make use of butter of craw-fish, for fowls *à la Cardinale*, or red and marbled *farces*. In England the eggs of lobsters are more frequently used, which are not amiss for *farces* of fish, and fowls, &c.

No. 14.—*Stuffing for Hare or Turkey.*

Take half a pound of beef suet, chopped very fine, some parsley, a little thyme, pepper, salt, and spices, the same quantity of crumbs of bread as of suet, an egg or two, and mix the whole with a little milk. It would not be amiss to put to it a very small bit of butter, and to pound the whole in a mortar for a short time. This *farce* may be used with baked pike, or with either roasted or boiled turkey, roasted hare, &c.; in short, with all such articles as will be mentioned in this work. If the taste of shalot is not objected to, it will be found to add to the flavour of the stuffing.

No. 15.—*Farce for Pies.*

Take an equal quantity of veal and fat bacon; chop them together, and season with pepper, salt, and all-spice, but no herbs, which only prevent the pie from keeping. If it is however to be eaten immediately, you may introduce some savoury herbs, a little chopped parsley, and shalots, and make a *pâté aux truffles*, or chop some truffles, which mix with *farce*. In pies made of game you may chop some ham, but in those made of fowl, the saltpetre gives a red colour to the meat, which can never look too white. For a *farce* to preserve game, fowl, &c. in tureens, proceed as follows: take a very light coloured calf's liver, cut it into square bits of about an inch in diameter, cut likewise half the same quantity of lean bacon from the breast, and a few bits of fat and lean ham, a small piece of butter, salt, pepper, spice, parsley, chopped fine, shalots and truffles (if at hand.) Fry all these ingredients gently over a very slow fire, stirring often with a wooden spoon. When the liver and the bacon are thoroughly done, drain off all the fat, and put them into a mortar, and pound them very well, and season very highly, as it is used to preserve and to stuff game, fowls, &c. in tureens. When you bake tureens of this description in the oven, take care that you place over the pot a bit of common paste, to close them hermetically, one hour more or less, according to the size of your pie or tureen. When done, take off the crust, squeeze the meat with a spoon all round, and clean the pot; then fill up with lard, and when cold cover it with clean paper, and label it with the title of contents.

This method not only keeps better, but is more mellow in the eating than the meat *farcée*.

No. 16.—*Farce for Sausages.*

Sausages are composed of only hog's flesh; but as it is not amiss to stuff turkeys with this *farce*, the author has thought proper to mention it here. Take all the tender parts of the meat, the sinews being left aside when the hams and breasts are cured, which will be found treated of in a separate article. Cut the whole of the meat into small dice; then cut nearly about the same quantity of fat into small dice also. Chop and mix them very fine together, fat and lean;

season with pepper and salt, allspice, and a little mint chopped very fine. All these ingredients give the sausages a very agreeable taste. When you use the sausages *directly*, you must moisten them with a little water or milk; they will keep two or three days, but then they should not be moistened. They are, however, not so good when kept, as they are liable to turn red directly.

CHAPTER V.

ENTRÉES OF BUTCHER'S MEAT.

BEEF.

No. 1.—*Blanquette of Palates of Beef.*

TAKE six or eight palates of Beef, rub them over with salt, and stew them in a *blanc*, till you can take off the upper skin. When the palates are thus skinned and done, cut them into the size of shilling pieces, and throw them into the *sauce à blanquette,* which is a *sauce tournée* reduced, that you have thickened. The palates of beef *en blanquette* are sent up to table either in a *casserole au ris,* or, a *vol au vent,* or a *timbal.* Observe, that the palates must be always well done before you intend to use them in any manner. This is a very difficult dish to dress, and is rarely sent up in perfection.

No. 2.—*Blanquette of Palates of Beef with Peas.*

This is made nearly in the same manner as that above; but previously to putting in the thickening, you take a few spoonsful of sweated peas intended for *entremets,* and reduce them with the sauce, that it may give the savour of the peas. Add a little salt and sugar. *Entrées* of this sort should be sweet, and not briny.

No. 3.—*Blanquette of Palates of Beef with Cucumbers.*

Prepare the palates of beef as for other *blanquettes*. Pare some cucumbers and cut them into the size of shilling pieces. Keep the *parings* to make a *purée*, which you throw into the sauce, to give it a taste of the cucumbers. Put the cucumbers into the *sauce tournée*, a little sugar, and let them do; then drain them, and reduce the sauce separately. When done, and the sauce is thickened, put the *liaison* to it;* throw into the sauce the cucumbers that are entire, and the palates of beef, and serve up in a deep dish, or in a *vol au vent*.

No. 4.—*Blanquette of Palates of Beef with Truffles.*

The palates to be prepared as above. Only in this case cut the truffles into the size of shilling pieces, and put them in butter and salt. *Sautez* them on a brisk fire, till done. Let them have one single boil in the sauce, before you throw in the thickening, then mix the palates and truffles together.

No. 5.—*Attelets of Palates of Beef à l' Italienne.*

Palates of beef are always prepared as directed at No. 1. The only difference consist in the cutting of them, and in the sauce with which they are sent up to table. Take some *sauce d'attelets* (see *Sauces*,) and after having cut the palates into square pieces of whatever dimension you may think proper, let them cool in the sauce. When quite cold, run a silver skewer through them in a row, and cover all the meat with some of the sauce. Make the *attelets* as smooth as possible with your knife. Next dip them into crumbs of bread, and make them quite square. Mind that both extremities are well covered with the crumbs; dip them a second time into an *omelette;* and

---

* As the cucumbers will always thin the sauce, do not put them in till you serve up. This *entrée* requires a little sugar.

again into the crumbs of bread; let both ends of the skewers be remarkably clean. Then fry the palates to a fine brown colour, and serve them up with a brown Italian sauce under it.

No. 6.—*Palates of Beef au gratin, otherwise en Paupiette.*

Have a good *farce à quenelles* ready; cut the palates in two lengthways, observing to keep them of an equal size and straight; spread some of the *farce* over the rough side, and roll them with the *farce* in, observing to garnish both hands with some of the *farce* neatly done; then put part of the *farce* into the middle of the dish, and erect all the slices of palates in the shape of a bastion, after having stuffed and rolled them. Cover the whole with layers of bacon, and put the dish into the oven, without allowing the contents to get brown. When the *farce* is done thoroughly, drain all the fat, take off all the layers of bacon, clean the dish well, and *mask* the meat with a thick *Espagnole*, well seasoned, and a little *ragout* in the middle.

No. 7.—*Miroton of Palates of Beef à la Ude.*

Use a cutter both for the palates of beef and truffles, which are made into pieces of an equal size. Dress them *en miroton*. Then take a sufficient quantity of mushrooms also of the same size, to make a border round the dish: put in the middle a *salpicon* of truffles, mushrooms, and palates of beef, and sauce the *miroton* with a pretty thick *Espagnole*. Before you use any of the preceding articles, they must be all done, and then put a palate and then a truffle alternately, to the very top of it. Keep the dish covered very warm to prevent its drying.

No. 8.—*Croquettes of Palates of Beef au velouté.*

Take all the trimming from the *blanquettes, mirotons,* &c. and cut them in square pieces. Have some mushrooms cut into small dice, which fry white in a little butter. Then moisten with a little thin *sauce tournée*, and let them boil gently on the corner of the stove, that you may skim off the grease. Next reduce this sauce with a pint of cream: when it has got thick enough, throw the palates into the sauce, and let them boil for a moment, that they may taste of the sauce. Let this preparation cool in a plate. When quite cold, roll the whole into *croquettes*, either round or oval; dip them once into crumbs of bread, then into an *omelette*, and into crumbs of bread again; then fry them till they are of a fine brown, and serve up with fried parsley. If you should not have quite enough of the palates, as weetbread, or the trimmings of fowl, will match the other ingredients very well. It is not the circumstance of being profuse in cookery that renders your cookery better, you may give a capital dinner at a small expense, if you turn every thing to advantage. When you have in the larder some *béchamelle* and mushrooms, cut some in small dice as well as the palate, and take the *béchamelle* in preference to make the *croquette* as above recommended.

No. 9.—*Beef's Tongue, Sauce hachée.*

Take a tongue that is quite fresh; let it disgorge, blanch it to take away any tripy taste it may have retained; then stew it in a good braize.* When done, flay it, cut it in two, spread it open, and *mask* with the *sauce hachée.* (See *Sauces.*) This is but a very common *entrée.*

No. 10.—*Miroton of Tongue with Turnips.*

Let the tongue be stewed as above, and then get cold. Next cut it into scollops, dish it *en miroton,*

* You must remember that every thing which is called *braize*, must be seasoned with carrot, onion, parsley, thyme, bay-leaf, and clove. (See *Braize.*)

and place the dish covered at the mouth of the oven. A short time before you send it up to table, glaze it with a light glaze, and pour into the middle *l'haricot brun*. (See *Sauces*.)

No. 11.—*Miroton of Tongue with Sorrel Sauce.*

Prepare the tongue as above, No. 10, only glaze it a little more and lay thicker. Pour into the middle the *purée* of sorrel.

No. 12.—*Miroton of Tongue with Spinach.*

The same preparation as above, only use spinach, and let them be richer and more liquid than for an *entremets*. It is necessary to observe, that when spinach is used as sauce, it must be more tasty and liquid than when it is used for garnishing round a tongue or ham. When for sauce, put a little more broth and seasoning, as it is to give taste and relish to whatever it is used with.

No. 13.—*Miroton of Red Tongue with mashed Turnips.*

This is not a French *entrée;* and is only mentioned here, because the author has seen it served at the table of men of acknowledged taste. Take the remnants of a tongue *à l'écarlate* that is quite cold; cut it into round slices, dress it in a dish, and put it into the oven for a moment. Then glaze it, and serve it up with mashed turnips in the middle. Never use broth to warm your slices of tongue, that spoils both colour and taste; put them in a clean plate, covered with one another, and as soon as they become warm, glaze and serve them forthwith, but never heat them in liquor.

No. 14.—*Pickled Tongue, glazed and bigarrée.*

This is a remove which is frequently used for family dinners. Take a large tongue *à l'écarlate*, boil it well, then flay it, glaze it, and, after having made it look quite neat, send it up with mashed turnips on one side, and mashed carrots, or carrots and spinach, on the other, &c.

––––––

Mashed Turnips or Carrots.—Peel some turnips, wash and boil them with salt and water; when properly done, press all the water out, and pound them well in a mortar, then put them into a stew-pan with a quarter of a pound of fresh butter, a little salt, half a pint of cream, and a tea-spoonful of flour to prevent the water from running out; mix and warm very hot, and use them when wanted. The same method exactly for carrots.

Never rub them through a sieve, for they then become a *purée*, and not a mash, and look dirty.

No. 15.—*Filets Mignons of Beef sautés à la Lyonaise.*

Take the inside fillet of a sirloin of beef, and scollop it of about the size of the palm of your hand. *Mark* them in clarified butter, with a little salt and pepper, in a *sautez* pan; when dinner-time is come, *sautez* them and turn them over; when done on both sides, drain the butter and put a little glaze in its stead. Keep stirring the meat in the glaze with a little lemon-juice, and a small bit of fresh butter. Dish it *en miroton*, and pour the *Lyonaise* in the *sautez* pan with the glaze. When you have mixed that well, put the sauce in the middle of the *filets mignons*, and serve up quite hot. You must give this dish only when you have a rump of beef; the small fillets left to that part is sufficient; it would be unnecessary and extravagant to spoil a sirloin. This dish is excellent at breakfast to those who like onions: it requires, however, very high seasoning.

No. 16.—*Filets of Beef marinaded à la broche.*

Take the same part as above, and take off the sinews. Then lard it, and pickle it raw with an onion and a shalot cut into slices, a little parsley, salt, pepper, vinegar, &c.; let it *marinade* one day. Then roast and glaze it. Serve up with a *poivrade*. This dish is dressed in this way for those who like vinegar. You must sometimes omit the vinegar, and put instead of it a little sweet oil; it prevents the meat from drying, and makes it tender.

It may be necessary to make a remark here, which is of consequence to the right understanding of the present work. We have two kinds of larding with bacon, that which is larded on the superficies (as a *fricandeau*), is commonly called *piqué*, while that which is larded with wood or iron larding pin through the meat with coarse bacon, is vulgarly termed *lardé:* the adoption of the term *larded* and *piqué* is recommended. A filet *marinaded* is *piqué*, and veal *à la bourgeoise*, or *beef à la mode*, is *larded*.

No. 17.—*Ox-Tail in Hochepot.*

The beef-tail being a very plain and common dish, is seldom sent up otherwise than as a tureen. See No. 21, *Deep Dishes*, page 72.) This dish has a detestable appearance, but when well drest is delicious eating. It requires to be well done, and is excellent either with peas, or as a *haricot* with turnips.

No. 18.—*Miroton of Beef.*

When you have some cold rump of beef left, cut it neatly into slices, and put them into a *sauté* pan, with a little *Espagnole* or *brown Italienne*, some salt and pepper, and a little broth. Give them a few boils, and serve up quite hot. This dish, when well managed, is excellent and economical; but observe, you must keep it always well covered, or it will become black and dry. The best way is to keep it under the sauce.

No. 19.—*Kidney of Beef with Champagne Wine.*

Take some kidneys that are of a nice light colour;

take off a little of the fat, mince it, and fry it white in a pan with a little chopped parsley, shalots, salt, pepper, &c. When it is done enough powder a little flour over it, and moisten with a glass of Champagne, or two or three spoonsful of *Espagnole.* It must not boil any more, for it would get hard. But you must keep it hot, and serve it up the same. We send this *entrée* up to table for breakfast only.

No. 20.—*Beef-Steaks with Potatoes, French fashion.*

Take some thin slices of rump of beef, flatten them, and season them with a little salt, pepper, &c. Dip those slices into a little butter, that the gravy may not drop out whilst broiling. You must have some parsley chopped very fine, and mixed with butter, salt, pepper, lemon, &c. When your beef-steaks are done, put the above ingredients under the steaks, and all round fried potatoes of a fine brown colour. Glaze the beef-steaks; you may serve them with different sauces, as mushroom, oyster, sauce *haché.* Beef-steaks are also served with oysters. (See *Sauces.*)

No. 21.—*Sirloin of Beef braized.*

Take that part of the beef that is between the rump and the first ribs. Turn it over on the *filet mignon,* and dress it in a good shape. *Mark* it in a large braizing-pan, with plenty of parings of veal, a large piece of the breast part of bacon, a small bit of ham, a few carrots, onions, some parsley-roots, a bunch of parsley and green onions, seasoned with thyme, bay-leaves, spices of all sorts, and a ladleful of good broth. Cover the sirloin with bacon first, and then with two sheets of white paper, to prevent the fire that you are to lay over it making the meat look brown. When you have closed the braizing-pan, stick some slips of paper all round, and stew the sirloin for four hours on a very slow fire. A moderately heated oven would be preferable. The braizing-pan must have boiled before you put it into the oven. (See *Sauces for the*

Godard.) You are to garnish with pigeons *à la gau-tier*, large *quenelles*, larded sweetbreads, and especially large cock's-combs, which slit into the fillet, when you are going to send up to table.

No. 22.—*Roast Beef.*

The author would recommend to the cook, to choose, in the first place, a well covered sirloin, not weighing more than twenty or twenty-four pounds; a larger piece is never well roasted, the time which it requires causes the outside to be too much done, while the middle remains quite raw. The meat must be covered for one hour only with paper, to prevent its taking too much colour; it is necessary to observe, that for large pieces the fire must not be too sharp, or the meat will be burned, before it is warm through; just before you take it off the spit, spread some fine salt over it, and send it up very hot with gravy only. This joint is often spoiled for the next day's use, by an injudicious mode of carving. If you object to the outside cut, take the brown off, and help yourself to the next; by thus cutting it only on one side, you preserve the gravy in the meat, and the goodly appearance likewise: by cutting it, on the contrary, down the middle of the joint, all the gravy runs out, and it remains dry and void of substance, besides exhibiting a most unseemly aspect when brought to table a second time.

No. 23.—*Brisket of Beef à la Flamande.*

See *Removes*, No. 3, page 75.

No. 24.—*Rib of Beef braized en Hochepot.*

Take about four ribs of beef: pare the thick part, lard them with thick bacon, and *braize* them in the same manner as you would do the rump. Send up with glazed onions, or cabbages, or *hochepot*, or a *sauce hachée*, round it. Observe that you are not to detach the ribs, which are to be served flat, as if they were mutton chops.

No. 25.—*L'Entre-Côte of Beef broiled, Sauce hachée.*

Take the slice which lies between two ribs of beef, flatten it well in a good shape, and broil it. If it be thick, you must have a gentle fire to heat it through; if it be thin, the fire must be brisk, or it will not get a good colour, nor eat so well. The *entre-côte* is most tender eating.

No. 26.—*Hachée of Beef.*

Take some of the beef left the preceding day, remove the fat and the skin, mince the beef about the thickness of a half-penny, and about the same size; spread over it salt, pepper, and flour, and moisten this with the gravy left from the meat; boil this *hachée* very little, for if it boil any length of time it will be hard and tough, but if it is only warmed it will be very tender.

When you make *hachée* for the servants, cut one onion, or a few shalots very fine, season with salt, pepper, bay-leaves and thyme; let the *hachée* boil one hour or more, and put the bones into it, which will give a capital taste. When you take the meat out to put into the larder, never forget to preserve the gravy in a basin to make a *hachée*, or to use as gravy under the roast; want of caution prevents your giving a good taste to common cookery.

CHAPTER VI.

MUTTON AND LAMB.

It is necessary to observe to the junior cook, that almost every thing which is made with mutton, may be made also with lamb; with this only difference, that lamb being the tenderest meat, requires less doing. If you make *haricot* of lamb, you must *sautez* the cutlets first, and then boil them in the sauce of *haricot* (see *Haricot*): the *epigram* is always made with lamb, as it requires a *blanquette* in the middle of the chop. Mutton is too highly coloured for it. Any observation respecting mutton is of importance, as it is more frequently served at dinner than any other dish. Be cautious, therefore, always to have your mutton very dark, and marble like. Young mutton is very pale, and has no flavour. You perceive the qualities of mutton when it appears very brown, and when the nerves of the leg are small and transparent. Young mutton is larger and whiter, the flesh on the neck being very dark and mixed with fat.

No. 1.—*Mutton Cutlets à la Soubise.*

Take a neck of mutton, and cut the chops one by one without flattening them; cut off some of the flat bone at the extremity of the chops. Put them into a stew-pan with all the parings, together with the parings of the onions for the *soubise*. Season the whole well with carrots, a bunch of parsley, and green onions, salt, and a very small quantity of spice, &c., throw in four or five spoonsful of good broth, to braize them. When done, drain them, and let them cool. Strain the liquor through a silk sieve. Then reduce it to glaze. Next pare the chops nicely, and put them with the glaze. This being completed, dish them *en miroton*, and pour the *soubise* into the middle.

Some persons take two necks of mutton, cut two bones to each chop, lard them with bacon, and *braize* them as above; but mutton being in general fat, is better without being larded. With regard to the two bones, you must take care not to let them be too thick, if they are too thick you can not dish them well.

Another, and a much better Method of preparing Cutlets à la soubise.

Cut the mutton chops a little thicker than when you wish to broil them. Pare them nicely, and put them into a stew-pan, where they may all be flat. Put an onion or two, a few carrots *tournées*, a little salt, a bundle of parsley and green onions, seasoned,* four or five spoonsful of good *consommé*,† and sweat the whole till it is entirely done. Then take out the roots, put in a little glaze, and reduce them over a large fire. When entirely *à glace*, take them out of the fire for a few minutes, then the cutlets, settle in glaze, take out the bones, trimmed and végétable, turn over the cutlets in the glaze, and take out the grease or fat, lay them on a cover to drain the fat, and serve up before they can get dry. This method is

---

* It may be necessary to remind the reader, that SEASONED means a composition of all sorts of herbs.

† Be on your guard against using old broth; if you have no fresh broth, put water. Old broth turns the cutlets red.

preferable to the other. You must not in either case, lard your chops with bacon. These cutlets may be served up with all sorts of *purée* or vegetable.

No. 2.—*Cutlets en Haricot Vierge.*

Prepare the chops as above. Braize them in the same manner. As many people object to onions, serve them with a *haricot vierge* instead of a *soubise.* (See *Sauces.*)

No. 3.—*Cutlets à la Minute.*

Take the best part of a neck of mutton that has been kept for a while. Cut the chops one by one, and pare them as nicely as you can. Season them with pepper and salt; dip them into some melted butter, and broil them over a brisk fire. Serve up with a very strong gravy of veal well seasoned. Observe that cutlets *à-la-minute,* to be good, must not be too much trimmed, and you must leave a little fat to them: they are dipped in butter to prevent them from drying and keep the gravy in it.

No. 4.—*Cutlets à l'Italienne.*

Take the best part of two necks of mutton, well mortified, to bring them very tender: trim them as small as can be, without wasting any thing, then laying them on the table, spread over each side salt and pepper. Have in a plate the yolk of one egg, take a paste-brush and dip it in the corner of the egg, rub the cutlets, one after the other, and rub them in the crumbs of bread; have some butter melted, but not clarified, dip the cutlets in the butter and in the crumbs of bread, then beat them in your two hands, and dip them again in the crumbs of bread, make them very equal with the knife, and put a little of the butter, in a thick *sautéz pan,* put the cutlets into it, and at the dinner time, put them over a very brisk fire, to *sautéz* them of a very good colour, observe, if the fire is not very brisk, they will take too much time in the cooking, and will be necessarily too much done: as soon as they acquire a colour they are done. Have some whity brown paper put over them and press them between two pieces, in order to extract all the fat, pass the paste-brush of glaze lightly over, and serve up with the *Italian sauce* very thin, spread over; this *entrée* will be in universal favour, if you are particular in the preparation of it.

No. 5.—*Cutlet with Purée of Mushroom.*

These are nearly the same as in No. 4. Only you serve the *purée* of mushroom, instead of the *Italienne* sauce, but do not *mask* with the sauce; glaze the cutlet, and drain them, and put the *purée* in the middle of it.

No. 6.—*Cutlets en Haricot brun.*

Many people braize and glaze them, and put the *haricot brun* in the middle, but I will explain the manner in which they are to be prepared, in order that they may taste of the turnips. Cut the chops as in No. 1, pare the bones nicely, then fry them in a little butter, of a nice brown colour, drain the butter, and make a *roux* very *blond;* that is to say, put into the same stew-pan a small bit of fresh butter and a spoonful of fine flour; put this over a moderate fire, and turn it with a wooden spoon till the flour is of a very nice brown colour, then moisten with some gravy of veal of a fine colour, well seasoned. When the sauce boils, throw in the chops, and the trimmings of the turnips, and a seasoned bundle of parsley and green onions; let them stew gently on the corner of the stove. Skim the sauce frequently: when the chops are nearly done, drain them in a clean stew-pan. Have ready some turnips turned in whatever shape you think proper, but they must not be too small for this *entrée;* drain the sauce through a tammy over the turnips and chops, which stew in this sauce with a little sugar; continue skimming frequently. When the turnips are done as well as the chops, keep them warm *au bain marie,* till you serve up.

N.B.—Some people fry the turnips in butter to make them brown, which is useless; as they will look very well, provided the gravy of veal is of a fine colour; but in case you have no gravy of veal, you put in an omelette-pan a small bit of butter, a spoonful of white pounded sugar, and the turnips: fry them till they are of a fine colour, then moisten and use them as specified above.

No. 7.—*Cutlets sautées à l'Essence.*

Pare them, as in No. 3, *mark* them in a cutlet or sauty-pan, with melted* butter. *Sautez* them over a brisk equal fire. Drain part of the butter; put one or two spoonsful of *Espagnole* and a little glaze in the cutlet-pan, with the juice of a lemon. Keep stirring the whole over the fire, but do not let it boil. Dish and send up instantly.

N.B.—If these are kept waiting they are spoiled. They are fine eating, however, for such people as like their meat under-done; but if they are over-done, they have no more savour than cork or leather.

No. 8.—*Cotelettes à la Maintenon.*

Pare the chops as in No. 3. Chop fine some sweet herbs, such as parsley, shalots, and mushrooms, which fry in a little butter. When they are done, fry the chops a little in that seasoning till nearly done, let them cool, then wrap them up in paper, and broil them over a slow fire. This *entrée* I can not much approve of, on account of the greased paper which is to appear at the table. But some persons like them. These cutlets are the same as *cotelettes du papillotte.* A few crumbs of bread and a little chopped ham are

---

* It is necessary to observe, when the butter is not to that clarified, it must be put in a stew-pan over a slow fire, and allowed to melt till the butter-milk settles at the bottom of the stew-pan. Let it not be too much done.

excellent additions, if put in the paper with the cutlets.

No. 9.—*The inside Filets à la Maréchale.*

The inside fillets of mutton are to be taken off from
under the surloin; take off all the fat; flatten the fillets
with the handle of your knife, then scatter a litle salt
and pepper, have a paste-brush dipped slightly in the
yolk of an egg, dip the fillets in the crumbs of bread,
and afterwards in the melted butter, make them of a
nice form with the knife, put them in a *sauty-pan*
with a little of the melted butter, the less the better, as
the fillet will take colour sooner, and be more quickly
ready. After having broiled them, or *sauté*, of a fine
colour, drain them in a sheet of very clean paper, to
take off the grease, and sauce them with the *maréchale.*
The *maréchale* for this is tarragon vinegar reduced in
a small stew-pan, and moistened with three or four
spoonsful of *Espagnole* sauce, and a little Cayenne
pepper.

No. 10.—*The inside Fillets marinaded au chev-
reuil.*

You must have the fillets of four saddles of mutton,
which of course produce eight *filets mignons.* Lard
them in the same manner as fillets of rabbits, next
pickle them in a *marinade crue,* such as thyme,
parsley, bay leaves, onions, salt, pepper and vinegar. When they have been lying for two or three
hours in this *marinade, mark* them in a *sauté*-pan
over layers of bacon; and bake them of a nice colour.
When done, glaze them, and serve them up with a
poivrade under them. Observe, that this *entrée* is
only to be served in a family, where you give saddle
of mutton to the nursery, or to the servants; in that
case, you take off the inside fillets. You may leave
the inside fat to the saddle, and only take off the filets.

No. 11.—*The inside Fillets with Purée of Sorrel*

These are to be pared and larded as in No. 10. *Mark* them as a *fricandeau*, by which is meant, that you must make a bed of roots in a stew-pan; these you cover with slices of layers of bacon; then lay the larded fillets on the bacon, and powder them over with a little salt. Moisten but little. They only require one hour to be done, between two fires, one at the top, the other at the bottom. When they are done, reduce the liquor and glaze the fillets with that glaze. Serve under them the *purée* of sorrel.

N.B.—They are also sent up with endive, or with the *Soubise*, or *Macedoine*, &c.

No. 12.—*Necks of Mutton en Aigrettes.*

Take the best part of two necks of mutton, pare the fillet, lard it as a *fricandeau;* take off the upper skin of the flank: then take a piece of cold veal, or a piece of cold *bouilli* beef, which cut round, a little larger than your hand. Wrap this beef up in a very thin layer of bacon. Next turn the mutton with the larded fillets downwards; and the fat upwards: mark this in the same manner as the inside fillets with vegetables. When they are done, glaze them of a nice colour, then take out the beef and the bacon, and in the middle pour a *Macédoine*, or any other sauce.

No. 13.—*The Neck of Mutton with Parsley.*

Take the same two parts as above: after having taken off the bones, take off also the sinews, as if you were going to lard them. Have in readiness a few branches of parsley, quite green, with which you lard the fillet only, but very thick, for when well done the parsley is diminished considerably, as it gets dry. Before you want the mutton it must be marinaded in oil and salt, an onion cut into slices, &c. The oil makes the parsley crisp, and preserves its green colour. Send up with a *poivrade* or an *Espagnole.* *(*See *Sauces.)*

No. 14.—*Les Carbonades à la Jardinière,*

Take a saddle of mutton, and cut off the skin that is over the fat without stripping the fillet. Cut the saddle in two, and each of these two into three or four; braize them as the mutton *à la Soubise;* do not leave too much fat, glaze them of a nice colour, and serve them with the *haricot,* or the *jardinière,* or endive, or spinach, &c.

N.B.—This *entrée,* although frequently sent to table in France, is not often introduced in this country. It may be sent up with sorrel, or with any sauce whatever; but it is too fat in general.

No 15.—*The Breasts of Mutton à la Ste. Menoult.*

These are to be braized with carrots, onions, spices, &c. When they are well done, drain them. Take out the bones and let the meat cool between two dishes, that it may be kept flat. When cold, cut them into the shape of hearts, rounds, or into chops, just as you like. Brush them over with the yolk of an egg, and then dip them into crumbs of bread; next dip them into clarified butter, and give them another coat of bread crumbs. Put them into the oven to give them a fine brown, and serve them up with a *sauce hachée,* or an *Italienne,* or *en haricot.* This is also a common dish.

No. 16.—*Musette of Mutton with Endive.*

Take a shoulder of mutton that has been kept for some while; bone it without taking off the thin skin that is found near the joint; powder it over with a little pepper and salt. Then pass a piece of packthread round, as tailors do round a button, fasten the packthread, and mould the shoulder of mutton quite round. You must preserve the knuckle so that it may resemble a bagpipe. Braize it, and season it well. After having drained and glazed it, send it up with either endive or sorrel.

N.B.—It may also be stuffed and larded, and a

flowret larded in the top part, and sent up with white beans *à la Lyonaise.* This is also a common dish.

No. 17.—*Sheep's Tongues with turnips.*

Take eight tongues of an equal size; let them disgorge in a little water and flour, and next blanch them. When thoroughly blanched, mark them in a stew-pan, to *braize* them. In case you should have a *braize* of beef, or of mutton, or any others, as they will all equally answer the purpose for sheep's tongues, when they are done, peel them and cut them in two. Dish them *en miroton,* and *mask* them with the sauce of the *haricot,* the turnips of course being put in the middle. It is customary, in French cookery, to call any thing made with turnips *haricot.*

No. 18.—*The same with Cabbage Lettuces.*

The tongues are to be braized as above, the same as those you wish to cook in any way whatever. Take a dozen and a half of good cabbage-lettuces, wash them very clean, and blanch them. When they are cold, and you have squeezed all the water out of them, open them in two, take off the stalks, powder a little salt and pepper over them; then shut them and give them a good form; mark them in a stew-pan, surrounded with layers of bacon: moisten them with a little *braize,* or a *poële,* or any thing to give them a good taste; otherwise take the pot-top, with a little broth and salt. When the lettuces are quite done, drain them, and squeeze them in a cloth to extract the grease. Dish them *en rosates,* namely, a tongue, a lettuce, and so on successively. Put a large tongue in the middle, to improve the look of the *rosate.* Another time, cut the tongues in two, and dish them *en miroton,* that is, one half of a tongue, and lettuce alternately. In this case, put a *jardinière* in the middle, and *mask** both the tongues and the lettuce with the *Espagnole*. This is likewise common *entrées*.

No. 19.—*Sheep's Tongues au gratin.*

Cut as many bits of bread in the shape of cocks'-combs, as you have tongues. Take some *farce fine*. (See Chap. 6.) Erect a little dome in the centre of the dish, and dress the tongues in the said *farce*, leaving however room enough betwen to place one of the toasts; then put the dish into the oven. When the *farce* and tongues are done, take them out of the oven, and drain all the grease; they must be covered with bacon, in order that they may not get dry (unless a mould may be procured to close hermetically;) you then put the toasts, or crouton, fried of a fine brown colour, between each tongue, and the sauce with a thick *essence*. Mind that the tongues must be *glazed* and *blazed* before, with whatever sauce you serve them.

No. 20.—*Sheep's Tongue à la Maintenon.*

The tongues are to be cut in two, and put into a *dusselle* or in fine herbs, the same as chops *à la Maintenon*. When you put any meat *en papillottes*, you must use as great a quantity of fine herbs as possible, (as No. 8,) and put to it likewise the ham chopped, and the crumbs of bread.

No. 21.—*Hashed Mutton, English Fashion.*

When you know that you have hashed mutton to make, be careful to keep some of the good gravy, then cut the skin off, and the sinews; leave as much fat as you can find in the inside of the leg; cut the meat into small flat bits, season with a little salt and fine pepper, spread a little fine flour over the meat, mix all very well, then moisten with the gravy; if you have no gravy, you must have a little broth and

* *Mask* signifies, cover with the sauce.

a small bit of glaze or portable soup; do not let it boil, for it will make the meat very tough.

No. 22.—*Minced Mutton with Cucumbers.*

Roast a leg of mutton that has been kept for a long time. When under-done, let it cool; when quite cold, pare the sinews, skin, fat, &c. &c.; next make a mince, which throw into the sauce with cucumbers *à l' Espagnole*, as follows:—

No. 23.—*Minced Mutton with endive.*

This is to be prepared in the same manner as all other minces of mutton. Only observe that minces of black meat, as we call them, require brown sauces; and that the meat must never boil a second time, as it would become tough.

No. 24.—*Sheep's Tails with purée of Green Peas.*

Disgorge the tails in water to draw out the blood; next blanch them, and *braize* them in an old *braize;* otherwise they are to be seasoned with carrots, onions, spices, &c. When done, drain and glaze them. Then let them get a little dry in the oven. Put the *purée* of green peas under them; the same if you use *purée* of sorrel.

No. 25.—*Sheep's Tails with à la St. Laurent.*

Braize them in the same manner as those above; drain them and let them cool. Mind to give them a pleasing shape. Next brush them over with the yolk of an egg, and dip them into crumbs of bread. Then dip them into melted butter and crumbs of bread again. Put them into the oven till they are of a fine brown, if your oven is hot enough; if not, broil and send them up with rich gravy, or an *Italienne.*

N. B.—The *entrées* of mutton, from No. 17 to this last number, are not very frequently sent up to table in England, but in France they are held in high estimation. The tails are served in different ways, the most commendable of which, is that with green peas, and *purées* of all sorts.

No. 26.—*Sheep's Brains en Matelotte.*

Detach the brains from the heads of about eight sheep, without breaking them. Put them into a large vessel with some luke-warm water; take off the skin and let them disgorge for two hours. When they are become quite white, blanch them in boiling water, vinegar, and salt; and when they are very firm, put them in very cold water, after which place some layers of bacon round a stew-pan, big enough to hold all the eight brains, add a small onion with one clove, a small bundle of parsley, well seasoned, and some salt, and cover them with some layers of bacon, and a round of paper; little broth is required, and a few slices of lemon, to keep them very white. Twenty minutes will suffice to boil them, but they must be boiled two hours or more before dinner, to acquire a flavour; then at dinner you must have ready some *croutons*, in quantity equal to the brains, stick them in the dish alternately, to leave room to put the brains in the spaces; *mask* them with the sauce of *matelottes*, mushrooms, and small onions, &c.

No. 27.—*Sheep's Brains à la maitre d'Hotel.*

Proceed entirely as above directed, with the *crouton*, glazed and stuck in the dish as above; and at dinner time, as soon as you have dished up the brains, take three spoonsful of *béchamel*, a good bit of fresh butter, a little salt and cayenne, some parsley, chopped thyme, and blanch the juice of half a lemon, then work the sauce over the fire, to render it very hot and serve quickly.

No. 28.—*Sheep's Trotters à la Poulette.*

Take a dozen of sheep's trotters well scalded. Wash them in warm water, and let them disgorge till very white, then put them in a *blanc*. (See

Calf's head.) When well done, take some *sauce tournée* well reduced, to help the thickening, into which you have put a little chopped and blanched parsley, with the juice of a lemon; then throw the trotters into this sauce after having them well drained. If you should happen to have no *sauce tournée*, make a little white *roux*, moisten it with good *consommé*, seasoned with a bunch of parsley and small onions, and a few mushrooms. Let this sauce stew on the corner of the stove; skim the grease, and after having reduced it to a proper state for the thickening to be thrown in, drain the sauce through a tammy, and put the trotters into it.

No. 29.—*Sheep's Trotters en Canelons.*

Take some sheep's trotters as above, and stew them in the same manner; but do not let them be overdone, as they are to be stuffed with a *farce*, which could not be done in the latter case. Introduce the *farce à quenelles* in the room of the bones. When the trotters are well stuffed, put them between layers of bacon, and moisten them with a *poële*. Stew them for half an hour only, on account of the *farce*. Drain them, and *mask* them with a sauce well seasoned, either white or brown, according to your taste. As these are to be served whole, when you bone them, mind you do not injure the skin, for they would not hold the force-meat that you must put in. Observe, that this dish is excellent, as well for the taste as for health. It is particularly good for weak stomachs.

No. 30.—*Sheep's Trotters Fried,*

Are to be prepared in the same manner as the preceding. Make a *marinade cuite*, and leave the trotters in it to *marinade*. Then drain them, and dip them into a paste; fry them of a fine brown, and when well drained send them up, with parsley fried green in the middle.

For a *marinade cuite*, take carrots, onions, a little parsley root, a clove, a little thyme, a bit of bay-leaf, and a shalot, which mix together. Fry them a little, but not brown, in a little butter. When the roots begin to colour, moisten with half water and half vinegar; let the roots and vegetables get quite done, season with pepper and salt, and drain it through a silk sieve over whatever you may choose to *marinade*.

No. 31.—*Sheep's Trotters Farce.*

Prepare the trotters as above, and when well done, put a little of the *farce à quenelles* well seasoned in the same manner as the other, dipped in one *omelette*. Observe, this fritter should be in a moderate heat, to afford time to prepare the *farce*, when done too quickly the meat will be raw. When fried of a good colour, drain them very well, and serve them up *masked* with a good *Espagnole*.

Paste for frying, *or batter.*—With regard to the batter intended for frying *marinades*, *beignet* of all sorts, as apples, apricots, peaches, *beignet* of cream, &c. put about four spoonsful of flour into an earthenpan, with a little salt, a little olive oil, and moisten with a sufficient quantity of water or good beer, that the paste may not curdle. When the flour is well mixed, beat the whites of two eggs, which mix with the paste, and then put in whatever you may wish to fry. This method is preferable to any other, except such as may be recommended for artichokes, orlies, &c. &c.

No. 32.—*Sheep's Kidneys broiled.*

Take some kidneys that have been kept for a while, cut them in two, and remove the thin skin that covers them, use a small skewer to keep them open, in imitation of two shells; powder them over with a little pepper and salt, dip them into a little melted butter, and broil them just as you are going to serve up. Broil the side that you have cut open first: when you broil the other side, the whole of the gravy issues on the upper part. Mind when you take them off the fire, that the gravy does not drop off. Have some parsley chopped very fine, mixed with fresh butter, the juice of a lemon, pepper, and salt; put a little of that mixture over each kidney, and send up to table in a hot dish.

N. B.—Kidneys are an excellent breakfast for sportsmen, but are seldom sent up to dinner. They must be eaten directly, as they lose their goodness by waiting. They have also the disadvantage of being uneatable if they are too much done, and a man that can not eat meat under-done should not have them at his table.

No. 33.—*Sheep's Kidneys with Champagne.*

Take six or twelve kidneys, according to the quantity that you wish to dress; remove the skins and mince them the thickness and size of a half-penny; have a little bit of lean bacon, cut in small squares, fry them in an omelette pan, with a very small bit of butter; when the bacon is of a good colour, put in the kidneys, taking care to move the pan frequently, to fry the kidneys equally; when they are done, strew over them a little salt and pepper, some parsley chopped very fine, and a very small bit of shalot, well chopped also, pour over a little flour; stir up all with a wooden spoon, then moisten with a glass of white Champagne or Chablis, (neither Madeira, nor Sherry,) a little glass of which should be very hot, but do not let it boil, otherwise the kidneys will not be eatable; add a little lemon, and a little Cayenne, and observe that those dishes should be well seasoned.

No. 34.—*Leg of Mutton braized, called generally De Sept Heures.*

See *Removes of Soup* No. 7, page 77.

No. 35.—*Leg of Mutton, farcie or stuffed.*

Take a leg of mutton, bone it without damaging the skin, cut off all the fat; then take some fat bacon, about one-third of the quantity of the inside meat:

chop the bacon and the meat together, season the whole well, with chopped parsley, *en chalotte*, and pounded spices; put this forcemeat into the mortar, when it is well pounded stuff the skin of the leg of mutton, sew it in underwise, wrap the whole in a cloth to give it a good shape, and braize it as a *gigot de sept heures*. Drain it a short time before you serve it up in order to be enabled to take off the packthread. Then glaze and serve up with the *Lyonaise*. The *Lyonaise* is as follows: take one quart of white haricot beans, put them into soft water for three hours, then put them into cold soft water to boil, with a very small bit of butter; when done, mince one very large white onion, and fry it in a half a quartern of fresh butter; when the onion is well done, put to it a spoonful of flour, moisten with some good gravy, and leave the flour to be well done; then put a few haricot beans with it, and rub it through a sieve or tammy; after this drain the haricot beans well, and put them into that *purée*, well seasoned with salt and pepper.

No. 36.—*Boiled Neck of Mutton.*

Take from the best part of a neck of mutton, the skin and the bones, which are unsightly. Boil it for an hour and a half. Then send it up with turnips mashed with a little butter and cream. This dish does not require any further observation; it belongs to plain English dishes.

No. 47.—*Boiled Leg of Mutton.*

The same as the above, only boil longer according to the size: and mind, not to boil it too fast, as it will be tough, and white; but if you boil it gently, it will be always good.

CHAPTER VII.

ENTREES OF VEAL.

It is necessary to observe, that the veal you intend to serve for dishes must always be very white and fat; what you use for sauces is not of so much consequence; but it is certain that very white veal is more healthy than common veal; red veal will disorder a great many stomachs, white never does.

No. 1.—*Veal Cutlets broiled, à l'Italienne.*

Take the best part of a neck of veal; cut the ribs one by one, flatten them, and pare them nicely, powder over a little salt and pepper, take the yolk of an egg, and with a paste-brush rub the cutlets with part of the egg, then dip them first in the bread crumbs, then in melted butter, and afterwards in the crumbs of bread again; give them a good form, and broil them on a slow fire, that they may get a fine brown colour. Send them to table with a brown *Italienne, Espagnole,* or gravy.

No. 2.—*The same, à la Vénitienne, dites aux fines Herbs.*

Take the same part as above; when the cutlets are well pared, take a quarter of a pottle of mushrooms, a few shalots, a little parsley, chop the whole very fine, separately, rasp a little fat bacon, and a small bit of butter, and stew these fine herbs on a slow fire. As soon as they are done, put the cutlets with them, and stew them over a small stove. When they are done, and well seasoned with salt and pepper, skim off as much fat as you can, put in a spoonful of *sauce tournée*, and thicken the sauce with the yolk of three eggs, mixed with a little cream, and the juice of a lemon: add a little Cayenne pepper to it.

No. 3.— *The same à la Dauphine.* *

Take six fine cutlets of veal, and pare them on one side only, but all on the same side: lard them like a *fricandeau*, only let the bacon be cut finer; let them be *braized* also in the same manner as a *fricandeau;* then reduce the liquor in which they have been stewed, with which you glaze them. Serve up with either endive or sorrel.

No. 4.— *The same, à la Mirepoix.*

Put a little fresh butter, a few small shreds of ham, a little thyme, the half of a bay-leaf, a few stalks or a bunch of parsley, into a stew-pan. Then put the cutlets, which have been pared and seasoned as above, over the ham and butter. Next sweat them on a very slow fire. When they are done, drain the grease; pour in two spoonsful of *Espagnole*, and one spoonful of *consommé*, to detach the glaze, and the juice of a lemon. Send up the cutlets covered with this sauce, after having taken out the thyme and bay-leaf. If you choose to serve up the ham, you must cut it into fanciful figures.

No. 5.— *Veal Cutlets à la Maintenon.*

These are to be prepared in the same manner as

* Observe, that part of the veal is always the best for *fricandeau*, which is intermixed with fat. The author never had any other *fricandeau* served at the United Service Club. The other way of making *fricandeau* is thready and dry.

described at No. 2. When they have been stewed for a short time with the fine herbs, let them cool; then cut some bacon into the shape of hearts, which you put on each side of the cutlets, to prevent the paper from catching fire; then wrap them well in the paper, rub the paper with oil, and broil them on a very slow fire on both sides.

No. 6.—*Veal cutlets à la Chingara.*

Pare six cutlets as above. Sweat them with a little butter and ham; when they have been well seasoned, and are done, cut some slices of tongue *à l'écarlate* of the size of the cutlets, which you glaze, and with which each cutlet is to be covered. Serve them up with an *essence* detached from the glaze of the cut-the cutlets.

No. 7.—*Veal Cutlets à la Dreux.*

These are to be cut very thick, and larded with large slips of ham cut square. Season and *mark* them wrapped up in bacon and carrots, onions, thyme, cloves, bay-leaves, &c. Lay the trimmings on the top, and moisten with two spoonsful of good broth; let them stew over a very slow fire for about two hours. When they are done, lay them in a dish to cool. Next pare them of an agreeable shape, and put them into the glaze of the liquor which you have reduced. When dinner-time is at hand, glaze them of a fine brown, and serve up with an *Espagnole*, or sauce *hachée* or any other sauce.

No. 8.—*Veal Cutlets à la Châlons.*

These are prepared in the same manner as those above, No. 7. The only difference is, that they are larded chequer-like, with pickled cucumbers, ham, and fat bacon, and that the former are larded with ham alone. Serve them up with a *sauce hachée* or *purée* of sorrel.

No. 9.—*Veal Cutlets,* à *la Financière.*

These are to be prepared, larded, done, and glazed as those à *la Dauphine;* put under them a *ragoût* à *la financière* (see *Sauces,*) and between each cutlet a large *quenelle.* (See *Sauces.*)

No. 10.—*Neck of Veal* à *la Cream.**

Take the same part as is used for the cutlets; cut the bones short enough to be enabled to roll the flanks underneath; give it a square shape, and *marinade* it for a couple of hours with oil, parsley, sliced shalots, pepper, salt, thyme, and bay-leaves. Fasten it on the spit, so that the shape is not altered, and then wrap it up in buttered paper. When roasted for about an hour and a quarter, take off the paper. Put in a small basin about a pint of good *béchamel,* well seasoned; put this basin under the neck of veal, which baste with this sauce till all the sauce adheres to it, then serve up with clear *béchamel* under it. The crust of this dish is the most relishing part.

No. 11.—*Neck of veal* à *la Mirepoix.*

Make a *mirepoix* as follows, with rasped bacon, butter, a bit of ham, thyme, bay-leaves, pepper, salt. &c. Fry the whole on a slow fire. When that is done, put the necks of veal fried with it; only stew it a little, and let it cool. When cold, take two sheets of white paper, butter one of them, and trim it with layers of bacon. Then lay the *mirepoix* over the bacon, and close the paper hermetically. Wrap the whole up in several sheets of paper; and bake it in an oven, which, however, must not be too hot. It will be done in an hour and a half's time. When done. take off the paper, and send up to table with an *Espagnole,* or an *Italienne.* As *mirepoix* is the name of the seasoned fat substance put round the meat to

---

* *A la cream* may sound absurd to an English ear; but as this sauce gives its name to the dish, it must retain the French appellation.

prevent its drying, and also to give it taste, you must remember to make no more than is wanted for the size of the *entrées* you intend to make. Half a quarter of a pound of butter, the same quantity of ham, thyme, bay-leaves, salt, pepper, &c. are sufficient for this.

No. 12.—*Neck of Veal à la Barbarie.*

Trim the neck of veal as above. Cut some black truffles into the shape of a nail, and with these lard the meat. Put them so as to represent a draft-board. *Braize* the meat as you would do a *fricandeau*, but it requires bacon on the top, that the veal may retain its white colour, and the truffles their black one. When done glaze it slightly, and serve under it an *Italienne* with truffles, or the *sauce hachée.*

No. 13.—*Neck of veal à la Ste. Menhoult.*

Braize a neck of veal, as above, but without larding it. Send it up glazed with any sauce you may fancy. If it is returned untouched, make a *sauce d' attelets*, with a little *sauce tournée*, and a little white *Italienne*, (See Sauces) which reduce on the fire. When the sauce is quite thick, throw into it the yolks of two eggs. Spread this sauce over the neck of veal, cover it likewise with crumbs of bread, then have a little melted butter, and strew some more crumbs over it, and moisten it by using the brush, dipped in the butter, and shake it over the neck to spread the butter equally all over. When the meat is thus well soaked, put it into the oven to give it a good colour, or use the salamander. Send it up with a *sauce hachée.*

N. B.—All the *entrées* of veal, such as *carrés, fricandeaux, côtelettes*, sweetbreads, &c. are served up with all sorts of *purées*, and *la Macédoine*, in the summer season. It is useless to multiply these articles when they may be explained more briefly; by changing the sauce, you change the appearance of the dish.

No. 14.—*Le Fricandeau aux differentes Purées.*

Fricandeau is a very good *entrée* when made with due care and attention, but it is seldom dressed as perfectly and scientifically as it should be.

To make a good *fricandeau*, the veal must be of the best quality, which you may know by the meat being white and not thready. Take off the skin of a *noix de veau*,* flatten it on a cloth or a clean towel, then at one stroke, level it with your knife, for a *fricandeau* that is cut off at several times, never looks so well. When you have pared the top part, turn it round, make slits in the middle, that it may taste more of the seasoning. Next lard it very thick, which in general, is not properly done in England. The consequence is, that the bacon not being laid sufficiently cross-wise, the shreds shrink, and can not be properly glazed. Never blanch the *fricandeau* after it has been larded, as some people do, but mark it in a stew-pan large enough to contain the *fricandeau*, besides plenty of roots cut into slices, such for instance as two carrots, two large onions, and some roots of parsley, besides a small quantity of mace, allspice, thyme, bay-leaves, and whole pepper. Put all these on the bottom of the stew-pan, with layers of very fat bacon on the top of the vegetables, as lean bacon gives a red colour to the *fricandeau*. When you have thus well covered the roots; erect a small dome in the centre, lay the *fricandeau* over the bacon, powder a little salt over it; and moisten with a sufficient quantity of broth to cover the roots without reaching the said *fricandeau*. Then put a great deal of fire on the cover of the stew-pan, keeping very little beneath the stew-pan. It is not amiss to ob-

* *Noix de Veau*—the leg of veal is divided into three distinct fleshy parts, besides the middle bone, the larger part, to which is attached the udder, is what is called *la noix*, the flat white part under it, *sous noix*, and the side part, *cóntre noix*. For these three parts the English have no name by which the French appellations may be rendered.

serve that the *fricandeau* being done in this way, retains a good shape, and all its gravy.

If you should wish to cook it as the author is farther about to direct, the moment it is *parti*, (which
signifies, when it begins to boil,) put it over a very
slow and equal fire, for three hours and a half, if it is
not very large. Baste it frequently with the liquor:
then take a needle *à brider*, which run through the
middle; if it gets in and comes out easily, the *fricandeau* is done enough. Now put a great deal of fire
over it to make the bacon firm, which otherwise
would break when you glaze it. The liquor must
be reduced to be used as glaze for the *fricandeau;*
it being more tasty than any other glaze. Serve up
with it such *purée* as the season will afford, or the
Macédoine, &c.

N.B.—The *fricandeau* may vary with regard to
the shape, but the flavour is always the same, if it is
done properly. If, for instance, a *fricandeau* is to
be served when there is a grand party, it is requisite
to give it another shape than for a family dinner.
Though an expensive dish when served alone, it becomes rather cheap if there is a grand dinner, as veal
in abundance is wanted to make the broths and sauces.
The *noix de veau*, besides glaze, will supply a very
elegant and good *entrée*. In the summer season,
give it the shape of a turtle. Cut of part of each extremity of the *fricandeau:* take the tops of asparagus, which you lay beneath, after having poured the
Macédoine into the dish. Have four braized lettuces
ready, put one at each corner, as sham claws. Asparagus and lettuces eat well with a *Macédoine*, and
of course they may be used without any danger of
their being disapproved of. In the winter season,
make *quenelles* of veal, which place instead of the
above-mentioned articles, and serve up with *Espagnole;* but the proper sauce is sorrel.

Another Method.

When the *fricandeau* is fully larded, split it

through the middle. Take a very large turnip, or a piece of cold veal, which has been used to make a sauce, cut either round or oval, wrap it up in bacon, and thrust it within the cleft, as you have done in the *fricandeau*. Mark this as the other, and let it be done in the same manner; but you should observe, that it will be done sooner. Glaze it. Take either French beans or asparagus; place them erect inside the two extremities of the cleft, and pour a *Macédoine* between, with a very large sweetbread larded and glazed over the middle, which produces a very pleasing effect.

The same may be done for a *fricandeau en puits*, with a *blanquette* in the middle.

No. 15.—*The Grenadins of Veal with the Purée of White Celery.*

We call *grenadins* small fillets of veal larded as a *fricandeau*, cooked and sauced in the same manner. Out of a *noix* of veal you may make two or three *grenadins* according to its size. Observe, only they should be cut off the long side of the flesh. In general, cut them out of a *noix de veau*. It is no easy matter to explain the manner of cutting them; let it suffice to say, that being much thinner than a *fricandeau*, they naturally are done in less time. They are served up with a *Macédoine*, or with all sorts of *purées*.

No. 16.—*The Noix of Veal en Bédeau.*

It is so called, because in France the parish beadles wear gowns of two colours, one half of one colour, the other half of another.

Take the *noix* of a young female calf, and trim it as follows. If intended for an *entrée*, choose the smallest you can procure; if for a *remove*, the largest that can be got. Flatten it a little, retaining the udder. Form a crescent on the border of the fat, and pare that part where there is no fat. Lard it as a *fricandeau;* let it be done in the same manner, only cover with bacon the part that is not larded, in order to keep it white, and glaze it slightly when done. Being done in the same style as the *fricandeau*, it is served up with the same sauces.

No. 17.—*Veal à la Bourgeoise.*

The only part which I could wish to recommend in this case, is the *cassis*,* which is fat, and a luscious eating. It is not generally sent up when there is a grand dinner; but for a family dinner it may prove very acceptable indeed. The plain way of cooking this I reckon the best, and will explain it accordingly. Take a stew-pan large enough to make the veal firm in a little butter, by frying; when it is of a fine brown colour all round, put in a few carrots, onions, spices, a little lean bacon, and two calf's feet, seasoned with pepper, salt, thyme, &c. Moisten with two spoonsful of broth, or water, and let the whole stew for a couple of hours on a very slow fire. When done, drain the fat, take out the spice, and serve up the veal with the roots and the gravy all round, and the calf's feet: this dish will only do for the country.

No. 18.—*Sweetbreads à la Dauphine.*

If you use round dishes, you must have four sweetbreads; if a long dish, three large ones will be sufficient. Mind, at any rate, to select them of a large size and very white. Pare the sinews and the fat; throw them into warm water, and let them disgorge, to draw out the blood, and make them as white as possible. When thoroughly disgorged, blanch them a little in boiling water to make them firm, that you may lard them with greater facility. As soon as they are larded, rub a stew-pan all over with butter, cut a few carrots and onions over the butter; cover this with some fat bacon, lay the sweetbreads over the bacon, powder them over with salt, and stew them with a great deal of fire on the top, and very little

---

* I call *cassis*, that part which is attached to the tail end of a loin of veal; the same part of beef is called the rump.

beneath. When they are of a fine brown, cover them with a round of paper, and lessen the fire on the top. If they are large, it will require three-quarters of an hour to do them. If they are too much done, they become soft, and are not so palatable. When properly done, drain them, and put them in a pan with some glaze, and the bacon beneath. Leave them in the glaze till dinner-time; then drain them afresh, and glaze them of a fine brown. Serve them up with sorrel or endive.

There is no necessity to moisten a sweetbread, as they have so much original moisture, that they will never be too dry.

No. 19.—*Sweetbreads à la Financière.*

These are to be larded and done in every respect as those above. Send up with a fine *quenelle* between or in the middle, and under them the *ragoût à la financière*, or the *ragoût à l'Allemande.*

No. 20.—*Sweetbreads à la Dreux.*

Let the sweetbreads disgorge till they are quite white. Then blanch them thoroughly, which is known by their becoming quite firm under your fingers. As long as you feel a softness in it, they are not blanched through; they want blanching thoroughly for this dish. Then set them to cool in cold water. Lard them with ham, chequer-like, very close to the level of the sweetbreads, mark the sweetbreads between layers of bacon the same as the other, and stew them for three-quarters of an hour. Next drain and glaze them, and serve up either with a *velouté*, or *Espganole*, or *purée* of sorrel, endive, or *Macédoine*, peas, &c.

No. 21.—*Blanquette of Veal with Cucumbers.*

Roast a neck, or a loin of veal. The leg part is tough and dry, as every one must know. When cold, cut it into scollops and put it into the *sauce blan-*

quette. (See *Sauces.*) Take six fine cucumbers, cut them into quarters, pare them about the size of the scollops, then take the parings and some other pieces, which mince with a little onion to make a *purée.* Fry the onions and the trimmings of the cucumbers together in a little butter: when the cucumbers are entirely melted, moisten with a *sauce tournée*, and stew them on the corner of the stove for an hour; skim off the grease, and rub this sauce through a tammy. Put the other whole cucumbers into some *sauce tournée*, and let them boil till done. Then put them in a small basin with a little salt, and a tea-spoonful of white vinegar, let them remain so for one hour, then drain them in a very clean towel, and put them in a hair sieve to drain. Put together the *purée* of cucumbers and the *sauce tournée* in which you have boiled the cucumbers; being sufficiently reduced, thicken it with yolks of eggs well beaten, and seasoned with salt and a very little sugar. When the sauce is well thickened with the aforesaid articles, and a little thick cream, put in the meat and cucumbers together, and keep the sauce hot, that the meat may have a better flavour. This *entrée* must be sweet, not too much so, but the sugar must predominate.

No. 22.—*Blanquette of Veal à la Paysanne.*

Roast the veal as above, cut it in the same way, reduce the *sauce tournée*, season well, put the veal into the sauce before the thickening; chop some parsley very fine, and put it in with the juice of half a lemon before you mix it with the thickening; stir the stewpan round without using a spoon, and send up to table quite hot.

N.B.—This is a very good method, but if you can cut your veal whilst quite hot, it will be a great improvement, as the sauce will then be better imbibed by the meat.

No. 23.—*Scollops of Sweetbreads with Green Peas.*

Take four fine sweetbreads, let them disgorge, and blanch them thoroughly. Next, cut them into scollops, as large as possible. Mark in a *sauté* pan with melted butter and a little salt. A quarter of an hour before you send up, *sautez* them over a stove, with a clear fire, turn them round, and when done, drain the butter, and put a little glaze into the *sauté* pan. Keep stirring the sweetbreads in the glaze; dish them *en miroton*, and send up the peas in the middle.

When you have sweetbreads of *desserte*,* cut them into scollops, make them hot in a little light glaze, and after having dished them *en miroton*, mask them with the peas. Scollops of sweetbreads are easier to dress, when you put between them a slice of fried bread cut round, and the green peas in the middle; without the fried bread they do not keep the shape in which you dish them.

No. 23.—*Scollops of Veal à l'Ecosse.*

When you have had a large party, and wish to practise a little economy after your previous expense, reserve from your dinner a small bit of the *sous noix de veau.* Cut some slices off it of the shape of a heart, which season with salt and pepper. Take the paste brush and the yolk of a single egg, rub the veal with it, and dip this into the crumbs of bread, afterwards in the melted butter, and again in bread crumbs. Put very little of the butter in a *sautez* pan, and put the slices of veal into it; fry them very briskly, of a very good colour, and drain them, and dress them one over the other round the dish, and serve over them a good *Italienne* sauce, or *Espagnole.* If you have no sauce, make a little in the following manner.

Receipt for the Sauce.

Put in a stew-pan a very small bit of fresh butter, a spoonful of flour, one shalot, and one or two mushrooms, if you are able to procure them; then fry them over a very slow fire till the flour becomes brown;

* *Desserte,* is when left from the table.

moisten with boiling water, salt, pepper, a bunch of parsley, thyme, cloves, &c.; add to these a small bit of *glaze*, and skim this sauce when well done; drain it through a hair sieve, and serve under the cutlets, &c.

No. 24.—*The Attelets of Sweetbreads à l'Italienne.*

Take some fine sweetbreads, as white as can be procured. Blanch them and stew them as directed above. When done, drain them; and when cold, cut them into squares of about an inch. Put those squares into a *sauce d'attelets*, and let them cool. When the sauce is cold, skewer the squares, alternately, with a bit of calf's udder ready done, using silver skewers, and give them as nearly as possible a square shape, all of a size. Then give them a good shape with the sauce, dip them into crumbs of bread only. Now give them a complete square shape, and dip them into an *omelette* of four eggs, whites and yolks beaten together with a little salt, cover them over again with crumbs of bread, which level with a knife. Next powder some crumbs of bread on the cover of a stew-pan, and lay the *attelets* over them. The moment you are going to send up to table, fry them of a fine brown, and sauce them with a brown or white *Italienne*, according to your fancy.

No. 25.—*Small Cases of Scollops of Sweetbreads.*

Let the sweetbreads disgorge and be blanched as above. When they have been lying for a time in cold water, make small scollops of them, and mix them with a *dusselle*, which is to be made in the following manner:—

Take half a pint of mushrooms, four or five shalots, a little parsley, and chop the whole very fine separately. Next rasp a little fat bacon, put a small lump of fresh butter. Stew the fine herbs over a slow fire, and put the scollops with them, seasoned with salt, pepper, and a little pounded spice. When done, drain all the fat; then put the scollops into small paper cases fried in olive-oil, and put to them a deal of seasoning, I mean plenty of fine herbs. Then stew over a few crumbs of bread fried in butter. Lay the paper cases for a moment in the oven, and when you are going to serve up, pour into each of them a little thin *Espagnole*, when you have squeezed the juice of a lemon; but contrive to drain all the fat, and serve very hot.

No. 26.—*Croquets of Sweetbread.*

Take such sweetbreads as have already been served, cut them into as small dice as possible. Have a good *velouté* reduced ready. Throw the dice of sweetbreads into the *velouté*, and give them a boil, that they may taste of the sauce. Then lay them on a plate to cool. When cold, roll them into any shape you like, round, oval, or long. Of all things avoid giving them the shape of pears, as some persons do, for in that case they must be more handled, without at all improving the quality. Serve up with parsley, fried green in the middle.

No. 27.—*Rissole of Sweetbread.*

Make the same preparation as for the *Croquets*, then take some of the trimming of puff paste, fill up with flour that it may not be too delicate, then spread the paste with the rolling-pin, very thin; moisten the part round the meat, with the paste first dipped in water; turn up the paste round the meat, and give it a good shape with your hand, take a paste cutter, and cut them all of an equal size, dip them in flour, fry them of a good colour, and serve up with fried parsley in the middle.

No. 28.—*Calf's Brain en Matelotte.*

Take three brains of an equal size. Strip them of the upper skin, let them disgorge in water; then blanch them in water, salt, and a little vinegar. When done, drain them, and put some slices of fat bacon round the stew-pan, put the brains *on*, or all round the bacon; season the braize with a bunch well seasoned, salt, pepper, one small onion, the juice of half a lemon, a small bit of butter, and a spoonful of broth; let them sweat on the fire for half an hour, where keep them till you serve up; have some bread fried of the shape of cocks'-combs, set it in the dish and put the brains between, and mask the brains with the *matelotte* sauce.

No. 29.—*Calf's Brain à la Maître d' Hôtel.*

Let them be prepared as above. Cut some bread into the shape of cocks'-combs, which fry in butter till of a fine colour. Dish them between each half of the brains, which you have divided, and *mask*** the brains with a *maître d'hôtel.*

No. 30.—*Calf's Brain with fried Parsley au Beure noir.*

The same as above with regard to the stewing. Fry separately some parsley very green, and likewise some butter in a frying-pan, till such time as it ceases sparkling. Then put the brains into a dish, with the parsley in the middle, and for the sauce, put with the brown butter a spoonful of vinegar, some salt and pepper, and pour it under the brains.

No. 31.—*Marinade of Calf's Brain.*

In case you should have any brains of *desserte*, make a *marinade cuite*, and give a boil to the brains in it. Then drain them and wrap them up in paste. (See *Paste for frying*, page 132.)

No. 32.—*Calf's Brain, Love-Apple Sauce.*

These are to be prepared and done as those above. Cut slices of bread in the shape of cocks'-combs, fry and glaze them, and dish them between the brains,

---

* *Mask*, means to cover it with the sauce.

with the love-apple sauce under them. Mind that the fried bread for those sorts of *entreés*, should be made of the shape of cocks'-combs, and put in the dish with a little white of eggs and flour mixed together, and put in a corner of the stove.

No. 33.—*Tendrons of Veal à la Jardinière.*

Tendrons are found at the extremity of the ribs. Previously to your detaching them, remove the dry bone which is next to them; then sever them from the bone, and scollop them in the shape of oysters. Set them to disgorge, that they may be made very white. Next blanch them through. Let them cool. When cold, *pare* them of a good form, and *mark* them in a stew-pan wrapt up in layers of bacon. Put in a carrot, an onion, a bay-leaf, a few branches of fresh gathered thyme, and salt and pepper; moisten them with good broth, or with a *poële*, if you have any, and let them stew for four hours as gently as you can. When they are done, drain them, and put them into a *sauté* pan with a little glaze. Keep stirring them over the fire that they may get the taste of the glaze. Dish them *en miroton*, and serve *la jardinière* in the middle.* The tendrons of veal require to be very well done, and are consequently, difficult to dress; then have some *croutons* of bread fried of a nice colour, which put them between; this will enable you to dish them more tastefully, and you must put the sauce, of whatever kind it is, into the middle, whether *maledoine*, peas, *jardinière*, cucumber, &c. &c.

---

* *La jardinière* means the gardener's wife: by this is understood, that any vegetable of a good appearance may be used for that dish; those most particularly used are carrots, turnips, asparagus, green peas, heads of cauliflowers, artichoke-bottoms, mushrooms, French beans, Windsor beans, &c. They are, however, to be used only in the spring, when they are in the highest perfection.

No. 34.—*Tendrons of Veal with Green Peas brown.*

Whatever sauce you may wish to serve the *tendrons* of veal with, they should always be dressed as directed above. They may be served in different ways, that is, either white or brown, which is explained in the article of Sauces. The *tendrons à l'Espagnole* are to be drained an hour before you send them up. When you have ascertained that there is no more fat left, put them with the peas, that they may acquire their flavour; give them one or two boils, then dish them *en miroton,* and *mask* them with the peas *à l'Espagnole,* with *crouton* as above.

No. 35.—*Tendrons of Veal with Green Peas, white.*

Braize the *tendrons* as above. When they are done, drain them, and glaze them in a *sauté*-pan. Dish them *en miroton,* and put the peas in the middle. (See the articles green peas, *white,* or *brown.*)

No. 36.—*Tendrons of Veal with Cabbage, Lettuce, à l'Espagnole.*

Braize and glaze the *tendrons* as above. Then take some braized lettuce. (See *Entreés of Mutton,* No. 18, page 127.) Dish the *tendrons en miroton,* that is, a *tendron* and a lettuce alternately, and *mask** with an *Espagnole,* putting the *jardinière* into the middle.

No. 37.—*Tendrons of Veal en Marinade, dites au Soleil.*

If you have any *tendrons* that have been sent to table, and are returned untouched, you can not send them up a second time dressed in the same manner, as they no longer retain their fine colour. Put them into a *marinade cuite,* and then in paste. (See *Paste*

Mask means to cover with the sauce.

for frying, page 132.) Fry them of a nice colour, and serve them up with a *poivrade*, or with love apple sauce.

No. 38.—*Tendrons of Veal en Chipolata, white.*

(See *deep Dishes*, No. 6, page 66.) They may also be served as *entrées*. Glaze them, and put the *chipolata* in the middle.

No. 39.—*Tendrons of Veal en Chipolata, brown.*

(See *deep Dishes*, No. 6, page 66.) They are also served as *entrées*, provided you have some deep dishes to contain all the ingredients and the sauce; for otherwise you had better not send them up. This dish is very well in a *casseralla d'argent*, or silver stewpan, (generally termed in this country *casserolle*); you may likewise serve it up in *a paté change*, or a very high border of *nouilles*. (See *Nouilles.*)

No 40.—*Tendrons of Veal with the purée of Chestnuts.*

The *tendrons* are served with all sorts of *purées*, either of peas, celery, sorrel, onions, mushrooms, &c.; but it is useless to repeat similar observations. *Tendrons* with a *purée* must always be glazed, and dished *en miroton* when served as *entrées*, with any sort of *purées* in the middle. Observe, that whenever you wish to give a good appearance to this dish, you must put between each *tendron*, a *crouton* of fried bread glazed, otherwise the *tendrons* will not dress becomingly.

No. 41.—*Calves' Ears farcies and fried.*

Take eight or twelve calves' ears, and let them disgorge. Blanch them, and be particular to clean away all the hair they have inside; then stew them in a *blanc*. (See *Calf's Head*, No. 10, *Removes.*) When the ears are done enough, that is, when you can stick your knife in them, drain, and let them cool; then in-

troduce a *farce fine* (See *Farces Fines, Entrees*
of Fowl *à la crême*) into the hollow part. Give the
ear the shape of a horn. Dip it into an *omelette*, and
crumbs of bread twice successively, and then fry them
till they are of a fine brown. Serve under them a
maître d'hôtel grasse, or love-apple sauce.

No. 42.—*Calves' Ears, Love-Apple Sauce.*

These are to be done as above directed, more particularly when they are very white, otherwise serve
them fried. Slit with your knife the part of the gristle all round. Cut the thickest side very flat, that
they may stand upright. Dish them *en fleurons
à blanc*, over the love-apple sauce. It is a difficult
matter to explain this dish accurately. Bind the
thinnest part of the ears in two, and split them several
times at equal distance. When you turn the *tendron*
on the other side, they have a beautiful effect and are
excellent eating.

No. 43.—*Calves' Ears with green Dutch Sauce.*

As above, very white, and the Dutch green sauce
under it. The green Dutch sauce is a *sauce tournée*
reduced, and a *verd de persil* in it, with the juice of
a lemon and a little Cayenne.

No. 44.—*Calves' Ears with the Ravigotte Sauce.*

Are to be done as those above, and slit in the same
manner, and served up with a *ravigotte*. The advantage of this *entrée*, is, that you can serve up the
same meat twice or three times, in different forms,
and with a different flavour.

No. 45.—*Calf's Liver Larded and Roasted.*

Take a fine calf's liver of a light colour. Lard it
as a *fricandeau*, and pickle it in vinegar with an
onion cut into slices, some stalks of parsley, salt, pepper, thyme, and a bay-leaf. When it has been marinaded for four and twenty hours in the pickle,

fasten it on a spit, roast it, and baste it frequently with the *marinade*. Then glaze it with a light glaze, as it is naturally of a black colour. Serve under it a brown *poivrade*. This is but a common *entrée*, but possesses an excellent taste when skilfully dressed.

No. 46.—*Scollops of Calf's Liver aux fines Herbes.*

Take a nice calf's liver as white as possible, cut it into slices of a good and equal shape. Dip them in the flour, and fry them in a black frying-pan, of a very good colour, with a little butter. When they are done, put them in a dish, and take some fine herbs which you have previously shaped fine, such as parsley, shalots, mushrooms, &c. Stew them slowly on the fire with a little butter, when the herbs are sufficiently done, add a tea-spoonful of flour, moisten with gravy, if you have any, or with water, and add a small bit of glaze. When done, put the liver in the sauce, which warm, but do not allow it to boil, add a little salt, pepper, lemon, and serve very hot.

This dish can not be served in this country, as nobody will sell the number required for a dish.

This is again a common *entrée*, yet it is very palatable. You may put the liver in the sauce; but mind that it does not boil. It is a dish for a breakfast *à la fourchette*.

No. 47.—*Les petites Noix d'Epaules de Veau with Sorrel.**

The *petites noix* in Paris are generally sold at the rate of a half a pound of meat. Ten or even twelve are required for an *entrée*, which is a very dainty dish for those people who know how to eat it. In general they are very fat, for which reason you are forced to send them up to table with the fat, as it keeps the *noix* mellow. Set them to disgorge as you

---

* These are to be found on the side of a shoulder of veal.

did the *tendrons*. Trim a stew-pan with layers of bacon, put in the *noix* after having blanched them, and give them a pleasing shape. Then moisten with a *poële*, and stew them for an hour on a very slow fire. Next drain them, and glaze them at two different times. Dish them *en cordon*, and put the sorrel in the middle.

No. 48.—*The Noix of Shoulder of Veal with Endive.*

These are dressed exactly in the same manner as those above; but you put endives, either white or brown, instead of sorrel.

No. 49.—*Calf's Feet plain.*

Take some nice white calf's feet, bone them as far as the joint; set them to disgorge, and stew them in a *blanc.* (See *Calf's Head.*) When they are done, drain them and send them up quite hot, with parsley and butter in a sauce-boat.

No. 50.—*Calf's Feet Marinade.*

Prepare the feet as above. Make a *marinade cuite*, and some paste for frying. Serve them up with fried parsley or a *poivrade* in the middle. (See *Sauces.*) This dish may be made very economically. When you make a calf's feet jelly do not let the feet be too much done, then make a *marinade cuite*, and put the calf's feet to boil in it for half an hour; let them cool in a good shape, put them in the butter to fry, and serve under the *poivrade*, or *tomata* sauce.

No. 51.—*Calf's Feet, farcis en Soleil.*

Stew a few calves' feet as above. When they are done, drain them. Then make a little *farce fine.* (In order to prevent too frequent repetitions of this kind, I have shown the manner of making the *farces* in a separate chapter.) When you have stuffed the middle of the calf's feet with the *farce*, give them a

round shape, then dip them into an *omelette* seasoned with pepper and salt, and into crumbs of bread
twice over, and fry them till they are of a fine brown.
Serve them up with fried parsley very green, and
send up the brown sharp sauce in a boat, or the sauce
tomata.

No. 52.—*Calf's Feet, à la Poulette.*

Stew them in a *blanc,* like those above. Dish them,
and pour the sauce over them. (See No. 27, *Entrées of Mutton,* for the sauce, page 130.) If you
were to put them in the sauce, they would not look
so well. Mind, drain them well before you put them
into the dish.

CHAPTER VIII.

ENTRÉES OF FOWL.

Observations.—When you have an opportunity of buying the fowls yourself, choose always white-legged ones; their flesh is finer, and the skin tender; they also look better at table. The manner of fattening fowls is, to separate them from the other chickens; mix together some oat-meal, milk, boiled potatoes, and bread, if you have any left from the table; add to the whole of it a little dripping; mind not to give them too much at a time, and not more than twice a day: above all keep them very clean. When they are sufficiently fattened, kill them or they will fall ill and die. When you find any of your poultry sick, chop a few leeks with their food, which will cure them; but when they become very fat, if you do not kill them they inevitably rot and die away.

No. 1.—*Fowl au Consommé, generally termed au gros Sel.*

Take a fine fat fowl, the flesh and skin of which are perfectly white; empty the fowl without making too great an aperture, singe it gently, and scald the legs, which are to be turned inside of the body; then lay on it a pretty thick layer of fat bacon, fasten it tight, and let it be boiled in broth, which must boil before you put it in, otherwise the fowl would lose its white colour. If the fowl is of a larger size, it will require an hour and a quarter before it is done enough; if it is of a common size one hour only will do. Next drain it in a dish, wipe off all the fat, and send it up with a little of the liquor in which it was boiled, and which has been reduced in the process from one quart to half a pint at least, with the addition of a little salt in the liquor, and put salt on the breast of the fowl.

No. 2.—*Fowl, or gros Sel.*

The same as above, with the only difference, that you lay both over and under the fowl some chrystalized salt, that has not been pounded.

No. 3.—*Fowl à la Villeroi.*

Take a fine fowl, which may be known by the connoisseurs by a skin of bluish hue marbled with gray: it is to be emptied and singed in the same manner as directed No. 1. Let it be trussed, the legs turned down outwards: inside of the body introduce a small quantity of butter kneaded with salt and lemon-juice. The fowl to be put into an oval stew-pan, with a layer of fat bacon: next pour some *poële* over it. (See *Sauces poële.*) Those articles which are *poëlez,** requiring to preserve their whiteness, are not to be kept on the fire so long as others. It requires only three-quarters of an hour for a fowl to be done in this style. A capon would require full an hour. To be served with *sauce à la financiére.*

Observation to be particularly attended to by the Cook.—As the POELE has no translation, it retains its name; it is indispensable in fine cookery, and is made as follows: Take one pound of beef suet, one pound of very fresh butter, and one pound of very fat bacon; cut the suet and the bacon into very large dice, put them into a stew-pan with two pounds of veal cut in the same manner, fried till the veal be-

* *Poëlez* is almost the same operation as *braizing,* the only difference is, that what is *poëlez* must be underdone, and a *braize* must be done through.

comes very white, and then moisten with about three
pints of clear boiling water, a handful of salt, one bay-
leaf, a few sprigs of thyme, one onion stuck with
three cloves, and a great bundle of parsley and green
onions; let the whole boil gently till the onion is
done, then drain it through a hair-sieve, and use it
for any thing that may want *poële*. The use of *poële*
is to make every thing boiled in it very white and
tasty: in the winter it keeps for a week, and is very
useful in the larder, particularly if you do not put in
any of the fleshy part of the bacon; otherwise, the
meat that you boil in it will turn quite red, on account
of the saltpetre used in curing the bacon.

No. 4.—*Fowl à la Montmorenci.*

The same care and attention are requisite in this
case as in the former. The fowl being trussed up,
you have some boiling water ready, then laying hold
of the fowl by the saddle, dip the breast only into
the water in order to give additional firmness to the
skin and flesh; next dip it into cold water. When
the fowl is quite cold, lard the whole breast in the
same manner as a *fricandeau* of veal, and put it into
an oval stew-pan, trimmed all round with fat bacon,
and moisten with the *poële*, but none at the top.
There must be a brisk fire over it, and a slow one
under it, the same as for a *fricandeau*, and it will be
done within three-quarters of an hour at most. Dry
the bacon with a salamander, glaze of a good colour,
and send up with *sauce à l'Allemande*, or a ragout
à la royale. A ragout is *à l'Allemande* when in a
sauce *à l'Allemande*, *à la royale* with the *béchamelle*,
and *à la finnacière* with the *Espagnole* sauce.

No. 5.—*Fowl à la Condé.*

Procure a nice fowl, singe and truss it up as above;
slit the breast, and introduce small slices of truffles
cut into the following shape into the slits that
you have made: cover the whole with slices of bacon,

and let it be stewed as above. Care must be taken, however, when you pour out the bacon, not to derange the symmetry. This dish requires to be garnished in imitation of a *chambord* with larded sweetbread, cocks'-combs, pigeons *à la gautier*, large *quenelles à la cuillière*, and *sauce à la financière*.

No. 6.—*Fowl à la Turque.*

Empty a fine fowl, and be particular in washing the inside of it with very hot water; if you leave any blood in it, the rice would be full of scum. Your rice having boiled a sufficient time in rich *consommé*, season it with salt, and introduce some into the body of the fowl, which you next roast, well wrapped up in layers of bacon, and in paper; it requires an hour to have it sufficiently done. Send it up with rice round the fowl, the same as you have used to put inside, only add to it two spoonsful of very good *béchamelle*, well seasoned; do not let it be too thin, and pour a little *velouté* over the fowl. Take particular care to keep the fowl white. If you want to make a very good and cheap dish, wash a quarter of a pound of Carolina rice in water, which you must pour away till it becomes quite clear, and the rice retains no odour. Have a good and white fowl well dressed, wash the inside with hot water, then put the fowl in an oval stew-pan with the rice, and an onion with two cloves stuck into it and some salt. Let it boil gently for an hour and a half, then take out the onion and the cloves, and skim all the fat. Serve this fowl with the rice, but mind that the rice must not be too liquid, or it will have a bad appearance. This dish is called *la poularde au ris*, and is very wholesome, excellent diet.

No. 7.—*Fowl à la Dreux.*

The fowl to be singed and trussed up as above. In order to give it additional firmness, use boiling water, as in No. 4. Cut some ham into long squares; lard the breast of the fowl in imitation of a small draft-board, put it into the stew-pan as above, and moisten with *poële*. The same time, and no longer is requisite for the fowl to be completely done. To this must be added, the *sauce à l'Allemande*. Observe, the pieces of ham must not be too large, and must be carefully stuck in at equal distances so as to represent a draft-board; when done, glaze the ham to make it shine.

No. 8.—*Fowl, with green Oysters.*

Singe and truss a nice fowl, and put it into a stew-pan, the same as in No. 3. When done enough, drain it, and send it up with oyster-sauce as follows.

Oyster-Sauce for Fowl or Turkey.—Take two dozen or more oysters, and take care to preserve all the liquor when you open them. Put them into a small stew-pan with the liquor, and add to it a spoonful of water. When the liquor boils, the oysters are done; stir them with a spoon, and put them to drain in a hair-sieve as you take them from the stew-pan with a spoon; let the liquor settle, and pour it off clear into another vessel; beard the oysters, and wash them again in the liquor, in order to remove all grit and sand; then put a pound of fresh butter into a stew-pan, with a spoonful or two of very fine flour; when the flour is fried a little, moisten with the oyster liquor, and a pint of cream: let this boil fifteen minutes, and add to it two spoonsful of *béchamelle:* if you have no *béchamelle*, put a small bit of glaze, or portable soup, well seasoned. Mind, this has no essence of anchovies, as for fish: it is the only difference. Mask the fowl with this sauce.

No. 3.—*Fowl aux Olives.*

Singe, &c. &c. a fine fowl as above, then take some olives, which are to be blanched till they are no longer briny. Next boil them in a thin *Espagnole*.

Skim the sauce and add a little lemon-juice, and pour it under the fowl. Serve up with some stuffed olives, without stones. Turn the olives with your knife, so as to take out the stone, and leave the olive whole.

No. 10.—*Fowl à la Crême.*

This dish is made out of a cold fowl, either roasted or stewed: you take off the breast and fleshy part of the fowl by cutting it square all through, with a little bread toasted and dipped in butter stop the aperture of the bottom. Then have the *farcé à la crême*, as directed in No. 5, with which fill the fowl; then make a kind of wall round the fowl with buttered paper, cover the same with bacon, in order that the fowl may not get too much colour. If this dish be placed on the flanks, some of the same *farce* may be served on toasts cut in the shape of hearts or lozenges, which are called *témoins*. These are to be baked in the oven, the same as the fowls, and the fat to be well drained. Send up with a thin *Espagnole* sauce, or *velouté*. The toast must be fried before you put the *farce* over it.

No. 11.—*Fowl à la Monglas.*

This is likewise a cold fowl of *desserte*, take off the breast as above. You must have ready either an *émincé*, or a *salpicon* pretty thick, which is to be introduced cold into the body of the fowl. Beat the yolks of two eggs, with a little fresh melted butter: then cover the breast of the fowl only with crumbs of bread, basted with clarified butter. Next give it a colour with the *salamander*, but you must be careful that it does not get a brown colour too soon. Now baste it with a little butter again: take the red-hot shovel to give the fowl a good brown colour on all sides. Serve a brown sauce under it, if you have applied a *salpicon;* and a *velouté* if you have used an *émincé;* it may also be called a *poulardi en surprise*. These dishes are very good and very cheap, as they are always made from the remains of yesterday.

Emincé or *salpicon* may be made with the same sauce; *salpicon* is a composition of different ingredients, and *émincé* is all of one sort of meat, either fowl or game.

> *Salpicon.*—Cut into small dices, some mushrooms, tongue, truffles, and *filets* of fowl; the truffles and mushrooms must be ready done, as well as the tongue and fowl; put all this into a very reduced *Espagnole*, and when cold use as directed.
>
> *Emincé*—is only the fleshy part of either fowl or game, minced and put into some *béchamelle* well seasoned; the difference between mince and dice is, that when you have a short allowance of meat, you are obliged to mince, as it requires no shape, and you may use whatever flesh you like, the dice require very good meat. When the fillets are eaten in the parlour, you must make the best of what is left. *Salpicon* is in general brown, minced fowl always white.

No. 12.—*Fowl à la Dubaril.*

This must likewise be a fowl of *desserte*,* but yet very white. Take off the breast, as in No. 11. Then take the fleshy part of a nice white roast fowl, which you cut into small square pieces of an equal size; you also cut some tongue the same: put these slices of fowl and tongue into a *béchamelle* pretty thick. Keep the fowl very hot. The moment you are going to serve it, pour the *émincé* inside the body of the fowl; thin slices of tongue, cut of the shape of cocks'-combs, should be put round the mince on the top of the fowl; serve under it a *ragoût à l'Allemande*, and poached eggs on the top of the mince.

---

* *Desserte* means what comes from the table, or is left at the parlour.

No. 13.—*Fowl à la Mirepoix, otherwise à la Cendre.*

Truss the fowl as in No. 1. Next mark a *mirepoix* without its being melted, that is to say, scrape some bacon, a little butter, a few slices of ham, with a little thyme, bay-leaves, salt and pepper.' Then spread the whole on a sheet of white paper: wrap the fowl up in this sheet of paper, and cover it with several other sheets: let the whole be closed hermetically, lest the grease should be lost: then put it into the oven if not too hot; if it should happen to be so, let the fowl be then covered with hot ashes, and over these have some live burning coals, but not too vivid for fear of the paper catching fire, which would spoil the fowl. It requires two hours for the fowl to be sufficiently done; when so, drain it well, and send it up with an *Espagnole* under it or *poivrade*, or a *sauce hachée.* This dish is seldom served, as it gives great trouble in the making.

No. 14.—*Fowl à la Cardinal.*

Take a nice white fowl, singe it, and take out the bones without destroying the skin. Next have a *farce à quenelles,** wherein you introduce a little lobster spawn well pounded to make it very red. This *farce* being made rather liquid, is to be injected, first between the skin and the flesh of the fowl, and then inside of the body. You then mould the fowl into an agreeable shape: next put it into an oval stew-pan well trimmed with sauce of bacon, and pour some *poële* over it; leave it on the fire for an hour and a half. As it has no bones left, it requires more time before it is done. Serve it up with a *sauce à l'Alle-mande,* to which you add some of the red to dye the sauce, or some love-apple sauce.

* *Farce à quenelles;* the necessity of preserving this appellation arises out of the multiplicity of different *farces* which are made, and are called in England *forced meats.* As this is a particular one, the professor must retain the proper name.

No. 15.—*Fowl à Campine, with raw Onions.*

Truss the fowl with the legs outwards, and roast it lengthways. It must be of a good colour. When done, slit the breast, cut raw onions in slices; which you introduce into the slits you have made, and send it up with a brown *poivrade* highly seasoned, and very hot.

This dish is of *Provençal* and Spanish origin; in general in warm climates they prefer strong eating, the onion should be sliced before, and remain in a plate ready to put into the fowl the moment it comes from the spit.

No. 16.—*Fowl à la Tartare.*

Take a fine fowl, turn in the legs as usual, then cut it in two, take the bones off from the back, cut the breast-bones off, break those of the legs, flatten the fowl with the back of your knife, and season it with salt and pepper: then take the yolk of one egg, and with a paste brush, rub the fowl all over; dip it in the crumbs of bread and in the melted butter in succession. Next broil it up to a fine colour, on a slow fire, that it may be done thoroughly. Send it up with the brown *Italienne.* Thrust your knife into it, to ascertain if it is well done; it requires an hour, or at least three-quarters, to be done properly.

No. 17.—*Fowl à la Chingara.*

Take a nice fowl of a fine white colour, singe and pick it well; then cut it into four equal parts, well trimmed. Next cut some thin slices of ham of a very good shape, put them into a buttered stew-pan, and put the four quarters of the fowl over them; let the whole simmer for a while on red-hot ashes: when the fowl is done, drain off the fat, and powder a little salt and pepper over it; you then detach the glaze made out of the gravy of the fowl and slices of ham; pour a little *Espagnole*, with the juice of a lemon, and send it up with the slices of ham over the four quarters, and four large fried pieces of bread between, of the same dimensions as the slices of ham. Mind, this is to be highly seasoned.

No. 18.—*Fowl with Tarragon Sauce.*

Take a fine fowl, truss it and *poële* it as in No. 3. When you are going to send it up to table, mask it with tarragon sauce, made as follows: put into a small stew-pan, a few branches of green tarragon, and a wine-glass of white vinegar; let it boil for ten minutes, then add four spoonsful of *sauce tournée*, and thicken with two yolks of eggs. Strain the whole through a tammy, and put to it a small pat of fresh butter, a little lemon-juice, some salt and pepper, and some leaves of tarragon cut like lozenges, and blanched very green; cover the fowl with this sauce.

All other *pluches*, such as leaves of parsley, chervil, &c. &c. are served up with whole *entrées*, by which is meant, that the fowl has not been cut in pieces. Then use any sauce you may fancy. *Pluches* may be made of different coloured sauces, but green leaves shine better in white sauce than in brown, and the majority of the nobility prefer white sauce.

No. 19.—*Fowl with Cauliflowers.*

The same as in No. 18; the only difference is, that you boil some cauliflowers in water with a little butter and salt. This you put round the fowl, and then *mask* both the fowl and cauliflower with a *velouté*. Mind that whenever you boil cauliflowers for the garnishing of *entrées* or removes, they should always be boiled in water, salt, and butter, (one hour before dinner time,) because they become very white in water so prepared, and lose their green appearance.

No. 20.—*Cutlets of Fillets of Fowl, with Crumbs of Bread à la Maréchale.*

Take four small fowls; cut off the fillets, without injuring the *filets mignons;* cut the merry-thoughts in two. Take off the *filets mignons;* pare them in the shape of hearts; and stick the merry-thought bones into the points of the hearts, to give them the appearance of chops: and do the same for all the rest. Season them with pepper and salt; then brush the fillets with yolks of eggs, and dip them into crumbs of bread; next dip them into melted butter, and then into crumbs again. Use your knife to level the bread and broil those fillets over a brisk fire. The fillets being very thin, require only to be lightly browned. Serve under them some thin *Espagnole* sauce well seasoned. [The author would here observe to the young and inexperienced cook, that when he has something thin to broil, the fire must be very sharp; and when something thick, the fire must be moderate, as it takes more time to be done through.] These fillets may be *sautez*'d in the same manner as the lamb chops or mutton cutlets. Take a very little melted butter in a *sauté* pan, and put it over a very sharp stove, which will do as well as boiling them. The *maréchale sauce* is better when you prepare it in the following manner:

Maréchale Sauce.—Reduce two spoonsful of tarragon vinegar to one; then add six spoonsful of *velouté* to it, thickening this sauce with the yolks of two eggs; work the sauce very well, finish with a small bit of fresh butter, salt, and a little Cayenne. Serve this sauce in preference to the other.

No. 21.—*The Wings of Fowls à la St. Laurent.*

Take three fowls, divide the breasts into two parts, take off the sinews and small bones, season with salt and pepper, &c. brush them as above with yolks of eggs, then dip them into bread, then in melted butter and bread again; next broil them in the same manner as above, well seasoned, and send them up with a thin *Espagnole*, or the *maréchale sauce.*

No. 22.—*Filets of Fowls sautés au suprême.*

Take off the fillets of three fowls, which will produce nine fillets, as two of the *filets mignons* are used to make a large fillet. You then prepare them all alike, and put them into a *sauté*-pan with some melted butter and salt, covered with a round of paper buttered, to prevent the fillets from drying and getting dusty. When you have *sautez* the fillets on a sharp fire, drain the butter, but be careful to preserve the gravy of the fowls with a small quantity of the butter: put four spoonsful of *béchamelle*, and two spoonsful of double cream. Let them warm gently without boiling, or the fillets would get tough: put likewise a spoonful of *consommé*, and taste if the seasoning is palatable. You must mind that this dish is a fine *entrée*, and must not be too highly seasoned. Send up with sliced bits of bread, fried in butter, and glazed over, which are to be placed between the fillets. The sauce to be poured over the fillets only, and the *croutons* of bread to be kept crisp.

No. 23.—*Scollops of Fowls with Cucumbers.*

Take off the fillets of three fowls, cut your scollops of the size of a half-crown piece, dip them into some clarified butter, in a *sauté*-pan, *sautez* them over a brisk fire on both sides, and throw them into sauce of cucumbers. The shortest way of making the scollops, and likewise retaining all the gravy, is to *sautez* the fillets just at dinner time, and to scollop them quickly.

No. 24.—*Scollops of Fowls with Essence of Cucumbers.*

These scollops are prepared in the same manner as those above, but the sauce is not the same; cut the cucumbers of the same shape and size as the scollops; keep the parings or trimmings of the cucumbers to make a *purée*. As this sauce must have a positive taste of cucumbers, put the cucumbers into a basin with a little salt, and half a glass of vinegar, let them *marinade* for one hour, then drain them upon a clean cloth, put them into a stew-pan with a small bit of butter, let them fry a little without colour; to drain the water from the cucumber, sprinkle a spoonful of flour over them, then moisten with *consommé* enough to let the fat rise on the top. Put a small bit of sugar, and a bundle of parsley and green onions. When the cucumbers are sufficiently done, drain them in a hair sieve, and put them by, covered with a plate. Now take the parings, fry them in a stew-pan with a little butter, moisten with the sauce in which you have boiled the cucumbers, skim off all the butter, reduce the sauce quite thick, taking care to add the juice of the cucumbers to be reduced with the sauce, and then put three spoonsful of good *béchamelle* with it; rub this through a tammy; keep this sauce very thick. Next *sautez* the scollops on both sides, but mind, as soon as they appear white they are done: lay the dish on its side, in order to drain off all the butter; put the fillets into the sauce, drain the cucumbers again, and put them to the fillets. If your sauce is quite thick, put to it a spoonful of double cream, a little salt, and serve in a deep dish with some *fleurons* of pastry round the dish; observe that this dish must be rather sweet. You must put a little sugar into it. The readiest mode of making scollops is to *mark* the fillets (without trimming them in the melted butter) with a little salt, and *sautez* them on a sharp stove till they are slightly done, then have a clean sheet of paper, cut the fillets in two, sideways, and scollop them with care and very quickly, to keep the gravy in; then put them in the sauce with the cucumbers, that they may acquire their flavour. Take care the *bain marie* does not boil, or the scollops will be too much done, and, in consequence, tough.

No. 25.—*Scollops of Fowls with Truffles.*

These are prepared as above, but at the moment when you put the fillets into the butter, the truffles must be ready peeled and cut of the same round form and dimension as the scollops will be. Season with a little salt; *sautez* the truffles and scollops a few moments before dinner-time; and put them into a *béchamelle*, to which you have added a little reduction of truffles. This reduction is made as follows: the trimmings of truffles are to be reduced in a little *consommé*, introduce some of this glaze into the scollops, and as it is always brownish, add three or four spoonsful of thick cream to the *sauté*, to make the sauce white; season it according to your palate. Do not forget to keep the sauce very bright. You must be very particular in the preparation of this dish, as it is one which distinguishes the fine cook. *Sautez* any truffles, whether fowl or game is not material, being almost similar, but take care that the meat and the truffles are both sufficiently done. The plan is, to put in the *sauté-pan* first the fillets, which you dip in the melted butter, and put in the *sauté-pan;* then when you have done them all, put in the truffles ready cut in slices; when the fillets have been *sauté,* you must leave the truffles a little longer in the *sauté-pan* over the fire, and keep stirring with a spoon to fry them equally, then put the scollops together, and give them a turn on the stove; raise the *sauté-pan* on one side, to drain the butter, then put the scollops in the sauce one hour before dinner to give the taste of truffles to the meat, and keep the sauce thick, as it is always easy to make it thin afterwards.

Observation relative to the Sautez in general. — Mind, you must never let the *sauté* be too much done, these *entrées* are very difficult to make in perfection. When they are too much done, they are not eatable. It is this point of perfection in the management of cookery, which distinguishes the *good* from the *bad* cook.

No. 26.—*Scollops of Fowl à la Conti, with Truffles.*

The same quantity of fowls as No. 25; the only

difference is, that you keep the *filets mignons,* which you lard, one half with bacon, and the other with truffles. You must take care that the *Conties* are not over-done. Those that are larded with bacon, must be well covered with fire, and those that are decorated with truffles must be wrapped up in bacon, and afterwards glazed. Give them the shape you please when you put them into the *sauté*-pan, either of garlands, *rosasses,* &c. The *Conties* must be put round the dish, when you have dished the scollops.

No. 27.—*Scollops of fowls with purée of Green Peas.*

These scollops are prepared, and done in the same manner as those above. When they have been *sautez,* put them into the *purée* of green peas.

No. 28.—*Fillets of Fowls à la Chingara.*

Take the fillets of three fowls, which you divest of the skin and sinews. Mark them as the above, with clarified butter in a *sauté*-pan, together with some slices of boiled ham, of the same size. *Sautez* them over a slow fire; but do not let the fillets be too long on the fire. Let the ham be of a fine colour; glaze it well, and dish it *en miroton.* Put three spoonsful of *Espagnole* into the *sauté*-pan, after having drained the butter, one spoonful of *consommé,* two pats of fresh butter, the juice of one lemon, some salt and a little Cayenne; glaze the bits of ham, and cover the fillets only with this sauce. Three fowls produce, in general, nine fillets, as you must make three with the inside fillet, the nine fillets will make a very small *entree;* but you must always add nine other things, either fried bread, tongue, or ham, otherwise the dish will be shabby: a good cook will always save a small bit of tongue, or ham; if he finds nothing else, he puts in its place some *crouton* of fried bread of the same shape as the fillets.

No. 29.—*Blanquette of Fowl marbrée.*

This dish is one which the Author does not approve of, but it is served at grand dinners. Take off the breast of three fleshy fowls, wrap them well up in bacon and paper, then roast them; do not let them be too much done. Next lay them aside to cool. Take off the flesh, first from one side, then from the other, which you cut to the size of a half-crown piece, as also some slices of a red tongue; then put into the dish that is to be sent up, a *miroton* of tongue and of fowl, that is, a slice of each alternately, and so on in a spiral line. Take care to keep the dish quite hot The moment you are going to send up, cover it with a *sauce à blanquette*, or *à l'Allemande*. These *entrées* should be made when you have much cold fowl in your larder, such as after a ball supper, for instance.

No. 30.—*Wings of Fowl à la Dauphin.*

If you have a very large dinner to send up, and use a great number of fowls, take eight fillets off from the same side, which makes no difference with regard to the expense; this dish looks better when the wings are all from the same side: prepare your fillets well, lard them with fine bacon, and then put them into the oven in a well-buttered stew-pan, in order to give them a good shape; when they have got a certain degree of firmness, lay them over slices of bacon, and put under the bacon a bed of vegetables, the same as for a *fricandeau*, with a little salt, and a good fire over them, in order that the larded part may be seized: the wings will be done in ten minutes; glaze them, and send up with whatever sauce you think proper. Endives with *béchemelle*, the *soubise*, and the *purée* of celery, and of green peas, are, however, preferable to all others.

No. 31.—*Boudin à la Reine.*

This dish is made out of cold fowls. Take the breast and fleshy parts of several fowls, which you

cut into small dice, all of an equal size. Throw those
dice into a reduction of *béchemelle,* and season them
well; next put them into a dish that they may cool,
and give them a good form with your knife. When
this preparation is quite cold, cut them into two equal
parts, which you make into *boudins,** of the size of
the dish: roll them into crumbs of bread; then dip
them into an *omelette,*† and roll them again in bread.
You must take care that the extremities are well covered with the crumbs, otherwise they would break
in the frying pan. When they are fried to a good
colour, drain them, wipe off the grease with a clean
towel, and serve with a thin *béchemelle* between.

No. 32.—*Croquettes of Fowl au Velouté.*

These are prepared in the same manner as the
Boudins à la Reine, but you must keep them rather
thick, to prevent their shrinking while frying. A
little fried parsley is to be put into the middle of the
dish, and you erect the *croquettes* round it. There
are several manners of rolling them, as in the shape
of a cork, of a ball, of a pear; the tail of which is
made out of a carrot, or some other substance, which
the author does not approve of; those which are the
best, are in the shape of a cork. You must press
pretty hard on the extremities, that they may stand
erect on the dish. To place them in a circular form,
with fried parsley in the centre, has a pretty effect,
though it is very plain.

Those that are in the shape of a pear, are called *à
la Dubaril.* There are also *croquettes* of sweetbreads, of palates of beef, of cocks'-combs: but they
are all much alike, as will be shown hereafter.

Croquettes of any kind ought to be made only with
remnants of fowl or game, as they require a great
quantity of flesh, but they may be made with what
is left from the preceding day.

* A long shape.
† *Omelette* consists of eggs beat together with a little salt.

No. 33.—*Hachi, or minced Fowl à la Polonoise.*

If you have any remnants of fowl, mince them, and put the minced meat into a good *béchamelle*, without suffering it to boil. Sometimes you may put the whole into a *vol au vent*, at another time into patties *en timballe;* another time you may put it in a *bordure*, with poached eggs over the minced meat. By this means you obtain a variety of dishes: you may likewise send it up in *croustades*, but these *croustades* bear the appearance of a dish of the second course.

No. 34.—*Legs of Fowl en Caneton. Duckling-like.*

After having prepared the fillets of several fowls, the legs should be turned to advantage: pull the bones entirely away from the white flesh; but take care not to destroy the knee: which must serve to make the beak of the duck. Cut the bone on both sides the joint, and keep the knuckle. When you have boned the thighs, stuff them moderately with a *farce à quenelles;* next sew them up with a little thread, and put them into the oven on a flat dish, put over these another flat dish with a weight on it, to give them a good shape. Leave them in the oven till they are quite firm, that they may retain their shape; next put them into a stew-pan, wrapped up with some bacon; add a few bits of carrot, an onion stuck with a clove, a little bay-leaf, thyme, salt and pepper. Put the knuckles to *braize* with this; when the whole has simmered gently on the fire for an hour, drain the legs and the knuckles, take off the thread, and stick the knuckle into the large part of the leg, and it will represent exactly the form of a duckling. Put under it a *purée* of green peas in summer; and at other times any kind of sauce, sharp or not.

The *sauce tomata*, or a *poivrade*, are very good with this dish, which is a saving one. When you use many fillets for a dinner, you should contrive to do something with the legs. If you are particular in binding the knuckle of fowl when you put them in the *braize*, you will be surprised how much it will resemble a duckling, when stuck properly in the large part of the legs.

No. 35.—*Legs of Fowl en Balotine.*

Bone the legs of the fowl; cut the knee entirely off, and the leg just above the joint: then roll the legs, and thrust the claws into the hole of the leg bone; tie them up quite round, and put them between two *plafonds*, with a pretty heavy weight over them, to give them a nice shape. When they are become firm, mark them between layers of bacon, and *braize* them in the common way: when they are done, drain and glaze them. Send up with any sauce you may fancy. The love-apple, or sharp sauce, will answer the purpose very well.

No. 36.—*Legs of Fowl à Orlie.*

Bone the legs of several fowls, and set them to be marinaded raw in an earthen pan with the juice of a lemon, a little parsley, thyme, bay-leaves, salt and pepper, &c. &c. When marinaded for three hours, drain them: then beat the white of an egg, mix a little flour with crumbs of bread, and dip the legs first into the white of the egg, and then into the flour and crumbs: next fry them, but mind, your dripping must not be too hot, for if it were so, the legs would get a colouring before they were done through. Serve up with the brown sharp sauce, or love-apple sauce.

This is a very excellent dish when you have had a large dinner the day before; you trim and bone these legs, and put them in the basin with *marinade* as before directed, but you must leave the skin very large, and trim them very round, so as to give them a good form; when fried, glaze them, and serve a *poivrade* or *tomata sauce* under them.

No. 37.—*Legs of Fowl à la Dreux.*

Bone the legs, fill up the vacuity, with a force-meat or *quenelle;* give the legs a round shape, then lard the upper part with small slips of ham, mark them between layers of bacon, and *braize* them as above. When they are done, glaze and send them up with whatever sauce you think proper. It is to be observed, however, that a glazed dish requires a white sauce, that the glazing may appear to greater advantage. These legs are to be put into a *sauté*-pan, on which you have spread layers of bacon. You also put the same over the legs, and cover the whole with the lid of a stew-pan, and over this put a heavy weight, to give the legs a good shape. When they are become sufficiently firm over a slow fire, or in the oven, take them out and *mark* them the same as any other *braize.**

* The *entrées* of legs of fowl are not in very great repute, but they are a very great saving of expense and nothing but prejudice can object to them; for when they are well made, they are excellent food, and make a very good appearance on table, as they can be served in so many different forms, and with such variety of flavour.

CHAPTER IX.

ENTRÉES OF FAT CHICKENS.

It is almost useless to describe what can be made
with fat chickens. Whatever can be made with
fowl, can also be made with chicken. The only difference is in the length of time requisite for dressing
them, a large one necessarily requiring more time
than a small one.

No. 1.—*Chickens à l'Ivoire.*

Take two chickens of the same size and equally
white; pick them well and singe them; then thrust
your fingers inside to pull out the breast-bone. Having mixed a little butter with the juice of half a lemon,
and some salt and pepper, introduce an equal proportion of this mixture into the body of each chicken,
and bind them up in a good-shape. Then put them
into an oval stew-pan, surrounded with layers of bacon:
next cut the juicy part of a lemon, and cover the
breasts of the chickens with thin slices of it and bacon. Pour some *poële* over them. The chickens
will be done in half an hour's time, and retain their
white colour. Drain them, take off the pack-thread,
and send them up with the *velouté*, or *béchamelle*.

No. 2.—*Chickens à la Villeroi*

Are dressed in the same manner as those above. The sauce, however, is to be an *aspic lié.* The *aspic lié* is the same sauce as the *marechale;* put in a stewpan three spoonsful of tarragon vinegar, let it reduce full half, then pour into it six spoonsful of *velouté,* a little salt and pepper, the yolks of two eggs, and mix this sauce very well. Add to it a very small piece of good butter, and work the sauce well, to make it as fine as possible. *Mark* the chicken all over.

No. 3.—*Chickens à la Montmorenci.*

Take two chickens of the same size, and equally while; bind them up as above; next have some boiling water, wherein you dip only the breasts of the chickens, to make the flesh firm. Then lard them the same as a *fricandeau,* and put them into an oval stew-pan, surrounded with bacon; though there is not to be any over them, moisten with the *poële,* or with some new broth, as old broth will turn any thing red. A large fire is required over the lid to seize the bacon; which having acquired a good colour, you remove the fire from over them, and let the chickens boil gently for half an hour: then drain and glaze them nicely, and serve up with a *ragoût à la financière.* Mind, they must be well done and drained; if any blood should remain in them, the sauce would be spoiled.

No. 4.—*Chickens à la Condé*

Are to be dressed as above, but it is useless to dip them into boiling water: slit them equally with a pen-knife, and introduce between the slits thin slices of truffles and of tongue *à l'ecarlate,* cut like a cock's comb ; then stew the chickens as mentioned above, and serve up with the *ragoût à l'Allemande.*

No. 5.—*Chickens à la Turque.*

Take two white chickens of the same size, empty them, and dress them up as above. Then have some rice well cleaned and blanched, and boil it in some *consommé.* When sufficiently swelled and very thick, season it well, and take one half of it, which you put inside of the chickens; stuff them as full as you possibly can, with the rump turned inside, to prevent the rice from bursting out: then spit the chickens, wrap them up in layers of bacon and paper, and they will be done in one hour. When done, lay them on the rice that remains, into which you may pour four spoonsful of *béchamelle,* and one spoonful of thick cream. Season the whole well. Mind that you have the inside of the chicken well washed with boiling water before you put the rice in, otherwise it will be full of scum, and will spoil the rice.

No. 6.—*Chickens with Italian Paste.*

Take two fat pullets as above, dress them in the like manner, but your Italian paste must be in a state of readiness, and made very thick, as it has less substance than rice: then stuff the chickens with part of the paste, and mix the remainder with some *béchamelle* as above.

No. 7.—*Fat Pullets aux Nouilles.*

Take a couple of fat pullets, which dress and prepare as directed in No. 1, and stew them in the same manner. The *nouilles* are made as follows: take the yolks of four eggs, five spoonsful of flour, a lump of butter of the size of two eggs, and a little salt; make a paste, which you moisten with a little water, yet let it be kept thick; work it hard with your hand, and spread it on the pastry-table with the rolling-pin; mind to powder a large quantity of flour when you cut the paste into long bits, to prevent their sticking to the pan: blanch the *nouilles* in water with a little salt. Drain them, throw them into cold water, and stew them in *consommé;* when they are done, drain them again, and toss them in a small quantity of *Alle-*

mande, or of *velouté.* You may also pour those sauces over the chickens. The paste may be cut into different shapes, as squares, lozenges, &c. &c. *Emincés,* or *blanquettes,* agree very well with the *nouilles.*

No. 8.—*Chickens à la Tartare.*

Take two very young chickens, singe and dress them *en poule,* by which is meant, that you make a hole above the joint of the leg, and thrust the claws into those holes: then split them in two, break the bones of the legs, and bone the backs and breasts, leaving as few bones as you possibly can; then mould the chickens into a round shape; season them with salt and pepper; take a brush dipped into yolks of eggs, and brush the chickens all over; next dip them into crumbs of bread; have some melted butter ready, dip them into it, and then into crumbs of bread again, and roll them equally, lay them on something flat, to give them a good shape; half an hour before you send them up, broil them on a clear fire; serve up with gravy, or an *Italienne.* Observe, that the legs are a long time boiling; ascertain if they are done before you send them up.

No. 9.—*Fat Pullets à la Givry.*

Dress two young pullets, and stew them as directed at No. 1. The *givry* is made in the following manner: take some small white onions, which you cut into rings; select them all of the same size, which you stew in a small quantity of *consommé;* take care your onions are not too much done, for they would break. Then spread these rings at an equal distance over the breasts of the chickens. Have a *verd de persil* (see *Sauces*) ready, and put a little in the centre of each ring; the remainder you mix with some *sauce tournée,* well reduced, and well seasoned; add a little lemon-juice, and a little Cayenne, and pour this sauce under the chickens.

No. 10.—*Chickens à la Barbarie with Truffles.*

Dress two young chickens as at No. 1. Cut small pieces of truffles in the shape of nails, make a few holes in the breasts of the chickens with a pen-knife, and fill them up equally with the prepared truffles. Then cover the chickens with layers of bacon, and stew them with a *poële*, as at No. 1, and serve up with an *Italienne* with truffles.

No. 11.—*Chickens à la Cardinal.*

Take a couple of fat chickens, very white, but mind that the skin is not injured, and pick them with the utmost care. Have some of the spawn of lobster ready pounded and mixed with a little *farce à quenelle;* introduce the handle of a small knife between the skin and the flesh, and thus separate the skin without tearing it; next introduce the red *quenelles* between the skin and the flesh very evenly; then truss the chickens in the common way and *poële* them as usual, but do not do them too much; let them stew gently, and pour under them a love-apple sauce, or a *poivrade*, or a *pluche*.

No. 12.—*Fillets of fat Pullets à la Royale.*

If you have a large dinner to serve, take the fillets of four chickens, and thus you obtain eight large fillets, and a similar number of *filets mignons;** flatten them with the handle of a knife that has been dipped in cold water, to prevent the knife breaking the fillets or sticking to them. Then use the knife to pull off the upper skin, which is very tough; take out the sinews from the *filets mignons*, put them into a *sauté*-pan, after having dipped them into butter; then powder them over with salt only, pepper being intended merely for highly seasoned dishes, but disagreeable to a dainty palate. When you are going to serve them, *sautez* them hastily, drain the butter,

---

* *Filets mignons* are the inside small fillets.

pour over them two or three spoonsful of *béchamelle*, and one spoonful of thick cream, which you keep stirring for a short time; then send up, dressed *en miroton*, with the *ragoût à la royale* in the centre, after having dished the fillets in a circle. The *ragoût à la royale* is white, and must be composed of the following articles: cocks'-combs, kidneys, mushrooms, small *quenelles*, and truffles, if you have any. Observe, that the sauce must be well seasoned.*

No. 13.—*Cutlets of Chicken à l'Epigramme.*

Take the fillets of five pullets, and pare them well; then take the small bone of the pinion, scrape it well, and stick it dexterously into the point of the fillets; season with salt and pepper. Brush them over with the yolks of two eggs, then dip them into crumbs of bread, next into some melted butter, and crumbs of bread again; let them be covered entirely. Broil them exactly at dinner-time. Then put the *filets mignons* in scollops, in a *sauce à blanquette*, with mushrooms, into the middle of the dish, and put the cutlets round the dish and send up. On other occasions you may *sautez* the *filets mignons* entire, and dish them between the cutlets, with a thin *Allemande.* You may put in this scollop some slices of truffles *sautez*, with the inside *filets*, called *filets mignon.*

No. 14.—*Fillets of fat Chicken, au Suprême.*

Take three small fat fowls, very white; clean and pick them well, scald the legs in boiling water; singe the chickens over the flame of a stove, then cut the fillets from the breast; flatten and trim the six large fillets: take the six small ones, and make three of them by sticking two together; lay them in a *sauté-*

* It is necessary to observe to the practitioner, that ragouts are few in number, viz. " *La Financiere,*" " *La Toulouse,*" " *L'Allemande,*" " *La Royale,*" " *La Godard,*" and " *La Chambord.*" Each of these ragouts have their different characteristics, and vary as well in appearance as in taste.

pan, and cover them with melted butter and fine
salt.. Just at dinner-time put the *sauté*-pan on the
stove, and *sautez* them on both sides; when they are
firm, they are done; drain the butter, but preserve
the gravy at the bottom of the pan; add to it three
spoonsful of *béchamelle* well seasoned, and move the
pan over the fire without letting the sauce boil: the
fillets will not be good if they have had the least
boil. Dress the nine fillets with a bit of bread fried
of a nice colour between each fillet, and pour the
sauce over them; but not on the fried bread; as that
must be crisp.

N.B.—Use the backs and legs of the fowls to make
the *consommé*, or soup *à la reine*.

No. 15.—*Fillets of fat Pullets sautez à la Lu-cullus.*

Take the fillets of four fat pullets, take off the *filets
mignons*, and pull the sinews from them, flatten them
with the back of a knife, and *mark* them in melted
butter. The larger fillets are to be garnished with
truffles, cut into small round slices, as in the *conties*.
Next make three round slits, in each fillet, and introduce the sliced truffles within each slit, though not
so far as to reach through the fillets, which would
break them. When your fillets have been garnished,
mark them in melted butter, and *sautez* them in
the usual way; mind, they must be only under-
done, by which is meant, that they are to retain somewhat of the reddish hue; but as they are to be kept
hot with the sauce, they will soon be thoroughly
done, and are always tender.

N.B.—For the sauce: strip the legs and loins of
the chickens, wash the inside of the lungs clean, and
put them into a small stew-pan with a few bits of ham,
half a shalot, and the parings of the truffles; let the
whole sweat for one hour, moistened with a spoonful or two of *consommé*. When the meat is done
through, pour over it some boiling hot *consommé*,
and let it boil for about an hour again, then drain the

whole on a double silk sieve; reduce the *consommé* to a light glaze: this will serve you for different purposes. When you have *sautez* the fillets, drain the butter; take four spoonsful of *béchamelle*, a little of the glaze of fowl and truffles, and a spoonful of thick cream; keep stirring the fillets in the sauce, and dish them alternately, a large fillet and a *filet mignon*. Pour the sauce over the parts that have no truffles on them, and that are not glazed; if you dress the dish with care, it will be very good. This dish will be found also under the head " GAME." It requires very great attention to be made in perfection. The fillets must

be sliced at three different places as follows.

When the truffles are put into it and dressed, it has a charming effect.

Be careful to have in a dish sauce sufficient to eat with every fillet.

No. 16.—*Scollops of Chicken, with Truffles.*

See *Scollops of Fowl*, No. 25, p. 169. You must always reduce to a glaze a little *consommè*, into which you have put the parings of the truffles. When reduced, strain it through a sieve, that the parings may not injure the sauce. Then use a small quantity of it with the sauce of the *sauté*, and add a little cream to whiten the sauce.

No. 17.—*Scollops of fat Pullets à la Conti, with Truffles.*

The same as above, with the difference only that you preserve the *filets mignons*, which you garnish with truffles, and mark them in a *sauté*-pan, in order to be enabled to give them the shape either of garlands, crescents, &c. &c. Butter the *sauté*-pan, and put in the *filets mignons* that you have larded with bacon: divide the thickest part of the fillets, preserve the right side point, turn over the two parts that you have divided, and give them the shape of a dart or arrow. Another time you may convert them into the shape of an S, and dish them round your scollops, which are dressed in the middle in the shape of an obelisk.

No. 18.—*Scollops of Chicken à l' Essence of Cucumbers.*

Mark the fillets of four fat pullets in a *sauté*-pan with some melted butter, and a little salt over them: cover them with a round piece of paper till dinner-time. The sauce is to be made in the following manner: take eight very green cucumbers, cut off the ends, and apply the tip of your tongue to taste them: if they should taste bitter, do not use them. Slice those only that are good about the size of a half-crown piece, take out all the seed, and put the parings, with a few minced cucumbers, to sweat in a little melted butter till they are melted; *marinade* the large slices with a little salt and vinegar, to draw the water from them, then lay those slices on a clean towel to drain, and put them into a stew-pan with four spoonsful of *sauce tournée*, a small bit of sugar, a little salt, and let them stew gently. When they are done, drain them on a hair sieve; then mix the whole of that sauce with the parings, and let it boil gently, in order to extract all the butter. When there is none left, reduce the *purée* till it becomes thick, then mix three or four spoonsful of *béchamelle*, and strain the whole through a tammy, like a *purée*. When dinner-time is come, put the fillet over the stove; after having *sautez* them, drain and scollop them, and put into the sauce, which must always be kept very thick. The moment you are going to send up, drain the cucumbers in a hair sieve, and put them with the scollops: mix a little cream with the scollops, taste whether they are well seasoned, and send up either with or without *conties*, according to your own taste. This dish should be rather sweet. When you have no *sauce tournée*, fry the cucumbers in butter. Spread flour over them, moisten with very good *consommé,* adding a bundle of parsley and green onions, a little sugar, and proceed as above. If you have no *béchamelle,* add three spoonsful of very thick cream which has been boiled, and keep the sauce thick, as it is easily made thin with a little *consommé* or broth.

No. 19.—*Wings of Chicken à la Maréchale.*

See wings of fowl *à la St. Laurent,* No. 21, page 167.

No. 20.—*Blanquette of Chicken à la Turque.*

Take a cold fowl or chicken and cut it into scollops, in the shape of half-crown pieces: have ready some rice, well washed, and which has been boiled in rich broth or *consommé;* let the rice be thick, make it richer with a few spoonsful of *béchamelle,* dish it *en buisson;* put the scollops of chickens *en miroton* up to the top of the *buisson;* keep the whole hot, well covered, and when ready to send up, *mask* with a *sauce à blanquette,* or a *béchamelle.*

To this dish I prefer the following.

No. 21.—*Sauté of Fillets of fat Pullets à la Turque.*

Take the fillets of three fat pullets, tear off the skin, and cut the sinews out of the *filets mignons;* stick two together, and then you will have nine fillets; put the whole into a *sauté*-pan, with some melted butter, and a little salt (never put any pepper into white made dishes,) cover them with paper to prevent the dust. At dinner-time have some rice ready that has swelled in rich *consomme;* the rice must be kept thick: mix two spoonsful of *bechamelle* with it, and a small bit of very fresh butter. This rice is dressed *en buisson* in the centre of the *sauté,* which is made in the same manner as the *sauté au suprême,* with the *filets* round it. Keep some of the rice a little thicker than the rest, mould in a spoon as many spoonsful as the fillets; dress them between, and keep the dish very hot. When the dinner is called for, sauce the fillets and the rice. This latter method is preferable.

No. 22.—*Sauté of Fillets of fat Pullets, sautez au Suprême.*

See No. 22, page 167, Fillets of fowl *au suprême.*

No. 23.—*Wings of fat Pullets à la Dauphine.*

See No. 30, page 172, Wings of fowl *à la Dauphine.*

No. 24.—*Boudins of Fillets of Chicken à la Reine.*

See No. 31, page 172.

No. 25.—*Boudins of Chicken à la Richelieu.*

Look into the Chapter of *Farces,* for the method of making *quenelles.* The *boudins à la Richelieu,* are the same thing as a *farce à quenelles,* made of either veal or fowl, rabbits, whitings, carp, &c. Sweat some white onions that are cut into small dice or fillet; when well done, drain them in a hair sieve, in order that there may not be the least particle of butter; work the *farce* with a wooden spoon before you put the onions in, to prevent their breaking, for it is requisite that the onions should remain entire in the *boudins à la Richelieu.* Next let this *farce* stand to cool. When it is quite cold, roll it in the shape of a rolling-pin of the length of the dish, and poach it in the following manner. After having rolled the *boudins,* rub with butter a stew-pan large enough to contain the *boudins* with ease; lay them over the butter; pour some boiling water with a little salt into the stew-pan, and let them boil gently, till you see they are swelled properly; then drain and let them cool. When cold, mould them of an equal size, then dip them into yolks of eggs well beaten, with a little salt, and then slightly into crumbs of bread, next into eggs again, and once more slightly into crumbs of bread: then fry them on a clear fire; they only want to get a fine colour: drain them with a clean towel, dish them, and pour over them an *Italienne.* Some people make use of the *sauce d'attelets;* in that case it must be poured hot over the *boudins.* When they are cold, and the sauce begins to cool, put some equally with your knife on each square. Dip them into crumbs of bread. Take care that you make them into regular squares; then prepare an *omelette*, by which is meant yolks and whites of eggs beat up with a little salt. The *boudins* are to be dipped only once into this preparation; give them a good colour by frying in very hot dripping; you may serve them sometimes with crumbs of bread, and sometimes white. Epicures will prefer them white, without the crumbs of bread, just at the instant they are poached.

No. 26.—*Boudins, or Pudding à la Sefton.*

Make some *quenelles* of fowl, in which you introduce some essence of mushroom, which mix with the *farce* in the same manner as the *boudins à la Richelieu;* then poach the *boudins.* When done, drain and put them in the dish; have some *béchamelle* very thick; *mask* the *boudins* with the thick sauce, and put over each of them the small fillets *larded*, which you must prepare in the following manner. In order to give the larded fillets a proper shape, take a piece of carrot, or a bit of bread of the same shape and size of the *boudin*, put over the carrot a thin slice of fat bacon, to prevent the fillets from smelling of it; bind the fillets over the carrot, and put them into the oven till they are firm; then glaze them; and put them over the *boudin* after having poured the sauce over, which must be thick; when the *boudins* are covered, put a spoonful of *consommé* and some of the *juice* of mushrooms to make the sauce thinner, and put it under.

No. 27.—*Quenelles of Chicken with clarified Consommé.*

The *quenelles* are to be rolled much about the size of a thick cork, and are to be put into a stew-pan rubbed with butter, as directed above. You must have ready some fowl *consommé* very clear, yet rich: drain the *quenelles* on a clear cloth, put them into a silver stew-pan, and pour the *consommé* gently over them, that they may not break, and that the *consommé* may remain clear.

Observation.—This dish is seldom called for in England. The other *quenelles* are made in the same manner but only of various sizes. There are *quenelles* called *à la cuillière*, or spoon, which are prepared in the following manner: take two spoons, one of which is always to be kept in hot water; fill the other with some *farce*, which you shape with a knife: when your *quenelle* is quite round, with the other spoon you take it out, and put it over some butter in a stew-pan, and so on with the rest. This manner of preparing *quenelles* is also practised in dressing *entrées* of fish. The *farce à quenelles* not only makes good *entrées* but is indispensably necessary in the making of *la Chambord, à la financière, le ragoût l'Allemande, la Godard, la Toulouse*, and all garnitures in general. The *quenelles* are a branch of cookery, which the author would select to try the knowledge of a cook, many cooks do not personally finish these dishes, but leave their attendant the care of them, by which means they are seldom well done.

No. 28.—*Risolles of Fowls.*

Risolles were formerly made with a *farce, fine,* either of fowl, or rabbit, (See *Farces.*) Spread some *feuilletage,** and lay at equal distances, balls of the *farce.* Then use the paste-brush over the paste, round the *farce,* and fold the paste, which you press all round, in order to make the borders stick close

---

* *Feuilletage,* puff-paste.

together. Then run a *videlle goudronnée* round the paste, so as to cut the *risolles* in the shape of a crescent. When you have about two dozen, fry them and send them up with fried parsley in the middle. Now the *risolles* are commonly made in the following manner: have some minced fowl, that is, the white fleshy part, which you put into a *velouté* reduced; give it a good seasoning, and then let it cool. When cold, divide it into small balls, and wrap them up in paste, fry them, and serve up garnished with fried parsley.

No 29.—*Croquettes of Chickens au Velouté.*

Take the flesh of roast chickens, which you cut into small dice of an equal size: put them into a *béchamelle* reduced, then let them cool, next mould them of the shape of a cork; dip them into an *omelette*, and then into crumbs of bread; lastly, fry them till of a light brown, and serve up with some fried parsley of a good green colour. This requiring a quantity of white flesh of chickens, is termed most naturally an *entrée de desserte*, remnants of cold chicken. The *croquettes* are better when made with some of the remnants of fowl, and sweetbreads. A good cook will never prepare *croquettes*, except he have something left in the larder, as it requires many little pieces of fowl; if he happen to have them in the larder, they may be made at a trifling expense.

No. 30.—*Fricassée of Chickens au naturel.*

Take a couple of fat chickens, empty them, and singe them till the flesh gets firm, in order that they may cut better, and the skin may not be injured, and cover every part of the chickens: some persons neglect this operation, but the flesh of chickens intended for a *fricassée* or a raw *marinade*, must be made firm. Next carve your chickens as neatly as possible and each will supply you with ten pieces. Take out the lungs, and the spungy substance that is within the loins, wash the members in luke-warm water; let them disgorge all the blood, and blanch them in boiling water, that the flesh may be made firm, and that you may give the members a good shape; drain them from that water, and put them into cold water; when cooled, trim them and put them in a stew-pan with a small bit of butter, till you have the *consommé* ready to moisten the *fricassée* in the following manner; put the trimming of the chicken in the water, wherein you have blanched the chicken, to this add the necks, the four legs, some parsley, green onions, a clove, a few bits of mace, one small shalot, and a bayleaf; let these stew well for one hour, and use them to moisten the *fricassée*. When the chickens have been fried lightly, dust a little salt and flour over them; mosten with the liquor they were blanched in. Let them boil for about three quarters of an hour: skim off all the butter and scum: then put the members into another stew-pan, reduce the sauce, and strain it through a tammy over the chickens. This stew-pan is to be put into a *bain marie* till dinnertime; then thicken the *fricassée* with the yolks of four eggs and a little cream: it is to be observed, that if the *fricassée* does not boil, the thickening will not be thoroughly done. Some people add a little lemonjuice, but others do not use any, and they are right, for lemon is admissible only in *fricassées* of a high relish. It must be particularly observed, that when you put lemon, you must put more seasoning, as salt, pepper, &c.

No. 31.—*Fricassée of Chickens à la Paysanne.**

This *fricassée* is to be prepared in the same way as that above, only boil four onions in it, which, however, are to be taken out again. Take about three dozen of small white onions of an equal size, peel without injuring them, blanch them in water first,

* *Fricassée* of chicken is a dish of as frequent occurrence as bread; if it is well done, it may be given for a trial dinner; very few cooks are able to make a good *fricassée*. The author considers this dish the most wholesome and the least expensive of any, as it requires only water to make it well.

next boil them in a little *consommé* with a little sugar and salt; they must simmer only. When done, leave them in the liquor. When it is dinner-time, put some chopped parsley into the sauce after having thickened it. Toss the *fricassée* gently, in order that all the members may be equally covered with the parsley, and dish it: then put the onions on a cloth to drain, that they may not thin the sauce, and put them with the sauce over the meat. Lemon in this *fricassée* is requisite, and you must give more seasoning to it than to that above; you must also add a little ground pepper, or Cayenne to it. The small onions should be boiled in a little of the sauce separate, and when they are sufficiently done, pour the sauce to the other, to be reduced; keep the small onions in the stew-pan covered, and put them in the sauce, well drained, the moment you are about to serve.

No. 32.—*Fricassée à la Chevalière.*

This is prepared in the same manner as No. 30, with this only difference, that you lard the fillets; which is a method not approved of by the author. You must cut off the *filets mignons* and the wings; the *filets mignons* only are to be larded, but keep the wings entire, and make the *fricassée* as usual: when it is dished with the sauce, lay the four *filets mignons* on each corner of the dish, with sweetbreads of lamb in the middle; by this means the members are all left entire except the breast. The small fillets are to be done by putting them into a buttered *sauté*-pan; sprinkle a little salt over them, and put them into the oven; as soon as they are white, they are done; glaze them of a nice colour, and serve up. The sweetbreads of lamb may be done the same, but they are longer doing. When you prepare a grand dinner, take the inside fillets of four chickens larded, and turn them round like a ring over the buttered *sauté*-pan; when done, put the round one over the leg, and the four others between; by this you have the *fricassée* complete in all its members, and the dish will be better garnished.

No. 33.—*Fricassée of Chickens à la St. Lambert.*

Make a broth of all sorts of vegetables.* Mark the *fricassée* as above, moisten with the vegetable broth, and proceed as usual. This *fricassée* instead of being white, is rather of a brown colour.

No. 34.—*Fricassée of Chickens à la Dauphine.*

If this is made on purpose for the day, the sauce must be very thick; let it cool, next pour the sauce equally over each member, dip them into crumbs of bread, equalize your pieces, and dip them into an *omelette*, and next into crumbs of bread a second time. Fry them till of a light brown, and under them serve a *velouté*. This dish is also an *entrée* of *desserte*. When a *fricassée* of chickens has been taken down untouched, serve it up again the next day in this manner.

No. 35.—*Marinade of Chickens à la St. Florentin.*

Take two very young fat chickens, singe them till they are firm; cut them in pieces as if for a *fricassée;* put them into an earthen-pot with a few leaves of parsley, a few slices of onion, a little salt and pepper; then squeeze a lemon or two over the limbs, and *marinade* them for a couple of hours. The *marinade* is to be stirred every now and then. At dinner-time drain the chickens, beat the whites of two eggs, and dip the pieces first into it, next into flour; cover them all over, that they may be made of a good equal colour; then fry them, but take care that the dripping is not too hot, for fear the chickens should be too brown and not done through; drain them on a clean

* The vegetables are carrots, turnips, onions, celery, parsley, &c. &c.

towel, and serve under them a *poivrade*, or love-apple sauce.

No. 36.—*Friteau of fat Chickens.*

This dish is prepared as that above, but is to be garnished with a frew fried eggs. Serve up with love-apple sauce. You must select very fresh eggs, and fry them in sweet salad oil. Observe, that you must use very little oil, otherwise the eggs will break to pieces; put a little oil into the corner of the *omelette* pan, and fry them one by one of a very good colour, and not too much; then glaze them, and garnish with them.

No. 36.—*Fricassée of Chickens à la Bardoux.*

This is prepared as that of No. 30. After having thickened your *fricassée*, take a few onions cut into dice. Sweat them in a little butter, but take care they do not get brown; drain them, put them into the sauce, and cover the *fricassée* with them.

No. 38.—*The Capilotade of Chickens.*

This is an *entrée* of *desserte*. Take two chickens that have been either roasted or *poëlé*, cut them as for eating, flay them and *mark* them in a stew-pan like a *salmi:* now pour a brown *Italienne* over them, and let them simmer gently over a slow fire, that the sauce may not stick to the pan. Then have thin slices of bread cut into the shape of flat pears, that you fry in butter till they are of a light brown: dish them between the members, glaze the fried bread, and pour the *Italienne* over the chickens only.

No. 39.—*Members of Chickens au Soleil, or Marinade cuite.*

This is also an *entrée* of *desserte*. The *marinade cuite* is to be prepared in the following manner: put a little butter into a stew-pan, with four shalots, an onion, and a carrot cut into dice, a little parsley, a few roots of ditto, a bay-leaf, a little thyme, clove, and some spice. Let the whole lay on the fire till the vegetables are of a light brown; then moisten with a little vinegar and water. When the *marinade* is done enough, season it, give it a high relish, then pour it over the members of the chickens; let the whole boil for a minute or two, and let it cool till dinner-time; drain the members, dip them into proper paste, (see *butter*,) and fry them. Serve under them a brown *poivrade*.

No. 40.—*Marinade of Chickens à la Orlie.*

This is the same as the *St. Florentin*, No. 35, with the only difference, that you mix a few crumbs of bread with the flour, into which the limbs are to be dipped.

No. 41.—*Minced Chickens à la Polonoise.*

Take the fleshy part of roasted chickens, chop it very small, and put the whole into a well-seasoned *béchamelle*. Send up in a *vol au vent*, or a *bord de plat*, with poached eggs over; if you have a deep dish, send them with fried bread round the dish only.

This *entrée* is made when you have a *blanquette*, or *sauté* left: chop altogether, truffles, chickens, &c., and denominate it, *haché de volaille*, either " *au truffle*," or " *à la Polonoise*."

No. 42.—*Blanquette of Chickens with green Peas.*

This dish is made out of roast chickens that have already been served up, otherwise it would be very expensive, as it would require five chickens at least to make it, and it would be but a small dish after all. Cut Scollops of chickens as large as possible, give them nearly a round shape; but it matters not whether they are of different sizes: put them into the *sauce à blanquette* as directed, with white peas, but not till you have thickened the sauce.

No. 43.—*Soufflé of Chickens à la Crême.*

This dish is also made of the remnants of roasted chickens; take off the white flesh, and mince it very small, and pound it in a mortar with a little *béchamelle,* and a good lump of fresh butter, and salt and pepper; with this, mix the yolks of four eggs. Strain the whole through a tammy, or a hair sieve; then beat the white of five eggs till made in a single body; mix these with the former preparation, and put the whole in the dish *à souffler,* or in a *croutade* that has been raised like the crust of a *pâté chaud.* It will be done in a quarter of an hour or twenty minutes, according to the quantity. It is to be observed, that if the oven is too hot, the outside of the *soufflé* will be burnt, although the inside is not done enough. This, therefore, must be carefully attended to.

No. 44.—*Gratin of Fillets of Chickens with Velouté.*

This is likewise an *entrée* of *desserte;* mince the flesh of cold roasted chickens, which you put into a *velouté* well reduced; then make a border to a dish, if you are without a deep one, about an inch thick, and put the minced meat in the middle. Your mince must be thick, and levelled with a knife; dust it over with crumbs of bread; pour some drops of clarified butter over the crumbs, then throw some more crumbs over, and again some clarified butter and crumbs of bread. Then give a colouring with the *salamander,* which you must hold at a distance, otherwise it would spoil the colour, which must be acquired gradually. Next cut pieces of bread in balls, and in the shape of corks, fry them in butter, with which alternately garnish your gratin all round, and serve up quite hot. Before you put the mince, pour some of the sauce into the dish, to reduce to *gratin.*

No. 45.—*Galantine of fat Chickens.*

Take a nice fleshy chicken, which empty and pick nicely. When picked neatly, bone it without injuring the flesh. Take some slips of ham and some truffles, which cut into bits of the same thickness at least, if you can not make them of the same length; cut the flesh of the chickens into fillets, and add a few slices of veal; of these form a kind of bed, in such a manner as that, when they are cut, the slices may be chequered; season with all sorts of spices, salt, &c., then close the skin of the chicken, sew up the back, and give it a nice shape before you put it into the stew-pan. You must have some calf's-foot jelly ready, for the chicken is much sooner done than the calf's-foot; then mark the chicken in a stew-pan, and cover it with layers of bacon; season it with salt and pepper, a bunch of parsley and small onions, some thyme, a bay-leaf, a clove, a little spice, a few carrots, a couple of onions, and some slices of veal; then mix a little broth and a small quantity of the jelly. The chicken must not boil above an hour.

Then take it off the fire, and let it cool in the liquor, that the slices may stick together by means of the jelly, for, were this neglected, the *galantine* would break to pieces on being cut. If you send it up hot, you may pour over it such sauce as you think proper; but it must be a brown sauce, or sorrel, or onions made brown in an *Espagnole:* however, it is much better to serve a *galantine* cold with jelly; take some of the liquor, beat the white of two or three eggs, which mix with the cold jelly after having skimmed off the fat; then again put the whole on the fire, and keep stirring till the liquor is white; then let it boil gently; next take the jelly off the fire, and lay it aside with a cover and fire over it: when quite clear, strain it through a cloth and let it cool, to be used when wanted. If you serve the jelly cold, season it with more salt and pepper, as above-mentioned.

No. 46.—*Boudins of Chickens à la Ude.*

Make these *boudins* with *quenelles*, like those *à la Richelieu:* dip them into crumbs of bread, and fry

them to a light brown: make on the top an oblong
square opening, empty the *boudins,* taking care to
preserve, however, a coat thick enough to admit a
salpicon of chickens, truffles, and mushrooms, cut
into small dice, and thrown into a well-seasoned *béchamelle;* take six *filets mignons,* as three are wanted for each *boudin:* give them the shape of the handle of a basket, after having larded them with bacon,
or decorated them *en conti,* as it is called.   Then
take a very large carrot, cut it of the same size as the
puddings, wrap it up in thin layers of bacon, put the
filets mignons over the carrot, and dust a little salt
over them: then put the whole into an oven; do not
let it be too much done; but of a light brown only.
Glaze them when ready to send up to the dinner;
pour the *salpicon* into the puddings with the sham
basket handles at an equal distance over the puddings:
mind, the fillets are not to be thrust in too far, that
they may really look like basket handles.   This dish
is intended for a grand dinner, when common dishes
are not to make their appearance.

No. 47.—*Grenade of Fillets of Chicken.*

You must have a mould ribbed like a melon; cut
very thin layers of bacon; line the mould with them:
then take fillets of chicken larded with bacon, and
others decorated with truffles.   Have sweetbreads of
lamb already done, one of which put between each
rib, and the thickest part of the *filets mignons.*
When you have thus arranged alternately one fillet
larded, and another decorated with truffles, cover the
whole of your fillets with a *farce à quenelles.*   Put
a thick *salpicon* in the centre, and cover it with the
farce: stick it with force-meat, then put the mould
au bain marie, or in the oven, in order to poach the
whole at once; next turn the *grenade* on a dish *à
entrées,* dry the larded slices with the *salamander,*
and glaze them.   When the fillets or slices are of a

light brown, uncover the rest, glaze them slightly, and serve them with an *Espagnole.**

No. 48.—*Turbans of Fillets of Chickens à la Sultane.*

Take the *filets mignons* of chickens, lard them with bacon; have ready a *farce à quenelles*, rather thick, which should be kept in ice, that it may acquire substance, and be more easily worked: cut a large piece of bread, which cover with thin slices of bacon; put the bread in the middle of the dish, then lay the *farce à quenelles* all round, of about three inches in height; stick the fillets in the *farce à quenelles;* they are not to be stuck perpendicularly, though at equal distances, leaving a separation between each fillet for the reception of cocks' kidneys. These are to be put in only when you are going to send up: cover your dish with an earthen pot, or a lid that closes hermetically. The turban is to be put into the oven, and when done, glaze the fillets with the *salamander.* Make small holes for the admission of the cocks' kidneys, which must be very white, and made to resemble so many pearls. If you have nothing to cover the dish, use layers of bacon; but a plain cover is preferable, as it is free from fat, and the *quenelles* are better and more easily poached.

Take out the large piece of bread; drain the fat off by means of crumbs of bread; and put into the centre of the dish a *blanquette* of chickens. (See *Blanquette.*) When in the season of truffles, garnish alternately with a *perle* or kidney, and a ball made out of a truffle, ready done; and then put scollops with truffles in the middle. A better method is now adopted, and here recommended. Have a sweetmeat-pot, buttered, and put it in the middle of the crust. You must make the crust with some remnants of paste, filled up with flour, and cake a little, to make it firm.

* The *grenade* is likewise a dish for grand dinners, and is excellent when well dressed.

Then put the pot in the middle, garnish all round with the *quenelles*, and stick the fillet as directed above. This method will be found easy, and when the turban is done in the oven, take off the pot and put the ragout in its room. But mind to drain all the fat, and make this dish very neat.

Observations to the Cook.—The author has in many instances altered clarified butter, by melted butter; but you must understand, that butter must be melted only, as, when you let it be quite clarified, it tastes greasy, and when it is only melted, the butter-milk goes down, and you use the butter with advantage, as you may use it several times, either to fry *croutons*, or for crumbs of bread, &c.

CHAPTER X.

ENTRÉES OF PARTRIDGES, YOUNG AND OLD.

No. 1.—*Whole Partridges à l'Espagnole.*

IT will be necessary to premise, in treating of game, that partridges in particular should be selected of the very young birds, the old ones being of no use in cookery. To demonstrate their inferiority, a young bird in Paris will fetch three shillings, while the other is not worth one. The only way of using the old birds, is to put them with cabbages or *purées* of lentils. They are good for *consommé* and glaze of game, but are too tough for any thing fine. Young ones, in general, have yellowish claws; but it will sometimes happen that the claws and legs are of a gray, or even of a bluish colour, and yet they may be tender. Look at the extremity of the wing; if it is sharp pointed and whitish, the bird is still tender; but if those marks do not exist, the bird is invariably old, and consequently unfit for use, except as above-mentioned; or for sauces, *consommés*, and cold patties. You should also be careful to remove the nerves when you bone them.

The size of the dish must determine the number of birds you are to dress; in general two or three are wanted; empty them as usual, and take care not to injure the skin: pick them well, cut off the sinew that is under the joints of the legs, truss the legs up towards the breast, and then dress up the birds in the following manner. First, put the packthread needle through the stump of the right wing, then through the thick joint of the leg, and next across the body; then again through the other stump; let the packthread be very tight ahd fasten the knot. Now from the back run the needle through the side beneath the leg, then above the pinion below the breast, so as to perforate the breast-bone: let the needle come out from the part parallel to that where first it was introduced, and then through the side to the back, and fasten the pack-thread. Give a good shape to the birds, which is an indispensable branch of knowledge in the art of cookery. A man can not be really a thorough good cook, unless he is practically acquainted with every branch of his art; and this branch of it is very important, though it is certainly not easy to teach how to truss poultry or game by any written direction: you may as well attempt to teach drawing without a master. Seasoning and *marking* may be explained, but practice alone can make a man perfect. Such, however, as have been initiated, may derive great advantage from such a work as this. Put the partridges between layers of bacon, and pour a *poële* over them. If you happen to have no *poële* ready, use some of the pot-top, with a little salt, parsley, and onions, well seasoned with spice, salt and pepper. They will be done in the course of twenty minutes, but let it be on a slow fire, drain and put them into the dish, and pour an *Espagnole* over them, in which you have put a little glaze of game, to give it the taste of game.

N.B.—All dishes of game require more seasoning than white fowl.

No. 2.— *Young Partridges à la Montmorenci.*

Take some young partridges, which empty, and truss as in No. 1, dip the breasts into boiling water; when made firm, dip them immediately in cold water:

next lard them with thin slits of bacon; mark them in a stew-pan with slices of fat bacon all round only, pour a little *poële*, or any other liquid, enough to immerse about one half of the birds. Have a brisk fire over them to seize the bacon; when they have been stewed for twenty minutes glaze them, and probe them near the back; if no blood issues, it is a sign that they are done enough. Drain them, glaze them a second time, and send them up with a *ragoût à la financière.**

No. 3.—*Young Partridges à la Barbarie.*

Truss the birds as in No 1; stuff them with chopped truffles and rasped bacon, seasoned with salt, pepper, and allspice. You should pound this mixture in the mortar, and when the truffles are reduced to paste, mix with them some whole ones that have been cleaned and peeled, and put the whole in the body of the bird: then cut small pieces of truffles in the shape of nails, make holes with a penknife in the breasts of the birds, widen the holes with a skewer and fill them with the truffles; let them be nailed in very regularly. Then *mark* them as in No. 1. They are to be stewed also in the same manner. Serve under them an *Italienne* with truffles.

N. B.—Take care to drain them well, otherwise the fat will spoil both the taste and look of the sauce.

No. 4.—*Young Partridges à la Dreux.*

This is nearly the same as the foregoing dish, only instead of using truffles you must lard with small pieces of ham: use the penknife to make the holes, as larding-pins would spoil the look of the birds,

* It will be needless to remind the reader, that every thing *larded on the top*, is called *piqué*. Larded is when you put bacon through the flesh. When you only lard the superficies you should say *piqué*: otherwise, you will have only one term to express two distinct ideas. The larding never glazes well. If you do not dry the bacon in the oven, put the glaze over lightly, and place it in the oven several times till it becomes of a fine colour.

which are to be served whole. *Mark* and stew as as above, and serve up with the *essence* of game.

No. 5.—*Young Partridges à la Crapaudine.*

Cut off the claws, after having emptied and picked the birds; make a hole below the joint of the leg; truss the leg inside of the body; singe the birds over the flame till the flesh gets firm; pinch the breast with your left hand; scollop the breasts without quite reaching the skin; turn the flesh over on the table; beat the bird flat; dust it with a little salt and pepper; then dip it twice into clarified butter and crumbs of bread; broil it, and send it up with an *Italienne*, or essence of game.

No. 6.—*Young Partridges à la Givry.*

In this case you add a *decoration* to the birds in the following manner, after having trussed and stewed them as in No. 1. At dinner time take rings of white onions, let them be stewed white in a litle *consommé*, then take a cutter of the same size as the inside of the rings of the onions, cut round pieces of truffles that have been *braized* with the birds; mind, the truffles must be of a very black colour: (the *parings* are to be chopped and mixed with the *Italienne;*) the round pieces of truffles are to be put over the breasts of the birds, three on each side, Mosaic fashion, and the rings of onions round the truffles, and one over the pouch. If the truffles do not stick well, use a little glaze to make them stick, as they are liable to fall off. Do not *mask* with the sauce, which must be poured into the bottom of the dish; the sauce must be an *Italienne* with truffles, mix with it a little glaze of game, to give the taste of it.

No. 7.—*Compotte of young Partridges à blanc.*

Take four young partridges, cut off the claws, and truss them with the legs inwards; next singe them. Then take a few pieces of the breast of bacon, which cut into the size of small corks, and boil in water for half an hour. Next fry them white, and take them off from the fire as soon as they are done. Now fry the partridges white also, in butter and the fat of the bacon. When they are quite firm, take them out of the stew-pan. Then throw a spoonful of flour into this butter; fry this flour white. Next pour in a little broth, till the sauce is thin enough to be skimmed, (for it is to be observed, that if a sauce is too thick it can never be skimmed,) then put in some *parings* of mushrooms, a bunch of parsley and green onions, and season with a little thyme, bay-leaves, a clove, a little salt; and a very small lump of sugar. Stew the birds in this sauce, the same as a *fricassée* of chickens; if onions are agreeable, put a few small ones to give a relish. When the *compotte* is done, skim off all the fat, and drain the partridges in a clean stew-pan; drain all the bacon and mushrooms, which you throw into the stew-pan with the partridges: reduce the sauce after it has been skimmed; strain it through a tammy over the birds, and put the stew-pan *au bain marie:* now take some small white onions of an equal size, which have been boiling in a little *consommé* with a very small bit of sugar; have also some mushrooms, fried white in butter; when the onions and mushrooms are ready, set the *compotte* a boiling; thicken the sauce with the yolks of four eggs, beat with a little cream and lemon juice; next put in the small onions, mushrooms, and bacon, with some *quenelles*, if you think proper to garnish your *entrée*. If the dish is of a large size, put a crust of bread, cut into the shape of cocks'-combs, in the dish between each bird, and send up with a good seasoning.

No. 8.—*Compotte of young Partridges à brun.*

Do exactly the same thing as in No. 7; instead of moistening with *consommé*, use gravy of veal. Fry the onions in a little butter till they are of a fine brown, then let them boil in a little gravy of veal; they should be of an equal size; give them a good colour. Add truffles and mushrooms, if you have any, and reduce the sauce till thick enough to *mask*.

No. 9.—*Partridges and Cabbages, dressed.*

Take a couple of old partridges, empty and truss them, with the legs inward; simmer them on the fire till they get firm. Blanch two cabbages that you have cut in halves, or in four if they are large. When they are well done, they reduce exceedingly. You must blanch the bacon with the cabbages, otherwise it will be too salt. When the cabbages are blanched, put them into cold water to cool; cut off the tops of the middle, squeeze them so as to leave no water; have also blanched about a pound and a half of breast of bacon with the cabbage; put this bacon into a small braizing-pan, and the birds close to the bacon. Next put in the cabbage, a few carrots turned round, two or three onions, a bunch of parsley seasoned, and a small quantity of allspice, bay-leaves, thyme, salt, and pepper: cover the whole with a few layers of bacon, and with a sheet of buttered paper; then moisten with a *braize*, if you have any; if not, take some of the pot-top, but in the latter case you must season a little more. Set the contents of the braizing-pan boiling, and this being done, put it over a slow fire for three hours and a half. Now take out the layers of bacon, the onions, and the carrots. Place a large sieve over a dish of the same size, turn the birds into the sieve, take a clean towel, mould the cabbages into a large roller, squeeze them so as to have no fat left; then take a plain mould, garnish it with very thin layers of bacon, make a kind of flower in the middle of the mould with the carrots, and put a border of small glazed onions all round the top; next take some of the cabbage with a spoon, with which fill the mould. At the same time let the birds be covered all over with the cabbage equally on all sides. Make a *rosasse* of carrots on each face of the mould, which fill to the brim. Then put it into the oven to keep warm. At dinner-time turn the mould into a dish, let it lay for a moment to drain out all the broth, and send up a nice *Espagnole* over it. Partridges with cabbages, in my opinion, are far superior when not put into a mould; squeeze the cabbage the same as before in a clean towel, to give it the shape of a large rolling-pin, then take the two ends of it to make a bed for the bird on the dish; cut the cabbages of an equal size, dress them round the partridges with a carrot between each cabbage; put also some sausages, and cover the whole when well dressed with a good *Espagnole* sauce, in which you have reduced a little of the liquor of the cabbages; if the cook has any ingenuity, this dish will be most excellent, and exhibit a beautiful appearance.

No. 10.—*Sauté of Fillets of young Partridges, au fumet of Game.*

Take four young partridges, rather stale, that they may have more flavour, and be more tender; flay them, take up the fillets, detach the *filets mignons* from the upper fillets, cut out the sinews of the *filets mignons*, and flatten the fillets with the handle of your knife dipped into cold water, the blade being also dipped into the same; pass it gently over the fillets, leaning heavy on the table, in order to take off the second skin of the fillets only: trim the fillets nicely, *mark* them with melted butter in a *sauté*-pan; lay the *filets mignons* over the others, dust a little salt, and cover the whole with a round piece of paper till dinner-time, then *sautez* the fillets over a very brisk and equal fire. With the remnants of the birds, put in a few thin slices of veal and ham in a small stew-pan, lay the remnants over the veal, and moisten the whole with a few spoonsful of *consommé.* Let the whole sweat on a slow fire, and when the meat is sweated thoroughly, moisten with boiling *consommé,* to which add a few mushrooms, if you have any, together with a bunch of parsley and green onions. Let the whole stew for an hour and a half; strain this *fumet* through a silk sieve, and reduce it to glaze, to use it when required. When the fillets have been *sautez*, drain the butter; then take four or five spoonsful of *béchamelle*, some of the above glaze of game, and keep stirring without allowing them to boil. Taste whether seasoned enough: pour a little thick cream to whiten the sauce, and make it mellower; have as many slices of bread cut into the shape of the fillets, fried in butter of a good colour, as you have large fillets; glaze the fried bread lightly, then dish the *sauté* in the following manner: a *crouton*, and next a large fillet with the thick end upwards, then a *filet mignon* with the point upwards, then again a *crouton*, &c. &c. as above. *Mask* the fillets only, not the *croutons*, and send up to table.

No. 11.—*Cutlets of young Partridges en Epigramme, with Truffles.*

Take five young partridges, flay them as above: take off, first the fillets, and next the *filets mignons;* tear off the second skin from the fillets, point the smallest bone of the pinion or wing, and stick it into the end of the fillet. Then season with salt and pepper; rub the fillets over with a brush that has been dipped into the yolk of an egg; then dip them into crumbs of bread, next into melted butter; and again into crumbs of bread; just before dinner-time broil them on a very sharp fire. *Sautez* the *filets mignons;* of which you make a *blanquette*, in which you must mix some glaze of game. Put *blanquette* into the middle of the dish, and the broiled fillets all round. *Mask* the fillets with some light glaze of game. If you expect much company, in order to give the dish a better appearance, put as many *croutons* between as you have *filets*, and add some mushrooms to the *blanquette*, mixed with the truffles. The truffles must be *sauté* with the inside fillet. Take out the fillets first, and let the truffles fry a little longer in the butter before you mix the whole.

No. 12.—*Sauté of Fillets of young Partridges à la Sefton.*

Take five or six young partridges, as tender as possible, and of an equal size, flay them, take up the fillets, and cut off the second skin. Next slit the fillets at three equal distances: have ready some truffles that are chamfered and cut into the shape of cocks'-combs, take about eight of these slices of truffles, lay them equally over one another, and introduce some into each of the slits that you have made, and next into the other two parts: take care not to make the slits too deep, do the same with regard to every one of the ten fillets. The *filets mignons* are only to be *marked* in melted butter; do not forget to pull off the sinews, to prevent the fillets from taking a bad shape while frying. *Mark* the fillets in a *sauté*-pan with butter and round slices of truffles of an equal size, and *sautez* the fillets when dinner-time is at hand. For the sauce, see *Sauce à la Lucullus;* next drain the butter, put the round truffles on the sauce, and keep the other halves to lay over the fillets. Make a kind of coronet with the large fillets, and dish the *blanquette* in the middle, standing nearly upright, by which is meant, that you are to press upon each intermediate one. This *entrée* has a fine appearance when dished properly.

No. 13.—*Croquettes of young Partridges.*

The same process as in No. 29, page 190. (*croquettes* of Chickens.) Only add a little glaze of game to the *béchamelle*. No. 29, page 190.

No. 14.—*Soufflé of young Partridges.*

Take the flesh of roasted partridges, which chop and pound in a mortar, with a few spoonsful of *velouté*, and a lump of butter: season the whole well. Mix with this *purée* the yolks of four or five eggs, and strain the whole through a sieve. Then put it into a basin. Beat well the whites of six eggs, which you mix lightly with the *purée*. Let the whole be put into a dish *à soufflé* and baked in the oven for twenty minutes: take care it does not burn at the top, which may be prevented by covering it with paper.

No. 15.—*Pureé of Game à l'Espagnole.*

This is an *entrée* of *desserte*. Take the fleshy parts of young partridges that have been in a *salmi*, chop and pound them well. Warm the sauce, in which some fried bread is left simmering. Then throw the pounded meat into the sauce. Strain the whole through a tammy. You need not put any seasoning, if the *salmi* is seasoned enough. If you should be asked for *purée* of game, you must make a sauce *à salmi*, the same as below, and put the pounded flesh of young partridges into the sauce. This *purée* is to be sent up in a deep dish, and covered with poached eggs.

This *entrée* is likewise very acceptable in a *casserole au ris*, a *vol au vent*, in *croustades, petits pâtés.*

No. 16.—*Salmi of young Partridges à l'Espagnole.*

Take five young partridges, rather stale, roast them under-done, but let them be covered with paper, for fear they should get brown while roasting; mind, they must be kept as under-done as possible. Then carve the birds as if for eating: by which is meant the wings, legs, and breast; flay them entirely, so as not to leave a particle of skin; trim them nicely, and *mark* them in a clean stew-pan; cover it, and let the whole cool till the sauce is ready. Take four or five shalots, some slips of ham, a carrot cut into dice, three or four mushrooms, a little parsley-root, a bay-leaf, a little thyme, two cloves, eight grains of corn pepper, and as many grains of allspice, fry all these ingredients in a stew-pan with a little butter, and when fried lightly, moisten with three glasses of Madeira wine, six spoonsful of *Espagnole*, and two

spoonsful of *consommé;* then put all the parings of
the birds, namely, the loins and skin, but not the
claws, as they would give a bad taste. Let them
stew for an hour and a half on the corner of the stove;
skim off the fat, put in a small bit of sugar to counter-
act the bitter taste of the lungs, and strain the sauce
through a tammy over the limbs; put the *salmi au
bain marie,* and send up with fried slices of bread
cut into the shape of a kite, or of bellows. If by
chance you are short of *Espagnole,* make a little
roux, and moisten with some gravy of veal, and a
few glasses of wine, Madeira in preference.

The following is a different way of making the
salmi, and which the cooks term *L'Ancienne;* it is
a good method, but does not look so well. Roast
and cut the partridges in the same manner as above,
making the sauce the same, but instead of putting the
trimmings into the sance, put it in the mortar pounded fine, and rubbed through a tammy; moisten with
the sauce, then put this *purée* over the members in
the stew-pan, warm them in the *bain marie* and dress
the *salmi* with *croutons* in the same manner as the
others.

No. 17.— *Young Partridges à la Monglas.*

This is also an *entrée* of *desserte.* Take three
roasted or stewed birds; they must be whole, not
damaged at all; cut out the whole of the breast in a
square piece, so as to form a square aperture: clean
away from the interior all the spongy substance, in
order to put a *salpicon* inside of the breasts of the
birds. The *salpicon** is to be made in the following
manner: cut into very small dice the flesh that you
have taken up; cut likewise small dice of tongue and
of mushrooms: if you have any truffles by you, a few
may be added. Reduce a little *Espagnole,* with

---

* As the meat taken from the body of the bird is not sufficient
to fill it again, if you have not some of the same sort of meat, it
is necessary to use the various articles mentioned, as tongue,
mushrooms, &c. to fill up the body.

which you mix some glaze of game. Put the dice of meat into the sauce, season well, and put the *salpicon* into the aperture. Lay with a paste-brush some yolk of egg all over, and put some crumbs of bread over the eggs, then some butter over that, and crumbs of bread again; use the salamander to give a colouring to the birds. Next keep the whole hot in an oven, and send up with an *Espagnole* of game. By putting a litle glaze of game in the brown sauce, it gives the taste of game.

No. 18.—*Young Partridges en surprise.*

Do as above, but instead of a *salpicon* make a mince of fillets of partridges only, with which stuff the birds. Dip them into eggs and crumbs of bread as above, fry them of a nice colour, and send up with a *suprême* of game. This sauce must be white, as you put some glaze of game into a white *béchamelle*, and use white sauce for the mince.

All dishes that are made with what is left in the larder, are economical; and if they are well managed and well seasoned, are very good, and of good appearance.

No. 19.—*Quenelles of young Partridges au fumet.*

Make the *quenelles* as directed in its proper place, only they are to be made of the meat of young partridges. You may send them up in different ways, *au consommé clair*, or *à l'essence*, or *au fumet*.

No. 20.—*Boudins of young Partridges.*

Make *boudins de quenelles* of young partridges: butter the bottom of a stew pan, lay the *boudins* over the butter, and pour some boiling water over them, with a little salt. When poached, drain them, and lay them to cool: when cold, dip them into an *omelette* and crumbs of bread: next fry them. Drain them well, till not a particle of dripping is left, and send up with a brown *Italienne* under it. If you wish to send them up broiled, you must use yolks of eggs, next crumbs of bread, then butter and crumbs again, before you broil them. But they are better with crumbs of bread.

No. 21.—*Quenelles of Partridges à la Sefton.*

Take the flesh of three very young partridges and make it into *quenelles*, as directed at that article. When the *quenelles* are made, and are quite cold in ice, mould three *boudins* of the size of the dish, and poach them in the usual way. For the sauce, take four spoonsful of *béchamelle*, and mix with it two spoonsful of glaze of game, three spoonsful of double cream, a little salt, and very little Cayenne; work the sauce very fine, and cover the *quenelles* with it. This *entrée* is most delicate, when well dressed.

CHAPTER IX.

RABBITS.

No. 1.—*Fillets of young Rabbits à la Orlie.*

It is to be observed, that warren rabbits only ought to be sent up to a good table, tame rabbits in general having no savour but that of cabbage; and you must be particular in using for table only young rabbits; this you may ascertain, by breaking the jaw between your thumb and finger; if they are old, they resist the pressure: feel also in the joint of the paw for a little nut; if it is gone, the rabbit is old, and not fit for fine cookery; in such case, use them to make rabbit puddings or pies.

Take four rabbits; detach the fillets, and *filets mignons:* cut the large fillets of an equal size: marinade them in lemon-juice, a little parsley, a shalot cut into slices, a little thyme, a bay-leaf, salt, pepper, &c. &c., leave them in that marinade for two hours. Drain, and dip them into the white of an egg that has been well beaten, and then into some flour mixed with a few crumbs of bread. Fry them of a fine brown, and serve under them a *poivrade,* or an *Espagnole* of game; observe particularly, that the fillets must be under-done.

The intelligence of the cook will inform him, that when the rabbits are too small to be filleted, he must make a *marinade* with the members of the rabbits, cut as follows: the shoulders, the legs cut to pieces, with the back, and the head, as many persons like to eat the brains; the small bones of the carcass must be thrown out, except you have broth in preparation, then put these trimmings in it, which will clarify your broth. When the rabbits are small, you must use several. This is an appropriate dish for a shooting party, being the produce of the sport.

No. 2.—*Turban of Fillets of Rabbits à la Sultane.*

Take the fillets of four rabbits; there will be eight; likewise the *filets mignons* and kidneys; lard the eight fillets with very small slips of bacon, all of an equal size. Have a *farce à quenelles* ready made out of the flesh of the legs of the rabbits. It would be requisite to have a kind of paste-cutter, very deep, or a sweetmeat pot to put into the middle of the dish, that you may raise the turban all round it; in this case the fat might be more easily drained, which is always very abundant, if you do not place a mould in the centre of the dish. Take a large piece of stale bread, cover it with a thin layer of bacon, lay it in the middle of the dish, and dress the *farce à quenelles* equally round on it; then with the handle of a wooden spoon *mark* eight ribs, leaving an interval between each, not straight, but rather sloping; put the fillets of rabbits inside each of those ribs; and after having skinned the kidneys, put them into four of the intervals, two by two; in the other four put fillets of truffles. You may give to this dish a superb appearance.

Mind to turn the pointed extremity of the fillets inside of the turban, otherwise they would not stick. Cover the whole with layers of bacon. If you have an earthen pan that may cover the whole hermetically, lay it over, without using the layers of bacon. The steam alone will prevent the fillets from getting dry. When the turban has been kept in the oven long enough to be well-baked, glaze the fillets of a light brown, and put them into the oven again; take the lump of bread out from the middle of the dish, and wipe off all the fat. When going to send up, put a *ragout*, made with *quenelles*, cocks'-combs, and mushrooms, in the middle of the dish, and sauce the outside with a very good *fumet* of rabbit. To make the *fumet* of rabbits, you must use all the rabbit-bones, with a little veal, ham, mushrooms, parsley, and green onions, &c. &c.; and when that *consommé* has been made in the usual way, reduce it, and then put some of the reduction with some *béchamelle*, to sauce the turban or any other *entreé* of rabbits with. Whether the sauce is to be *white* or *brown*, you must always give it the taste of rabbits. To make the turban in a more clean and efficient manner, have some trimmings of paste, which spread of the size of the inside of the dish. Bake it in the oven, and when done, dress the turban upon this paste; when the turban is quite ready to serve up, put it on the dish, which prevents it dirting the dish, and the *entrée* will not be so greasy.

No. 3.—*Mince of Rabbits au fumet.*

This is an *entrée de desserte.* Take the fillets of roasted rabbits, pare the sinews, then make a mince, but hold your knife on a slope, that the thin slices may curl like shavings; put the mince into a reduced *velouté* or *béchamelle*, mixed with some glaze of game; do not forget to pour into the mince a little thick cream, to give it a white colour, and make it mellower. You may put the mince either in a *bordure*, a *vol au vent*, a *casserole au ris*, a *turban*, a *grenade*, a *gratin*, *petty patties*, *petites casserolettes au ris*, &c. &c.

No. 4.—*Scollops of Rabbits aux Truffles, the same à la Conti.*

Take five rabbits; detach the fillets, tear off the sinews, then scollop the fillets, keeping your knife on a slope; flatten them with the handle of your knife; put the scollops into a *sauté*-pan with some melted butter; have ready some truffles peeled and cut into slices of the same size as the scollops will be, mix them with the rabbits in the butter, salt, and pepper. *Sautez* the whole a little while before dinner-time, drain the butter, and put the scollops into the sauce, in order that the truffles may give their flavour to the sauce, and likewise to the meat. Garnish the edges of the dish with a *conti*.* The best and most expeditious manner, is to *mark* the fillets with the truffles in the *sauté*-pan, without previously scolloping them; put some salt as before, and put the *sauté*-pan over a sharp fire about twenty minutes before dinner-time; turn the fillets equally on every side, then take a sheet of clean paper, scollop the fillets very quickly, and putting them again in the *sauté*-pan, let them remain on the fire a few minutes with the truffles; drain the butter in a basin, and put the scollops in the sauce in the *bain marie* to acquire the flavour of the truffles, &c.

No. 5.—*Blanquette of Rabbits with green Peas.*

Take four rabbits; detach the fillets, *sautez* them whole in melted butter with a little salt and pepper; next cut them on a sheet of paper, of the size of a shilling, and put them into the sauce *blanquette aux pois.* (See *Sauces.*) This *entrée* is sent up in a *vol au vent*, a *casserole* with rice, &c. &c.

No. 6.—*Scollops of Rabbits au fumet.*

Take five rabbits; detach the fillets, *sautez* them in melted butter. When done cut them as for a *blanquette*, and put them into a sauce made as follows: make a *consommé* with the remnants of the rabbits; put a few slices of Westmoreland ham in a small stew-

* I call *conti*, some of the *filets* larded with small bacon, or decorated with truffles; they must be done in the following way: Take a *sauté*-pan, and put on the bottom of it some slices of fat bacon, lay your *conti* on the top of them in any shape you think proper, and powder some salt over; put them into a hot oven, and as soon as they are firm, glaze them, and serve them round whatever they may be wanted with.

pan, with some pieces of veal, &c. put the bones of the rabbits over them; then moisten with two spoonsful of first broth. Let the meat sweat thoroughly, till, on thrusting your knife into it, neither scum nor blood issue. Then fill the stew-pan with boiling broth, seasoned with a bunch of parsley, green onions, thyme, bay-leaves, and a few mushrooms. When the *consommé* is done enough, put a small lump of butter into a stew-pan on the fire, and as soon as the butter is melted, throw in a spoonful of flour: let the flour fry a little in the butter, without, however, getting brown. Next moisten with the *consommé*. Let this sauce boil gently on the corner of the stove for an hour. Skim the grease off carefully, then reduce the sauce, and thicken it with the yolks of three eggs well beaten with some cream. Strain this sauce through a tammy over the scollops, and send up quite hot. This *entreé* may be served either with or without *contis*, in a *casserole* with rice, a *vol au vent*, or a *bordure* of mashed potatoes. This sauce being made in the same way as any other sauce for *blanquette*, if you should have any other *entrées* that require white sauces, by keeping a little of this, you will save at once expense and trouble.

No. 7.—*Scollops of Rabbits à la Conti.*

See No. 6. Only keep four fillets, which you divide into eight pieces, cross-ways. Flatten them a little with the handle of your knife; lard them with thin slips of bacon. Then butter a *sauté*-pan. Give the above pieces whatever shape you may think proper, powder a little salt over them, and bake them. Do not let them be too long in the oven; glaze them nicely, and dish them round the scollops. In the country, when you have plenty of rabbits, you should use the fillets for the parlour, and make a pie or pudding for the domestics with the legs and shoulders.

No. 8.—*Young Rabbits en friteau.*

Take several very young rabbits; skin them and cut them in four, according to the size; let them be marinaded as in No. 1, of this Chapter. Drain them and dip them into flour; then fry them till of a light brown. Serve up with a *poivrade,* or a love-apple sauce.

No. 9.—*Rabbits à la Vénitienne.*

Take three or more young rabbits; skin and empty them nicely, then cut them into pieces in the following manner: take up the shoulders, then the head from the neck, divide the back into four parts; take off the legs on each side of the saddle, and cut them into two pieces. Have ready half a pottle of mushrooms chopped very fine, with parsley and shalots the same. Put a small lump of butter into a stew-pan with a little rasped bacon: put the sweet herbs on the fire with a little salt, pepper, and allspice: let them stew for a short time on a slow fire. When sufficiently fried, put in the rabbits, make them get firm with these sweet herbs, till they are sufficiently done. Take the limbs out from the seasoning, lean the stew-pan sideways to skim the fat that comes uppermost, put a spoonful of *sauce tournée,* or if you have none, add to it a small tea-spoonful of flour, moistened with a spoonful or two of *consommé,* let it boil a few minutes, and make a thickening of the yolks of four eggs; put the juice of a lemon and a little Cayenne pepper: stir the sauce well: if it happens to be too thick, make it thinner with a spoonful of broth: keep it quite hot, throw the members into the sauce again, and send up quite hot. This sauce must be rather highly seasoned.

No. 10.—*Rabbits en caisses*

Make cases of paper, either square or round; do the rabbits as above with sweet herbs; when nearly done, put them into the paper cases and the sweet herbs over them, with the rasped crust of a two-penny French loaf, to absorb the fat. Then put the paper cases into an oven. Before you send up, squeeze over it the juice of a lemon, and pour in a few spoonsful of *Espagnole.*

No. 11.—*Giblottes of Rabbits.*

Take two young rabbits to make a *giblotte;* but observe, they must be both alike as to quality; if you put a young one with an old one, the young one will be done to rags, when the other will scarcely be done at all. Skin them, and cut them into pieces as above. Have ready some pieces of breast of bacon cut into the shape of small corks, which are blanched in order that they may not be briny. Fry them in the stew-pan with a little butter, to give them a light brown colour. Take the bacon out of the stew-pan, and put the members of the rabbits into it; when made firm, take them out also; throw a good handful of flour with the butter into the stew-pan, let it get a little brown; next moisten with some gravy of veal. Let the sauce boil a little, to see whether it is not too thick; if so, you will never be able to skim the fat off, and accordingly it will never be of a good colour. When sufficiently stewed, put in the members, bacon, a bunch of parsley and green onions, thyme, bay-leaf, clove, &c. &c; and when the sauce has boiled for an hour, put the members into another clean stew-pan, and drain the sauce through a tammy, then take some turned mushrooms, and some small onions, and fry them white in butter; let them boil for a quarter of an hour in the sauce. When you are going to send up, dish first the members, next the small white onions, and then the bacon and the mushrooms over. Take off the fat and scum, otherwise there can be no good cookery; and cover the whole with the sauce when reduced.

No. 12.—*White Giblottes of Rabbits.*

Do as above, but after having dredged with flour, and moistened with *consommé,* let the whole stew for above an hour. Next take off all the scum and fat: shift the members into another clean stew-pan; reduce the sauce, strain it through a tammy over the members, lay the *giblotte* on the fire, and when it boils, thicken it with the yolks of four eggs, and the juice of a lemon. This sauce, although white, must be highly seasoned. Note, if you want to make the *giblotte* whiter, disgorge the rabbits, and blanch them.

No. 13.—*Fillets of young Rabbits en lorgnettes.*

Take the fillets of four young rabbits that have been skinned; lard them with thin bits of bacon; when larded, make an opening on the thickest part, by thrusting your knife nearly to the very extremity. Then run the knife in, but no farther than the middle; and so on with the rest. Put a little butter into a *sauté*-pan; thrust your finger into the opening, and put into it some carrot or turnip to keep it open; give those parts the shape of a *lorgnette,* or eye-glass; put them for a moment into an oven, that they may take a good form. When firm, *mark* them in a stew-pan, over a bed of minced roots and vegetables, covered with bacon, seasoned with salt, pepper, thyme, bay-leaves, &c. &c. and moisten with two spoonsful of *consommè.* Let the whole stew for a quarter of an hour or twenty minutes; drain the fillets, reduce the liquor, to which add a little glaze of a light colour, and send up with *endives au velouté,* or a *soubise.* (See *Sauces.*) Dish *en miroton,* and pour the sauce in the middle. Mind, this sauce must not be too liquid.

No. 14.—*Hot raised Pie of Rabbits.*

Take one or two rabbits, according to the size of your pie. Skin and empty them; then detach the legs and shoulder, which you cut into halves: from the head to the tail cut out four pieces of an equal size; then chop a shalot, a little parsley, and a few mushrooms, and stew them a little: next put the members into the butter with the sweet herbs till the flesh is quite firm, then season with salt, pepper, and spices. In the course of a few minutes drain the butter. Then raise a *croustade*, (see *Pastry;*) put the limbs into it, and put the whole into the oven. When the crust is baked enough make a round opening, lift up this kind of cover, and just as you are going to send up, pour into the pie a *ragout à la financière* over the rabbits. Be careful to drain the fat that may have remained.

N.B.—The above is the true manner of making a raised pie of rabbits. Many people make a pie-crust which is commonly called *croustade;* and after having emptied it, put in a *giblotte*. The former method, however, is preferable, as it retains better the flavour of rabbit.

No. 15.—*Quenelles of Rabbits.*

This *farce* is made like the generality of *quenelles:* the only difference is, that you take the flesh of rabbits instead of any other meat. The legs, in general, are used for making the *quenelles;* the fillets will supply you with another *entrée;* so will the legs occasionally. The bones and the *parings* are used to make the *consommé* and sauces. As the legs are tougher than the tender fillets, they should be pounded for a longer time, and rubbed through a tammy, on account of the number of nerves and sinews.

No. 16.—*Gratin of Rabbits.*

This is an *entrée* of *desserte;* * take a couple of roasted rabbits; take off the whole of the fleshy parts; then *pare* those that have sinews about them; mince the meat very fine, and put this *mince* into a *béchamelle* reduced; take a little of the liquor, which *gratinez* (by *gratiné* is meant, to boil it in a silver

* *Desserte* is any any thing left from the preceding day.

dish till it sticks at the bottom without burning.)
When the preparation is cold, stick a border of soft
bread all round the inside of the dish, and put your
mince into the middle: level it well with a knife;
then powder crumbs of bread over it, which baste
with butter; and then put crumbs a second time, and
baste with butter again. Then make it brown all
over with a salamander, because if you were to put
the dish into an oven hot enough to give it a colouring, the *gratin* would burn. Keep it hot, and send
it up either with slices of bread fried in butter all
round the dish, cut in the shape of corks, or with
flowrets made of puff-paste.

No. 17.—*Soufflé of Rabbits.*

This is also an *entrée* of *desserte.* Take off the
flesh of roasted rabbits, chop it very fine, and pound
it: pour into it a few spoonsful of *velouté*, season it
well. Break half a dozen of eggs, the whites on
one side, the yolks on the other, throw the beaten
yolks into the *purée*, which put on the fire a little,
that the eggs may stew, but take your stew-pan off
from the fire as soon as you perceive they are done;
then add a small bit of fresh butter, and work the
whole well. Next beat the six whites well, and pour
them also into the above preparation, which you put
into a *soufflé* dish, and then into the oven ten or
twelve minutes before you send up. In case you
should not have a dish *à soufflé*, you must use a
croustade or pie-crust.*

No. 18.—*Croquettes of Rabbits.*

Cut the meat of young roasted rabbits into dice,
which throw into a *béchamelle* reduced, adding a
little glaze of game. Let this cool, then roll it into
whatever shape you please, either into balls, or

---

* By pie-crust, I mean here, the crust of a pie which has been
served up and returned unbroken. It can then serve again for
a *soufflé*.

in the shape of a cork, or of a pear: but, in my opinion, those that are the least handled are the best. Fry them and send up as other *croquettes*, garnished with fried parsley in the middle of the dish. It is necessary to observe respecting *croquettes* or any other thing made use of in cookery, that the less you handle them the better. Put the preparation of the *croquettes* in a flat long dish; equalize with the knife the preparation till you have it of the thickness required: mark with the knife the number of *croquettes* you intend to make. Then take them from off the dish, and roll them in your hand as little as possible, and put them in the crumbs of bread and roll them again in the *omelette,* and make them of equal sizes in a cover of a stew-pan till such time as you wish to fry them.

No. 19.—*Boudins of Rabbits à la Reine.*

Prepare in the same manner as the *croquettes:* roll the meat into large *boudins;* dip them into eggs and crumbs of bread, and fry them. Serve under them a *velouté,* with a little glaze of game. For *croquettes* or *boudins à la reine,* made of fowl, rabbits, or game, if you should have by you some sweetbreads, they will be a great improvement to them, as they make them more mellow and delicate.

No. 20.—*Boudins of Rabbits à la Richelieu.*

Take some *quenelles* of rabbits, and fry some white onions of a light colour. Put them into a hair sieve to drain the butter, and then mix them with the *quenelles:* let them cool, and roll it into two *boudins* of the same length as your dish. Poach them in boiled water with a little salt; when done, drain them on a clean cloth, and let them cool.* Next dip them into an *omelette,* and then in crumbs, and fry them

* You may serve them, when hot, covered with a good *béchamelle:* they have not so good an appearance, but they are better eating.

till they are of a light brown. Send up with an *Italienne* under.

No. 21.—*Legs of Rabbits à la Maintenon.*

Bone the legs of the rabbits. Have ready some sweated herbs, the same as for *Maintenon* cutlets, with a little rasped bacon, salt, pepper, spices, &c. Stew the legs in those herbs till they are done through. Let them cool. When cold, cut slips of paper of the size of the legs; or they may be a little larger. Then take small layers of bacon, lay one on the paper, and the leg over the bacon; then a little seasoning, and another layer of bacon; wrap the whole in the paper, which is to be plaited equally all round with the back of the blade of the knife. Then broil them over a slow fire, and send up hot, with no other sauce but the seasoning of the herbs inside.

No. 22.—*Rissoles of Rabbits.*

Take the remnants of roasted rabbits, with which make a *farce fine*. (See *Farce Fine.*) Spread on the table some puff-paste, but do not let it be too rich; cover it, at equal distances, with little lumps of *farce;* moisten the paste all round the *farce*, then fold it in two; lean upon it all round with your fingers that the paste may stick; then with a rowel cut it and fry it till it is of a fine brown colour. You may occasionally dip them into eggs, and then powder them over with crumbs of bread; they by that means fry of a better colour, but it makes the crust thicker. You must always send them up with fried parsley in the middle of the dish.

No. 23.—*Boudins of Rabbits à la Lucullus.*

Make *boudins* of rabbits with *quenelles* of the same length as the dish; poach them in milk and butter, and a little salt, or boiled water and salt. When done enough, drain them on a clean towel. Cut one side flat, that they may dish well; have a little *bécha-*

melle reduced, and pretty thick, which whiten with a little thick cream. *Mask* the *boudins* with this sauce, but do not use more than is requisite for *masking:* in the middle you are to serve a *ragoût à l'Allemande*, which is the same thing as a *Toulouse*. You must have six fillets larded equally. Take a very large carrot, cover it with thin layers of bacon, and lay the fillets over the carrot with a little salt: let them stand a moment in the oven till they are firm: then glaze and dry them with the salamander: glaze them a second time: then lay a fillet at each end of the *boudin*, and one in the middle. Mind that you keep this *entrée* well covered, for otherwise it would not be of a fine colour; the *béchamelle* would dry up, and consequently it would not preserve its white colour.

No. 24.—*Fillets of Rabbits à la Maréchale.*

Take the fillets of four young rabbits; divide each of them into two pieces in order that they may not be too long: flatten them with the back of your knife, that they may be sooner done; let them be of an equal size; season them with salt and pepper; then brush them over with the yolks of eggs, and dip them into crumbs of bread, next into melted butter, and then again into crumbs of bread, but so as to lay very evenly. Press the fillets between both your hands, in order to melt the butter, and that the crumbs may stick equally all round. Broil them on a brisk fire, always observing that the thinner and the more tender the objects, the more brisk must the fire be; for if it were not so, the fillets would get over-done, without being of a nice brown. Glaze and dish them *en miroton, mask* them with the brown *Italienne*, mixed with a small quantity of glaze of game.

No. 25.—*Fillets of Rabbits à la Pompadour.*

Take the fillets of four young rabbits; cut each fillet into two, lengthways, and keep them as long as possible. Make a *sauce d'attelets* (see *Sauce d'At-*

telets,) put the fillets into the seasoning, after having dusted them over with salt and pepper. Let this preparation cool, without however getting quite cold, yet sufficiently so as to enable you to lay some round the fillets. Next dip the fillets once into crumbs of bread: then break three eggs into an earthen pan with a little salt, beat them, throw in the fillets, dip them again lightly a second time into crumbs of bread, and fry them of a nice colour. Dish them in the shape of a pile, which could not be done if they were not kept crisp. Send up with the *sauce à la Pompadour* in the middle.

No. 26.—*Attereaux of Rabbits à l'Italienne.*

Take the fillets of four young rabbits; cut them into pieces of an inch square; then have some mushrooms, parsley, and shalots, chopped fine; put them to fry gently in a small bit of butter over a slow fire till they are done, then put the bits of rabbits to fry gently in those herbs; and when nearly done, drain them, and season them with a little salt and pepper; take the sweet herbs with which they have been stewed, and make a *sauce d'attelets* in the following manner; put a spoonful of flour to the herbs, and mix it well with a wooden spoon; moisten with a few spoonsful of good *consommé*, let the whole boil till the flour is quite done; skim off the butter; reduce the sauce thick, and then thicken it with the yolks of two eggs; throw into this the square pieces you have prepared; then let them get quite cold; next take some silver skewers, have a few pieces of calf's udder ready done, of half the breadth of the pieces of rabbits, but not so thick; run a skewer first through one of the pieces of rabbit, dipped into the sauce, and next through a piece of the udder, and so on; observing, however, to have a piece of rabbit at each end. Do not stuff the *attelet* too full, for some of it must project at each end. Put plenty of the sauce, and give a square shape to the above preparation; then dip it into crumbs of bread; next, when of a good shape, into an *omelette* well seasoned: and into crumbs of bread a second time; then fry it till of a fine colour, and send up with a brown *Italienne* mixed with a little glaze of rabbit, or the white sharp sauce.

There are many *entrées* of rabbits, which I omit mentioning in this present edition, such as the *bressole, pains* of rabbits, *profitrolles*, &c. &c. which are now quite out of fashion, for fashion prevails in our art as in all others. A veteran cook may still make good dishes, but they will not catch the eye, as the phrase goes. In the common way, many *entrées* may be made with the legs of rabbits; but as many dishes of game are not to be sent up at a time, provided you have fillets, it is better to use the legs for *farces* or petty patties, or *croquettes*, &c. &c.

No. 27.—*Rabbits and Onions.*

As this dish is of the English school, it will not require many observations; but the author would recommend that old rabbits be never used, as they always spoil both the taste and the look.

Take one or two rabbits, skin them and skewer them as for boiling; put them into warm water in order to extract all the blood: when they are very white, boil them in boiling water and a little salt, to prevent them from skimming. An hour is sufficient to boil them if they are young: the sauce as follows: peel a dozen of white onions, cut the tops and the tails off, then cut them into six pieces, put them to boil in boiling water and a little salt; when nearly done, drain them on a sieve, put them into a clean towel, squeeze out the water, then chop them very fine on the table; put them into a stew-pan, with half a quarter of a pound of butter, let them fry to drain the water away: then put half a spoonful of flour, mix well together, and moisten with cream or milk, according to your means; cream is preferable: next let this sauce reduce on a sharp fire, put some salt and pepper to it, and make it rather thick. Drain the rabbits, and cover them with this sauce.

No. 28.—*Rabbit Soup.*

This soup is made almost in the same way as the soup *à la Reine.* Take the fillets of four rabbits to make an *entrée,* and with the legs and shoulders make the soup as follows: put them into warm water to take out the blood; when quite clean, put them into a stew-pan with a bundle of parsley and a ladleful of good broth; put all this to simmer over a slow fire; when done through, moisten with some good broth. Season it of a good taste, and let it boil for an hour only: if you let it boil too long, the soup will be brown: next take the meat out of the broth, drain it, and let it cool, then pick all the meat from the bones, and put it into the mortar, with four yolks of eggs boiled hard, and the crumb of a penny loaf soaked in a little broth; pound all this very fine; rub it through a tammy, moisten with the broth, and when done, add to it a pint of double cream that has boiled; mix altogether, and serve up. Take particular notice, that this soup must be very white; sometimes you give it with vermicelli, sometimes with pearl barley, sometimes with rice; on all occasions, each of these articles must be done separately in broth, and put into the soup afterwards. If you should be with a nobleman who has an abundance of rabbits, you may use also the fillets, as the soup will then be whiter and better.

No. 29.—*Fillets of Rabbits à la Ude.*

Take the fillets of five rabbits, and make some *quenelles* with the legs and inside fillets, seasoned rather high; then split the *fillets* in two, (first cutting one side of the fillet so as to make it wider, and then the other side;) when the fillet is very wide, spread some salt and pepper lightly over it, then put some of the *quenelles* in the aperture; then wrap up the *fillets* together to hide the *quenelles,* have some *sauce d'attelet* the same as the fillets *à la Pompadour,* crumb it in the same manner, and fry it of a very good colour in a frittee, (not too hot,) allowing space enough to the *fillets* and the *quenelles* to be thoroughly done. This is a very good and delicate dish, but requires great care to bring it to perfection; serve under it a very clear *Italienne brune*, well seasoned.

N. B.—Make the fillets as flat as you can, because they are more easy to dress on the dish.

No. 30.—*Rabbit Pie.*

Put into the bottom of a baking dish a few slices of ham, veal, or beef; cut the rabbit into as many bits as you like; season each bit with salt, pepper, pounded spices, &c.; put them in a dish as close as possible; add a glass of broth if you have any, if not, a wine glass of water and a drop of white wine; cover this dish hermetically with a good crust, and bake it in a hot oven for an hour and a half, then use it; whether hot or cold you will find this dish very good. If you would give the crust a good appearance, you must mould one whole egg in a gallipot, and beating it with a brush, dress the paste with it all over.

CHAPTER IX.

I⊤ is proper to observe, that hares are fit to be sent up to a nobleman's table, only when they still show their age. In order to judge of their age, feel the first joint of the fore claw: if you find a small nut, the animal is still young: should this nut have disappeared, turn the claw sideways, and if the joint crack, that is a sign of its being still tender; if not, it is only fit to be made *en daube*, or *en civet:* but if very tough, a *daube* is preferable; yet it is a very insignificant dish, particularly as it requires high seasoning; it is too nourishing to be sent up to the table of any nobleman, or of a real epicure.

No. 1.—*Hare en Daube.*

After having skinned, emptied, and washed off the blood of a hare, cut it through the middle. Have ready layers of bacon well seasoned with chopped parsley, spices, salt, and pepper. Lard the hare as thick as you can; put slices of bacon into the bottom of a stew-pan, cover them with the bits of hare, tie up a large bundle of parsley seasoned with thyme, bay-leaves, sweet basil, a clove, and common spices, a few carrots, four large white onions, two calf's feet, and a few pieces of breast of bacon; season the whole with salt, pepper, &c. and a few roots of parsley. Moisten with a couple of spoonsful of broth, and a pint of white wine; cover the whole with a round of buttered paper, to prevent the hare from getting dry: close it hermetically, and let it stew for three hours as gently as possible: then take it off the fire; drain the hare; skim the liquor, strain it through a silk sieve, and let it cool, that it may be eaten cold, though it may be served hot, with a garnish all round. In this latter case make a *roux* with a little flour and butter; when of a very light colour, moisten it with the liquor in which the hare has been stewed, and let it boil enough for the flour to be done, and then send it up, plain as it is. To make potted hare proceed as above. When the hare is stewed, remove the vegetables and the bones, take all the flesh, as well as the bacon, place it in a mortar and pound it very fine; when you find it becomes smooth, rub it through a sieve, then put this paste in some small pot, and place it in the oven covered with paper; when it becomes very hot, take it out, and let it cool; melt some butter, and pour it over the paste to prevent its drying, and cover it with paper to preserve it. This is a very good thing for breakfast or luncheon.

N. B.—If you wish the jelly to look bright, break a couple of eggs into it, before it is hot; beat it over the fire till it begins boiling, then lay it aside with a cover and a little fire over it; when limpid, drain it through a cloth, and let it cool, to be used occasionally.

No. 2.—*Civet of Hare, served as soup.*

Skin and empty the hare, but take care not to waste the blood. Cut off the two legs, and divide them into two or three pieces; cut the body into equal pieces; be particular in preserving the blood, to be used as follows. Take half a pound of the breast of bacon, cut it into small square pieces about an inch thick, blanch them in water, and put them into the stew-pan, with a small lump of butter; let them fry till they are of a fine brown; take out the bacon, and put the pieces of hare into the stew-pan; stew them in the butter till firm; then take them out and make a *roux*, with a little flour, which must not be kept too long on the fire. Moisten with about a quart of broth, and a pint of red wine; put in the pieces of hare, the bacon, a bunch of parsley, &c. seasoned with pepper, salt, spices, and a few white onions, to give a relish, together with some trimmings of mushrooms. Let the whole boil for an hour, and try whether the pieces of hare are done. Skim the fat off the sauce; then put the members into a clean stew-pan, one after another, as also the bacon; then skim the sauce well, reduce it to a good substance, that it may stick round the hare; and put the sauce over the members through a tammy. You must have ready some white onions fried in butter till they are of a light brown; then stew them in a little *consommé*. Have likewise some mushrooms stewed in butter, and put them with the onions to take off the butter. Now the blood and liver, that have been kept apart, are to be poured in the sauce as a thickening. You must not let the sauce boil, or else the blood would in some measure curdle, and the sauce would not be of the same dark brown colour. *Civet* must appear as black as possible; then put in the onions and mushrooms, and send up highly seasoned. The *consommé* in which you have boiled the onions and the mushrooms, must be reduced, and put with the sauce.

Sometimes you take all the flesh of the worst bits, as the shoulders, the legs, the head, &c. leaving merely the back, cut in four or five pieces, then take out the bones, pound the flesh very fine, and rub it through a tammy moistened with the sauce. In this case, you should pound the onions, mushrooms, &c. and warm the soup in the *bain marie*, leaving in it, the best pieces of the *fillets*. This is a delicious soup.

No. 3.—*Fillets of Hare, with the blood.*

When a hare has been skinned, thrust your knife all along the spine, always taking care to lean towards the bone. Detach with your fingers, the fillet from the neck down to the legs; leave the thick fleshy part to the leg: then introduce your knife, the sharp side towards the tender part of the fillet, and your thumb towards the skin; press with your thumb on the sharp side of the blade of the knife, in order that it may not cut the part which contains the sinews; then pull towards you the fillet, and the sinew will remain attached to the leg. This operation being performed, lay the fillets on the table, and flatten them with the back of your knife; *mark* them in a *sauté*-pan with melted butter, and dust a little salt and pepper over them. At dinner-time *sautez* the fillets, drain the butter, and scollop the fillets; put the fillets into a *sauce de civet*, which you have made with the remnants, as it will require at least a couple of hares to make scollops. Mind you preserve the blood of both in order that the sauce may be black, or of a dark brown. The members may serve for soup. When you wish to make soup, take the parts from which you have cut the *fillets* and make a *civet;* the sauce is to be made by the same process. (See *Civet* above.)

The best and shortest method is to *sauté* the *filets* whole, and scollop them after they are finished; it is better, as it retains the gravy, and is made quicker.

No. 4.—*Fillets of Hare en Chevreuil.*

Take the fillets of three hares, according to the size of your dish, detach the fillets, and lard them with bacon cut very equally, then put them into a deep vessel, with salt and pepper, a little parsley, two onions cut into slices, a bay-leaf, a little thyme, a glass of vinegar, and half a glass of water. Let all this be *marinaded* for a couple of days, and then drain the fillets, and *mark* them in a *sauté* pan, with a little butter: bake them under-done, and glaze them with a light glaze, as they are always dark enough. Send them up with a *poivrade* under.

You should observe what has already been noticed, that *larded* is not the proper word, *piqué* is the term, as larded is when you lard the meat quite through, but *piqué* is what is seen every day at the poulterers.

No. 5.—*Pain of Hares, Boudins of Hares, roasted Hares.*

The author will merely remark, that *boudins*, *quenelles*, minces, &c. can be made of hares, although in England it is more customary to serve them roasted. They are, however, very good, when dressed as *entrées*. Hares for roasting ought always to be tender. After being skinned, make a stuffing in the following manner; take a good handful of crumbs of bread, with the same quantity of beef-suet well chopped, a little chopped parsley, a little thyme, salt, pepper, two eggs, a little butter, a little milk, and a shalot; mix up these well into an oval shape, with which stuff the belly of the hare, and sew it up. Stick the fore legs under the belly, and double the hind-legs under the belly also, then skewer them well, the head stands erect as if the hare was running; skin the ears. If it is an old hare, it will be good for nothing; if young, three-quarters of an hour will do it. Serve it up with gravy, and some currant jelly in a sauce-boat; mind that you stop the spit with the belly towards the fire, or else the stuffing will not be done. Some persons like a *poivrade* under it. (See *Brown Sharp Sauce.*)

No. 6.—*Hare Soup.*

Take two hares, young ones are the best; skin them, and wash the inside well, separate the limbs, legs, shoulders, &c, and put them into a stew-pan with two or three glasses of port wine, two onions stuck with four cloves, a bundle of parsley, a bay leaf, a couple of sprigs of thyme, ditto of sweet basil, marjoram, and a few blades of mace: put the whole over a slow fire on the stove. When it has simmered for an hour, moisten with some very good boiling broth, till the meat is entirely covered with it; then let the whole simmer gently till the meat is quite done. Strain the meat, put the broth through a hair sieve: put the crumb of a two-penny loaf to soak in the broth. Take all the flesh of the hare from the bones, and pound it in a mortar till fine enough to be rubbed through a sieve, moisten with the broth, and season according to your palate. You must not make the soup too thick: and be particularly careful, when you have occasion to warm it up again, not to let it boil, as boiling spoils it.

Observe, whenever you wish to make hare soup in perfection, you should preserve all the blood in a basin; when you are ready to serve up, keep the soup very hot, and pour the blood to it till it is thickened. Take care that the soup does not curdle. This addition will make the soup black. Do the same with the scollops, &c.

No. 7.—*Another way of making Hare Soup.*

On another occasion, you may select some of the best pieces, as the rump, shoulders, &c.; as soon as they are done enough, take out what you intend to put whole into the soup, and put it into a stew-pan with some of the liquor, to prevent it from drying and getting black. When your soup is quite ready, and you are going to serve up, put the reserved members into the tureen, and pour the soup over. See another method, No. 2.

Entrées of red-legged Partridges, or Bartavelle's.

This sort of partridge is very scarce in England; when you meet with them, cook them in the same manner as the other partridges.

Quails and Cailleteaux.

The *cailleteaux* are young quails, but owing to their enormous price in England they are very seldom, if ever, to be procured at the poulterers. An *entrée* of fillets of young quails, beside its costing too dear, is never attempted; the expense would be extravagant, without any other merit.

Quails in my opinion have no flavour, and from the circumstance of confinement and bad feeding are never very fat; it is only their rarity that makes them fashionable.

No. 1.—*Compotte of Quails.*

Take six or eight quails, according to the size of your dish. Cut the claws off, empty the birds, without making too large an opening. Truss them *en poule*, that is to say with the legs inward. Have a dozen pieces of bacon cut into the shape of corks, blanch them in order to draw the salt out: then let them fry in butter till they are of a light brown; next take them out of the stew-pan to make room for the quails, which stew till they begin to be of a light brown also, and then take them out. Make a *roux*, which moisten with a ladleful of gravy of veal; add a bunch of parsley and green onions, some small white onions (if approved of), mushrooms, &c. As soon as the quails are done, take them out of the stew-pan, and let the bacon stew till thoroughly done. Skim the sauce well, and strain it through a tammy over the quails: then dish the bacon, mushrooms, and small onions, and send up quite hot and well seasoned. This dish will not do for an English dinner.

No. 2.—*Compotte of Quails, white.*

This is made in the same manner as the *compotte* of partridges, with the only difference that you use broth instead of gravy of veal; thicken the sauce with yolks of eggs, and serve the onions white, the same as the mushrooms, &c.

No. 3.—*Quails with Peas.*

Empty, singe, and truss six nice quails; put them into a stew-pan wrapped up in layers of bacon: moisten with a *poële*, if you have any; if not, with two spoonsful of broth, a bunch of parsley, seasoned with bay-leaves, thyme, a clove, &c. Stew them for twenty minutes over a very slow fire. Drain them well, and let them boil for a moment with the peas and bacon. (See *Sauces, Green Peas, brown, or white.*) Next dish them, and reduce the peas, which, the quails having been boiled in it, would be too thin to *mask* with.

No. 4.—*Quails au Gratin.*

Bone six quails, pick them nicely: take a little *farce fine* or *quenelle*, made in preference with the flesh of young rabbits; fill the bodies of the quails with the said *farce:* then raise a kind of dome on a dish, and with a spoon make room for the birds: next make an opening in the middle; let it be either round or square, according to the shape of the dish. Put a sweetmeat pot within the opening; cover the birds with layers of bacon, and put the dish into the oven for about a quarter of an hour, or twenty minutes at most, till the birds are done. Drain the fat carefully, take out the pot; then take six slices of bread cut into the shape of cocks'-combs, which you fry in butter till they are of a light brown, and put them one by one between the birds. Serve a *ragoût à la financière* in the middle, and *mask** the birds and the *gratin* with a good *Espagnole* well reduced.

No. 5.—*Quails à la Bourguignotte.*

Mark the quails as directed No. 3: when done, drain them well, and let them boil for a couple of minutes in the *bourguignotte* (see *Sauces*); leave them in the sauce during an hour, when the stew-pan

---

* *Mask*, signifies cover with the sauce.

is to be put *au bain marie*, that the birds may taste of the sauce and truffles.

No. 6.—*Quails à la Crapaudine.*

These are dressed and cooked in the same manner as pigeons, or partridges *à la crapaudine*. Serve them up with an *Italienne*, or a *consommé à glace* over them.

Woodcocks and Snipes.

Woodcocks, the same as snipes, are good only when they are fat. They are cooked but in very few ways. The most delicate parts are the legs and the intestines. The fillets of woodcocks, for those persons who do not like their meat under-done, are tough and without savour. They are held in high estimation when roasted, or *en salmi*. A *pureé* of woodcocks is also served occasionally. They may, however, be dressed in as many ways as young partridges. When roasted, you must always put a toast under them, to receive the intestines, which generally drop out while roasting, unless paper is used to secure them. Take care to stop the spit when the back is towards the fire, because the legs are to be well done, and the fillets under-done.

No. 1.—*Salmi of Woodcocks.*

The same operation is required as for the *salmi* of partridges. Instead of boiling the trimmings in the sauce, take out the members, as you do in the *salmi* of partridges, and pound the remainder and trimmings in a mortar, till you can strain it through a tammy. When you have skimmed the fat from the sauce, and given a good seasoning, moisten the pounded meat with it; then strain it through a tammy, and put it over the legs in a *bain marie*. The *salmi* must be made hot, but without boiling. Serve up with it slices of fried bread cut into hearts and glazed.

No. 2.—*Salmi of Woodcocks à l'Espagnole.*

If you have any roasted woodcocks left, cut them as for eating; *mark* the members in a stew-pan; make a sauce as for *salmi* of partridges: put the *parings* into the sauce to boil for an hour: when the sauce has been well skimmed and there is no fat left, strain it through a tammy over the members. Let it be made hot without boiling, and serve up with slices of fried bread between the members. This *salmi* will be good only if the birds are not too much done; when game is over-done, it is of no value as good cookery; this *salmi*, when returned from the table, makes excellent *hachis à la turc*, or *purée* of game. When dinner comes down, remove the sauce and put the members in a plate; the next day place all the flesh in a mortar, and when well pounded, mix with it the same sauce; add to it a little *Espagnole*, or *consommé;* rub this through a tammy, and warm it at dinner time in the *bain marie*, and serve in a *vol au vent*, a *casserolle au ris*, or *patés.*

No. 3.—*Croustade of Purée of Woodcocks.*

If you have any *salmi* of woodcocks left, drain all the sauce, mince the flesh well, and pound it in a mortar; then moisten it with the sauce, and warm it, to know whether the *purée* is too thin or too thick: then strain it through a tammy, and put it *au bain marie;* then work it with a small lump of very fresh butter. Cut eight slices of bread into hearts all of an equal size: try them on the dish, to see whether they form a regular flower; then cut another slice quite round to put in the middle over the points of the hearts: this completed, make a deep incision all round the upper part, without, however, its being cut through; then fry them in clarified butter till of a light brown: as soon as they are fried, cut the middle out, to leave as little crumb as possible. Keep them hot, well wrapped up in a clean sheet of paper. When ready to serve up, work the *purée*, and pour it into the *croustade.*

You may send up this *purée* in a *bord de plat* with poached eggs, or in a *vol au vent*, &c.

No 4.—*Salmi of Woodcocks à la Lucullus.*

For this dish, you must be particular in having the woodcocks very under-done; then take out the intestines, and with the addition of two or three fat livers of fowls, make the following *farce:*

Take a dozen of mushrooms chopped very fine, a shalot and some parsley, the same; fry these herbs in a small bit of butter; when they are nearly done, put the fat livers, and the intestines of the woodcocks, to fry with them; and when done, put the whole into a mortar, and pound the whole very fine; season with salt and pepper, &c.; then, as three woodcocks give you six fillets, cut six bits of bread of the same shape, fry them of a nice colour; then spread the *farce* equally divided over the six *croustades* of bread; put them into the oven, and when they are of a good colour, serve them between each of the *filets;* as for the sauce, you make it with the trimmings as usual for *salmi;* this, well managed, is a delicious dish. The sauce must be made early, so as to keep the fillets in it to prevent them from drying: then warm them without boiling, for boiling would make the dish good for nothing.

No. 1.—*Plovers.*

Plovers are hardly fit for any thing but roasting. Sometimes, however, they are prepared *à la bourguignotte*, which is indeed the only way of making a *ragoût* of plovers. In this latter case, empty and truss them as neatly as possible: *mark* them in a stewpan with layers of bacon; moisten them with a little *poële* or with broth; when done enough, let them simmer a little in a *bourguignotte*, and serve up hot with a garnish. See *Bourguignotte* in the sauces.

No. 2—*Capilottade of Plovers.*

If you have any roasted plovers left, and are short of an *entrée*, cut them in halves and pare them: flay them, put them into a stew-pan with two spoonsful of *Italienne*, a glass of white wine, a little salt and pepper. Let them simmer for one hour, and dish them with fried slices of bread between. Skim the sauce, squeeze the juice of a lemon, and *mask* the members with the sauce. This dish must be highly seasoned.

Pigeons.

There are pigeons of various sorts; namely, tame pigeons, wild pigeons, and wood pigeons. The former are most in use, although wild pigeons are good either boiled or roasted; but if made *ragoûts* or *fricassées* of, their flesh is too black. Small pigeons *à la gautier* or *squabbs*, are of great service for garnishing, but they make very indifferent *entrées*, as they are seldom well prepared by the poulterer in this country.

No. 1.—*Compotte of Pigeons, brown.*

Take four or six pigeons, according to the size of your dish; after having picked them clean, cut off the sinew below the joint of the leg: empty them without taking out the liver, but feel with your finger if there is any grain left in the paunch. Truss the legs inwards, and make an incision in the back, that they may disgorge. Then put them into a stew-pan with some lukewarm water, to draw out the blood: next *mark* them in layers of bacon, and stew them as you would do chickens. When done, drain them, and send up with a *ragoût a la financière.*

No. 2.—*Compotte of Pigeons à la Paysanne.*

Truss your pigeons as above, and wash them clean in warm water. Cut half a pound of breast of bacon into small slices of about an inch; blanch them first, and then put them into a stew-pan with a small bit of butter; when they are of a nice light brown, take them out to make room for the pigeons, and when they are become firm, take them out also. Throw a good spoonful of flour into the fat that is in the stew-pan, and let it become of a light brown colour; then pour either a little broth or warm water into it to dilute the flour; season with salt, pepper, spices, a bunch of parsley and green onions, a few mushrooms, and some small white onions. Then put the pigeons into this sauce, and let the whole stew gently. Next skim off the grease, put the pigeons into another stew-pan, with all the ingredients to garnish them nicely. Reduce the sauce, and strain it through a tammy over the pigeons; serve up hot: add to it a small bit of *glaze* to give more flavour to this dish.

No. 3.—*Pigeons à la Crapaudine.*

Pick the pigeon, cut off the claws, truss them with the legs inwards, and then with your left hand press on the breast, and scollop one half of the flesh of the breast: turn it down on the table, flatten it well with your knife, dust it over with salt and pepper, break the yolks of two eggs into a plate, brush the pigeons all over with them, then dip them into crumbs of bread, next into melted butter, then into crumbs of bread again, which you level as smooth as possible. Now broil the pigeons on a slow fire, that they may get thoroughly done without being burnt. Ascertain when they are done enough, by thrusting the point of your knife into the fleshy part of the leg. If no blood issues, then they are done enough. Serve under them an *Italienne* or some rich gravy. This being a common *entrée*, I shall explain a method of making a *sauce piquante* in a moment.

Sauce piquante.—Chop a dozen of shalots, which put into a stew-pan with two spoonsful of vinegar;

boil till there is no vinegar left: then put in a little broth, or gravy of roast meat, with raspings of bread, salt, pepper, &c. Let this boil for a short time, pour it over the pigeons, and send up hot; if you put to it a small bit of glaze or portable soup, it will give it a good taste.

No. 4.—*Pigeons au Soleil.*

Truly these are not well named, for they shine but very little indeed. It is an *entrée* of *desserte*, and that is saying enough. If you have any pigeons left, either roasted or otherwise, cut them in two, and put them into a *marinade.* (See No. 39, page 194. *Entrées of Fowl.*) When they have simmered for half an hour in the *marinade*, let them cool, drain them, and put them into a paste for frying. (See page 132.) Fry them of a good colour, and serve up with fried parsley in the middle, if you like, or a *poivrade*, or a *sauce piquante.* (See *Sauces.*)

No. 5.—*Cutlets of Pigeons à la d'Armagnac.*

Take eight pigeons, as you may make one *entrée* with the loins and legs, and another with the *fillets.* Take the flesh off the breasts, and make a *farce* of it, with the same quantity of calf's udder, or calf's suet ready boiled, but somewhat less of the *panada.* Put the whole into a mortar, but observe that with the *panada*, plenty of herbs, shalots, parsley, mushrooms, &c. are required. When the *farce* has been well pounded, use a couple of eggs to give it more substance: then bake a little bit in a tartlet mould, in order to taste whether it is sufficiently seasoned. Spread the whole on a *plafond* well buttered, and very even, about the thickness of a mutton chop; then let it cool. When cold, either with a cutter or with your knife, cut the minced meat into the shape of cutlets, without however detaching it from the *plafond:* this being done, put the *plafond* over something hot, merely to melt the butter. Then take the bones out of the pinions, which scrape well, and stick them into the extremity of the mock *cutlets;* dip them into an *omelette,* and into crumbs of bread, and fry them; but do not let the dripping be too hot, that the cutlets may have sufficient time to be done through without being burnt. Dish the cutlets *en miroton,* with either fried parsley, or *Italienne* in the middle; send a brown *Italienne* separately in a boat.

No. 6.—*Cutlets of Pigeons à la Maréchale.*

Take the fillets of eight pigeons, flatten them with the back of your knife, scrape the bone of the pinion, and stick it into the point of the cutlets: dip the cutlets into melted butter: after having seasoned them with salt and pepper, dip them once only into crumbs of bread, but very even and smooth; broil them till they are of a nice colour, and send them up with rich gravy, or an *Italienne* or the *maréchale* sauce.

No. 7.—*Pigeons à la Toulouse.*

Pick, empty, truss, and singe six young pigeons: *mark* them in a stew-pan trimmed with layers of bacon: moisten with a little *poële;* let them stew for sixteen or twenty minutes. Then drain and dish them; *mask* them with a *ragoût à la Toulouse.* (See *Sauces.*)

No. 8.—*Pigeons à la Financière.*

For this *entrée* you must procure young pigeons *à la gautier* or squabbs: singe them slightly. Melt about half a pound of butter, squeeze the juice of a lemon into the butter, and then let the pigeons be fried lightly over the fire twice or three times only. Then put the pigeons into a stew-pan trimmed with layers of bacon; pour the melted butter and lemon-juice over them, and then cover them well: it is also requisite to pour in a spoonful of *poële,* to prevent their frying. Sweat them for a quarter of an hour over an equal fire, and drain them; dish them nicely, and cover them with a *financière* sauce. Mind to have them well disgorged of all their blood before you put them into the butter.

No. 9.—*Pigeons à l'Aspic clair*.

Take six pigeons *à la gautier*, which cook as those above, No. 8. When done, dish them with large craw-fish between each pigeon, and use the *aspic* for sauce.

No. 10.—*Pigeons cooked in all Manner of Ways*.

As the author does not pretend to make a show of extraordinary knowledge, by introducing a multiplicity of names and of *entrées* which are no longer in fashion, he will only observe, that pigeons in general are rather used for *garnitures* than for *entrées*. In the first case, they are prepared as directed in No. 8. They may be dressed with peas, white or brown, *marinade*, or love-apple sauce, &c. &c. The only science consists in preserving their white colour. The shape is always the same; and with respect to the sauce, every one has his choice and taste.

For the *godard*, or the *chambord*, as also for the generality of great *garnitures*, pigeons *à la gautier* are requisite.

A pigeon pie is a very plain dish, which is left to the management of common female cooks. To make a pigeon pie, put a few thin slices of beef in a dish, and the pigeons over them, well seasoned with salt, pepper, and spices, the yolks of a few eggs within the intervals, and a spoonful of broth; cover the whole with plain paste, or with puff-paste, &c. &c.

Ducks, Wild Ducks, &c.

Ducks are fit to be sent up for *entrées*, only when they begin to be plump; they are good towards November, when they are plump and fat; but those that are sold in London in May, June, or July, are nothing but skin and bone. Ducks, the same as wood-cocks, require the fillets to be under-done; but in that case the legs would be nearly raw, as they require a much longer time to do. Care must therefore be taken to stop the spit when the back is turned towards the fire. The legs and breast, by this means, will be equally done.

No. 1.—*Duck with Turnips.*

After having emptied, trussed, and singed the duck, *mark* it between layers of bacon, and moisten either with a *poële*, or broth, with a little salt. Stew the duck for three-quarters of an hour if it is a young one; if old or tough, it will require an hour: when done, drain it, and let it simmer in turnip sauce to take the taste of turnips. When ducks begin to grow old, by keeping them a few days they become tender; roast the duck of a nice colour. When under-done, cut it in five parts, the two wings, the two legs, and the breast; cut six turnips in the shape of olives, fry them in butter with a little powdered sugar, to give them a good colour; when they have got a good colour, mix a spoonful of flour with them; moisten with half broth and half gravy of veal; season with salt and a little pepper, a bundle of parsley, and green onions; skim; when the turnips are done, put them into a stew-pan separately, and put a very little sauce with them. In the remainder of the sauce boil the duck till well done; then skim off the fat, reduce the sauce, and serve all together.

No. 2.—*Duck with small Green Peas.*

Prepare and cook the duck as above. When done, lay it with the green peas. When the duck is too large, it is not to be served whole, but cut into four or five pieces; namely, the breast, the two wings, which otherwise are called fillets, the two legs, and the back. Pare all the members properly, and make the sauce in the following way: take two quarts of very fine fresh green peas, put them into a pan with

clean water, and half a quarter of a pound of fresh
butter; mix the butter up with the peas, drain the peas
by taking them out of the water with your hand,
otherwise all the dirt would go into the cullender;
let them dry; next put into a stew-pan half a pound
of the best part of a breast of bacon, cut in squares of
an inch, and a very small bit of fresh butter; fry the
bacon of a nice colour, then drain the fat, and put in
the peas to sweat gently. When they are all very
green, put half a spoonful of flour, and moisten with
boiling water. Add the members of the duck, with
some salt, and a little pepper, a very small bit of sugar,
and a bundle of parsley and green onions. When the
duck is done, serve the members covered with the
peas, and take great care to skim off the fat.

No. 3.—*Duck with the purée of Green Peas.*

Prepare the duck as above, and send it up with a
purée of green peas over it, (see *Purée verte*) or with
a *hochepot*. (See *Hochepot*.)

No. 4.—*Ducklings à la Bigarade.*

This *entrée* requires plump fleshy ducks: pick,
empty, and truss them well, with the legs stuck upwards. First roast them under-done, and make inci-
sions in the breast, what the French call *aiguillettes;*
pour the gravy that issues from the duck into the
sauce, which must be ready made, in order that you
may send up quickly; a thing to be particularly attended to. With respect to the appropriate sauce, see
Sauces. If you are allowed to serve up fillets only,
then you must have three ducklings at least. Roast
them under-done; when properly done cut them into
aiguillettes, that is, four out of each duck; put them
into the sauce with the gravy that runs from them,
and send up without loss of time, and quite hot. As
soon as you have put the *aiguillettes* into the sauce,
squeeze a little juice of *bigarade* (bitter orange) over
the whole; keep stirring well, and serve up the fillets
in the sauce. This is a dish for an epicure of the

daintiest palate. Do not think of dishing *en couronne*, to give it a better appearance, but send it up in the sauce, and they who eat it will fare all the better. *Mignonette*, or coarse pepper, is required in this sauce, and the *entrée* altogether must be highly seasoned. Before roasting the duck, blanch a handful of sage with a couple of onions cut into quarters; chop them; season them with a little salt and pepper, and stuff the duck; by so doing, it will acquire additional savour.

No. 5.—*Salmi of Wild Duck.*

If you roast a duck on purpose, let it be under-done. Pare it whilst hot, and let the parings simmer in the sauce. Then stain the sauce through a tammy over the members, and let them be made hot without boiling. The sauce is made in the same manner as that of the *salmi* of partridges, or as follows: cut four shalots into several pieces, a small bit of ham, a few bits of carrot, some parsley roots, thyme, bay-leaf, three cloves, a few blades of mace, five allspice, and a small bit of butter; fry all this in a stew-pan till the ham has acquired a little colour, then put a little flour to it, fry it a little more to do the flour, moisten with a glass of wine, either red or white, a ladleful of good veal gravy, and salt and pepper; put all the trimmings of the duck to boil with this sauce; skim off all the fat, reduce the sauce, and put it over the members through a tammy to warm them only; when you send up, squeeze the juice of a lemon over. This *entrée* must be highly seasoned; add a little Cayenne, and do not let the members boil.

No. 6.—*Members of Duck, with the purée of Lentilles.*

Poële the members as directed in No. 1. Drain them, and *mask* them with the *purée* of *lentilles*. (See *Purée* of *Lentilles*.)

No. 7.—*Duck with Olives.*

This *entrée* is admired only by the Italians. *Poële* the ducks as directed in No. 1. Pour over them the *sauce aux olives*, which in my opinion is no great treat. Take a bottle of French or Italian olives, cut the kernel out, but mind to preserve the shape of the olive; blanch them in boiling water to take off the salt: if they are not too briny, put them into a very good *Espagnole* sauce, with the juice of a lemon, and a little Cayenne. Serve this sauce with duck only.

No. 8.—*Capilottade of Duck.*

If you have any roasted ducks left, and are called upon for one *entrée* more, cut the ducks as for eating, flay them, and let them simmer in a thin *Italienne*. Fry a few slices of bread, cut into the shape of a kite, and send up with the juice of a lemon.

If you should not have any *Italienne* ready, mince a few shalots, boil them in vinegar, make a litte browning (*roux*,) which you moisten with broth or even water, and mix a little glaze, seasoned with salt and pepper: put the shalots into the sauce; let it boil a few minutes; then put the duck into the sauce to heat, but without boiling, and give it a high seasoning. Such common dishes are always to be highly seasoned.

A general Observation relative to Cookery.—Any thing which has been roasted before, if boiled, will become tough: do not therefore allow it to boil, if you would have it tender, except in the case of a common *hachi*, which the longer it boils, the better.

Larks.

No. 1.—*Larks au gratin.*

Take eighteen larks, as fat as possible; pick and bone them; next, season them with salt and pepper, and stuff them with a *farce fine* or a *farce à quenelles;* the former, however, is preferable. Dish them nicely, and put some of the *farce* into the dish. Put slices of fried bread cut whimsically between the

birds, so ⬠ or so 〰. When the larks are

put all round the dish, if there are any left put them into the middle: but these latter are to be raised higher than the rest. Cover the whole with layers of bacon, and leave it in the oven for twenty minutes. Then take off the bacon, drain the fat, and serve up with an *Espagnole* of a nice colour, and well-seasoned.

No. 2.—*Caisses of Larks.*

Bone the larks as above; and stuff them with *farce fine.* Have ready small paper cases dipped into warm oil. Give the larks a round shape, put into the cases some of the *farce*, and put the larks over. Next put them on a *plafond* with some buttered paper over them, for fear they should dry while baking. When baked enough, dish them. If there is room enough, pour into the cases a little *Espagnole* and lemon-juice; mind to drain all the fat out before you put in the sauce.

No. 3.—*Hot raised Pies of Larks.*

Bone the larks as above: dress the pie crust, put the *farce* in the bottom and the birds over the *farce:* then fill the crust with *farce*, close the pie, but leave a little hole at the top, to prevent the crust from breaking. Let it be made of a light brown colour. When done, take it out of the oven, take off likewise the top crust, or cover, drain the fat, then pour a *ragoût à la financière* into the pie. Do not put the top crust on again: send up hot with high seasoning: which brown *entrées* require more than white ones.

No. 4.—*Larks en Croustade.*

This dish would find few admirers, as birds in *croustade*, and even hot-raised pies, are very seldom called for. The nobility of this country like to see what they are eating; they fear to meet with something they do not like in a hot raised pie, which they accordingly seldom touch. The reason of it is obvious, and justifies their aversion: the aforesaid hot pies being generally economical *entrées*, made of legs or such other parts of either fowl or game. People in general never taste any part but the fillets. Larks in *croustade* must be done beforehand. Put the birds into *croustades* fried of a light brown, the inside part of which you take out with a cutter: into the vacuity put first a little *farce*, and the lark over it. Keep the birds hot till you serve up.

Pheasants.

It is no easy matter to meet with a pheasant possessing that exquisite taste which is acquired only by long keeping. The damp of the climate prevents their being kept so long as they are in other countries. The hens in general are more delicate. The cocks show their age by their spurs. They are only fit to be eaten when the blood runs from the bill, which is commonly six days or a week after they have been killed. You may then either roast, or make *entrées* of them. The flesh of a pheasant is white, tender, and has a good savour if you keep it long enough; if not, it has no more savour than a common fowl, or a hen.

No. 1.—*Salmi of Pheasants à l'Espagnole.*

These articles in general, which after having been roasted, are to be put into a sauce, require to be under-done, and especially pheasants. After having trussed them nicely, spit them. They will be done in half an hour's time. If small, take the bird from the fire at the expiration of that time. When cold, flay and cut it, as for eating, and put the parings into the *sauce à salmi*. If you have two pheasants, you must not use the legs, but to give flavour; as the breast of a pheasant is generally very fleshy, cut each side in three pieces, and pare them of a nice shape, cut likewise some slices of bread of the same shape and size, and fry them of a nice brown; put the flesh into a stew-pan covered, to prevent it from drying, and keep the trimmings to put into the sauce as follows: cut four shalots, a small bit of lean ham, some parsley-roots, a small bit of carrot cut into dice, some thyme, bay-leaf, six cloves, mace, ten grains of allspice, a small bit of butter; fry all this in a stew-pan till the ham has a good colour; if you have no brown sauce, put a spoonful of flour; moisten with two glasses of Madeira and a ladleful of gravy of veal; season with salt and pepper; put the trimmings to boil with this, and skim off all the fat; if it should taste a little bitter, correct with a very small bit of sugar. Keep this sauce thick enough to cover the meat: put it over the flesh through a tammy, and let it warm, but it must not boil. This dish, when well made, is most excellent: if you like to make it with truffles, put the trimmings of them to boil with the sauce: have some truffles cut of the size of a nutmeg, and put them separately to boil in clean sauce; when done, put the sauce of the truffles with the other, and put the truffles in the middle of the dish, when you send the dinner up.

No. 2.—*Croquettes of Pheasant.*

The operation is the same as for all other *croquettes* of fowl, or game; it is only to be observed, that *croquettes* of game must be stronger (i. e. higher in flavour) than those of poultry. You must not forget to mix a little glaze of game, which makes the only difference. Serve up, garnished with fried parsley.

No. 3.—*Hachi of Pheasant à la Polonoise.*

Use the same method as for *hachis* of poultry, or of game. Garnish with poached eggs, but remember to put into it some of the glaze of game.

No. 4.—*Soufflé of Pheasant.*

See No. 14, page 209, *Soufflés* of Partridges. In general all *entrées* that are made of partridges, may likewise be made of pheasants; such as *aux choux, à la Monglas, à la Barbarie,* otherwise *en petit deuil, à la Givry, à la Crême,* &c. &c.

No. 5.—*Cutlet of Pheasant au Fumet.*

Take the *fillets* of three young pheasants, and keep all the small bones to stick on the point of each cutlet. Prepare six cutlets with each pheasant, two with large *fillets*, and one with the *fillets mignons.* Flatten and trim them of a good shape, and crumb them as above-directed; broil them, and serve under *Italienne brune,* or brown *fumet* of game.

No. 6.—*Escallopes of Fillets of Pheasant with Truffles.*

Take the *fillets* of two very young, but well kept pheasants, do not use them when fresh killed, as they have no *fumet* you may as well cook an old fowl; then put those fillets in a *sauté*-pan with some melted butter, and put with them some truffles cut in slices of the shape of a penny, of very moderate thickness; spread some salt over lighty, and cover with a round of paper till dinner time; when ready to serve up, put the *sauté*-pan on the fire, and do the fillets equally on both sides. Then have a sheet of clean paper on the table, scollop the fillets of equal shapes, and let the *truffles* fry alone a little longer; then put the scolloped fillets once more together, and give them a little turn over the fire; put the *sauté*-pan on one side, to drain the butter; with a hollow spoon take the meat and truffles, and put them in a *béchamelle,* after mixing some of the essence of game and truffles. If you prepare this one hour before dinner, the taste will be admirable:—sooner, the flesh will turn red.

CHAPTER XIII.

CARP.

No. 1.—*Broiled Carp with Caper Sauce.*

You must never use fresh-water fish unless it is alive, and you kill it yourself. When you have given a few strokes on the carp's head with a large knife, thrust your knife under the scales, beginning at the tail, and proceed to cut right and left. All the scales on one side must come off at once, in a piece. Then do the same on the other side, and about the belly. When the scales have been taken off properly, and none are left, the carp must be white; then take off the gills, without damaging the tongue, which is one of the most delicate parts of the carp. Make a small incision in the neck, as if you were going to cut off the head; make another in the belly, but in a contrary direction, and as small as possible. Then with your fore-finger draw out the roe, intestines, and guts. Wash the carp well, till there is no blood left, and wipe it well; slit both sides of the back, and let it *marinade* in a little oil, salt, and pepper, for about an hour, or a little more. Now lay it on the gridiron over a very slow fire, that it may have time to be well done through. When broiled on both sides, serve it with caper sauce, into which you put a spoonful of essence of anchovies. If the carp has a soft roe, put it again into the body with a little chopped parsley, mixed with a small lump of fresh butter, salt and pepper; then sew the belly up, for fear the contents should drop out, and broil all together. When the carp is done, cut off the thread, and *mask** the fish with the sauce.

Sauce *au carp* for fish is made as follows: put in a saucepan or stew-pan, about a quarter of a pound of very fresh butter, a large tea-spoonful of flour, a little salt, a little nutmeg, very little pepper, a tea-spoonful of white vinegar, a little water sufficient to thicken the sauce, a small bit of *glaze*, and then put this on the fire, and stir it till the sauce becomes very smooth; taste it, and add to it a spoonful of fine capers without any of the vinegar.

No. 2.—*Carp Farcie, baked.*

After having cleansed and prepared a carp as above, take up one-half of it, and with the flesh make a *farce* (see *Farce de Carpe*,) with which you cover the other half, after having taken out the bones. Give it a pleasing shape. Then, with a very small spoon, figure scales over it, and put it into the oven on a baking-pan. Take care it does not get too dry. When it is of a fine brown colour, cover it, and ascertain if it is done, by running your knife between the *farce* and the fish. Send it up to table with anchovy sauce, or *sauce hachée.*

No. 3.—*Carp au bleu, and au Court-bouillon.*

Take a very fine carp, cut off the gills, but keep the tongue. Then make as small an opening as possible to empty it, and wash it well, till no blood is left. Then boil some vinegar, and when boiling hot, pour it over the fish, that the scales may crisp. Next wrap the carp up in a cloth, and stew it in a *court-bouillon*. When done drain it, and serve it with anchovy sauce and capers.

---

* *Mask*, means to cover it with the sauce.

Court-bouillon.*

Take three carrots, four onions, six shalots, and two roots of parsley, which pick and wash. Mince them. Put a small lump of butter into a stew-pan, with the above roots, and fry them till they begin to get brown. Moisten next with two bottles of red wine, a bottle of water, a handful of salt, some whole pepper-corns, and a bunch of parsley and green onions, seasoned with thyme, bay-leaves, sweet basil, cloves, &c. Let the whole stew for an hour, and then strain it through a sieve, to use as occasion may require. If you should have no wine, put in some vinegar. The *court-bouillon* is better after having served several times than on the first day. It is a famous thing for stewing crawfish.

No. 4.—*Carp á la Chambord.*

Take a very large carp, scale and empty it, as directed in No. 1. Have the soft roes of other small carp, which put into the body of the large one, after you have seasoned them with chopped parsley, salt, pepper, and spices. Sew up the belly of the carp, and lard two squares on the back with very small pieces of bacon, and cover the parts that are not larded with bacon. Next lay the carp in a fish-pan, with two ladles of *court-bouillon*, and put it into the oven, but mind it must be basted frequently with the *marinade*. When it is done, drain it, but take care you do not break it. Glaze the parts that are larded, and dish it with *la chambord* and its garnish.

The *chambord* is a dish very seldom served in this country, as the English nobility prefer sea-fish to any fresh-water fish, except the perch. The *chambord* is the same sauce as the *financière;* you have only to reduce a little of the *marinade* in which you have done the fish, whether carp, or jack, &c. and put into

---

* This is a very good thing in a Roman Catholic family during Lent. It is always good, only add a glass of wine to it every time you use it. Use it for *marinade*, &c. &c.

it some essence of anchovies, Cayenne, and lemon juice. All sorts of garnish are required: lambs' sweetbread, cocks'-combs, mushrooms, truffles, *quenelles*, small pigeons called squabbs, &c.

No. 5.—*Matelotte of Carp à la Royale.*

Take several carp, which cleanse as directed in No. 1. Cut them into thick slices; first cut off the head, but never forget to take out the stone which is at the top of the spine, exactly about the neck, for it has a most nauseous bitter taste. Next cut the remainder into three equal parts, and wash them well, then lay them on a clean towel to drain, after which put them into a stew pan just large enough to contain the quantity of fish you wish to cook. As you are to boil the fish with wine only, if you were to take too large a vessel, it would require too much wine, which would be wasted. Sprinkle a little salt over the fish. Pour only as much wine as is requisite just to cover the carp, and let it stew over a large fire. As soon as the wine boils, if it is good, or unadulterated, it will catch fire. Red wine of course is used. Then take your pan from off the fire, and leave it on the corner of the stove, and make a sauce in the following manner:

Put a quarter of a pound of butter into a stew-pan, and make a *roux* by mixing a little flour. When the *roux* begins to get brown, put in two large onions cut in quarters, and let them fry till they are entirely melted. Then moisten with some of the wine in which the fish has been stewing; add a large bunch of parsley and green onions, seasoned with allspice, thyme, bay-leaf, &c. Pick a pint of mushrooms, wash them well, turn the finest and throw them into a little water and lemon-juice to keep them white. The parings are to be used for the improvement of the taste of the sauce, from which skim off all the fat; then strain it through a tammy over the carp, which you must have drained well beforehand. You must have ready some small onions, fried brown in butter, and stewed separately in a little broth; and some mushrooms likewise stewed separately. Then dish the carp with the head in the middle. You must also have some soft roes stewed separately in vinegar, that they may be quite firm; with these garnish the *matelotte*. Next have a dozen of toasts made of rasped crust of bread, a few *quenelles*, and a few crawfish, and dish the *matelotte* rather high in the middle. Let the sauce boil, and put in a good lump of butter kneaded with a little flour, two spoonsful of essence of anchovies, and the juice of a lemon. The sauce must be rather highly seasoned and thick, that it may cover well and adhere to the fish. The small onions and mushrooms are not to be omitted, but put them over the fish.

In general, a *matelotte* must have eels mixed with it: as the carp alone are not so good as the eels, but they are of better digestion; mind that eels require longer cooking than any other fish. *Quenelles* are generally used as the garniture of a *matelotte*.

No. 6.—*Matelotte of Carp à la Marinière.*

After having cleansed the fish as directed No. 1, put it into a vessel that will stand a large brisk fire. Moisten with some red wine according to the quantity of fish: put some small onions fried white in butter into the vessel, with salt, pepper, spices, a bunch of parsley and green onions well seasoned.* Let the whole boil till you see the fish is done. Handle some butter and flour, which you drop in small portions into this sauce in order to thicken it. Have likewise some toasts, which put round your dish in the sauce. Season it well, and serve up quite hot, rather highly seasoned.

---

* A bunch seasoned, is when thyme, bay-leaf, spices, cloves, &c. &c. are added.

No. 7.—*Petits Pâtés of Farce of Carp.*

See *farces* for the flesh, and *pastry* for the paste.
These are only served in Roman Catholic families,
on fast days.

EELS.

No. 1.—*Matelotte of Eels.**

Take one or two live eels; throw them into the fire.
As they are twisting about on all sides, lay hold of
them with a towel in your hand, and skin them from
head to tail. This method is the best, as it is the
means of drawing out all the oil, which is unpalatable. Cut the eels in pieces without ripping the
belly: then run your knife into the hollow part, and
turn it round to take out the entrails. Wash them
well, that no blood may remain. *Mark* the pieces
of eel in the same manner as you do the carp. The
eel is longer in doing, but the process is the same.
It will frequently happen that a *matelotte* is made of
all sorts of fish, such as carp, tench, pike, and eels.
The carp is sooner done than any of the other mentioned fish; but they are, notwithstanding, always
cooked together, when they can be procured.

No. 2.—*Tronçons of Eels broiled à la Tartare.*

Skin the eels as above, cut the *tronçons* or pieces
about four inches long, make a *court-bouillon* or
marinade. Stew the eels in this *marinade*, and

---

* The Author has been accused of cruelty, in recommending
the burning alive of eels. He could not be supposed to advocate
a practice which he owns savours of unnecessary torture; but as
this work is devoted to the explanation of the refinements of
cookery, he has introduced this method amongst the rest, leaving it to be adopted or not, as may be seen fit by the practitioner. Undoubtedly, the blue skin and oil which remain when the
eel has been skinned in the ordinary way, renders it highly in-
digestible.

when they are done let them cool, then brush them over with yolks of eggs mixed with a little salt, and dip them into crumbs of bread, then into clarified butter, and strew over them crumbs of bread again. Boil them of a fine colour, or bake them, and serve them up with a *remoulade sauce.*

Observe, that eels contract very much when done; you should therefore cut the *tronçons* long enough to be about three inches after being done; take care to have the bone out on both sides before you add the crumbs of bread.

Remoulade Sauce.—Put into a mortar, a spoonful of very fine chopped shalots, the yolks of two boiled eggs, a spoonful of mustard, salt, pepper and a little Cayenne, pound the whole well, then put gently one or two spoonsful of fine Lucca oil and a little vinegar: rub this sauce through a tammy, and put the yolk of a raw egg, to prevent its turning oily: if you wish the sauce to be green, put a *verd d'Epinard* into it, and some scented vinegar, as Tarragon, or elder, &c. &c.; if you have any *béchamelle,* you may add a spoonful.

No. 3.—*Tronçons of Eels à la Poulette.*

There are some people who cook eels *à la poulette,* in the same manner as a *fricassée* of chickens; it is better, however, to stew them in a *marinade,* and then to make the sauce *à la poulette* separately, by taking some *sauce tournée,* which you reduce till it can take a thickening   Mix it with parsley chopped very fine, and small onions, if approved of; but then they are to be done separately, and stewed in a little broth and salt.   Drain them, and put them into the sauce after having thickened it.   Let it be seasoned pretty highly with salt, pepper, and the juice of a lemon.   Let the eels continue in the sauce for ten minutes before you send the dinner up to table.   If you should have no *sauce tournée,* make a little white *roux,* (see *Sauces*), moisten with either water or broth, to which add a bunch of parsley and green onions, pepper, salt, a small white onion, a few mush-rooms, and a little glaze. When your sauce has been boiling for half an hour, that the flour may be well done, take out the parsley and onions, skim the sauce, mix a little chopped parsley and the juice of a lemon with the thickening, and serve up hot over the eels.

No. 4.—*Eels baked.*

Prepare the eels as above, but open the belly in order to draw out the intestines and blood. Roll it round, put a stuffing into it, and fasten it with a skewer. Then bake it in a *marinade*, or a little *court-bouillon.* When it is of a brown colour, glaze it, and serve under it an *Italienne*, with which you mix half a quarter of a pound of butter. Add to it a spoonful of essence of anchovies.

No. 5.—*Tronçons of Eels larded and glazed.*

This *entrée* never looks well, as the *tronçons* will not stand upright. Strip the eels, however, as above, cut the *tronçons* of an equal size, and lard them. Next *mark* them in a stew-pan rubbed round with butter. Have ready a *marinade*, and moisten with a few spoonsful only. When the eel is done, contrive that the *tronçons* shall not be crooked, and glaze them of a fine brown. Send them up with caper sauce, to which you have added a spoonful of essence of anchovies.

PIKE.

No. 1.—*Pike à la Polonoise.*

See No. 24, page 94.

No. 2.—*Pike with Genévoise Sauce.*

After having merely emptied and washed the pike, without scaling it, *mark* a *marinade* with carrots, onions, parsley roots, thyme, bay-leaves, sweet basil, cloves, and a few stalks of parsley. Stew all these in a little butter over a slow fire. When the roots are become tender, moisten them with Madeira wine, and let the *marinade* stew on. When it is done enough, strain it through a sieve over the pike, which you have taken care to lay in the narrowest vessel you can procure, so as to use no more wine than is requisite for the sauce. Mind not to put much salt, as the moistening is used for the sauce. When the pike is done, drain it immediately, that you may scrape off all the scales on both sides. Then put it back into the vessel where it was boiled, and pour in a little of the liquor to keep it warm, and to prevent its getting dry. Make a *roux*, but not too high in colour, which *en maigre* you must moisten with wine alone; but *en gras* you add two good spoonsful of gravy of veal, with some parings of mushrooms, and a bunch of parsley and green onions. Let these stew till the sauce no longer smells of flour. Then strain it through a tammy, and add a good lump of butter kneaded with flour, a spoonful of essence of anchovies, and the juice of a lemon.

N. B.—You must use white wine in preference to red; it will then differ, besides, from a *matelotte*.

No. 3.—*Pike with Dutch Sauce.*

Scale the pike and take off the gills, without opening the belly. You must empty it at the head. Make a *farce*, with two handfuls of crumbs of bread, and the same quantity of beef-suet (*en maigre* you use butter instead of suet), the yolks of two eggs, or two whole eggs, a little milk, a large quantity of chopped parsley, a little thyme, salt, and pepper, and shalots chopped very fine, if approved of. Mix this very fine, and put the whole into the belly of the pike. Then trim a *plafond* or baking-dish, with layers of bacon, that the pike may not burn and stick to it. Fasten the fish's tail in its mouth with a little skewer. Break a few eggs into an earthen pan, with a little pepper and salt. Brush the pike all over with the beaten eggs, and powder it over with crumbs of bread; then baste it all over with clarified butter, and powder it with crumbs of bread again: baste it afresh with butter, and then bake it in the oven till it is of a fine colour. Send it up to table over a cloth, and serve up separately the Dutch sauce. If you send up two pikes, let one be green, and the other yellow. The green one is made by mixing a large quantity of chopped parsley with the crumbs of bread, before you powder the fish over with them.

No. 4.—*Baked Pike, French way.*

Prepare the pike as above, but instead of stuffing it with the aforesaid *farce*, stuff it with a *farce à quenelles*. Mind you bind the head, which is liable to break. Make a *marinade*,* a small quantity will do, as it is improper that pike should be drenched with it; indeed there will be quite enough if it reaches the middle of the fish. Baste it frequently with some of the moistening, that it may take a fine colour, which is not easily obtained, as you have not used crumbs of bread. When it is done, drain it. Take some of the *marinade* to *mark* a butter sauce in this way; put a good lump of butter and a spoonful of flour into a stew-pan; moisten with the seasoning, but do not allow the sauce to boil. Add to this a spoonful of essence of anchovies, and the juice of a lemon. Serve the sauce under the fish without *masking*.† If the pike is not of a fine colour, you should add some fine capers to the sauce; and in that case, *mask* the fish over with it.

No. 5.—*Pike, Sauce à Matelotte.*

Empty it as directed No. 2. Stew it in a *marinade au vinaigre,* and *mask* it with the *sauce à matelotte,* after having removed the scales, as in No. 2. The

---

* See *Marinade.*
† *Masking,* or covering with the sauce.

sauce matelotte is to be made with red wine. If you wish to make a *matelotte* of pike, do it in the same way as the other *matelottes;* boil the fish in wine, and use the wine to make the sauce as usual.

No. 6.—*Fillets of Pike à la Maître d'Hôtel.*

Take up the fillets of a moderate-sized pike, divest them of the skin, and cut them into equal pieces, that they may be dished nicely. Mark them in a *sauté-* pan with some melted butter, pepper, and salt. When just going to send them up to table, *sautez* them over a large fire, that they may be white and firm, and turn them on the other side. When they are done, drain and dish them *en miroton,* and serve them up with the *maître d'hôtel à poisson;* the same as for fillets of soles.

No. 7.—*Fillets of Pike à la Maréchale.*

Take the pike and skin it as above. Cut the fillets in the shape of cutlets, and powder a little salt and pepper over them. Beat the yolks of two eggs in a pan, with which brush the fillets over, and then strew crumbs of bread over them. Next dip them into melted butter, and into crumbs of bread, to give them a second coat. Make those crumbs quite level. Last-ly, broil the fillets over a slow, but equal fire. Dish them *en miroton,* and send them up with a white *poivrade.* Put into a small stew-pan two spoonsful of Tarragon vinegar, let it reduce to half, and add to it three spoonsful of *sauce tournée;* thicken it with the yolk of an egg, add to it half a quartern of fresh butter, some salt, pepper, and the juice of half a lemon; work the sauce to make it smooth.

No. 8.—*Fillets of Pike à la Turque.*

Prepare the fillets as in No. 6. Wash some rice quite clean, and blanch it. Make it swell soft in some good *consommé.* Let it be done thoroughly, keep it thick, and season it well. Add a few spoonsful of *velouté,* and a little thick cream, still preserving it thick and firm, that it may be dished in a pyramid or dome, in the centre of the dish, and the fillets all round. *Mask* the fillets, but not the rice. You may serve up either with the *maître d'hôtel,* or the *ravigotte.* (See *Sauces.*)

No. 9.—*Pike à la Chambord.*

Exactly the same thing as carp, No. 4.

PERCH.

Perch is a fish that is held in high estimation. Its flesh is white and delicate; it is easily digested, and is particularly recommended to those invalids who have a weak, debilitated stomach.

No. 1.—*Perch à la Water-fish.*

Empty the perch. Wash it well in several waters. *Mark* in a stew-pan a white *marinade,* composed of shreds of parsley and of parsley roots, a few carrots, and two or three green onions cut into fillets. Stew the whole in a little butter. When the roots begin to get soft, moisten with boiling water, and a glass of white wine, salt, pepper, &c. Let the whole stew well, and pour that *marinade* over the fish, which stew for about ten minutes. Then drain and scale it nicely, preserving, however, the red fins. When the perch is quite clean, stick those red fins into the partition of the fillet, to show what the fish is. As it is very liable to break, put it with care into a *sauté*-pan, covered with some of the liquid, to keep it warm; reduce the remainder of the liquid almost to glaze; have some parsley roots cut as for *Julienne* soup, some leaves of parsley blanched very green, and two spoonsful of good *béchamelle;* add to it the reduction, some salt, pepper, the juice of half a lemon, and half a quartern of fresh butter: after having drained the perch, dish it, and cover it with the sauce.

No. 2.—*Perch plain boiled, or Water Suchet.*

Empty and wash the perch as above. Trim a stew-pan with parsley roots, a bunch of parsley, a little salt, and a few grains of corn pepper, which you must count, that you may take every one out when the water has boiled for half an hour. Put the perch into the water, and boil them speedily, that they may be more firm. Then take out the bunch of parsley, and throw into the liquor some leaves of parsley that have been blanched very green. Serve up the fish in a deep-bottomed dish, with the liquor and the roots, which must be cut into fillets of about an inch long, and an eighth wide, send up with slices of bread and butter on a plate; the liquor must be rather salt.

No. 3.—*Perch à la Maître d'Hôtel.*

Let them be prepared and cooked as above. Remember that you must preserve the red fins, which you stick into the middle part, instead of leaving them in their natural place. After you have drained the fish, *mask* it with a *maître d'hôtel.*

No. 4.—*Perch plain boiled, Dutch Sauce.*

After having emptied the fish, scale them well, and boil them, with water and salt, for a quarter of an hour. Serve them up on a cloth, with parsley quite green all round, and send up the Dutch sauce separately.

TENCH.

Tench is a fish which real epicures think very little of; yet it is more admissible in a *matelotte* than in any other way. However, it may be dressed either broiled, *au court-bouillon*, or *farcie*, the same in every respect as a carp. (See *Carp*.)

No. 1.—*Fried Tench.*

After having scaled and emptied the tench, split the back of the fish, but take care not to touch the belly, for if you do, it will divide. Let it pickle for three hours in vinegar, salt, pepper, stalks of parsley, and onions. Then drain it and dip it into flour. Fry it of a fine colour, and quite firm. The dripping must be very hot. This you try with a drop of water, which being thrown into the dripping, occasions a noise, if it is in a proper state. Send it up to table on a cloth, with fried parsley all around; if you have a soft roe, fry it likewise, and serve it in the middle.

TROUT, AND SALMON-TROUT.

Trout is never good unless it is caught in running water; indeed it is seldom to be found elsewhere. It is to be cooked or dressed in the same manner as salmon, and is generally better and more delicate.

No. 1.—*Trout au Court-bouillon.*

Empty the trout without making a large opening in the belly. Wash it well; wrap it up in a cloth, fasten both ends with a bit of packthread, and bind the middle, or body, but not too tight. Then stew it in a *court-bouillon*. (See *Court-bouillon*.) When the trout is done, drain it, unfold the cloth, and send it up to table on another clean cloth, with green parsley all round. Send up the Dutch sauce in a boat.

No. 2.—*Trout with Genévoise Sauce.*

After having emptied the trout, fasten the head with packthread, and stew it (without having removed the scales) with *marinade*. This is to be dressed exactly in the same manner as the pike (see

Pike à la Genévoise,) only put a little more cloves with this sauce, and make it with red wine instead of white. All red fish must be dressed with red wine in preference to white. When the trout is done, take off the scales and skin, and put it again to warm with some of the liquor, and serve with the sauce over it.

No. 3.—*Fillets of Trout à l'Aurore.*

Take up the fillets of three trouts with the skin off. *Pare* them in the shape of hearts. Put them into a *sauté*-pan with melted butter, salt, and pepper. *Sautez** them on a clear fire, turn them over, and when they are done, dish them *en miroton,* and *mask* them with the *sauce à l'aurore.* *Sauce à l'aurore* is the white sharp sauce: put some lobster spawn to make it red, the sauce *à la l'aurore* with the fish, is the same sauce as that which you will find before under the name of *maréchale,* only when *à l'aurore,* you add to it butter made red with the spawn of lobster, which must be rubbed through a tammy or a sieve.

No. 4.—*Baked Trout.*

Having emptied and scaled the trout, put a stuffing well seasoned into the belly, then turn it round, with its tail fixed in its mouth. Put the fish in a small quantity of *marinade,* so that it may be just covered. Baste it frequently, and let it be made of a fine colour. When it is done, reduce one-half of the liquor in which the trout has been stewing, put in a good lump of fresh butter kneaded with flour, with a little essence of anchovies, a few fine capers, salt and pepper, if the sauce is not sufficiently seasoned; but be careful when you use anchovies, not to put too much salt. Then squeeze the juice of a lemon, drain the fish, send it up to table, with the sauce under it, but without *masking,* or covering.

* *Sautez* means, set them to fry briskly.

No. 5.—*Trout plain boiled.*

After having emptied, scaled, and washed the fish, have some boiling water ready, into which put the trout with a good handful of salt only; but no vinegar, as it spoils the colour of the fish. When it is done, drain it well, and serve it up on a clean cloth, garnished with parsley. Send up the lobster sauce separately in a boat, or the Dutch sauce. The length of time it should boil, is left to the judgment of the cook; the size determines the time. But be cautious, that when the fish remains long in the water, it loses its flavour and quality; for this reason, take care to boil it precisely at the time it is wanted.

LAMPREY.

Although very few people are partial to this fish, some, however, like it *en matelotte;* it is then to be cooked in the same manner as the eel. You must notice, however, that the lamprey requires a very long time before it is done. Make a *sauce à matelotte* (see *Sauces*) wherein you let your fish simmer for an hour and a half, or two hours if the fish is of a large size.

No. 1.—*Craw-Fish.*

Craw-fish is good only when it does not spawn, for then it is most nauseously bitter. Wash it well in several clean waters, till the water remains perfectly limpid and bright. Trim a stew-pan with a few slices of carrots, onions, roots and stalks of parsley, thyme, bay-leaves, two cloves, salt, pepper, a glass of vinegar, and some water. Let the whole stew for an hour, drain it through a sieve, and put the live craw-fish into the seasoning to boil. Keep stirring them almost without interruption, that they may be done all alike, for twenty minutes. Keep them in the seasoning till you send them up to table, as they take a better flavour.

No. 2.—*Craw-Fish à la Poulette.*

When the best craw-fish have been sent to table plain, take the smaller ones and pick off the lesser claws; cut the large ones in half, beard them, pick the tail; put all these in a cloth, and shake them well, that there may be no water left. Then take two spoonsful of *velouté*, (see *Sauces*,) a quarter of a pound of butter, some pepper and salt, chopped parsley, a little *cavice*, and the juice of a lemon. Toss the craw-fish in this sauce, which must be thick, and send up to table quite hot.

No. 3.—*Bisque of Craw-Fish.*

This is a *potage* which is sent to table on gala days only, when you are obliged to make a frequent change of *potages*. Take the best craw-fish you can procure, according to the quantity you may want. Five or six dozen at least are generally requisite. If you boil the craw-fish expressly for the occasion, you must not put vinegar. Lay aside two dozen and a half of the finest tails, that remain whole. The rest, with all the meat, and flesy parts of the inside, pound in a mortar with the flesh of the breasts of two roasted fowls or chickens. Previously, have soaked or boiled in rich broth, the crumb of two French penny loaves. Put that also into the mortar, with the yolks of three eggs boiled hard. Pound the whole together. Next put the shells of the craw-fish to boil in a little broth; then take some of the liquor to dilute the *purée* with, which rub through a tammy. Now boil a pint and a half of cream, which you keep continually stirring round, in order to prevent a scum from rising. Pour that cream into the *potage*, and season it well. Have the red spawn of a lobster well pounded, dilute it with some of the broth, and mix it with your soup, or *potage*. Keep it hot, without its boiling. Soak a few rounds of bread, which lay at the bottom of the tureen. Pour your *bisque* into the tureen, over the bread; place the tails that you have laid aside previously, all round the tureen over the soup, and serve up hot. Mind the soup is not to be too thick; and season it of a good flavour.

No. 4.—*Craw-Fish for Entrées.*

Your craw-fish, in this case, must be dressed as directed in No. 1 They never serve but for a garnish, and then the small claws must always be taken off. Mind that you beard the fish, take off all the small claws, and that is of a fine colour. Thus prepared, they may be used for either *chambords*, *godards*, *matelottes*, *fricassées*, *pâtés chauds*, *aspics*, &c. &c.

There are many other sorts of fresh-water fish that seldom are sent to table, which are found in sleeping waters, and which accordingly shall not be mentioned here. Those who fancy them, however, may either broil or fry them, as they would a carp.

Aloze, Shad.

This fish is held in high estimation in France, and especially in Paris. It must be scaled, emptied, and washed nicely. Next it is to be *marinaded* in a little oil, with pepper and salt. It is necessary to split it, that the salt may penetrate. Broil it on both sides over a slow fire. It will be done in the course of one hour. When it is done, let it be served with caper sauce, or with sorrel, not *purée*, but what is called *farce*.

CHAPTER XIV

SALT-WATER FISH.

No. 1.— *Turbot.*

A TURBOT of a middling size is preferable to any other. When very large, the meat is tough and thready. It is customary in France, and the same must be done in every country, to empty the fish, and to wash out all the blood.

Some gentlemen are much mistaken with regard to the freshness of the turbot: the author has ascertained by many years' observation, that a turbot kept two or three days is much better eating than a very fresh one: it certainly depends much on the quality of the fish, but if it is boiled with care and attention, its having been kept is a great improvement to it. If you are obliged to wait after it is done, it is better not to leave the fish in the water; keep the water boiling, but put the fish over the steam, covered with a damp cloth. When the dinner is called for, dip the fish again into the water; by this means it never loses its quality. It is of great consequence to boil the white fish always in clear pump water; it makes the fish eat better, and keeps it whiter and firmer.

No. 2.—*Fillets of Turbot à la Maréchale.*

Take the fillets of a moderate-sized turbot, skin them, and cut each fillet into equal pieces, either oval or in the shape of hearts. Season them with salt and pepper. Then beat the yolks of two or three eggs in a plate, and brush the fillets over with them, next dip them into crumbs of bread, then into clarified butter, and next into bread again. Boil them till they are of a fine colour, on a slow but equal fire. Dish them *en couronne*, and pour over a white sharp sauce. See *sauce maréchale*, only remark, when for fish you must put more butter.

No. 3.—*Fillets of Turbot à la Crême.*

This is an *entrée* of *desserte.** When the turbot is returned from table, immediately take up the fillets, and skin them; you must do this while they are hot, as it will occasion a great waste to trim them when cold. The next day you must scollop your fillets, as equally as possible. Have a *sauce à la crême* quite hot; put the fillets into it, and keep them hot, and in due time send them up in a dish garnished with a *bordure*, or in a *vol au vent*.

The cream sauce may be made in two different ways; first, if you have *béchamelle* in the larder, put into a stew-pan three spoonsful of it, a quarter of a pound of very fresh butter, two spoonsful of very good cream, some salt and a little Cayenne: mix the whole well, and put either the sauce over the fish, or the fish into the sauce, if it is for a *vol au vent*. If you have no *béchamelle*, put into a stew-pan a tablespoonful of flour, a quarter of a pound of butter, two or three spoonsful of cream, salt, a little Cayenne, and a small bit of glaze. Do not let this sauce boil, only melt it till it is thick, and season high.

No. 4.—*Gratin of Fillets of Turbot au Velouté.*

This is another *entrée* of *desserte.* Proceed as above, No. 3. Cut a few slices of bread, one inch broad and a quarter of an inch thick. Dip them into an *omelette* of one single egg. Stick them on the border of a dish, which lay on the corner of a little

---

* *Entrée* of *desserte*, is what is left from the preceding day.

stove. As you stick on the bread, turn the dish; when you you have completed the circle, put a spoonful or two of *velouté* on the dish, and let it *gratiné* in the centre of the dish. Next take more of the same *velouté*, to which add a quarter of a pound of butter, and mix this on the stove without boiling. Keep this sauce thick; pour into it a little thick cream; season it well; put your scollops into the sauce, and the whole into the dish in which you have *gratiné* the *velouté*. Now level with your knife, and strew crumbs of bread over them equally; heat a bored ladle, put a small lump of butter into it, and baste the scollops with it; let them have another coat of crumbs of bread, baste them again, and let them get a good colour with the salamander. When the *gratin* has got a good colour, take off the slices of bread that you had previously stuck round the dish, to make room for others that have been fried in butter of a fine colour. If you have a deep dish, the first border will not be wanted, only the second, which makes the dish look better; if you trim and fry your bread nicely, it makes a beautiful *entrée*.

No. 5.—*Vol au Vent d'Escalopes de Turbot, au bon Buerre.*

This is an excellent *entrée* of *desserte*. Be particular in cleaning the fillets of the turbot when returned from table, as directed No. 3. Cut them in scollops, and put them into a stew-pan, well covered to prevent their getting dry. With regard to the sauce, take six spoonsful of *sauce tournée*, which reduce with two spoonsful of *consommé*. When the sauce is reduced, thicken it with the yolks of two eggs, and refine your sauce with at least a quarter of a pound of the best butter, or more. If you should have any thick cream, put in a little, as it will make the sauce mellower; lastly, season well, put the scollops with the sauce, keep them hot, and send up the whole to table in a *vol au vent*. (See *vol au vent.*)

No. 6.—*Petites Timballes of Fillets of Turbot à la Vénitienne.*

This is an *entrée* of *desserte*, held in high estimation. It requires but very little flesh of the fish to make it. Cut whatever is left of the turbot into dice, as small as possible. For the sauce, take three spoonsful of hot *béchamelle*, to which add a good lump of butter, salt, white fine pepper, a little parsley chopped very fine, and well squeezed in a towel, that it may not give a green colour to the sauce. Then put a little *cavice;* that of Mackay's, which is the best, is the composition which agrees the most with all fish sauces, particularly when kept many years. Keep stirring your sauce, which is generally called working it. We call it *vanner*, taking up the sauce in a ladle, and pour it perpendicularly into the stew-pan, repeating the operation frequently, and very quick, to make the sauce transparent. When it is mellow, and of a good taste, throw in the small dice of turbot, keep them hot, and when ready to send up to table, garnish the little *timballes** with the turbot. Let them lay for a moment in the oven, and serve them up hot. If you have no *béchamelle*, you must make use of the sauce *à la crême*, or *bon Beurre*, No. 5, of this article.

No. 7.—*Turbotin broiled with Caper Sauce.*

After having emptied and washed the fish clean, make an incision in the back, down to the bone; then wipe it quite dry; next lay it in a dish to *marinade* in salt, pepper, and sweet oil; put in very little oil, as it requires only sufficient to prevent it from drying. Half an hour, or even three-quarters of an hour before dinner-time, broil the fish over a slow fire. It is requisite to lay some straws on the gridiron, to prevent its making black streaks on the turbot, which broil on both sides, and serve up with caper sauce.

* *Timballe* is the pastry made in the *dariole* mould.

BRILL.

This is very delicate, and very luscious eating when broiled with caper sauce. It is to be cooked exactly in the same manner as the *turbotin*, No. 7. It is also eaten like turbot, and is almost as good. When very fresh, you may use it for fillets, and for every *entrée* the same as turbot. (See *Turbot*, plain and cooked.) The brill is very delicate, and as good as the turbot, and may be used more frequently for fillets, as the price is not so exorbitant, and the fillets are more delicate than those of turbot.

No. 1.—*John Dory.*

John Dory is a hideous looking fish, but the meat is very delicate. Cook it in the same manner as the turbot; and when broiled, send it up with caper or anchovy sauce.

No. 2.—*John Dory boiled, with Lobster Sauce.*

John Dory is boiled exactly the same as a turbot; and the sauce is the same. Put parsley round it, particularly in the opening of the head.

SALMON.

Salmon from the Thames is the most esteemed and sells accordingly. Salmon is served indiscriminately, plain, or as an *entrée, entremets,* &c. Crimped salmon fetches the highest price, and is the only one introduced at the table of a true connoisseur.

No. 1.—*Slices of Crimped Salmon, with Lobster Sauce.*

See *Salmon*, No. 5, page 88.

No. 2.—*Slices of Crimped Salmon boiled, with Caper Sauce.*

Marinade your slices of salmon in a little olive oil, with salt and pepper. Three-quarters of an hour before you send up, broil them on a very slow fire, on both sides. When it is done, take off the skin, and drain it on a clean towel to draw out all the oil. Dish it, and *mask* it with the caper sauce. Let it be understood that your gridiron must be put on a slope, with a *plafond* under the fore-feet to receive the oil, which, if it fell into the fire, the smoke of it would spoil the fish, and besides fill the kitchen with smoke and stench. (The sauce as in No. 4, page 88.)

No. 3.—*Cutlets of Salmon sautez à la Maître d'Hôtel.*

Cut some slices of salmon in the shape of chops. Put them into a *sauté*-pan with some clarified butter, pepper and salt, and *sautez* or toss them when dinner-time is come, over an equal fire. Drain the butter well, and dish the slices of salmon *en couronne.* Send up with a *maître d'hôtel.* For salmon, you must not use any cream, as this fish is already heavy for the stomach; put into a stew-pan three spoonsful of *sauce tournée* well reduced; add to it the thickening of one egg, and refine the sauce with a quarter of a pound of Epping butter, some salt, a little Cayenne, the juice of half a lemon, and some parsley chopped very fine; work this sauce very fine, and use it when wanted. As it is not the object of the author to swell his volume, unnecessarily, two or three articles will often be found under one head, as in the article, salmon *à la maître d'hôtel,* but you may give it with six different sauces, as *maréchale, Dutch caper, maintenon, ravigotte,* &c. &c.

No. 4.—*Salad of Salmon.*

This is an *entremet* which is recurred to on economical principles, when there is any salmon left.

Let it cool, and cut it nicely into hearts, or square lozenges. Decorate these with fillets of anchovies, pickled cucumbers, fine capers, and chopped eggs, to which add a few hearts of lettuce. Then make the sauce as follows: if you should have some jelly, make a kind of *mayonaise.* Put three spoonsful of oil, one spoonful of vinegar, with an equal quantity of jelly, seasoned with pepper, salt, and chopped *ravigotte.* Beat all these over ice, till they are of a white colour, and decorate your salad with this *mayonaise,* and a few lumps of jelly, cut of different shapes. Avoid making any decorations that are liable to tumble down. A plain good salad is eaten in preference to any other. Grand decorations are intended to ornament the centre of the table, whereas what is to be eaten must be plain and good. Above all things, avoid introducing artificial colours. Nature has supplied you with nasturtium, red and white beet-roots, beans of two colours, white and green, chervil, Tarragon, burnet, &c.; besides, you have white or yellow *omelettes.* Never put any fish into a salad of fowl, for if the fowl taste of fish, what will you have your salads *maigres* taste of? In summer-time, you have asparagus, artichoke-bottoms, cauliflowers, &c.

Salmon is also cooked in various other ways, which ought not to be done. This fish being oily, will not admit of so many metamorphoses. The author has seen salmon-pies sent to table, petty patties, and scollops of salmon in paper cases, *croquettes* ditto, and *bonne morue,* all which *entrées* are good for nothing; and the best proof of the truth of this assertion is, that no one will ever taste them. If, notwithstanding, you would wish to try, the process is the same as for dressing turbot, or haddock. However, if you will follow his advice, you will never attempt any other *entrées* but those herein described. When a good slice happens to be left whole, you may serve it with a butter of *montpelier;* this is very relishing, and may be made as follows: take about eight good *anchovies,* a quarter of a pound of fresh butter, some *ravigottes,* as chervil, burnet, Tarragon, a few shalots, and a very little garlick; blanch these herbs in boiling water and salt, put them in cold water, and when quite cold put them into the mortar with the rest of the articles before named; add to it the yolks of six eggs boiled hard, with salt and Cayenne: rub this through a sieve, after being well pounded, and use it for any sort of fish that you intend to serve *au beur de montpelier;* if you like to have it very green, make a *verd de parsley,* the same as directed for the *verd d'épinard.*

No. 5.—*Salmon, with Genévoise Sauce.*

Scale, empty, and wash your salmon clean. Then follow the method prescribed at No. 6, page 11.

No. 6.—*Salmon, matelotte Sauce.*

Make a *marinade,* in which stew the salmon. When it is done, pick off the scales carefully. Pour the *marinade* over the salmon to keep it hot. Then make a *sauce matelotte* in the following manner: put a good bit of butter and two spoonsful of flour into a stew-pan, and make a *roux.* When it begins to colour, throw four or six onions into your *roux,* and let them melt: keep stirring with a wooden spoon. Then moisten with a bottle of red wine; add a few spoonsful of the *marinade* in which you have stewed the salmon, some trimmings of mushrooms, a bunch of parsley and green onions well seasoned, and a small piece of glaze; season the whole, and put a little sugar to correct the acidity of the wine; skim the grease, and keep the sauce thick. In case it should not be thick enough to *mask* with, add a small bit of butter kneaded with flour, a quarter of a pound of fresh butter, some essence of anchovies, the juice of a lemon, and some salt and pepper. Drain the fish, and *mask* it with the sauce, after having strained it through a tammy.

STURGEON.

Sturgeon is an excellent fish if firm; as soon as you find it soft and flabby, never attempt to make any thing good of it; it will become red and of bad flavour. Take care never to let it boil when it is in the oven.

No. 1.—*Roast Sturgeon.*

See No. 29, page 96.

No. 2.—*Baked Sturgeon.*

The same process as above. Make a *marinade*, either with wine or vinegar, and pour it into a vessel large enough to contain the fish, which cover with buttered paper, to prevent its getting too high a colour. Baste frequently with the *marinade*. When the sturgeon is done, have the sauce made as No. 29, page 96, and use it to *mask* the fish.

No. 3.—*Sturgeon à la Ude.*

Boil the sturgeon in salt and water. When it is done, drain and *mask* it with the following sauce: reduce in a small stew-pan four spoonsful of elder vinegar. When it is half reduced, put in six spoonsful of *velouté,* or rather a quantity proportionate to the size of the fish, half a spoonful of *cavice*, thicken the sauce with three yolks of eggs, and add a quarter of a pound of butter, and some salt and pepper. Work this sauce well; drain the fish and *mask* it with the sauce. In order to keep it thick and white, mix with it a little thick cream.

No. 4.—*Blanquette of Sturgeon à la Paysanne.*

When you have some roasted sturgeon returned, keep it to make a *blanquette.* Pare some round pieces nicely of the size of half a crown, and put them into a *sauce à blanquette,* to which you add a little chopped parsley, and the juice of a lemon. This *blanquette* is sent to table like all others in a *vol au vent,* or a *casserole au ris.*

No. 5.—*Blanquette of Sturgeon, with Green Peas.*

If you have any sturgeon left, that is still very fresh, make a *blanquette* with peas, which not requiring to be highly seasoned, will admit only of fish which is extremely sweet. After having simmered the peas as they are always prepared for the second course, take three spoonsful of *sauce tournée,* and reduce it with four spoonsful of the peas: add a very small bit of sugar. When your sauce is very thick, put to it a thickening of two yolks of eggs, then put the sturgeon to it, and serve either in a *vol au vent,* or in a *bordure* of potatoes. Observe, that in this *entrée* the seasoning must be very mild.

No. 6.—*Croquettes of Sturgeon.*

Sturgeon is a fish absolutely resembling veal; when fresh, it is as white as the finest veal. If it is red, there is nothing to be done with it. If there is any returned, of a very good white, but not a sufficient quantity to make a *croquette,* make small *timballes* (see *Pastry*): cut the sturgeon into dice, and put them into a sauce similar to that mentioned in No. 6.—*(Timballes de Turbot.)* After having cut enough fish into dice to make the *croquettes,* take a *béchamelle* reduced, and some mushrooms cut into dice, to which add a small lump of butter, salt, &c. and put the fish into that sauce. Let them cool, and then dip them into crumbs of bread, as prescribed for other *croquettes.* Serve some fried parsley in the centre of the dish.

COD.

No. 1.—*Cod with Oyster Sauce.*

After having emptied the cod, you must open the sound or white skin of the belly, wash it careful all along the bone, that there may be no blood remaining. Mind that the fish is absolutely white, then lay it on a fish plate, and put it into the kettle with salt and boiling pump water; as soon as you see the fish boil fast, slacken it, and let it boil more gently, or else the outside will be done and the middle will be raw: as it it is not easy to fix the time that it ought to remain in the water, you must judge according to the size of the fish; when done, drain it, and serve it on a napkin garnished with green parsley. (See *Oyster Sauce*, No. 96, p. 42.)

No. 2.—*Cod with Cream Sauce.*

Prepare and boil the cod as above. But after having drained it, take the skin off, and mask the fish with the cream sauce which follows: put into a stewpan half a pound of very fresh butter, and a spoonful of flour; moisten this with a pint of cream; add some salt, a very little Cayenne, and one spoonful of essence of anchovies; put all this on the stove, and let the sauce thicken without boiling; work it well, and cover the fish with it.

No. 3.—*Scollops of Cod en bonne Morue.*

This is an *entrée of desserte.* If you have any cod left, take up all the flakes, taking care to leave no skin nor bones. Have a cream sauce as above, or else take three spoonsful of *béchamelle* and a good bit of butter; work them over the stove, and season with pepper and salt. When the sauce is well mixed with the butter, put in the scollops, and stir them well, that the fish may imbibe the sauce properly. Let the fish stand a moment till it is cold; then make a *bordure* round the dish, with slices of bread fried in butter. Dish the scollops, level them smooth with your knife, dust them over with crumbs of bread, and baste them with butter; repeat both these operations; use the salamander to give the fish a colour, and serve up with toasts of bread, one round, one oblong, alternately, so as to be ornamental.

No. 4.—*Vol au Vent of Scollops of Cod à la Crême.*

This is another *entrée of desserte*, but much the same as that above, it is as good as if it were fresh made, which, by the bye, should always be the case when company is invited. Make the same sauce as for that above, only keep it a little thinner. Put your *vol au vent* into a dish, and put in the scollops only when you are going to send your dinner up. *En maigre* use the cream sauce, p. 284. If you put in the fish too soon, it makes the paste soft.

No. 5.—*Scollops of Cod à la Maître d' Hôtel.*

Make a *maître d' hôtel*, into which put the scollops; season them pretty high, and add the juice of a lemon. Send them up to table quite hot, for a cold dinner is good for nothing, particularly fish.

No. 6.—*Crimped Cod and Oyster Sauce.*

This dish is boiled like the other fish, but it should be observed, that sixteen minutes, and sometimes not so much, will suffice to boil it; when the pump-water boils, put the fish on the lining, and scatter a good deal of salt over it; as soon as it begins to boil, put it at the side of the fire, allowing it to simmer gently, try with your knife, between the bones, if it is done, and drain and serve immediately; the sauce should be separately.

SALT COD.

No. 1.—*Salt Cod à la Maître d' Hôtel.*

The black skinned ones are generally reckoned the best. Be particular in having the salt well soaked out, put the fish into cold water, and put it on the fire. Let it be done in a large vessel that it may have plenty of room. The moment it is beginning to boil, take it off the fire, and keep it in the water well covered: it then will be tender, but if it should boil, it will be tough and thready. Make a *maître d'hôtel* with half a pound of butter, a spoonful of flour, four or five spoonsful of water, and a little salt. Taste the fish, and if required put a little more salt and pepper. Then put it on the fire without allowing it to boil. When the sauce begins to thicken, work it well, that it may be more mellow. Have some parsley chopped very fine, mix a pinch of it with a little glaze and the juice of a lemon. Then taste the sauce. If it be too brown, put in a little thick cream, which will make it both whiter and more mellow. Take away the skin and bones of the fish, and put it into the sauce, shaking it gently for fear of breaking it. Send it up either in a *vol au vent*, or in a deep dish, with *croutons* of puff-paste. Sometimes, if you give this fish as a fish-dish, serve it with the skin down in the dish. Drain all the water, and *mask* with the *sauce à la maître d'hôtel*, and garnish with fried potatoes round the fish.

No. 2.—*Salt Cod à la Provençale.*

After having drawn out the salt, and done the fish as above, pound two or three heads of garlick, which throw into a stew-pan with two spoonsful of oil, a quarter of a pound of butter, a little salt, and some coarse pepper. Continue shaking the stew-pan with its contents. Put in the salt fish quite hot, and keep shaking till the whole is well mixed together. If you should find that it is not mellow enough, add a little oil, and a spoonful of *velouté*. Such *entrées* require to be highly seasoned, and will induce the guests to send the bottle round freely. Do not neglect the juice of a lemon.

No. 3.—*Salt Cod with Cream Sauce.*

The same process as No. 2, p. 284. You may send it up to table in a *vol au vent*, &c.

No. 4.—*Salt Cod à la Bonne Femme.*

This is the same thing nearly as No. 1. Only boil some potatoes, and let them stand till they are cold; turn them into corks, and then cut them into round slices much about the size of a half-crown piece, which put with the sauce and salt fish. Taste and season well.

No. 5.—*Salt Cod à la Lyonaise.*

The same process as usual; boil it in water. Cut some onions into dice, which fry in butter till they are very brown. Dust them over with a little flour. Moisten with milk or cream. Let the onions be well done; mix a good lump of butter, and season the sauce of a good taste. Put the fish into the sauce, and serve up quite hot.

No. 6.—*Salt Cod plain, Egg Sauce.*

Draw out the salt, and boil it as above, in the French way. Have some parsnips well done, which dish round the fish. Boil a few eggs hard, chop them, and throw them into melted butter, which send up in a boat.

WHITINGS.

No. 1.—*Broiled Whitings.*

Empty the whitings, scale them, but mind that you preserve the liver, which is very delicate. When you have washed and wiped them clean, slit the back on both sides. Beat the yolk of an egg with a little salt and pepper, and rub some of it over the whitings with a brush. Then dip the fish into crumbs of bread, next into melted butter, and then into crumbs of bread again. Broil them of a fine colour, and serve up. The sauce is to be sent up separately in a boat, whether it is a *maître d'hôtel,* anchovy sauce, or melted butter. Send up the sauce separately; for if you were to pour the sauce over the fish, the whiting would not prove palatable, and the sauce would get too thick.

No. 2.—*Fillets of Whitings à la Orlie.*

After having scaled, emptied, and washed the whitings, take up the fillets. Pare them nicely on both sides, without damaging the skin. Cut each fillet in two pieces of an equal size, and put them into an earthen pan with a few stalks of parsley, and a few shalots shredded, some salt, pepper, and the juice of a lemon; stir the whole in the lemon juice. Let it *marinade* for about three hours. Then drain the fillets on a clean towel. Next beat the whites of two eggs, so that they may stick to the fillets. Mix some crumbs of bread and flour, dip the fillets into the whites of eggs, and in the crumbs of bread and flour, and fry the whole just before they are wanted, in very hot dripping, that they may be served up hot, with white sharp sauce. See *maréchale* or *ravigotte.*

No. 3.—*Quenelles of Whitings.*

The same process as for other *quenelles.* The mixtures are the same. You may make a vast number of *entrées* with *quenelles* of whitings, such as *quenelles à l'Allemande,* in a *vol au vent,* a *casserole au ris,* and *boudins,* either *à la Ude* or *à la Richelieu,* which you have poached and cooled. Brush them over with an *omelette* and crumbs of bread, and fry them. Serve under it an *Italienne,* refined with a good lump of butter, &c. All *entrées* of fish require some additional butter in the sauce.

No. 4.—*Boudins of Whitings à la Ude.*

Make a *farce à quenelles,* as for other *quenelles.* Take the spawn of a lobster, which pound well, with a little butter, and rub it through a sieve. Mix the

whole well with the *farce à quenelles.* Then mould
two *boudins* of the length of your dish. Poach them.
When they are done, drain them on a clean towel;
then have the tail of a very red lobster, and scollop
it in several pieces. Next slit the *boudins,* and cover
them with white *béchamelle,* then introduce the
pieces of lobster in the same way as if you were making a *conti,* observing to put the red part upward.
When the *boudins* are equally decorated, lay them
in a dish, cover them hermetically, and put them for
a moment in the hot closet to keep them hot. For
the sauce, take two spoonsful of *béchamelle.* Work
it well with a quarter of a pound of butter, seasoned
with a very little Cayenne, some salt, and a little
lemon juice. Keep it rather liquid, in order to *mask*
the intervals between the *contis* of lobster. If you
pay proper attention to the making of this *entrée,* it
will not merely afford a pleasing appearance, but will
also be found a relish for the epicure.

No. 5.—*Fillets of Whitings broiled à la Maître d'Hôtel.*

Take up the fillets of four whitings, after having
washed them clean. Cut each fillet in two, brush
them with yolks of eggs, seasoned with pepper and
salt, and dip them into crumbs of bread, and next into clarified butter. Broil them of a fine brown, dish
them *en miroton,* and sauce them with the *maître
d'hôtel.*

N.B.—Fillets of whitings never answer when
sautez, as they have not substance enough; and indeed I do not altogether approve of their being dressed in that style.

No. 6.—*Paupiettes of Fillets of Whitings.*

Take up the fillets of four whitings, and *pare* them
equally. Spread some *farce à quenelles* over the white
side; then roll the fillets. Erect a small dome with
some of the same *farce,* in the dish you mean to send
up your fish in. Lay one row of fillets round the

dish. Put *farce* enough to support the second middle row, and finally put one or three fillets in the centre of the dish, according to the space that is left. Sprinkle a little salt over, then cover the fish with buttered paper, that the fillets may bake without getting dry. They will be done in the course of twenty minutes. Then take them out of the oven, and wipe the dish clean. Put a good lump of butter, about a quarter of a pound, into an *Italienne*, with a little essence of anchovies; work the sauce, season it well, and *mask* the fillets with it.

No. 7.—*Whitings au gratin.*

After having scaled, emptied, and washed the whitings, wipe them clean. Preserve the liver. Take a silver dish, if you have one, if not, a baking-pan. Rub the bottom over with butter, and sprinkle it over with parsley and mushrooms chopped very fine, over which lay the whitings. Then take some rasps of bread, that are not burnt, and sprinkle them over the whitings, with pepper, salt, and grated nutmeg: then again dust them over with sweet herbs; namely, parsley and mushrooms, chopped very fine. (If shalots are approved of, you may add some.) Next lay small lumps of butter on the whitings; pour into the dish a glass or two of white wine, and bake them in a hot oven. They will be done within a quarter of an hour, or twenty minutes, according to their size. Serve them up with the juice of a lemon, and no other sauce. This is a very palatable dish, but a common one; if there is too much sauce, reduce it on a stove, as it must be very short, as it is called *au gratin* because it is a short sauce.

No. 8.—*Whitings Fried.*

According to the French fashion, you must not flay the whiting, only slit and dip them in flour, and then fry them in very hot dripping, and serve them without any sauce. In England they take off the skin, and fasten the tail in the mouth; they are then dipped in an *omelette*, then in a little flour and crumbs of bread. Fry them of a fine colour, and serve them up on a cloth, garnished with parsley, and send the shrimp sauce in a boat.

Shrimp Sauce.

Put into a stew-pan a quarter of a pound of fresh butter, a tea-spoonful of flour, a small glass of water, some salt and pepper, and a spoonful of essence of anchovies; put this on the stove; as soon as the sauce is thick, take it off, and put in the shrimps, after having well washed them.*

SOLES.

No. 1.—*Soles au Water Suchet.*

Take some very fresh soles; scale the white side, and skin the black one. Empty out all the intestines, and wash the fish in several waters. When they are quite clean, boil them in a *water suchet*, which is made as follows:

Take some roots of parsley, and cut them into slices as for a *julienne*, about the eighth of an inch thick, and an inch long. Put these roots into some water with a bunch of parsley, green onions, and a little salt, and let them stew for an hour; then stew the soles in this water. When they are done, have ready some leaves of parsley, (without stalks,) which have been blanched separately in salt and water. Drain the soles, and mind that the parsley-roots, cut into slips as above mentioned, must be preserved. Then put the soles into a tureen, or a deep dish, with some of the liquor in which they have been stewed, and which you strain through a silk sieve. Throw in the roots of parsley, and the leaves likewise, and send up

---

* Never neglect to *season* your sauce; without seasoning, cookery goes for nothing.

the *water suchet* without any bread in it; but in a separate plate send up a few slices of rye bread and butter. This broth must be salt, like sea water.

No. 2.—*Paupiette of Fillets of Soles.*

The *farce* must be made of whiting, the flesh of soles not blending with any other ingredient; you may keep the skin on the white side of the soles, provided you scrape them well; spread the *farce* over the inside of the fillets, and roll them as you do the *paupiettes* of beef palates, or fillets of whiting. Dish alternately a white fillet and one without the skin, as they look ·better so: do them in the oven as other *paupiettes;* drain the butter, and serve.

Use the same sauce as for whitings, (see No. 6, page 288), or white sharp sauce, (No. 25, page 12).

No. 3.—*Fillets of Soles sautez à la Ravigotte.*

First scale the soles, and wash them, but do not empty them. Take up the fillets, by running your knife first between the bone and the flesh, then between the skin and the fillet; by leaning pretty hard on the table, you may be sure they will come off very neatly. Cut them in two. *Mark* them in a *sauté-*pan with some melted butter, and dust them over with pepper and salt. When dinner-time is come, *sautez* them over a very brisk fire, turn them over, and when done, drain them on a sheet of white paper. Dish them either *en couronne*, or *en miroton.* Cover them, and keep them hot. Do not forget to drain the water which has issued from the fillets, before you pour the sauce over them. (See below, *Ravigotte à la Crême.*)

Ravigotte à la Crême.—Put into a small stew-pan three spoonsful of very thick *béchamelle* or *sauce à la crême,* one tea-spoonful of *cavice,* one ditto of elder vinegar, one ditto of vinegar *à la ravigotte,* and a quarter of a pound of very fresh butter; mix all this with salt and a very little Cayenne, add a tea-spoonful of parsley, chopped very fine, that has been blanch-

ed in salt water, that it may be very green, drain it
on a sieve, and press the water out of it, in order to
keep your *ravigotte* sauce thick enough to cover the
fillets. You must make this sauce very smooth and
palatable; as the *cavice* darkens the sauce, add to it a
spoonful of double cream.

No. 4.—*Fillets of Soles à la Orlie.*

The same process, and the same sauce as for fillets
of whiting, No. 2, page 287.

No. 5.—*Timballes of Fillets of Soles à la Vénitienne.*

When you have served soles, either fried or boiled,
you must preserve a sufficient quantity to make one
entrée on the following day. *Pare* well the skin,
and cut the meat into small dice. Take two spoonsful of *béchamelle*, which mix with a quarter of a
pound of very fresh butter; add to it a little parsley,
chopped very fine, a tea-spoonful of *cavice* (from
Mackay's), and half a tea-spoonful of elder vinegar.
Keep the whole hot, without boiling. Put the small
dice of fish into this sauce, season it with pepper and
salt; fill the little *timballes*, and serve up quite hot.
The *timballes* are to be made in *dariole* moulds.

No. 6.—*Vol au Vent of Fillets of Soles with Cream Sauce.*

This is another *entrée* of *desserte*.* *Pare* the skin;
cut the soles into round pieces of the size of half-a-
crown. Then have a *sauce à la crême*, or else four
spoonsful of *béchamelle*, mixed with a quarter of a
pound of butter, a little salt and pepper. Let the
sauce be made hot, without boiling, put the soles into
it, and then the whole mixed into a *vol au vent.* The

---

* *Entrée* of *desserte*, means something left from the preceding
day.

sauce must be kept rather thick, for fear of making the crust soft.

No. 7.—*Fillets of Soles à l'Aurore.*

Take up the fillets of four soles: skin them on both sides. Have ready a *farce à quenelles*, made of whitings, with the spawn of lobsters put in, to make it look reddish. Spread this *farce* over each fillet, then roll them in the same manner as the *paupiettes*. Next skewer them with silver skewers, three to each skewer; dust a little pepper and salt over them. Season the *farce* rather high. Lay the skewered fillets in a baking-pan, cover them with layers of bacon, and bake them. When they are done, take off the skewers, *pare* the *farce* that has over-reached, and dish them neatly. With a part of the pounded lobster's spawn which you have kept aside, mix two spoonsful of *sauce tournée,* deprived of all fat, and a good lump of fresh butter; drain the whole through a tammy, in order that it may be fine. Add to it a little essence of anchovies, with pepper, salt, and lemon-juice. Keep the sauce very hot, and *mask* the fillets with it. Observe, all the bacon must be taken off.

No. 8.—*Soles à la Miromesnil.*

Take three soles, scale them on both sides, and empty them nicely without injuring the flesh. Make an incision on the black side. Fry them without dipping them into flour. When they are done, drain them on a clean cloth; open the place where you have made the incision, cut the bone near the head and tail, and draw it out. Let the fish cool. Make a *maitre d'hôtel* cold; that is to say, mix a lump of butter with some parsley chopped very fine, pepper, salt, and the juice of a lemon. Divide the butter into three equal parts, and put one part into the opening of each sole, close the opening, and make the whole stick by means of the yolk of an egg; put a few crumbs of bread at the joint. Then dip the soles into an *omelette* of two eggs, and next into crumbs of bread, equally on all sides. When dinner-time is come, fry the soles in hot dripping. They are done as soon as they have got a colour. The sauce is found in the sole itself. This is what we call in France an *entrée bourgeoise*.

No. 9.—*Aspic and Salad of Fillets of Soles, with Butter of Montpelier.*

Butter of Montpelier.—Take a handful of chervil, tarragon, burnet, and green onions; wash them very clean, and blanch them in boiling water, with a handful of salt to keep them as green as possible. When they have boiled six minutes, take them out, and put them into cold water till quite cold: you must have ready some hard-boiled eggs; drain the herbs, and squeeze all the water out; put them into the mortar, and pound them very fine; add the yolks of eight eggs, ten or twelve anchovies, cleaned and boned, two spoonsful of fine capers, a very little garlic, some salt, a little Cayenne, and a little nutmeg; pound all this till very fine, then add half a pound of very fresh butter, a spoonful of sweet oil, and a spoonful of elder or tarragon vinegar; taste if the seasoning is very palatable. Rub it all through a sieve, and to make it of a greener colour, add some green of spinach; you must be particular in observing that none of the different herbs should predominate: put this butter into ice, and you may use it for borders of salads of fish, &c. &c. When you want to make this butter red, you must infuse all the herbs in a little boiled vinegar, and use lobster spawn to colour it, instead of the green of spinach.

It is occasionally requisite to dress soles on purpose, to make either *aspics*, or salad; in this case it is better to fry them with the skin, rather than take up the fillets and *sautez* them. When they are fried, the fillets come off neater, and without any scum. If, however, you have sent up to table an *entrée*, or a dish of fillets of soles, that has been returned untouch-

ed, you may make a salad with them. Pare them
nicely. Endeavour always to procure some green
salad, of any sort, to dish them with. Nature will
always supply you with agreeable colours, without
painting what is intended to be eaten. I like to see
a bed of fresh salad, or of mustard seed, on a dish.
Then dish the fillets *en miroton;* ornament them with
beet-root, nasturtium, small white onions stewed, chervil, pickled cucumbers, and red turnip-radishes; but
above all things, take care not to lose time in orna-
menting the salad, and do not pour the sauce over the
decoration. (The sauce for a salad is to be found underneath.) The *aspic* of *fillets* of *soles* is hardly admissible except at balls, when the multiplicity of
dishes may require their being introduced; but in
general it is a very indifferent article. Salad is always preferable. First, put a little *aspic* into a mould
to acquire a substance, and when it is chilled, make
some ornaments with the whites of eggs boiled hard,
some black truffles, some gherkins, or beet-root.
When you have made decorations, with all sorts of
eatable things, pour in some of the liquid *aspic* gently, to settle all this together, and put the mould in
the ice; when the *aspic* is frozen again, put the *fillets
au miroton* over the *aspic;* but mind when you return the mould that the *miroton* is on the right side;
then fill up the mould with the *aspic,* very near the
top of the fillets of soles; let it freeze, and when it becomes quite stiff, put some of the *mayonaise* all round
the fillets, or some of the *montpelier* butter, and add
some more *aspic,* quite cold, otherwise the butter will
dilute in the jelly, and will appear muddy; fill the
mould to the rim, and let it freeze; at dinner-time,
dip a rubber in hot water, with which rub the mould,
and turn the *aspic* on the dish. When judiciously
made, this is a pretty dish, but should never be attempted by a clumsy person, who would inevitably
bring disgrace on the art.

Salad Sauce.—Take the yolks of four eggs, boiled
hard, put them into the mortar with a spoonful of
mustard; pound this very fine, add to it salt and pep-

per, two spoonsful of vinegar, and three of sweet oil;
you may also put a spoonful of tarragon or elder
vinegar. If you have in your larder a good jelly of
meat, you may occasionally put some to it, but do
not put any cream, as some do, for it is very unwholesome; you may put some chopped herbs, as
chervil, tarragon, burnet, &c. if approved of. In
making salad sauce, you should be cautious not to
use any of the herbs mentioned without consulting
the taste of your employer.

No. 10.—*Croquettes of Fillets of Soles.*

Several books mention *croquettes* of *salmon*, and
croquettes of cod, which are certainly not eatable.
Sturgeon and soles are the only two fishes which have
a sufficient firmness to allow of their being made into
croquettes. The oftener a fish is presented to the
fire, the more unpalatable it becomes. With regard
to the *croquettes* of soles, reduce the sauce, cut the
soles into small dice, and throw them into it, season
them well, and put the whole preparation into ice.
When cold, cut them into equal parts on a dish. Roll
them either round or oval, but never into pears; dip
them into an *omelette* of two eggs, put a little salt,
and then dip them into crumbs of bread, fry them
of a good colour, and serve them up with crisp fried
green parsley in the middle.

No. 11.—*Fillets of Soles à la Turque.*

Take off and *sautez* the fillets as directed before.
Have some rice swelled, and made soft in good *consommé;* mix it with a few spoonsful of good *béchamelle,* to put in the middle of the dish: this rice must
be thick, in order that it may be dished in a pyramid.
To *mask* the soles take three spoonsful of *béchamelle,*
mixed with a quarter of a pound of butter, a tea-spoonful of *cavice,* and a little salt and pepper. Work this
sauce well, and *mask* the fillets only. The rice is to
form the centre of the turban, as implied by the title.

FRESH HERRINGS.

Herrings are an excellent fish; but the flesh is so delicate that no cook attempts to dress them otherwise than broiled or fried. Those with soft roes are the most delicate. You know them to be very fresh, when the eyes are very red, and the scales shine bright. You must broil them over a brisk fire, but never wash them. Wipe them well, empty and scale them carefully: cut off a small piece of the tail and of the head, to prevent them from burning. Send them to table with mustard sauce in a boat.

Soft Roes of Herrings, in Cases.

Have a paper case, either round or square, its size must be suited to the dish you are going to use; spread some butter over the bottom. Broil eight very fresh soft-roed herrings, and when well done, take out the roes, and put them without breaking into the case. Sprinkle over them a little pepper, salt, rasped bread, and finely chopped parsley; put a few small bits of butter over them in different places, and bake them in a hot oven. When they are done, put a little *maître d'hôtel* into the case, with the juice of a lemon. Send up quite hot, and very firm.

This dish can never be properly prepared if you do not take the precaution to wash the herrings; scale them very well, and wipe them first with a damp cloth, and afterwards with a dry one, then broil them very sharply, so as to keep the soft roe ver y firm. Act as before directed. The case should be made of strong foolscap paper.

PIPER.

This fish is not in the repute which it deserves; for when it is well dressed, it is superior to any other; but it should be used when very fresh

No. 1.—*Baked Piper, Dutch Sauce.*

Empty and clean this fish as you do every other, then make a good stuffing in the following manner: two handsful of crumbs of bread, the same quantity of beef suet, well chopped, parsley, and a little thyme chopped very fine, two whole eggs, a drop of cream, a small bit of butter, salt, a little Cayenne pepper, and a very little spice, ground very fine; mix this very well, and put it into the belly of the fish, and sew it up; bind the tail of the fish to the mouth, and fasten it with the skewer, then rub the fish all over with a brush dipped into the yolk of an egg; sprinkle over some salt, then some crumbs of bread, and baste with clarified butter: then put this to bake in a very hot oven, in order to give it a good colour. When done, drain it, and serve up with Dutch sauce.

No. 2.—*Fillets of Piper à la Sefton.*

Take one large piper, or three small ones, strip the flesh from the bone, and divide it into fillets of the same shape, then put them into a *sauté*-pan with melted butter, as for other fillets, with salt and pepper; when it is dinner time put them on the stove, or into the oven; when done, drain them, and dish them the same as fillets of soles, and the sauce is the same; but they are better eating than either soles or whitings.

No. 3.—*Fillets of Piper à la Maître d'Hôtel.*

The same as No. 2, only you must use the *maître d'hôtel* instead of *white sharp sauce.*

No. 4.—*Fillets of Piper à la Orlie.*

The same as Fillets of Whiting, No. 2, page 287. Observe that the piper is best when red.

RED MULLET.

This fish is in great repute, and deserves it, for the delicacy of its flesh: you may boil them; but in general, to eat them in great perfection, you must wash them well, but not empty them: drain them very dry in a clean cloth; then have some buttered paper and a little salt, wrap them well in it, and put them into the oven, or broil them if you have no oven. They may be eaten with lobster sauce, or anchovy sauce alone; send them to table without the paper.

You may dress them in another way, by putting them in the oven in a buttered baking dish, and covering them with buttered paper; when they are done, serve them over the following sauce:—

A description of *Genevoise:*—Put in a small stew-pan, a little bit of butter, a few pieces of ham, cut in dice, a few leaves of mace, two cloves, a little thyme, a few bits of mushroom, some parsley roots, one shalot, cut in four, and a small bit of carrot; fry them on a slow fire till they become a little brown, then moisten with a glass of good Madeira, and put but little sugar; reduce the wine to half the quantity, add to this a spoonful or two of good *Espagnole*, skim away all the fat, put the sauce through a tammy, and add to it a bit of fresh butter, about a quarter of a pound, add to this the gravy from the fish. Season the sauce of very good taste, with salt, pepper, lemon, &c., and if the sauce should not be thick enough, add a small bit of butter, with a little flour.

MACKAREL.

No. 1.—*Mackarel broiled à la Maître d'Hôtel.*

Mackarel is a fish generally esteemed by all ranks of people. The rich eat it on account of its good savour, the poor because it is cheap. It must not be washed, when intended to be broiled. Empty and wipe it well. Open the back, and put into it a little salt and oil. Broil it on a gentle fire; turn it over on both sides, and also on the back. With the point of your knife try if it is done, by detaching the bone from the flesh. Send it up with a *maître d'hôtel* melted, in a boat. When you wish to eat them very good, and have the taste of the fish, they must not be washed; only pull out the gills, and empty the intestines; then wipe them clean and dry them with a damp cloth; next make an incision on the back, put over them some salt and pepper, and a drop of sweet oil, to prevent them from sticking to the gridiron; broil them well, and then put into the back some butter, kneaded with chopped parsley, pepper, salt, and lemon, &c. as directed above.

No. 2.—*Mackarel boiled.*

When the mackarel have been emptied and washed clean, put them into boiling water, with a handful of salt, and let them boil very fast that they may be firmer. When they are done, drain them and serve them on a cloth with green fennel all round. For the sauce, blanch some fennel in salt and water. When it is quite soft, drain it, chop it, and mix it with the melted butter. Gooseberries are also used for the sauce. Blanch them, when soft lay them in a hair sieve to drain. Squeeze them with a wooden spoon, and strain them through a hair sieve. Throw the *purée* into a stew-pan with a little sugar and butter, and when hot, send up the sauce in a boat.

No. 3.—*Fillets of Mackarel à la Ste. Menhoult.*

Take the fillets of three mackarel, cut each fillet into two. Pare them equally, season them with pepper and salt; then take the yolks of two eggs, beat them well, and rub the fillets over with the brush: dip them first into crumbs of bread, next into clarified butter, and then into crumbs of bread again. Broil them of a fine colour, and serve them up *en miroton* with a white sharp sauce in the middle. (See *Maréchale*, or *Maître d'hôtel.*)

No. 4.—*Fillets of Mackarel sautez à la Maître d'Hôtel.*

Take the fillets of three mackarel, cut them in two, *mark* them in a *sauté*-pan with some melted butter, salt, and pepper. At dinner-time *sautez* them on both sides. When they are done, drain, take off the blue skin; dish, and *mask* them with the *maître d'hôtel.*

No. 5.—*Fillets of Mackarel à la Ravigotte.*

Sautez them the same as above. For *ravigotte à la crême,* see *Ravigotte à la crême,*

No. 6.—*Timballe of soft Roes of Mackarel à la Sefton.*

Take the soft roes of four large mackarel. Do not wash the fish, for the roes then would turn black and soft. *Mark* the roes in melted butter, without any salt; cover them with the butter, and bake them in the oven, or let them sweat on a stove. Take care not to break them. When they are done, lay them on a sheet of white paper to drain: dust a little salt over them, and cut them into small dice as neatly as possible. Put these into *petits pâtés,* which keep hot, and make the following sauce, which is to be put afterwards into the *petits pâtés.* Take two spoonsful of *béchamel,* add a little bit of butter with pepper and salt. Refine this sauce with some thick cream. Keep it hot, fill the *pâtés* in which the soft roes are, but mind that it is liquid enough to penetrate the roes. Above all, send up quite hot. This *entrée* is much esteemed by the daintiest epicures.

N.B.—If you have a grand dinner, four mackarel will make two *entrées* without any connoisseur having occasion to find fault, as they will both differ in flavour as well as in form and appearance.

Observe, that you give the soft roes for *pâtés*, and the fillets for a dish of *fillets* of *mackarel*.

No. 7.—*Soft Roes of Mackarel in Cases.*

Take six very fresh soft-roed mackarel. Broil them till well done, then take the roes from them, and put them into small cases, with parsley chopped fine, a little rasped crust of bread, salt, pepper, and a little butter; then put them into the oven; when they are very hot, send them to table with a drop of white sharp sauce, and the juice of a lemon. This will only make a small dish, but when you want to make it larger, put more soft roes, and use the mackarel for *fillets* as a fish dish.

VIVE GRILLÉE. SEA-DRAGON.

Sea-dragon is a fish that is seldom eaten in England, although in France it is frequently sent up to table. Towards the gills there is a most venomous bone. We always broil it, and serve up with a butter of anchovies, a *maître d'hôtel* or a *provençale*.

ANCHOVIES.

Anchovies are a salt fish of great utility, and of frequent necessity in cookery. Essence of anchovies is a thing which a skilful cook must use with great care, as it is not always made with the fish only, but also with the brine of it, which consequently makes it very unhealthy. Make butter of anchovies yourself, in the following manner: for a dozen of anchovies, a quarter of a pound of fresh butter will do. First wash the anchovies, so that no slime whatever may remain. Take off the bones and fins. Pound the meat with the butter. When well pounded, rub the whole through a hair sieve, and secure it in a gallipot well covered. Use butter of anchovies when wanted, for either *canapés*, salads, fish sauce, &c.; anchovies are very seldom used with meat.

SMELTS.

Smelts are most generally fried. After they have been cleaned and emptied, wipe them very dry, and dip them into an *omelette* of two eggs, and into crumbs of bread mixed with flour. Fry them of a fine colour, and send them up with fried parsley round them.

SKATE.

No. 1.—*Skate with Caper Sauce, French fashion.*[*]

Stew the skate in a *marinade*, that is to say, in a vessel with water, vinegar, salt, pepper, a sliced onion, parsley, green onions, bay-leaves, and thyme. When it is done, pick it neatly, and remove it into another clean vessel; pour over it some of the liquor in which it has been boiling, then drain it and send it up to table, either entire or in pieces, with caper sauce; or in hearts, *masked* with the same sauce.

No. 2.—*Skate au Beurre noir.*

Fry some parsley very green. Dish the skate according to your fancy. For an *entrèe* you must either cut it into the shape of kites, or rounds. Put the fried parsley in the middle of the dish, and the *beurre noir* under the fish.

---

[*] It may be proper to notice, that in France, where the fish is not so fresh as in this country, they are obliged to season this preparation more highly to hide the stench of the skate.

No. 3.—*Skate plain boiled.*

Take off the skin. Boil it in salt and water, and send it up on a clean cloth, with shrimp sauce, or any other sauce in a boat.

No. 4.—*Small Skates fried.*

When the skates are very small, pickle them in vinegar, salt, pepper, a sliced onion, some parsley, and lemon-juice for about an hour. Next drain them and dip them into an *omelette*, and then into flour. Next fry them in hot dripping, and send them up either with or without sauce. This fish is very seldom used for *entrées* in England; when it is boiled with *marinade*, the skin must remain while boiling, otherwise the colour of the *marinade* will dye the fish: take off the skin after it is done, and dress it in the dish immediately.

MIROTON OF FLOUNDERS A L'ITALIENNE.

Cut each flounder in two, and take out all the small bones. Butter a dish *d'entrée*, and dish the flounders *en miroton;* dust them over with salt, pepper, grated nutmeg, chopped mushrooms, parsley, green onions, and raspings of bread: to which add a little butter. Then bake them. When they are done, drain the butter, and send them up with an *Italienne* or caper sauce; add a little essence of anchovies and lemon-juice. This fish, as well as plaice, is seldom used for *entrées* in England. When you give them as fish, they are to be dressed the same as soles, either fried or boiled.

PLAICE.

See Flounders. Plaice can only be fried, or made *en miroton* as above.

LOBSTER.

Lobsters are boiled in the same manner as craw-fish, but they would have a better savour if sea-water could be had to boil them in. Several *ragoûts* are made of lobsters. Pies for *entrées; salades* for *entremets;* fish sauce, and minces in the shell, &c. You must pay attention to the proper time required for boiling a lobster; if you boil it too long, the flesh becomes thready and disagreeable; and if not done enough the spawn is not red through: this must be obviated by great attention.

No. 1.—*Small Timbals of Lobster, au velouté.*

Cut according to their size, the white flesh of one or two lobsters into small dice; put them into a sauce similar to that of *pâtés* of fillets of soles, and serve them up quite hot. This is an *entrée.* The spawn will serve for fish sauce, or for any other use; as *quenelles* or salads, &c. &c.

No. 2.—*Scollops of Lobster in the Shell.*

This is an *entremet.* Take one or two lobsters, according to the size of the dish, or the number of people you have to dinner. Cut the lobster in two without breaking the shell. Clean the inside of the shell, cut the meat of the lobsters into small dice, and preserve the kind of *farce* that is inside. Then take one or two spoonsful of *velouté,* a small bit of butter, a little salt and Cayenne peper, and keep stirring the whole over the fire. When it is quite hot, throw the meat and the kind of *farce* that you found in the lobster into the sauce, and lay the whole in the shells. Level with your knife and strew over crumbs of bread twice, and keep basting with a little melted butter. Give it a colour with the salamander, and keep the scollops very hot. Never let it colour in the oven, as it would taste too strong.

No. 3.—*Lobster Sauce.*

See No. 56, page 25.

No. 4.—*Salad of Lobster.*

See Salad of Fillets of Soles and *mayonaise;* the sauce is to be found among the other sauces. The shape you give to the salad depends on the dish you use. Jelly of meat is not properly used for salads of fish, unless it is as an ornament. Roots and vegetables are more appropriate; and the salad sauce only, or the butter of Montpelier. Lobster may be dressed also without any sauce: merely break the shell, and give an agreeable shape to the dish by putting the body in the middle, the tail cut in two on each side, and the claws at the ends; the flesh of this fish is very firm, and can be used in cookery for *petits pâtés* of all kinds.

MUSSELS AU PERSINET, DITES A LA POULETTE.

Wash the mussels; be particular in taking off all the threads that are found about the joint of the shell, and be cautious of the small crabs, as they are very dangerous eating. Put the mussels into a stew-pan over a brisk fire, and keep them covered that they may be done equally. When they are done, take off one of the shells, dip the mussel into the liquor that has issued from them, in order to wash off the sand. When they have all been picked, let the liquor stand, drain it, pour it into a clean vessel, and then make the following sauce:

Put a small lump of butter with a spoonful of flour into a stew-pan, and make a little white *roux*, to prevent the flour getting brown; moisten with the above-mentioned liquor, add a small bunch of parsley and green onions, and stew them for half an hour. Then take the bunch out, and replace it with a little parsley chopped very fine. Next take the yolks of two or four eggs, according to the quantity of the mussels, to thicken the sauce, which season well, but be rather sparing of salt. Mix the mussels with the sauce; let them be just hot through, and squeeze the juice of a lemon into the sauce, which must be thick, in order to adhere to the mussels. They are dangerous eating in the dog-days.

CRABS

Are prepared and cooked in the same manner as lobsters, but are eaten with oil and vinegar, after having arranged the meat in fillets, and the small claws all round.

OYSTERS.

No. 1.—*Scollops of Oysters.*

The English green oysters are the best that are known. After having opened them, boil them in their own liquor, but do not let them be too much done. Next beard them and return them into the liquor, out of which you take them with a bored ladle. Let the liquor stand, and drain it from the sand. Make a little white *roux*, moisten with the liquor, and when the sauce is got pretty thick, add a spoonful or two of cream, and a spoonful of *béchamelle:* put the oysters into this sauce and season them with salt and pepper. Next put them into the shell used for that purpose, strew them over twice with butter and crumbs of bread; give them a good colour with the salamander, and serve them up very hot with the juice of a lemon. You may grate a little nutmeg over them if you think proper; but never omit parsley chopped very fine. Some people add mushrooms, which are no improvement.

No. 2.—*Small Oyster Patties à la Sefton.*

Pick out the smallest oysters you can find, and boil and beard them as above. Make the sauce also in the same manner, only add to it a little cavice and butter, and a little pepper and salt. Have about two dozen of small patties ready; fill them with oysters and as much sauce as they will hold; have also some crumbs of bread fried of a fine colour, strew some over the small pies, which dish *en buisson.* Serve them up very hot. This addition of the fried crumbs gives a very pleasant taste.

No. 3.—*Small Patties à la Française.*

After having boiled the oysters, beard them, and cut them into dice. Have some mushrooms also cut into dice, which you fry in a little butter dusted over with flour. Moisten with some of the liquor of the oysters, one or two spoonsful of *consommé,* two spoonsful of cream, and let it reduce. Add a small bit of butter; season well with salt and Cayenne pepper; throw the oysters into the sauce, and fill the patties, which must be in *dariole* moulds, otherwise called *timbals.*

No. 4. —*Oyster Sauce.* (See No. 96, page 42.)

If you should be in a hurry, *mark* in a stew-pan a good lump of butter, a spoonful or two of flour, moisten with the liquor of the oysters, and put the sauce on the fire, but do not let it boil. When it is thick, throw in the oysters, with a spoonful of the essence of anchovies, a little *cavice,* a spoonful of thick cream, and serve up.

No. 5.—*Oyster Sauce for Entrées.* *

After having stewed the oysters as above, make a white *roux,* into which you put a few small onions,

---

* Such as fowl, turkey, chicken, &c.

mushrooms, a bunch of parsley and green onions. Moisten with some of the liquor, and a few spoonsful of *consommé*, which reduce over a large fire. Then add a pint of cream, season well; keep the sauce pretty thick, strain it through a tammy, put in the oysters whole, and use it with such articles as require oyster sauce; the only thing to be observed is, that when it is for fish, you must use essence of anchovies.

No. 6.—*Attelets of Oysters.*

This *entrée*, which is no great favourite, has found its way into this work, on account of its being occasionally called for. Stew the oysters as above. Have a *sauce d'attelets*, moisten with some of the liquor, and let it stand to cool. Then skewer the oysters according to the size of your dish, and with your knife spread the sauce all round. Throw crumbs of bread over the oysters; next dip them into an *omelette,* and then into crumbs again. Fry them of a fine brown, and serve them up without any sauce; if any, the sauce made with the oyster is the best.

The *sauce d'attelets* is made as follows: fry some herbs (as parsley, shalots, mushrooms) in a little butter, put a spoonful of flour, moisten with the liquor of the oysters, season it well, reduce the sauce, then thicken it with the yolks of three eggs, and pour it over the oysters. Let the whole stand till cold, and then make the *attelets* in the same way as other *attelets;* the sauce must be only *béchamelle* with the taste of oysters: do not omit the seasoning, salt, pepper, &c.

Observation relative to all sorts of Fish Sauces.

Fish sauces should always be *thick enough* to adhere to the fish. When the sauce is too liquid it is abominable: of the two, the thick is preferable, as you can make it thinner at table, by adding some of the cruet sauces.

OF EGGS IN GENERAL.

Eggs are indispensable in cookery. They are used for a prodigious number of *entrées, entremets,* and sauces.. Eggs are the original of all pastry, as well as of creams. The author will proceed to show the manner in which they may be used, either for first or second courses. You should, however, be particular in the use of them, a single bad one will spoil a very large dish, and when you make *biscuit, liaison, œufs brouillés, &c. &c.,* you should break them, and smell them one after the other: when you remove the yolk from the white you should have a small basin to break them in separately.

No. 1.—*Omelette Moëlleuse.*

Break eight eggs into an earthen pan with a little pepper and salt, and a sufficient quantity of water to melt the salt. Beat the eggs well; then throw an ounce and a half of fresh butter into a frying-pan, and melt it over a brisk fire: pour the eggs into the pan, which is not to be kept too close to the fire. Keep turning continually, but never let the middle part of it be over the fire, for it is always rather too hot. Gather all the border together, and roll the *omelette* before it gets too much done. The middle part must always be kept mellow. Roll it equally with your knife before you dish it, and take care not to let the pan soil the dish, in turning out the *omelette* into it.

No. 2.—*L'Omelette aux fines Herbes.*

The same preparation as above, with the addition only of a little parsley chopped very fine. Some people mix a few chopped shalots likewise, which may be done if approved of.

No. 3—*Small Omelettes with Ham.*

Mark these *omelettes* as above. If you have some ham which has served as a remove, mince about a quarter of a pound of it, which you throw into a little very thick *Espagnole.* Then make small omelettes of about two eggs each. Before you roll them, put in a spoonful of the minced ham. You may make four or six, according to the size of the dish. Take care not to put too much salt; and if the ham is briny, do not put any salt at all. You may put four or five omelettes to one dish. (This is a second course dish.)

No. 4.—*Small Omelettes with Sorrel.*

Make small *omelettes* as above. Have some sorrel ready stewed, which you put on each of the *omelettes* before you roll them, the same as above with ham. Give them a pleasing shape and colour. The same number as above.

No. 5.—*Omelette with Kidney of Veal.*

If you have remaining the kidney of a roasted loin of veal, chop it, and put it in an *omelette*, prepared as in No. 1. Make it mellow, and season it properly with salt.

No. 6.—*Small Omelettes with Sweetmeats.*

Make small *omelettes* as above. Let them be done properly. Put in the sweetmeats before you roll the *omelettes*, and lay them on the cover of a stew-pan. When they are all made, sprinkle over them a little finely-pounded sugar, and then use the salamander to glaze them of a fine colour. *Omelettes* are always second course dishes, called *entremets.* The only sweetmeats used in these dishes, are currant jelly, or apricot marmalade.

No. 7.—*Fried Eggs*.

Break some fresh eggs into a dish, without damaging the yolks, and powder them over with a little pepper and salt. Then fry some butter; a quarter of a pound will do for a dozen of eggs. When the butter is completely fried, pour it over the eggs, and then put the eggs into the frying-pan, which keep at a little distance from the fire, for fear the eggs should stick. When they are done at the bottom, use the salamander for the top, till they turn white. Then dish without breaking them, and pour over them a little vinegar.

No. 8.—*Eggs au Miroir*.

Butter the dish in which you are to send up the eggs, break eight of them, but mind that they are fresh, seasoned with pepper and salt: then cut small pieces of butter over the eggs, and use the salamander, and a small fire under, till they are quite white. They must not be too much done.

No. 9.—*Poached Eggs*.

Boil some water with a little vinegar. Take some fresh eggs, and break the point of the shell with your knife, that the egg may drop into the water without breaking. Turn with the shell to gather all the white round the yolk. Never poach more than four at a time. As soon as they are done, take them out, one at a time, and throw them into cold water. When you have poached the number you want, *pare* them well. Then with your finger rub them gently over in the water, that they may be very neat and white. They must be very soft. These serve for a great number of *entrées* and *entremets*. They may be served with sorrel, spinach, gravy of veal, clarified gravy, &c. &c.

No. 10.—*Fried Poached Eggs.*

You must have a *sauté*-pan made on purpose for this dish, with little round holes in it, to fry the eggs in boiling oil. They fry better and are drier, when you use oil instead of butter. Fry them soft, but of a very brown colour, and before you send them up, powder a little salt over them and glaze them.

No. 11.—*Eggs à la Tripe.*

Make a little *roux* with flour and butter; fry a few chopped onions in the same stew-pan before the *roux* is made brown. Moisten with some good boiling milk, pepper and salt. Let the flour and onions be well done, and keep the sauce rather thick. Next have ten eggs boiled hard, cut them in quarters or in round slices, and put them into the sauce. Stir gently, that the yolk may not separate from the white, and serve up.

No. 12.—*Eggs à la Maître d'Hôtel.*

Make a little white *roux* as above. Moisten with some good boiling milk, pepper and salt: let these stew for half an hour. Throw a quarter of a pound of fresh butter into the sauce, with a little parsley chopped very fine. Cut the eggs into the sauce, and send up to table quite hot. Add the juice of a lemon.

No. 13.—*Eggs à l'Aurore.*

Cut a dozen of hard eggs in two; take the yolks from them, which strain through a hair sieve, then make a *sauce* as follows: mark, in a stew-pan, a quarter of a pound of butter, half a spoonful of flour, with pepper and salt, a little nutmeg, and half a pint of cream. Then stew this sauce till thick, but do not let it boil. Chop half the whites of the eggs, and throw it into the sauce. Next dish the whites, pour the yolks over them equally, baste them with a little butter, and use the salamander. Then serve up.

No. 14.—*Eggs en surprise.*

Cut a dozen and a half of eggs (boiled hard) in two. Take all the yolks and pound them in a mortar, with a quartern, or if you choose with half a pound of butter, with which mix a little cream, pepper, salt, and grated nutmeg. When you have pounded about half an hour, add two raw eggs to thicken the *farce.* Then *pare* out the inside of the whites, and fill one-half of them again with the *farce.* Next mix some chopped parsley with part of the *farce,* and fill the other half of the eggs. Erect a little dome in the centre of the dish with some of the *farce,* and trim it all round with the stuffed eggs; contrive to give them a pleasing appearance. Next put them into an oven for ten minutes, and send them up quite hot. In paring the inside of the whites, you must leave only just enough to keep in the *farce.*

No. 15.—*Croquettes of Eggs.*

Cut the white of a dozen and a half of eggs (boiled hard) into small dice. Strain the yolks of six eggs through a hair sieve. Cut a couple of onions into dice, sweat them white in a quarter of a pound of butter, then put a spoonful of flour to fry; moisten with boiling milk, and season with salt and pepper. Next throw both the whites and yolks into the sauce. Let them cool, and cover them with crumbs of bread, as you do all other *croquettes.* If you were to put in all the yolks, the *croquettes* would get too dry; the remaining yolks may be used for salads, &c. Season of a good taste, and put fried parsley in the middle.

No. 16.—*Andouilles of Eggs.*

Cut the whites of eggs boiled hard into fillets as long as you can make them: cut a few truffles, onions, and mushrooms the same, sweat the whole except the eggs, in a little butter. When done put the ingredients in a hair sieve to drain the butter. Next make a *sauce à la crême,* which must be rather thick, mix the liquor in which the truffles, &c. have been sweated, with the sauce, and set them boiling. When it is thick enough, put the fillets of eggs into it, and let it cool over ice. Make two *boudins*, which you dip into an *omelette*, as you do the *boudins à la Reine*. Fry them, and send them up with fried parsley between the *boudins*. These make a very good *entrée* when you are short of dishes in the country. All the preceding dishes, from No. 7 to this last, are *entrées*.

No. 17.—*Eggs à la Neige.*

Beat some whites of eggs, which boil in milk, with a little salt. Cut them all of a size with a spoon, and drain them. Then boil a pint of cream. When it boils, throw in the thin outside peel of half a lemon, a little sugar, and a very small quantity of salt; let the lemon steep. Then beat the yolks of four eggs with the cream, and let it thicken on the fire. When the cream is thick enough, strain it through a tammy, and *mask* the eggs *à la neige* with this sauce. Another time, instead of lemon, use leaves of rose or almond laurel; although in England it is considered poisonous, a small quantity is never injurious.

No. 18.—*Les Cocottes.*

Put a little fresh butter at the bottom of small China cups, called *cocottes*. Break a fine new-laid egg over the butter, with a little salt and some coarse pepper. Lay these over some red hot ashes, and then use the salamander till the eggs are done soft.

No. 19.—*Egg brouillés.*

There are various sorts of eggs *brouillés*, namely:—with *champignons*, with *cardes*, with truffles, with cucumbers, with verjuice, with broth, and with asparagus heads, which are made as follows:—

Break eight eggs into a clean stew-pan with half a quarter of a pound of butter, and a little salt and pepper; beat the eggs till the whites and yolks are well blended. Then put the stew-pan on a slow fire, and keep constantly stirring with a wooden-spoon; mind that the eggs *brouillés* are never to be grumous or clotty. A spoonful of broth or sauce makes them more delicate, and add whatever you intend to put in it, from the various names above.

No. 20.—*Eggs and Bacon.*

This may appear a common and vulgar dish. It is, however, a palatable one, and well calculated for the keen appetites generated by shooting, or the chase. Prepare it as follows:—Break with great care the number of eggs you intend to fry, (more than ten or twelve will never fry well.) Then break them without injuring the yolks; fry the butter till it becomes very hot, and throw the eggs gently in the pan; fry them very well, and do not let them be too much done; add some salt and pepper, and with the salamander slip the eggs dexterously on a dish; fry some bacon separately, and put it round the eggs. Serve very hot.

ENTREMETS OF VEGETABLES

General Remark on Vegetables.

ALTHOUGH the various sorts of vegetables are so numerous, the cook is not unfrequently left with a scarcity of dishes for the second course, as most of the better sort make their appearance at the same time of the year. Winter is a season of peculiar difficulty for *entremets* of vegetables, as the nobility of this country do not use any of the dry-floured vegetables; you are therefore left with only *cardons*, spinach, salsifis, brocolis, and potatoes; and in this short list of vegetables, little variety is left for the table except in the different ways of dressing.

No. 1.—*Cardons à l'Espagnole.*

This dish, which is first introduced amongst the *entremets* of vegetables, requires great attention, and no small share of skill in the art of cookery. It is not much relished in England, but in France it is held in the highest estimation. It is always one of those selected for the trial of a cook.

In the first place, you must select a few heads of *cardons* all very white. Cut each leaf into slices of six inches long; with the exception, however, of those that are hollow, which are tough and thready. Beard them of their prickles, and blanch them, by putting the thickest leaves into boiling water. When you have given these a few boils, put in the leaves of the heart; turn the middle stalks into large olives, and blanch them likewise. Then try a piece in cold water, to see whether the slime which is on the surface will come off by rubbing. If so, take them off the fire immediately, and throw them into cold water, as they are done enough; or you may cool the boiling water, by pouring in cold till you are able to bear your hand in it, to rub off all the slime. This being done, wash them clean, and throw the *cardons* into a *blanc*, give them a single boil, and leave them in the *blanc*. Whenever you wish to use them, drain a sufficient quantity. *Pare* both extremities, and mark them in a stew-pan with four spoonsful of *Espagnole*, and four spoonsful of *consommé*, a little salt and a little sugar. Let them boil over a sharp fire, that they may not be done too much; be sure to skim off all the fat. Dish them nicely. Strain the sauce through a tammy before you *mask* them. Send them up to table quite hot with a cover over them to prevent their getting dry.

The *cardons* mix very well with eggs, and when you have any returned from table, they will warm up again very well, if you are particular in taking them off to put them in the larder, in this case they are too much done; use them to make *les œufs brouillés*, *œufs cardé*, which you should make only when you have *cardons* left from the parlour. This is a capital *entremet*, and may be selected as one of the finest efforts of cookery.

No. 2.—*Cardons à l'Essence with Marrow.*

Proceed as above. Take a few pieces of beef marrow all of a size, which you put in warm water to draw out all the blood. When thoroughly disgorged, blanch and stew them in water with a little salt, and a few slices of lemon to keep them white. When done, drain them in a clean towel, and put them into the essence, which is nothing but some *Espagnole* reduced; unless you have some essence, or *Espagnole*, as mentioned among the sauces. Drain the fat, and do not forget to put a little sugar; which is requisite in all dishes of *cardons*, as it improves them greatly. *Cardons* are not unfrequently bitter.

No. 3.—*Cardons au Velouté.*

The same preparation as in the two preceding articles. Take some out of the *blanc*, trim, and stew them in a little *consommé*, and when they are done, drain and sauce them with some *veloulé* or *béchamel*.

No. 4.—*Cardons à la Sauce blanche.*

The same preparation as above; only sauce with the *sauce blanche*, or French melted butter.

SPINACH.

No. 1.—*Spinach au Consommé.*

You must take particular care when the spinach is picked, that no stalks or weeds are left amongst it. The least oversight may cause the spinach to be good for nothing, notwithstanding all the trouble you might take in cooking it. It must be washed several times in a great quantity of water. Then boil some water in a vessel large enough for the spinach to float with ease. Put a great deal of salt, that it may preserve its green colour, and press it down frequently with a wooden spoon, that it may be done equally. When it has had a few boils, try whether it can be squeezed easily between your two fingers: then without loss of time, put it into a cullender to drain the water. Next throw it into a great quantity of cold water to keep it green. When it is quite cold, make it into balls and squeeze it well. Then spread it on the table with your knife to ascertain that no improper substance is left among it. Chop it very fine, put a good piece of butter into a stew-pan, and lay the spinach over the butter. Let it dry over a gentle fire, and next dredge it with a spoonful of flour Moisten with a few spoonsful of *consommé* and let it stew briskly, that it may not turn yellow. Make it rich with a small piece of glaze. If you intend to send it up as an *entrée* with a ham, or a tongue, &c. you must mix a few spoonsful of *Espagnole*, and let it be well seasoned. Some people like nutmeg, in that case you may grate a little into it. Spinach thus prepared may be used with a *fricandeau*, sweet breads of veal and breasts of veal or of mutton.

No. 2.—*Spinach with Cream.*

Blanch and prepare it as above, only use cream instead of broth. Boil the cream before you throw it over the spinach. If it should curdle, the cream only is lost; whereas, otherwise, you would lose the spinach, butter, and all. Spinach with cream requires a little sugar and nutmeg. It is needless to repeat, that a little salt is also requisite, as there can be no good seasoning without it. You must always have fried toasts of bread round the spinach when you send it up to table, or some made of puff-paste flourets; but mind that they must both be fresh made.

No. 3.—*Spinach French fashion.*

This dish in Paris is called *à l'Anglais*. The spinach is to be blanched as above. Squeeze it well, and pound it in a mortar; then *mark* it in a stew-pan with a little butter. Leave it for three-quarters of an hour on a very slow fire till very dry. Next throw in a quarter of a pound of very fresh butter, with salt, and grated nutmeg. Work the spinach well till it is thick, but take care the butter does not turn to oil, and serve very hot.

No. 4.—*Croustades of Spinach.*

This dish is introduced merely for the sake of variety. Cut some bread into hearts, which you slit all round. Fry them in butter. Arrange those hearts

in the form of a rosette. Next cut a round of
bread, which slit in the same manner, and place it in
the middle, over the points of the hearts. Fry these
till they are of a fine brown, then cut out the interior,
take out all the crumb, and fill the vacuity with spinach, either with cream or *consommé*. Observe, that
when spinach is dressed to put under meat, whether
fricandeau or sweetbread, &c. it must be more seasoned than when dressed for *entremets*, and a little
more liquid, as it is like sauce. Spinach is often used
in sweet dishes to dye the almonds, or make the green
colour of the *biscuit marbré*. You pound in the
mortar some of the spinach, and squeeze the juice out
of it by pressing it through a towel; put the liquor in
a small stew-pan, and place the stew-pan in a *bain
marie* to poach. When the green is settled at the
bottom of the stew pan, drain it through a silk sieve
and use it for almonds, or whatever requires green.

ENDIVE.

No. 1.—*Endive with Gravy of Veal.*

Wash and clean twelve heads of endive, and be-
ware of the worms, which generally are found in the
heart. After having taken off all the green part of
the leaves, wash the endive again in two or three
different waters, and blanch them to take off the bitter taste. Then throw them into cold water, and
when quite cold, squeeze them till there is no water
left in them, then chop them very fine Next stew
them in a sufficient quantity of gravy to cover them
entirely, to which add a little salt, and a very small
lump of sugar to qualify the bitter tart taste of the
endive. Ascertain if they are done enough, by
squeezing a bit between two fingers; if very tender,
they are done. Then add two spoonsful of *Espagnole*

reduced, and use them either for *entremets* under poached eggs, or for *entrées*, such as minces of mutton, *muzettes* of mutton, *carbonades*, *fricandeau*, sweetbreads, fillets of fowl, &c. &c.

No. 2.—*Endive au Velouté.*

The same preparation as above, but instead of gravy use *consommé*, and in lieu of *Espagnole* take *béchamel.* Endive must always be stewed in broth, or gravy, or *consommé.* The sauce must not boil when you pour it over the endive, especially if it is cream sauce. If you wish the sauce to be white, add some thick cream to it. Endive is a very wholesome vegetable, but you take off from its quality by adding to it strong seasoning, by which it becomes an epicurean sauce; it is, however, very strengthening, and of easy digestion.

No. 3.—*Endive à la Française.*

The same preparation again as in No. 1. When the endive is done in the broth as above, reduce it quite dry; put in a quarter of a pound of fresh butter, a little salt, nutmeg, and pepper. Mix all together, and serve up very hot.

CAULIFLOWER.

Cauliflowers are never good but when white and hard, and are never used in French cookery when they begin to run to seed.

No. 1.—*Cauliflowers à la Sauce blanche.*

After having torn off all the green leaves, it is requisite you should open the cauliflower to remove the snails or other insects, which are liable to creep towards the heart. For this purpose, leave the cauliflower in cold water for an hour. Next throw it into boiling water, with a little salt and butter. This vegetable being very tender, is soon done. If you wish to boil it beforehand, take it off the fire when only half done, as its being left in boiling water will soon finish it. Drain them separately, without breaking them; dish them in the shape of a large cauliflower, and pour the sauce over them. (See *Sauce blanche.*)

No. 2.—*Cauliflower au Velouté.*

The same preparation as above, with the only difference that you use *velouté* instead of *sauce blanche.* You make the *velouté* by putting a small bit of butter in *bechamel.*

No. 3.—*Cauliflowers with Parmesan Cheese.*

Prepare and dish the cauliflowers as above. Next *mask* the top with a little thick *béchamel,* powder some rasped Parmesan cheese over them, and melt a little fresh butter, which pour gently in different places. Then stew them over with crumbs of bread and rasped cheese again, to which you give a fine colour with the salamander. Wipe the border of the dish, mix a little Parmesan cheese with some *velouté* and a little fresh butter, work the sauce, season it well, and pour it gently all round the cauliflower. If you should happen to have neither *béchamel* nor any other sauce ready, a little melted butter with some glaze in it, will answer the same purpose; but it is more liable to turn to oil.

No. 4.—*Cauliflower à l'Espagnole.*

The same preparation again as in No. 1. When the cauliflowers are done, drain them, and put them to simmer a little in a stew-pan with a few spoonsful of *Espagnole.* If you serve them in a silver stew-pan, it is requisite that the cauliflower should be boiled in the same, as they would break if you attempted to shift them into another vessel.

N. B.—Cauliflowers intended for *entrées* are to be prepared as in No. 1, and they always look whiter if boiled beforehand.

SALSIFIS.

This root, when black, we call *salsifis;* if white, it goes by the appellation of *scorsonary.* This latter is by no means so tender or palatable as the former; however, both are prepared and dressed in the same manner. Scrape them gently, so as to strip them only of the outside peel. Then cut them into pieces of an equal size, of about four inches, and throw them into water with a little vinegar, or lemon-juice, to prevent their getting black. When you have scraped a sufficient quantity, boil them in water enough for them to swim with ease; put a little salt and a small bit of butter, and juice of a lemon. They will generally be done in three-quarters of an hour; yet it is better to ascertain the fact by taking a piece out of the water, and trying with your knife whether they are done enough, which is the case when the knife penetrates easily. Drain the *salsifis*, and send them up with whatever sauce you think proper. It is generally served with *velouté*, or *sauce blanche*, or French melted butter.

No. 1.—*Salsifis au Velouté.*

The same preparation as above. Only observe that such sauces as are sent up with vegetables, must always be refined, and thickened with fresh butter; never forget salt and a little Cayenne.

No. 2.—*Salsifis à l'Espagnole.*

The same preparation as in No. 1. Only use *Espagnole* instead of *sauce blanche*.

No. 3.—*Fried Salsifis.*

Make a batter as follows: take six spoonsful of flour, a small pinch of salt, a spoonful of olive oil, and beat the whole with beer, enough to make it into batter, but do not make it too liquid. Then beat the whites of two eggs, and when well beaten, pour them into the batter, which you keep stirring gently. Next put the vegetables, that are done beforehand and well drained in a cloth, into the batter; take them out again one by one, and throw them into the dripping. Use a skewer, to prevent their sticking together. When fried of a fine colour and crisp, send them up with fried parsley in the centre of the dish, and a little pounded salt sprinkled over the vegetables.

No. 4.—*Salsifis en Salade or Aspic.*

Take *salsifis* enough to fill a mould of the size of the dish; then boil them in the same way as the others; drain and cut them of the length of the mould; dress them like a *Chartreuse*, dip them into a little aspic, to stick them together all round the mould, and fill the middle with a salad of small bits of *salsifis* all of the same size; then season with salt, pepper, a little oil and vinegar, and a little *aspic;* put also some parsley chopped very fine; toss the whole, and put it in the mould into ice. At dinner, dip a rubber into hot water, rub the mould all round with it, and turn the salad out on the dish to serve up. If you can procure a few French beans very green it will make the salad appear better; white haricot beans are likewise very useful.

ARTICHOKES.

Artichokes are fit to eat only when young and tender. Such as are intended for *l'estouffade*, or *la barigoule*, or plain boiled, must be full grown; the sprouts are used when to be fried *à la Provençale, à l'Itali-*

enne, &c.   You ascertain that they are good, by the stalks breaking without being thready.

No. 1.—*Artichokes au Naturel.*

According to the size of your dish,* boil a certain quantity of artichokes in salt and water only, after having washed them in several waters: remove all the insects that swarm about the leaves, and trim them of all the bad leaves; ascertain whether they are done enough, either with the point of a knife, or by tearing off one of the leaves.   If the knife penetrates, or the leaf comes off with facility, then you may be certain that the artichoke is done.   Shift it instantly into cold water, that you may take out all the inside; first take off the top all of a lump, then empty the choke, set the top on again, and send up as hot as possible, with a *sauce blanche,* or French melted butter in a sauce-boat.

No. 2.—*Artichokes à l'Estouffade.*

These are prepared as in No. 1, but boil them only till you are enabled to empty them of all the choke. When emptied, drain them well.   Then have some olive oil boiling, in which fry the surface of the leaves. When they are of a fine brown colour, wipe off all the oil, and *mark* the artichokes in a stew-pan trimmed with layers of fat bacon, and a few slices of ham; powder each artichoke with a little salt, and add to them a few carrots, onions, and a clove.   Next cover them with thin layers of lean bacon.   One single spoonful of broth will be sufficient to moisten the whole. There must be but a very small fire underneath, and a very brisk one on the top.   The artichokes will be done in three-quarters of an hour's time, if they

---

* *Another Method.*—Take of artichokes a number not exceeding five, because when the dish is too full, it does not look well. Cut all the points of the leaves, and trim the bottoms very neatly, rub the bottoms with the juice of a lemon to prevent it turning black, and when you have boiled them, empty the middle, and serve them very hot with plain melted butter.

are young and tender; but as not unfrequently there
are old ones among the number, it is better to ascertain
with the point of a knife whether they are really
done enough. Next drain all the grease, dish them,
and send up with an *Espagnole*, and the juice of a
lemon in the inside of each of them.

No. 3.—*Artichokes à la Barigoule*

Are prepared in every respect like those of No. 2.
Only have some sweet herbs, such as mushrooms,
shalots, and parsley chopped very fine, which you fry
white in a little butter. When they are done, without being made too dry, season with pepper, salt, and
the juice of a lemon. Then divide those herbs, and
put them inside the artichokes, which you stew as
above. When done, drain them from the fat upon a
clean towel, and send up with a brown *Italienne* in
the inside.

No. 4.—*Artichokes à la Provençale.*

Choose some artichokes that are very tender, cut
them into four equal quarters, *pare* them nicely,
and rub them over with some lemon, that they may
preserve their white colour. Throw them into cold
water, the quantity to be in proportion to the size of
the dish, in which you are to serve the *entremets.*
Trim a stew-pan with a little olive oil, salt, and pepper, or butter, then put the artichokes all round, and
set the whole to stew over some red-hot ashes, or to
bake in a moderately hot oven. When done, drain
the artichokes, and serve them up with French melted butter in them, to which add a little glaze, and
the juice of a lemon; or otherwise some *Espagnole*
worked with a small lump of butter, and the juice of
a lemon.

No. 5.—*Fried Artichokes.*

Let the artichokes be tender, and cut into quarters
as above. Rub them over with a lemon to keep them

white. When they have been well washed and drained, so that not a single drop of water remains, throw them into an earthen pan, with some pepper, salt, and the juice of a lemon. Next take four spoonsful of flour, three entire eggs, a tea-spoonful of olive oil, and keep stirring the whole with a wooden spoon till the leaves are well imbued. Then have some dripping, which must not be too hot, so that the artichokes may be done through of a fine brown colour. Throw the artichokes into the dripping piece after piece, and use a skewer to prevent their sticking together. When they are done and crisp, lay them on a towel to drain, and send them up with fried crisp green parsley. The paste will do better if you take care to make it an hour before you begin to fry them. The paste dilutes and goes into all the leaves. Trim the artichokes so as to make the leaves open.

No. 6.—*Artichokes à l' Italienne.*

These are also to be cut into quarters, and boiled in water enough to enable them to swim with ease; with a little salt and butter. When done, drain them well, and lay them all round the dish with the leaves outwards. Then take some *Italienne*, with which you mix a small bit of butter, and pour the sauce over the part that is to be eaten, but not over the leaves.

No. 7.—*Artichoke bottoms.*

Artichoke bottoms require to be turned very nicely, and the most tender leaves are to be left on, that the inside of the artichokes may be kept more clean. Blanch them in salt and water. When they are so far done that you may pull off the leaves, and empty the choke without breaking the bottoms, take them out of the water, and throw them into cold water, that you may strip them entirely of the leaves, and remove the choke. Then make a *blanc* in the following manner.

Blanc for Vegetables and Cardons in general.

Cut about half a pound of fat bacon into large dice, as also a little beef suet: take half a quarter of a pound of fresh butter, a little salt, and the half of a lemon cut in thin slices, and put the whole into a sufficient quantity of water to cover whatever you wish to put into your *blanc*. Let this *blanc* stew for half an hour before you throw in the artichoke-bottoms, which are also generally done in the same space of time, yet the most certain method is to use the point of your knife to ascertain if they are done enough. Send them up with whatever sauce you may think proper. They likewise serve to *garnish* either *fricassées* of fowls, *ragoûts*, white or brown, &c. they are always to be boiled in this way, in whatever sauce you may serve them.

No. 8.—*Artichoke-bottoms en Canapés.*

These, when cold, are served for *entremets*. Pour on the centre of each artichoke-bottom some anchovy butter, or Montpelier butter, and decorate the whole with capers, pickled cucumbers, beet-root, &c.; and when ready to serve up, pour over them a salad sauce, garnished with cresses between. It will be readily perceived that over a flat bottom of artichokes it will be very easy to make some decoration with Montpelier butter, gherkin, anchovies, capers, hard eggs, white and yellow, &c.; it rests entirely to the judicious sagacity of the artist; make salad sauce always for this *entremet*.

FRENCH BEANS.

No. 1.—*French Beans à la Poulette.*

French beans must be young and tender. The fruiterers and green-grocers of this country sell them by the hundred when they are unfit to eat; but they are fit to be eaten only when they are sold at market by the measure, as they are then young and tender. They are to be boiled in salt and water, over a large fire, that they may retain their green colour.

The *poulette* is made with a little *sauce tournée*, which you reduce, and next thicken with the yolks of two eggs, to which you add a little parsley chopped very fine. When the thickening is done enough, add to it a good lump of fresh butter, which you work well, a little pepper and salt, and the juice of half a lemon. Drain the beans well, so that no water remains; dish them lightly (as the sauce should penetrate thoroughly,) and send up with the sauce over them.

No. 2.—*French Beans à la Lyonaise.*

These are to be prepared as above. Next cut some onions into slices; fry them of a fine brown colour, take two spoonsful of *Espagnole*, and work it with a good lump of fresh butter. After having drained the onions and beans, pour them into the sauce, keep stirring, season them well with salt, and a little pepper; serve up hot over the beans.

No. 3.—*French Beans à la Française.*

After having boiled the beans as in No. 1, drain and lay them on the fire in a stew-pan, to dry all the water. When entirely dry and quite hot, add to them a quarter of a pound of fresh butter, a little pepper and salt, and the juice of half a lemon; keep moving the stew-pan without using a spoon, as that would break the beans. If the butter should not mix well, add half a spoonful of *sauce tournée*, and send up hot.

No. 4.—*French Beans à la Provençale.*

These are to be boiled as above. Take two small pieces of garlic, which squeeze on the dresser with a wooden spoon, mixed with a little fresh butter. Let the beans be made quite dry, as in No. 3, and then put in the garlic with a quarter of a pound of butter, and keep stirring the beans till the whole is well combined. Mix some herbs chopped fine with the above, such as parsley and shalots, or green onions, to which add a little good olive oil. Keep stirring, and if you do it properly the oil will form a pomatum. Lastly, season it well, with the addition of the juice of a lemon, Serve up hot and with great expedition, that no oil may drop.

WHITE BEANS.

No. 1.—*White Beans à la Maître d'Hôtel.*

White beans when new and fresh, must be put into boiling water. But if they are dry, they must be soaked for an hour in cold water, before you boil them. Then boil them in cold water, and replenish with cold water also, which makes the rind or coat tender. White beans must be well done before you dress them *à la maître d'hôtel*, which is done as follows: trim a stew-pan with a quarter of a pound of fresh butter, a little parsley chopped very fine, and some pepper and salt, over which lay the beans, well drained. Keep moving the stew-pan without using a spoon, for fear of crumbling the beans. Then squeeze the juice of half a lemon, and send up quite hot.

No. 2.—*White Beans à la Lyonaise.*

Cut a few onions into dice, and fry them in a little butter till they are of a light brown colour; then add to them two spoonsful of *Espagnole.* Let the onions be well done; season them with pepper and salt; drain the beans that have been done as above, then throw them into the sauce, and serve up hot; if you have no *Espagnole* sauce, when you have fried the onions, add to it a spoonful of fine flour, and moisten with good gravy, or broth, and a little glaze, then boil it very well, and put the beans in as directed.

No. 3.—*The Purée of White Beans.*

The beans, which must have been boiled beforehand, are to be mixed with the following preparation: chop some onions, and fry them lightly in a little butter, put a little flour to fry in the butter, and when done moisten with a spoonful or two of broth. Let the onions be thoroughly done. Next let the beans boil in that sauce for half an hour, season well, without pepper, however, and strain them through a tammy. Reduce the *purée* over a brisk fire, skim off the white scum, and before you serve up, refine the *purée* with a bit of very fresh butter, and two spoonsful of thick cream. This *entremet* is to be garnished with fried crusts of bread all round.

No. 4.—*The same as above, brown.*

Is prepared in the same manner as that above, with this difference, that the onions are to be fried brown, and moistened with some *Espagnole*, or gravy of veal; in case you should not have any, as soon as the onion is of a fine brown colour, throw in a spoonful of flour, and moisten with a little gravy of veal, and broth; let the flour be well done, and set the beans to boil in it for half an hour, that the taste of both may be well mixed; next rub the whole through a tammy, and give it a good seasoning. Remember that brown sauces are always to be more highly seasoned than others. This *purée* is made either for *entremets*, or for sauces; when intended for sauce, it should be liquid, and still more liquid for soup; it makes excellent soup, only moisten with the water in which you have boiled the beans, and add a bunch of parsley and green onions, when you mean to use the water for broth or soup.

ASPARAGUS.

Observation.—Asparagus is a very wholesome vegetable; do not eat them except they are fresh gathered, as they produce the contrary effect, and are of very bad taste; when used fresh they are mildly aperient; never put them in water to preserve them, unless you immerse them perpendicularly with only about half an inch plunged in water. This method will keep them tolerably fresh: there is nothing, however, like having them fresh gathered.

No. 1.—*Asparagus with Sauce blanche, dites en Bâtonets.*

Asparagus are always boiled in salt and water, whether intended for *entrées* or *entremets.* The water in which they are boiled is always impregnated with a nauseous bitter taste; for which reason asparagus is never used in soups or garnish, but at the very last moment before sending up the dinner. They must boil over a large fire, in order to preserve their green colour. Those served *en bâtonets* are cut according to the size of the dish. A toast of bread is generally put under the asparagus, to raise them on the dish, and to receive the water which may issue from them. Send up separately some melted butter in a boat.

No. 2.—*Asparagus Peas.*

If the asparagus are properly dressed, they must taste like green peas. Take some young asparagus, which pick with great care; then cut them into small equal pieces, avoiding to put in such parts as are hard or tough. Wash them in several waters, and throw them into boiling water, with a little salt. When the asparagus are nearly done, drain them first through a sieve, and next wipe them quite dry with a towel. Then put them into a stew-pan with a small bit of butter, a bunch of parsley, and green onions, and *sautez** them over the fire for ten minutes. Now add a little flour, and a small lump of sugar, and moisten with boiling water. They must boil over a

* *Sautez* means, toss them in the stew-pan, to do them equally.

large fire. When well reduced, take out the parsley and green onions, and thicken with the yoiks of two eggs beaten with a little cream, and a little salt. Remember that in this *entremet* sugar must predominate, and that there is to be no sauce. Asparagus are always dressed in this manner, when to be served as *entremets;* but for *entrées*, throw them into some good *sauce tournée* well reduced. Give them a few boils over a large fire, then powder a little sugar, and make a thickening of one egg. The sauce must be made thick, on account of the asparagus always giving out a certain quantity of water that will thin the sauce.*

CUCUMBERS.†

No. 1.—*Cucumbers farcis.*

Take four or six cucumbers, according to the size of your dish; cut them into the shape of a screw, which is done by leaning with your thumb on the blade of your knife whilst cutting the cucumber, at an equal distance. When you have thus turned the outside, empty the inside with a scooper. Take great care not to bruise the cucumbers, which when prepared, you throw successively into some water. Now blanch them, and cool them in cold water; drain them; then take a little *farce à quenelles*, or some *godiveau*, (see *Farces*), with which fill the cucumbers. *Mark* them in a stew-pan with layers of bacon, under and above, and a little salt and pepper;

---

* I shall observe here, the quantity of dishes and soups that asparagus serve, either for flavours or garnish; such as, " *macédoine,*" "*jardinière,*" "*pointes d'asperge,*" " *salad,*" " *aspics,*" &c.

† Cucumbers are a very cool plant, but of very great use in cookery; they are useful in first and second courses, and may be dressed in a great many different ways; they are of very easy digestion, and may be recommended as very healthy food.

moisten with some good *consommé*, and let them stew, but not too long. Lay them on a towel to drain, and send them up with a fine *Espagnole* almost reduced to glaze.

No. 2.—*Cucumbers à la Poulette.*

Cut some cucumbers in the shape of half-crown pieces, *marinade* them for half an hour in a little salt and vinegar; next drain them in a towel, and lay them in a stew-pan with half a quarter of a pound of butter. Fry them white over a brisk fire, and then powder them over with a little flour. Next moisten with a little broth, and let them be reduced without breaking. When sufficiently reduced, add a little chopped parsley, a little sugar, and a thickening of three eggs or more, according to the quantity of the cucumbers, together with a little salt; you may also put a little pepper if you like it. It would be useless to recommend the necessity of seasoning, as it is known to constitute the difference between good and bad cookery. Either salt or sugar must predominate in some respects. Mind to skim off all the butter before you reduce.

No. 3.—*Cucumbers cardon fashion.*

Cut cucumbers lengthways of the size of the dish; empty the seed, and slit the outside, that it may bear the appearance of a cardoon; blanch them in boiling water; next stew them in some *consommé* with two or three spoonsful of *Espagnole*. Let them boil over a sharp fire, and take care the sauce does not become skinny. If the cucumbers should give a bitter taste, put in a little sugar. This dish is a very wholesome one for weak stomachs. The cucumber for sauces or dishes of the first course are explained in the articles relative to made dishes, those served as *entremets*, or as garnishings, are here merely inserted.

SEA-KALE.

This plant is not known in France. It is to be boiled in salt and water, and after being well drained, sent up with either a *sauce blanche*, a *velouté*, or an *Espagnole;* it has a great resemblance to asparagus, but is only used for second courses. It is a common practice with the female cooks, to serve under them a piece of toasted bread to soak up the water, but when you drain them well on a clean cloth, they do not require the toast.

BROCOLI.

Brocoli are no other than green cauliflowers. They are dressed in the same manner, and sent up with the same sauce. (See *Cauliflowers*, Nos. 1, 2, 3, 4, pages 322, 323.)

POTATOES.

No. 1.—*Potatoes à la Maître d'Hôtel.*

Wash the potatoes clean, and boil them with the skin, in salt and water. When they are done, let them cool, then turn them in the shape of big corks, and cut them into slices as thick as two-penny pieces, for if the slices were too thin, they would break in the sauce. (For the *Maître d'Hôtel*, see Sauces.) If you should have no sauce ready, make a butter sauce, mix with it a little chopped parsley, pepper, salt, a little glaze, and the juice of a lemon, if acid is required. Mind that the sauce is neither curdled nor too thick, and that it is mixed well before you put the potatoes in it.

No. 2.—*Fried Potatoes.*

These are to be turned when raw, and cut of the same thickness as in No. 1; then fry them in clarified butter. If you should have any goose dripping it would do better. When the potatoes are fried of a fine brown colour, and crisp, drain all the grease on a towel, and serve them quite hot on a napkin, or in a deep dish, for this *entremets* can not be dished nicely in any other way. Do not forget to sprinkle them over with a little pounded salt.

No. 3.—*Purée of Potatoes.*

Take some potatoes well boiled and well drained, pound them in the mortar, moisten with good broth and salt, then rub them through a sieve; when done, put the *purée* to warm in a stew-pan, and add a quartern of fresh butter to it: *purée* must be thinner than *mash*; put fried bread round it. Sometimes you may use cream instead of broth, but it is not so healthy, and is much dearer.

No. 4.—*Croquettes of Potatoes.*

After having boiled the potatoes in water to take off the tartness, boil a pint of milk, in which infuse half the peel of a lemon, a lump of sugar, and a little salt. It is hardly possible to determine exactly what quantity of potatoes is requisite for a pint of milk; however, the mash must be made rather thick. Let it cool, and then roll it in the shape you like best, either corks, pears, or balls. Then crumb them as other *croquettes* with an *omelette* and a little salt; and then crumbs of bread, repeating both operations twice. Give them a pleasing form, fry them of a fine colour, and send them up, but without any fried parsley. In this dish sugar must predominate, as it is one of the class of sweet dishes.

You may sometimes make the *croquettes* as directed, but without crumbing them; have some whites of eggs frothed, into which dip them only, and fry them; when of a good colour, glaze them with sugar and serve very hot.

No. 5.—*Casserole of Potatoes.*

Instead of a rice *casserole*, make a *casserole* of potatoes. The potatoes must be well done; then mix some butter and cream well with a little salt, and make the whole into a thick mash. Dish it, and make an opening in the centre. After having given it a fine brown colour in the oven, wipe your dish clean, and pour in the *ragoût, macaroni,* or *fricassée,* &c. Keep the mash very thick to prevent its breaking when the *ragoûts* are in it.

No. 6.—*Soufflé of Potatoes.*

The *soufflé* requires the potatoes to be well done also. When they have boiled a sufficient time in water, strain them through a hair sieve, and put what comes through the sieve into a mixture of milk, sugar, lemon-peel, a good bit of butter, and a little salt, as in No. 4. Work the whole with the potatoes, and add the yolks of six eggs. At the moment you are going to send up the removes of the soups, beat the whites of the six eggs, and mix them with the rest of the preparation, add to it a small bit of butter. Put the whole into a *soufflé* dish, or into a pie-crust that has been made before-hand. The *soufflé,* however, is better in a dish, as you can not get it so well done in paets. Glaze with a little pounded sugar and the salamander. Send up speedily for fear the *soufflé* should fall.

The *fécule* that are sold at Sporel's, in Piccadilly, are sooner done. Take three or four spoonsful of flour of potatoes, and mix them with good milk, a little salt, lemon-peel and sugar; keep this preparation thick, then proceed as before directed, with the white and the yolks.

No. 7.—*Gateau of Potatoes.* [*]

The same preparation as for the *souffle*, with the only difference, that you put some crumbs of bread into a mould. First, you must put some clarified butter into the mould, so that it may be spread all over; this being done, put two or three large handsful of crumbs of bread, and spread them equally on all parts of the mould. Then dip a brush into some hot butter, and sprinkle it gently over the contents of the mould, which strew over a second time equally with crumbs of bread; that the *gateau* or cake, may be made of a fine colour. You may occasionally add dried currants, or dried cherries, sometimes flavour it with *noyau, marasquin,* or *vanilla, &c.* to create a variety of names and tastes. When you turn the mould, be particular not to break the cake.

No. 8.—*Biscuits of Potatoes.*

Take fifteen fresh eggs, break the yolks into one pan, and the whites into another. Beat the yolks with a pound of sugar pounded very fine, scrape the peel of a lemon with a lump of sugar, dry that, and pound it fine also, then throw it into the yolks, and work the eggs and sugar till they are of a whitish colour. Next, whip the whites well, and mix them with the yolks. Now sift half a pound of flour of potatoes through a silk sieve over the eggs and sugar. Have some paper cases ready, which lay on a *plafond,* with some paper underneath. Fill the cases, but not too full, glaze the contents with some sugar, which must not be pounded too fine, and bake the whole in an oven moderately heated.

With this quantity of paste, you may make one good cake, and twenty-four cases. The biscuit in the mould is made with the same paste, but you put some

* Not unnecessarily to increase the bulk of the present work, the author has given, in the above recipe, directions for a plain one, but you may vary them *ad infinitum,* by putting different tastes, *rose, vanilla, caffe, lanan, orange,* &c. &c.

melted butter in a mould of the shape you fancy; then take some very dry, pounded white sugar, and after having spread the butter all over the inside, throw the pounded sugar into it, and turn the mould all over to equalize the sugar; throw a few cinders on a baking dish, and put the mould over them to prevent its burning in the oven; put the paste gently into it, taking care not to fill the mould too full, and bake it in an oven of a moderate heat. It should be of a good colour. Take it out of the mould as soon as you bring it from the oven. One hour will suffice to bake if thoroughly.

N.B.—The cases are to be baked on a *plafond*, where there has been no sugar; otherwise the paper would be soiled.

The flour of potatoes may be easily made by yourself, by first peeling some raw potatoes, and then rasping them into a great vessel of clean cold water. When the potatoes have produced a sediment at the bottom of the pan, drain off all the water gently, and fill the pan again with very clean water, then stir up the sediment, and let it settle again. When settled, drain off all the water, and put the sediment on a clean cloth till it is quite dry. Keep it in a clean pot for use.

YOUNG, OR NEW GREEN PEAS.

We have in France a proverb; "Eat green peas with the rich, and cherries with the poor." In fact, peas are only fit to be dressed in the French way, when they are young, extremely fine, and well selected. If they have been gathered a long time, they must undoubtedly be coarse and hard, and have lost their savour. If you wish to eat them in a state of perfection, you should do as Lord S. does, have them gathered in the morning, and dressed on the same day, in the following manner:

No. 1.—*Peas French fashion.*

For a large dish, take three quarts of green peas. Throw them into an earthen pan with a quarter of a pound of fresh butter, and plenty of cold water. Handle the peas with the butter till they stick together; then drain them, take them out of the water by handsful, and throw them into a cullender, that neither water nor any kind of filth may remain. Next stew them over a moderate fire, with a bunch of parsley and green onions. When they have recovered their green colour, powder them over with a little flour; stir the peas before you moisten them with boiling water, till they are entirely covered with it, which you reduce quickly on a large fire. The moment you perceive there is no moisture or liquor remaining, dip a small lump of sugar into some water, that it may soon melt, and put it with the peas, to which add a very small quantity of salt. The author has already said (see *Asparagus Peas*,) that sugar must predominate; however, green peas without salt would taste very insipid, although the persons who eat them are not sensible of there being any. Next take about a quartern of butter, which knead with a spoonful of flour. Mind that the peas are boiling when you put the kneaded butter in; thicken them with it, and remember, that when green peas are properly dressed, there must be no sauce.

The practitioner should study this article repeatedly, if he would cook the peas in perfection: when they are fresh gathered, they should be handled with the butter as above, and placed on the stove to simmer or sweat; it is well to toast them frequently: when they are done, if too much liquid remain, reduce them quickly and add the sugar, the salt, (but no water,) and the flour, as before. If the peas are not of the best quality, moisten them with the boiling water, and proceed as before directed.

No. 2.—*Stewed Green Peas with Bacon.*

The same preparation as in No. 1. The bacon is

to be cut into pieces one inch square, and always take from that part of the breast, which in France is called *petit lard*. Sometimes the pieces may be cut in the shape of corks, according to fancy. Blanch these for half an hour in water, to take off the briny taste; then fry them of a fine colour, and drain all the grease. Next stew the bacon, with the peas in the same manner as in No. 1. But instead of flour, put in only a little water. When the peas are nearly done and reduced, add to them a spoonful of *sauce tournée*. If you wish them to be of a brown colour, use some *Espagnole*, and never omit a little sugar. Unless the peas are served as sauce, or an *entrée*, there must never be any sauce in the dish; and observe, when they are for *entremets*, that there must be no sauce at all.

No. 3.—*Peas plain boiled.*

Set some water boiling. When it boils, throw in the peas with a little salt. When done enough, drain them, and empty them into a stew-pan, with a good bit of butter, and a little salt. Keep stirring till the butter is melted, and season with a little more salt, and pepper also, if approved of. Send up hot, but take care the butter does not turn to oil.

No. 4.—*Green Peas à la Paysanne.*

Mark the peas as in No. 1. Then take a few cabbage and cos lettuces, a good handful of parsley, and a few green onions. Wash them clean, and break them with your fingers instead of chopping them. Drain the lettuce, parsley, and onions, and sweat them with the peas over a very slow fire. You need not put any other moisture but the butter; take care to stir the stew-pan repeatedly, to prevent the vegetables from burning. When they are done enough, add a little pepper and salt, without any thickening, as for peas dressed in a different way.

No. 5.—*Of Peas in general.*

When very busy, it is requisite that you should have all the peas intended for *entrées* or for *entremets*, marked in a stew-pan. Sweat them all together, take a certain quantity for your first course, and reduce the remainder the moment you finish the *entremets* for the second. Peas, to be dressed French fashion, must be very young, and of an equal size, for if of different sizes they never will adhere well. Have a sieve made of ozier or of cane, through which they must be sifted; such as can not come through are used for soups, *purées*, &c. or to be plain boiled.

WINDSOR BEANS.

No. 1.—*Windsor Beans à la Poulette.*

Windsor beans are to be served at a good table, only when very young, and fresh gathered. Boil them in salt and water. When nearly done, drain them, and stew them in a little *sauce tournée*, with a bunch of parsley and green onions, a little savory, chopped very fine, and a small lump of sugar. When the beans are sufficiently reduced, throw in a thickening made of the yolks of two eggs, and a little thick cream. Send them up in a short *sauce*, and properly seasoned.

No. 2.—*Windsor Beans à la Poulette.—Another Method.*

When the beans are large, you must take off the coats, and boil them in salt and water; cook them as above, and send them up with a short sauce.

No. 3.—*Beans and Bacon.*

Windsor beans are served as an *entrée* in the summer season. Take a piece of streaky bacon, and boil it for a couple of hours. When ready to send up, take off the rind, and dry the bacon with a red hot shovel. Powder the bacon over with raspings of bread. Give it a pleasing shape, and lay it over the beans that have been boiled in water and salt only, without any sauce. Send up separately in a boat, some chopped parsley in melted butter. Beans are likewise an excellent garnish to ham: when young, serve them plain round it, and cook them as directed at No. 1.

TURNIPS.

Turnips are of the greatest utility in cookery, as they are used for seasoning all the soups, for a great many *entrées*, and also for *entremets*, as follows:—

No. 1. — *Turnips with Sauce blanche.*

Turnips only find their way as *entremets*, in winter-time, from a want of other vegetables. Cut them in the shape of pears or balls; boil them in salt and water, and butter, and when done enough, drain them, and send them up with a *sauce blanche*, to which you may add a little mustard if approved of.

No. 2. — *Turnips glazed, Pear fashion*

Select a few fine turnips; turn a sufficient number to cover, or to fill the dish; stew them in a little broth with a little sugar, which you reduce to glaze, and add to it a little glaze. When equally glazed, dish them; take a spoonful of *Espagnole* to detach the glaze that remains in the stew-pan, with a small bit of butter twice as big as a walnut, which you work with the sauce. Pour the sauce over the turnips without masking them, after you have given it a good seasoning.

No. 3.—*The White Purée of Turnips.*

If you want to make a *purée* very white, you must mince the turnips, blanch them in boiling water, drain and sweat them over a very slow fire, in a little butter, to prevent their getting brown. When they are done enough, add two or three spoonsful of *bechamelle*, strain them *en purée* through a tammy, reduce and send them up, surrounded with fried toasts of bread.

No. 4.—*The brown Purée of Turnips.*

Instead of blanching the turnips, sweat them on a slow fire, in a little butter. Take care that they do not burn. When they are well done, moisten with three spoonsful of *sauce tournée,* and one spoonful of gravy of veal. Give them a good seasoning, rub them through a tammy, and send up as above with fried toasts of bread. Never omit putting in a small lump of sugar before you serve up, to overcome the bitter taste of the turnips.

CARROTS.

Carrots are like turnips, to supply the scarcity of vegetables at a particular time of the year, when vegetables are dear and scarce.

No. 1.—*Carrots à la d'Orleans.*

Take a few young carrots, turn them of an equal size, and cut them in slices of about the eighth of an inch thick, and blanch them well. Next lay them on a towel to drain; put them into a stew-pan with a lump of sugar and a little broth, and let them boil over a large fire. When reduced to glaze, add a good bit of fresh butter and a little salt. Mind that the butter must adhere to the carrots when you serve up, as no sauce must be seen.

No. 2.—*Purée of Carrots.*

Mince some young carrots; blanch them to take off the tart taste, and use the same process as for the *purée* of turnips.

No. 3.—*Soufflé of Carrots.*

Make a thick *purée* of carrots, but instead of broth use water, in which put a great deal of sugar, half a spoonful of flour, a little salt, and a good bit of butter; let all this boil till very thick, then put the yolks of six eggs, and mix all well together. The moment you are ready to send up, beat the whites of the eggs, which you throw in with the rest, and put into the oven for a proper time, in the vessel which you wish to use.

CELERY.*

No. 1.—*Céleri à l' Espagnole.*

Cut a dozen heads of celery of the length of your dish *à entremets;* blanch them; and *mark* them in a stew-pan between two layers of bacon. Moisten with a spoonful of broth, and let them boil gently; when done, drain all the fat. Lastly, dish the celery, and send it up with an *Espagnole,* rather thick. If the celery could be boiled after being drained in the sauce for about half an hour, it will have a better taste.

No. 2.—*Céleri with Sauce blanche.*

Cut a dozen heads of celery as above. Let them stew in a little butter, salt, and water. When done

* This is a very heating, but easily digested vegetable; it will be found of great use in cookery, as it is to be seen in so many preparations, *soups, salads, sauces,* and *entremets* of all descriptions.

enough, drain them, and serve up with the sauce *blanche*. If you would have the celery very white, blanch it in boiling water to take out the green; then put it in a *blanc* as you do for the celery sauce, as before directed, it will then become as white as possible.

No. 3.—For the *purée* of celery (see *Sauces.*) In general, all *purées* are made by the same process.

SWEET ENTREMETS.

APPLES.

Observation.—The grand difficulty is to find good apples, and such as will bear cooking. In general they break as soon as they feel the fire, the golden pippins are excellent for *entremets,* but they are small, and generally dear.

No. 1.—*Apples à la Portugaise.*

Take a dozen of fine rennet apples; take care that they are not injured. Peel them equally, and push the core out with a vegetable cutter. Let them boil in a very thin syrup, without being too much done. Then make a marmalade with some other apples, but let it be very white. (See *Marmalade.*) This marmalade must be made of a good thickness. Lay the apples in a hair sieve to drain, that no syrup may remain, and next dish the marmalade, which you level with your knife. Lay the apples round the dish at an equal distance, and in such a manner as that they may be more elevated in the centre. In the cavity of each apple place a preserved cherry. If you should have any apricot marmalade, generally called apricot jam, you may use some to decorate this *entremet* as your taste may suggest, or your means allow. It would be a long and unsuccessful task to undertake to teach dressing and decorating by a book; the ingenuity and understanding of the learner will be his best guide.

No. 2.—*Miroton of Apples.*

You must take at least two dozen apples, and of that sort particularly which stands the fire best. Golden pippins are generally the best. Peel them and cut them into slices about the size of a dollar. Take a deep dish, otherwise your *miroton* would sink in it, and not look well. Put a little marmalade on the bottom of the dish, in order to stick down the apples, one above another, all round the dish. Fill up the middle of the dish with the most defective slices of the apples. Now lay another bed of apricot marmalade, to prevent the apples from slipping down. Next lay a second bed of apples, and some marmalade again, so as to form a complete spiral line. You must close the centre with a slice of apple which is to be slit. Next bake this in a moderately hot oven. When the apples yield to the pressure of the finger, it is a sign of their being done enough. Lastly, sprinkle over the apples a little pounded sugar, and glaze with the salamander. Remember that you must give the apples a fine colouring.

No. 3.—*Suédoise of Apples.*

Make a marmalade of apples as compact as possible. Then take small pieces of apples cut into corks, and of different colours. To dye them you need only dilute with syrup a little carmine or saffron, and give them a boil. Next let the apples cool in the syrup, that the colour may be spread equally over them. When you dish the *suédoise*, first spread some marmalade over the middle of the dish, and next arrange the apple corks symmetrically, viz. one white, one red, one yellow, and so on. As the rows ascend, make the next always narrower, and decorate the top with cherries of a pink hue, green-gages, angelica, &c. Have some apple jelly, with which cover the *suédoise*, and put it into ice to cool. When the *suédoise* is decorated in an agreeable form, use some jelly for garnishing, and place it gently over and round the *suédoise.* The jelly must be of a sufficient substance not to run down the fruit.

No. 4.—*Chartreuse of Apples and Fruit.*

A *Chartreuse* is the same thing as a *suédoise,* only instead of raising the fruit with the hand over the marmalade, you oil a mould of the same size as the dish you intend to use, and arrange symmetrically fruit of different colours, such as angelica, preserved oranges, lemons, &c. ; in short, whatever may offer a variety of colours. Apples and pears are in more general use for the outside, but then they must be dyed as directed above, No. 3. When you have decorated the middle or bottom, proceed to decorate the sides. Next use some thick marmalade of apples to consolidate the decorations. When you have made a wall sufficiently strong that you may turn the *Chartreuse* upside down, take the whitest apple jelly you can procure, some stewed pears cut into slices the size of a half crown piece, and some cherries, &c. and mix the whole with the jelly, so as to represent a *Macedoine.* Do not fill the cavity too full with the *miroton,* as you are to close it with apple marmalade that has more substance in it. Then turn over the *Chartreuse* and dish it. Glaze the fruit over with some thick syrup. This syrup gives additional lustre to the colours, and a fresh gloss to the fruit.

No. 5.—*Turban of Apples.*

Take some real rennets or golden pippins, cut them into equal quarters, and stew them in some thin syrup. Mind they do not break. Boil some rice in cream, with a little lemon, sugar, and salt. Let the rice be done thoroughly, and kept thick. Then let it cool. When it is nearly cold, take a large piece of bread, or rather an empty gallipot, which you put in the centre of the dish, lay the rice all round till you reach the top of the gallipot. Next take the pieces of apples that have been drained of all the syrup over a sieve, thrust them into the rice, sloping towards the right in the first row, and towards the left in the second, and so on till you reach the top of the turban, which you put into the oven that the apples may be made of a fine colour. When you are ready to serve up, remove the gallipot, wipe off all the butter, and decorate the apples with some hard currant jelly, green gages, cherries, &c. which may sometimes be about the middle of the dish, and pour into the middle a *crême patissière,* that is made as follows:

Crême Patissière.

Take a pint of cream and a pint of milk, boil and keep stirring them with a spoon. When boiled, add about two ounces of sugar, a little salt, and the peel of a lemon. Let this peel infuse till the cream tastes of the lemon; next beat the yolks of eight eggs with the cream, and do them on the fire, stirring all the while with a wooden spoon. When the cream is become very thick, pour it into a hair sieve and rub through with the wooden spoon. When entirely strained, put it into a pan to serve when wanted. If you wish your *crême patissière* to be very thick, you must put more eggs to it. This *crême* is termed by the generality of ladies in this country *custard.* The custard, will, however, be found under the head of creams and jellies.

Another Method, called Frangipane.

Throw four spoonsful of flour into a stew-pan, and beat the flour with four entire eggs, and a pint of cream, and take care the flour is well mixed: add a little salt and a little sugar. Now rasp the peel of a lemon with a lump of sugar, and scrape it into this preparation. Lay the whole on a slow fire, and keep continually stirring, for fear the contents should stick to the stew-pan. When the mixture has been on the fire for a quarter of an hour, blanch a dozen of sweet almonds and the same number of bitter ones, which pound very fine, and moisten a little, that they may not turn to oil. When reduced to a kind of pomatum, mix them with the *frangipane*, and try whether it tastes well. This you may use for *tourtes tartelettes, gateaux en dariole*, &c. &c. (See *Pastry*.) Observe that sugar must predominate in all sweet *entremets*, but they must not be too sweet.

OF RICE FOR ENTREES AND ENTREMETS.

Carolina rice is generally the best. It must be observed, that rice which has been wetted by the sea, has lost its savour, and of course is unfit to be made use of for *casseroles* with rice. You must in the first place pick the rice, and wash it by rubbing it within your hands in several waters, till the water has not the least stain. Then smell it, for if it should smell of musk, which is often the case, it must be washed in hot water, and then in cold water again, till the bad smell is entirely gone. Next lay it in a sieve to drain for use when wanted.

RICE FOR ENTRÉES.

No. 1.—*Casserole of Rice.*

After having picked the rice well, wash it first in lukewarm, and next in cold water, as directed above. After you have well drained it throw it into a stewpan of a proper size, that it may swell with ease: moisten with some pot-top.* The broth must be previously drained through a silk sieve, in order that the rice may be kept very clean. Mix it with a large quantity of grease, and some pieces of fat ham, in order to make the rice more mellow; add a little salt. As the rice must swell very much, use a sufficient quantity of broth to produce that effect. Lay the

---

* *Pot-top,* fat.

rice on a very slow fire, and mind to stir it frequently that it may not stick. Taste it to ascertain whether it is well seasoned, and done enough; you then strain it through a cullender, and level it well with a wooden spoon. Take off the fat that issues from the rice, and pour it into the mould which you select for the *casserole:* when all the parts of this latter are well covered with grease, drain it by turning the mould upside down, then put some rice all round the mould; put a piece of soft bread in the middle, and cover it with rice, squeeze it in equally with your spoon, and let it cool. When the rice is become firm, dip the outside of the mould into boiling water. Have a little *pâte brisée,* which fraem of the size of the mould; turn the mould over the paste; make an opening with a knife in the top; and flatten the paste all round with a spoon; then put it into the oven, which can never be too hot for a *casserole,* for if the oven is not hot enough, the *casserole* is liable to break; baste it with the grease, and when it is become of a fine colour, take it out of the oven; open it gently; then cut the bread into small pieces with a penknife, that you may take it out without injuring the *casserole;* next remove the rice that sticks round, but do not empty it too much, for fear it should not bear or resist the weight of whatever you intend to throw in. You generally put into these *casseroles,* white and brown *ragoûts, blanquettes, émincés, fricassées* of pullets, macaroni, and scollops of fish that have already been sent up to table, &c. &c.

No. 2.— *Cassolettes of Rice.*

The rice is to be prepared as above, No. 1, but must be put into smaller moulds, those called *dariole* moulds. Mind that the *cassolettes* are to be quite cold before you take them out of the mould. The best method of filling up the *cassolettes,* consists in taking a carrot, which you cut of a proper large size, to make a hole in the rice, this hole you fill up with a mince of fowl, *à la béchamel.* This mince must be thoroughly cold. When you fill up the mould with the rice, close it without allowing any of the mince to be mixed with the rice, in which case the *casso-lettes* would break in the dripping when you fry them. To prevent this accident, the dripping must be very hot. It is to be observed, that in making *cassolettes*, the rice must be made quite firm; and that they require something of a white colour to be added; as a *mince au velouté,* or a *salpicon* of palates and of mushrooms *à l'Allemande,* or fillets of fish *à la béchamelle.*

N. B.—You may likewise give them a light colour in the oven, the same as other *casserolles* of rice, but frying is the best and the quickest.

No. 3.—*Le Gateau de Ris, or Rice Cake.*

After having prepared the rice as in No. 1, take some good cream, which you boil first, to ascertain that it will not curdle; the quantity must be proportionate to the size of the mould you intend to use. For a quarter of a pound of rice take a quart of cream, which however is not always sufficient; this depends on the rice swelling more or less: in this case add a little milk to it. When the cream has boiled, take the peel of a lemon, which infuse in the cream for a quarter of an hour; take the peel out before you pour in the rice, which lay on a very slow fire till it bursts, or swells; when well swollen add a little salt, and some sugar, according to your own palate; the sugar, however, must predominate, the salt being only intended to remedy the insipid taste that is inseparable from sweet *entremets.* Sugar must entirely predominate in articles for a dessert, but in *entremets* it is to be used moderately. When the rice is done enough, and properly seasoned, break eight eggs, and mix the yolks with the rice; next beat the whites, which pour gently into the preparation; put also a good bit of butter; then clarify about a quarter of a pound of butter, and when it is completely clarified, pour it into the mould; turn the mould round, that the butter may be spread equally on all sides of the mould, which you then turn upside down for a moment: then put crumbs of bread into the mould, and contrive to have them likewise spread equally all over the mould; now dip a small piece of paper into the butter, sprinkle some butter all round the mould, and put some more crumbs of bread. This being done to your satisfaction, pour the rice into the mould, and put it into the oven, but mind it must not be too hot. An hour is required for your *gateau* to be baked enough. Turn it upside down in the dish, and serve up.

N. B.—You may sometimes put with it preserved cherries, raisins, or currants, &c.

No. 4.—*Croquettes of Rice.*

The rice is to be prepared as in No. 3. When it has swelled in the cream, and is properly seasoned, let it cool; then roll it into *croquettes* in the shape of a cork. Next strew over them crumbs of bread (by which is meant that you dip them first into an *omelette*, and next into crumbs of bread). Roll them several times in the crumbs in what form you please, and mind that they are made of a fine colour. When you have fried them of a good colour, you may glaze them on one side with pounded sugar, by using the salamander. Send up with fried parsley, of a nice colour, in the centre. It may be necessary to remark, that you may multiply these *entremets* by the variety of the different odours which may be used, as *vanilla, citron, lemon, orange, caffé, chocolate, &c.*, and the *noyeau, maraschino, oil of roses*, &c.

No. 5.—*Soufflé of Rice.*

The same preparation as in No. 3, only in that case you keep the rice rather more liquid, and put the whites of two more eggs; that is to say, in a *gateau* you put eight yolks and as many whites, whereas in a *soufflé* you put only six yolks and eight whites, and a little more butter, to determine the *soufflé*.

No. 6.—*Rice gratiné.*

Take two ounces of rice, which wash and pick, &c.
Then let it swell in hot milk, as cream, when used
for *entremets* of this sort, would turn to butter.
When the rice is well done, pound half a dozen of
sweet almonds, and the same quantity of bitter ones;
when you have made them into a paste, rub them
through a tammy, and mix them with the rice, together with a little sugar, and a very little salt. Then
put the rice into a silver pan or porringer, or silver
casserole, and leave it to *gratiner* on a slow fire for
three quarters of an hour or more. Instead of using
the lid, only cover the pan with a sheet of paper, to
prevent the dust and the steam. Serve hot; if you
put a cover to it, the steam will prevent its *gratin.*

No. 7.— *Turban of Rice.*

Prepare the rice as in No. 3. Have some apples
cut into quarters, and stewed in syrup. Take particular care that the quarters are kept whole. Dish
the rice; put a gallipot in the middle, to form a vacancy, into which you are to pour by and by a vanilla
cream. Dress the rice round the gallipot, and level
it with the back of a spoon. Next place the apples
round the rice, till you have reached the summit of
it, and put the whole into the oven, but only leave
it there time enough to dry up the syrup which sticks
round the apples. Next decorate with sweetmeats
of different colours, such as green-gages, apricots, and
cherries; and when you are ready to send up, remove the gallipot, and fill the vacancy with the vanilla cream.

N. B.—Many *entremets* are made of rice *crême*,
which, by the bye, is no more than flour of rice,
which is like any other flour, except that it swells
more than others. You may make *soufflés* of it, and
give them whatever taste you think proper. They
must be always sweet.

No. 8.—*Croquettes of Rice with Apricot Marmalade.*

Prepare the rice as in No. 3: form a *croquette*, take the handle of a wooden spoon, make a hole in the *croquette*, which fill with marmalade of apricots. Then close it up with some of the rice, put crumbs of bread as you do in all other *croquettes*, and fry in the same manner.

No. 9.—*Croquettes stuffed with Apples.*

Prepare the rice as above, and repeat every other operation, except that you must have rennets cut into small corks, and well stewed in syrup. Drain them well, and put them into the *croquettes* instead of marmalade.

No. 10.—*Soufflé of Apples in a bordure of Rice.*

Prepare your rice as in No. 3. Keep it of a strong solid substance, dress it up all round a dish, the same height as a raised crust, that is to say, three inches high. Give a pleasing shape to the rice, and let it be levelled smooth; have some marmalade of apple ready, made very thick; mix with it six yolks of eggs and a small bit of butter; warm it on the stove in order to do the yolks; then have eight whites of eggs well whipped, as for biscuits, mix them lightly with the apples, and put the whole into the middle of the rice; put this into the oven, which must not be too hot. When the *soufflé* is raised sufficiently, send it up, as it would soon lower. If you wish to make a kind of pap, take a spoonful of flour, a pint of milk, a little salt, lemon and sugar: let the whole boil well, then mix it with the apples and the yolks of four eggs: the whites are to be poured in afterwards: next bake the *soufflé* in the oven. This method is safer than the former, and is not deficient in delicacy.

No. 11.—*Charlotte of Apples mixed with Apricots.*

The *Charlotte* has been so called after the name of the original inventor, yet there is no doubt but his

successors have made great improvements on the
original. To make a *Charlotte*, take a dozen of rennets; but if you use a very large mould, you must take
more. Cut them into quarters, peel them, and put
them into a pan with a lump of butter, a little cinnamon, the peel of half a lemon, and a little pounded
sugar. Stew all these ingredients over a brisk fire,
but without allowing them to burn. When the apples are nearly done, take them off the fire, mix with
them half a pot of marmalade of apricots, and throw
the whole into a mould trimmed with slices of bread
dipped into melted butter; cover the marmalade with
bread that has also been dipped into butter. Now
bake the *Charlotte* in an oven that is pretty hot;
give it a good colour and serve up hot. It is useless
to recommend that the top of the *Charlotte* must be
decorated; it must always be so. To garnish the
Charlotte, put some clarified butter all round a plain
mould, then cut the crumbs of bread in any shape
you think proper; to keep all the apples confined in
the mould, the neatest and prettiest way, is to cut
the bread with a plain round cutter, and lay them
over one another all round; they must be dipped into
clarified butter before they are put into the mould;
then put the apples, and cover them, give a good colour, drain all the butter, and serve very hot and
crisp.

OF NOUILLES IN GENERAL.

Nouilles are made with a paste as follows:—Put on
the table about half a quarter of a pound of good and
very fine flour, make a little hole in the middle of
the flour, and put into it a little salt, a small bit of
butter, the yolks of three eggs, and a little drop of
water, mix this paste very well, and spread it on the
table with the rolling pin, then cut in a small bit,
about a line in size, and an inch in length; pour some
flour lightly over these pieces to prevent their adher-

ing together, then blanch them in boiling water, after which, drain them through a cullender, and use them as directed hereafter.

Nouilles are very useful, as they are served as *potage, entrées, entremets;* but as they have been ex plained under their proper heads, the author will pro ceed to speak of the *entremets.*

Croquettes of Nouilles.

When they are prepared and blanched, take a pint of milk, boil it with a little salt, a small bit of sugar, and the peel of half a lemon; when the milk boils, put the *nouilles* into it, and reduce it till it becomes very thick, put them into a cold dish, and when perfectly cold, shape them as you do the rice, sometimes crumbing, and sometimes frying them, only dipping in white of eggs; frost and glaze them with sugar of a good colour.

OF CREAMS IN GENERAL.

No. 1.—*Coffee Cream.*

It is necessary to observe in this first article, that all Creams are made in the same manner; the taste and colour only varying. Take a pint of cream and a pint of milk, and boil them together. When boiled, throw in a small lump of sugar, and a little salt; next roast the coffee in the *omelette* pan, or in a coffee roaster. When well and equally roasted, throw it burning hot into the cream, cover the stew-pan, and let it infuse till it gets quite cold. If you wish to pour the cream into cups or any other small vessels, you must measure the quantity of cream, but for a mould it is unnecessary; put the yolk of an egg to every cup; rub the cream twice through a tammy, in order that the egg may be well mixed with it, and next put the cups into a pan containing water enough to reach to half the height of them; cover them, and put a littie fire over the lid of the pan to prevent any steam dropping into the cream. As soon as the cream is done, let it cool, and take care to secure the cups from dust, &c. When you make the cream in a large mould, put more eggs.

No. 2.—*Lemon Cream.*

The same preparation as above; but when the cream has boiled, instead of coffee, throw in the peel of a lemon, which you leave to infuse, with the addition of a little salt and sugar. If intended for a cream in moulds of a large size, you must use a greater quantity of eggs; as for instance, sixteen eggs for two pints of cream or milk.

No. 3.—*Chocolate Cream.*

For an *entremet*, take a quarter of a pound of vanilla chocolate, rasp it very fine, and throw it into a pan to melt with a little water. When melted, mix and beat it with some cream, which you have boiled as above, and a little salt. Except in creams of fruit, as pine-apple, apricots, raspberries, &c. a little salt is always requisite, but very little however. If you wish to make an ice cream, instead of sixteen eggs for a quart of cream, only put eight, which put on the fire to thicken, but take particular care to prevent its curdling: as soon as you take it from the fire, mix with it a little melted isinglass, and rub the whole through a tammy. Now try a little of the preparation in a small mould over ice. If you should find that the cream has not substance enough to allow of being turned upside down, you must add a little more isinglass.

It is to be observed, that the isinglass must previously be melted in a little water. (See *Method of Melting Isinglass*, page 362.)

No. 4.—*Cream à la Vanille.*

Take one or two sticks of vanilla, which infuse in some boiling cream; next put in the eggs as you do for other creams. If you are making a *fromage à la glace*,* you must put a smaller quantity of eggs, as isinglass is to be put to stiffen it; and keep constantly stirring the cream on the fire, while the eggs are doing. Mind that the eggs are not overdone. When you perceive the cream is getting thick, put the melted isinglass in, and rub it through a tammy, then put it into a mould, and into ice. When you wish to make the cream more delicate, let it get cold; then put it into a vessel over ice, before you put any isinglass into it, and whip it; when quite frozen, put in cold melted isinglass: this method requires less isinglass, and the jelly is much lighter.

No. 5.—*Cream au Thé.*

Boil a pint of cream and a pint of milk, into which throw a little salt and some sugar; the latter must, however, predominate. When the cream boils, throw two or three spoonsful of good tea into it, give it a boil, put in ten yolks of very fresh eggs, and proceed as usual upon the fire, till the cream becomes thick; then put in the isinglass, &c. If your mould is small, eight eggs are sufficient.

No. 6.—*Orange Flower Cream.*

Instead of tea, infuse a large pinch of orange flowers, and when the cream has got the flavour, put in the eggs, &c.

No. 7.—*Cream à la Genet, dite au Caramel.*

Melt about an ounce of sugar in a confectionary pan. Let it reduce till it is brown, but mind to keep continually stirring, to prevent the sugar from getting a bitter taste. When quite brown, dilute it with a little water, to which add a little sugar to qualify the bitter taste. When melted, take a quart of cream that has boiled, throw the *caramel* into it, and put a

* Sometimes erroneously called *fromage bavarois.*

sufficient quantity of sugar to make it palatable. If you wish to have the cream iced, pour in the yolks of eight eggs; but if you intend to have it with eggs only, you must use twelve. In the first case, when the eggs are well mixed, put the stew-pan on the fire to thicken the cream; and when it begins to thicken, stir it well, and throw in the isinglass that you have melted previously: then put it into the mould and ice it. You must let it cool first, or it will melt the ice, and the mould will be liable to tilt over, and the cream fall out. It is not customary in this country to use cream without isinglass, therefore it is not particularly necessary to recommend the method of making them with eggs only; it is sufficient to say, that when you intend to put no isinglass into the cream, you must put more eggs, and it must not be done till it is put into the mould; butter the mould with clarified butter, then put the cream into it, to be poached in boiling water, with fire on the lid to prevent the steam from falling in. With respect to the multiplicity of names, they are derived from the peculiar flavour of the cream; there is no difference in the manutation. Thus rose cream, vanilla cream, lemon cream, orange-flower cream, marasquin cream, pine apple cream, &c. &c. derive their respective appellation from the flavouring ingredient. They are all made alike.

No. 8.—*The manner of Melting Isinglass.*

To melt a quarter of a pound of isinglass, take a little more than a pint of water, into which throw the twelfth part of the white of an egg; beat the water well till it becomes white; throw the isinglass into that water, and lay it on the stove over a very slow fire. If you keep it covered it will melt more easily. Take care it does not burn, for then it can never be made clear, and, besides, it would have an unpleasant taste. For a larger quantity put more water, but not more white of egg. Some people put in the peel of a lemon, which is wrong; however, you may squeeze the juice of it into it if you want the isinglass to be clear, but for cream it is useless. Always put isinglass cautiously; in order to make cream or jellies in perfection, always try a little in a small mould. If the jelly should not be firm enough, add a little more isinglass. It is impossible to determine the exact quantity that is required for creams or jellies, as the dishes and moulds are never of the same dimensions. The best method therefore is to try by tasting. A medical man once demanded of the author why cooks had not weights and measures, the same as apothecaries? To which he incontinently replied: " because *we* taste our recipes, whereas *gentlemen* seldom taste those they are mixing; therefore they must have exact measures."

No. 9.—*Egg and Water Cream.*

Boil a pint of water with half a quarter of a pound of sugar, a little corriander, a little cinnamon, and the peel of a lemon. When all these ingredients have been well infused, break the yolks of eight eggs, which you mix and beat with that preparation; then rub it through a tammy, and put it into small cups to thicken *au bain marie*. Put but very little fire under, as there must be some on the covers, to prevent the water of the steam from falling into the cream. The cream must not boil too long, and only gently, for fear it should curdle. This cream agrees very well with weak stomachs, and is specially recommended to young ladies of feeble constitutions.

No. 10.—*Eggs au Bouillon, and reversed.*

Take some good *consommé*, of the particular sort you wish to use, whether of game or of fowl: do not put any sugar to it. Measure a cup full of it to every yolk, and make this cream thick, in the same manner as you do all others. If you wish to make it with reversed eggs, use two yolks of eggs for each *dariole* mould, and proceed as above; with the only difference, that you must butter the moulds lightly inside with some clarified butter. Boil the eggs in moulds instead of cups, and when they are hard enough, turn them upside down in the dish: serve up with some *consommé* thickened with the yolks of two eggs, and poured over as sauce. This *entremet* is greatly admired by the amateurs of game, as it gives a very peculiar flavour to the different species of game used in the preparation—

œuf au consommé de la preaux,
œuf au fumet de perdreaux
œuf au fumet de bécasser, fesant, &c.

Eggs *au consommé de Gibier les petits pots*, as those above, but put in the smaller cream-pots.

No. 11.—*Eggs à la Neige.*

Take the white of six eggs, which will be enough for an *entremet;* whip them till they get thick; have some milk boiling over the fire in a large stew-pan; poach several spoonsful of the whites in it, and when done enough, drain and dish them; next make a sauce to pour over them in the following manner: take some of the milk in which you have poached your eggs, then put a little sugar, a little orange flower, and a little salt; mix the yolks of four eggs with the same, stir the whole on the fire till the milk is made thick, put it through a tammy, and mask the *neiges* with that sauce.

No. 12.—*Italian Cream.*

Boil a pint of cream with half a pint of milk. When it boils, throw in the peel of an orange and of a lemon, to infuse with half a quarter of a pound of sugar and a small pinch of salt. When the cream is impregnated with the flavour of the fruit, mix and beat it with the yolks of eight eggs, and put it on the fire to acquire an equal thickness. As soon as it is thick enough, and the eggs done, put a little melted isinglass in it, strain it well through a tammy, and put some of it into a small mould, to try if it is thick enough to be turned over. If not, add a little more isinglass, and put the preparation into a mould on ice. When quite frozen, and you wish to send it up, dip a towel into hot water, and rub it all round the mould, to detach the cream, and turn it upside down on a dish. By this means the cream is brighter, and the dish not soiled. If you whip the cream before you put it into the mould, it makes it more delicate and more mellow; but you do not put the isinglass in the cream before the cream is nearly done. In concluding the article on creams, his readers may probably be surprised at the scarcity introduced; when it is considered, however, that the author has intentionally shortened this article by recommending variations of flavour with the same preparation, it will be found that the number of changes which may be made with the same receipt, on which they are all grounded, will equal, if not exceed that of any publication expressly devoted to the exposition of the subject.

No. 13.—*Pine-Apple Cream.*

Infuse the rind of a pine-apple in boiling cream, and proceed as usual for other fruit. You must only use the rind, for the pulp of the pine-apple being acid, the cream would curdle.

No. 14.—*Cabinet Pudding, or Chancellor's Pudding.*

Boil a pint of cream, in which put to infuse a little lemon peel, and a little salt. Pour the cream while boiling over a pound of buiscuits *à la cuilliére,* and let them soak. Next add the yolks of eight eggs. Then beat the whites of six eggs only: some persons add a little brandy, but that I disapprove of. Butter over a mould, and decorate it with preserved cherries. When you send up the first course, pour the above preparation into a mould, and put it *au bain marie.* Observe, that if the mould is large, you must use more eggs. Make a sauce as for the eggs *à la neige*, into which squeeze the juice of a lemon: or make a sauce with arrow-root as follows; dilute a spoonful of arrow-root with white wine and sugar, and lay it on the fire to boil; keep it liquid enough to mask the mould, and let the dried cherries that are around be full in sight.

N. B.—This pudding can be made of remnants of Savoy biscuits, or *brioche*, or the crumb of a penny loaf.

No. 15.—*Pudding à la Bourgoise.*

Butter a mould all over in the inside, then stick symmetrically some dried cherries all round the inside, cut some slices of bread and butter, and spread some black currants over, then put them one over the other in the mould, till you have filled it, then have in a stew-pan some milk which has been boiled beforehand, into which infuse some lemon peel, add a little sugar, and a little salt, mix with this five or six eggs, and taste it to see if the sugar predominates. Put this quite cold into the mould, and put this mould into a stew-pan *au bain marie* for one hour. When done, try all round if the pudding will come out easily. Turn it round on the dish, and serve with the arrow-root sauce over.

No. 16.—*Soufflé, or Cake of Tapioca.*

Tapioca is an article that swells very much, and which requires a long time to be done thoroughly. If you boil it over too brisk a fire, it will become tough; if over a very slow fire, it will be as mellow as marrow, and then it is extremely pleasant to the palate. Boil a pint of cream and a pint of milk with a little sugar, and a very little salt. Then infuse the peel of half a lemon; but if the taste of orange flowers, roses, or vanilla, &c. should be more agreeable, use them in preference, according to the taste of your employer. Put a quarter of a pound of tapioca into the cream, and let it boil over a very slow fire. When it is done, throw in a piece of butter, and break the yolks of six eggs, which you beat up with it, and let them do over the stove. When you send up the first course, beat the whites of the eggs, pour them gently with the rest, and set the whole into a moderate oven. If you wish to make a cake, sprinkle a mould twice over with clarified butter and crumbs of bread: mix with the preparation some dried cherries and currants, and proceed as you do for a *soufflé*. When done, turn the mould upside down in a dish, and send up hot.

No. 17.—*Tapioca gratiné.*

Put half a quarter of a pound of very clean tapioca, with a quart of hot milk, a small bit of sugar, a very little salt, and one leaf of almond laurel; let this boil gently over a slow fire; when the tapioca is done, put it into a silver stew-pan, and set it on a pretty sharp stove fire to *gratiné;* let it stick very much to the bottom of the stew-pan; take out the laurel leaf, and serve it up with a cover over; but mind to cover the stew-pan with a skewer and a sheet of paper, to prevent the dust from flying into it.

No. 18.—*Croquettes of Chestnuts à la Ude.*

Take fifty good chestnuts, and put them into a hot oven, observing that you must cut each of them with the point of your knife, to prevent them from bursting. When well roasted, clean them, and put half of them, (taking care to choose those parts that have colour) into the mortar, with three ounces of butter and a spoonful of cream; rub this paste through a hair sieve, then mix with it the same quantity of butter as before, a pinch of salt, three ounces of sugar, and a quarter of a pint of cream; put the whole over the fire in a stew-pan to dry like royal paste, or a *choux;* when it has acquired a little consistence, put to it six yolks of eggs, and give to the preparation the taste you think proper, as lemon, vanilla, *cédrat*, coffee,

&c.; let this paste go to the fire again after you have put the yolks of the six eggs; stir it well with a wooden spoon till it is rather firm; then butter a dish, and spread this paste over, equally, with your knife; cover this with a sheet of buttered paper, and let it cool; when cold, cut it with a knife, and take half of a chestnut, and make the paste into the shape of a big chestnut; put some crumbs of bread over the *croquettes*, then dip them into three eggs beaten up with a little salt, and into the crumbs again; give them a good shape, fry them of a nice colour, and serve them without fried parsley as a sweet dish; sometimes dip them into eggs only without crumbs; they are more delicate. Put fine sugar over them after they are fried.

SOUFFLÉS FOR ENTREMETS.

It will be sufficient to observe on the subject of *soufflés*, that they are all made in the same manner, and that they vary only in the taste you give them. If sent up in proper time they are very good eating, if not, they are no better than other puddings.

No. 1.—*Soufflé of Potatoes with Lemon.*

Bake a dozen potatoes in the oven; when they are well done, open them, scoop out the most floury part, and mix it with half a pint of cream that has boiled, and in which you have infused the peel of a lemon: to this add a little sugar, a large bit of butter, and a little salt; the taste of the sugar, however, must predominate; yet observe, that the less sugar you use the lighter the *soufflés* are. Now break six eggs, throw the yolks of four only into the potatoes, beat the six whites, which pour gently with the above preparation into a *soufflé* dish, and put it into the oven, which must not be too hot. When the *soufflé* is done enough, powder a little sugar over it, and use the salamander; *soufflés* must be served up the moment they are ready, for they are liable to sink.

No. 2.—*Soufflé of Orange Flower.*

Dilute a little flour with half cream and milk; set this pap on the fire to boil; when the flour is done, put a little salt, a little sugar, and a small quantity of pounded orange flower, mix well, and then add a good bit of butter, the yolks of six eggs, and mix the whole well. Next beat the six whites, and mix them with the rest: then bake the *soufflé* as above, and when it is baked enough, glaze it and send up.

No. 3.—*Soufflé of Ground Rice.*

Wash and pick a certain quantity of rice; when it has lost all improper flavour, lay it in a hair sieve to dry before the fire; when quite dry, pound it and sift it. Take two spoonsful of the flour, and dilute it with a little cream and milk; boil them on a slow fire, and give whatever taste you may think proper. Of course you must add butter, sugar, salt, beaten whites, &c. as to all other *soufflés;* then send up.

No. 4.—*Soufflé of Bread.*

Boil some milk with a little cream, to which give any taste you think proper. Throw into it the soft part of two or three fresh rolls to soak, rub the bread through a sieve, and proceed with the eggs, butter, sugar, &c. as Nos. 1, 2, and 3.

No. 5.—*Soufflé of Coffee.*

Boil a pint of cream with a pint of milk, to which add a little sugar and a very little salt. Take a clean *omelette* pan, or a coffee roaster, and roast in it a quarter of a pound of coffee on a slow fire. When it is equally roasted, throw it into the boiling cream, that it may acquire a proper taste of the coffee. Use this cream to make either bread *soufflé*, No. 4, or potatoe *soufflé*, No. 1, &c. &c.

No. 6.—*Soufflé of Chocolate.*

Take a quarter of a pound of chocolate, which cut as small as you can, and melt it on the fire in a little water. When it is entirely melted, throw it into the *soufflé* preparation, No. 4, the same as all others.

Vanilla *Soufflé*,   Pine-Apple *Soufflé*,
Saffron *Soufflé*,   Rose *Soufflé*,

and generally all other *soufflés*, are prepared in the same manner. The question is, to make the preparation well, and above all things to beat the whites of the eggs very well, for on that alone depends the rising or falling of the *soufflé*.

OMELETTE SOUFFLÉ.

Break six eggs, put the whites into one pan, and the yolks into another; rasp a little lemon peel or orange flowers, beat the yolks well, add a little sugar and salt, and next beat the whites well *en neige*, and mix them with the yolks lightly. Then put a lump of butter into an *omelette* pan on the fire; when the butter is melted, pour the *omelette* into the pan; when is is firm enough on one side to hold the liquid part, turn it over on the dish you send up; then bake it in an oven, or use the Dutch oven. When it is well raised, glaze it, and sent it up immediately, for it would soon lower. Mind, it must be covered hermetically with a large fire over it, otherwise it will not rise. To this you may give whatever flavour you think proper; but the plainer the better, when served very hot, and very high.

PANCAKES, FRENCH FASHION.

Put into a stew-pan or basin, two ounces of fine flour, three ounces of sugar, a few macaroons of bitter almonds, a tea-spoonful of orange-flower water, a little salt, a pint of cream, a glass of milk, and the yolks of five very fresh eggs. Mix the whole well; then clarify two ounces of butter, and with a hoop of clean paper put some into the pancake pan; put a very little of the mixture into the pan at a time; let it be well done on the one side only, and turn the first one on the bottom of a silver plate; and do the same alternately with the others; arrange them in an agreeable form, and when you are about finishing, glaze the last with fine sugar, and salamander it; put the plate on a dish, and send up very hot. If you have a very hot oven ready, you may put the pancakes in it for ten minutes; after which, glaze them *à l'Allemande*, and serve very hot.

Pancakes.

Put into a pan four spoonsful of very fine flour, a pinch of salt, a spoonful of fine sugar, the peel of a lemon chopped very fine, and two eggs; dilute the whole of this with a pint of cream, melt a small bit of fresh butter in a stew-pan, throw it into the preparation, and then have a pancake pan very clean, put a very small bit of butter into it, let it get hot, put a spoonful of the mixture into the pan, turn round the pan, that the pancake may be done equally, then give a sudden jerk to turn the pancake on the other side; let it be well done on both sides; lastly, roll and glaze them with fine sugar. They must be made quickly, as there must be many to make a dish. Under this head, you will find many varieties, all of which, however, resolve themselves to this:—In some, you put *apricot marmalade;* in *currant-jelly, &c. &c.* They are all similar.

JELLIES OF FRUIT.

It is to be observed, that all jellies made of what is called red fruit, must be worked cold, and be put on ice very promptly. If you were to use a tinned mould, the tin would alter the red into a dead blue colour, and also spoil the taste; but if you use earthen moulds, the jellies will always look and taste as they ought.

It is also advisable to clarify the isinglass while it is melting: there is less waste, and the jellies have a brighter appearance. (See the manner of melting *Isinglass*, page 362.)

No. 1.—*Strawberry Jelly.*

Put some strawberries into an earthen pan, squeeze them well with a new wooden spoon; mix some pounded sugar with the fruit, and let them infuse for an hour, that the sugar may draw out all the juice; next pour in a little water. If the strawberries are very ripe, squeeze the juice of two lemons to restore the acid taste of the strawberries, for such preparations as are too sweet are insipid. Put all this into a bag that is nearly new, that the juice may be strained clear and limpid; mix some melted isinglass with the juice, but mind that the whole must be very cold. Now put half a spoonful of the jelly into a mould over ice, to ascertain of what substance it is. If thick enough, put the whole into the large mould in ice, and cover it also with ice, but no salt, for it would spoil the bright colour of the jelly.

Some people clarify the sugar, and when it is quite limpid and very hot, they throw their strawberries into it. This method is good enough, but then the jelly does not keep the taste of the fruit so well. You may try either way. When the strawberries have been infused in the sugar, and they have discharged their colour, strain them through a bag, mix the isinglass, and lay them in ice. Cover the mould with ice also.

No. 3.—*Raspberry Jelly.*

Raspberries are prepared in the same manner as strawberries, either hot or cold. They are also liable to lose their colour. It will not be amiss to repeat, that the isinglass must be thrown in very cold;

but the best way of all is to put the fruit into the mortar with some sugar, and mix them together; add a little water, put the whole into a jelly bag, and when the juice has been through, mix the cold isinglass with it. Mind, that you must avoid bruising the small kernels which are in the raspberries, as they would destroy the cleanliness of the jelly; press the fruit only to extract the juice; recollect, it is the same with all fruit, particularly the red, as follows:

No. 3.—*Red Currant Jelly.*

The same preparation as above, either hot or cold.

No. 4.—*Currant Jelly with Raspberries.*

The same as above, only mix some raspberries with the currants.

No. 5.—*White Currant Jelly*

The same operation as for red currants.

No. 6.—*Orange Jelly.*

Eighteen oranges are requisite to make a good jelly. Peel lightly six oranges, and throw the peel into a little water, which lay on the corner of a stove, without allowing it to boil, for fear it should taste too bitter. Cut the oranges in two: have a silk sieve and a lemon squeezer, both which dip into cold water, or otherwise they would absorb the juice of two oranges at least. Squeeze the oranges into the sieve over an earthen pan. This being done, pour the infusion of the peel through the sieve; next take a pound of sugar or so, in proportion to the acidity of the oranges, break it in a confectionary pan, pour a drop of the white of an egg into about a pint of water, whip it till it gets white, pour it over the sugar, and set it on the fire. When the sugar becomes frothy or scummy, throw a little more water in. Skim the sugar, let it reduce till it begins to bubble; and then pour in the juice of the oranges. The heat of the sugar will clarify the jelly. Do not let it boil, but as soon as you perceive a yellow scum, skim it, and pour the jelly into a bag. Next mix some melted isinglass, either hot or cold. This jelly must not be made too firm, and especially avoid introducing any colour into it, as it is almost always yellow. Why should you wish to make it red? Some people add brandy to it, which is wrong, the natural flavour ought never to be adulterated. If the oranges should be too ripe, mix a little lemon-juice to make them acid.

No. 7.—*Lemon Jelly.*

Lemon jelly is made exactly in the same manner as that of oranges. However, it requires a little more attention, for you must smell all the lemons you use, for fear they should be musty; besides, the lemons being more acid, require a larger quantity of sugar. In every other respect the process is the same as above.

No. 8.—*Mosaic Jelly.*

Boil half a pint of cream; when it boils, infuse the peel either of an orange or of a lemon, according as you wish to decorate the jelly with either. When the cream has imbibed the flavour of the fruit, put in a little sugar. Break the yolks of four eggs, which you beat with the cream, lay it on the fire to thicken, and then put in some isinglass that has previously been melted. Strain the whole through a hair sieve, and put it in a basin, well covered, on some ice, in order that it may get quite firm. Now take the mould which you intend to use, brush it lightly with oil all over the inside, and then cut the white cream jelly with a knife, in the first place, and next, with small tin cutters. Decorate the mould without putting it on ice, for the damp would prevent the decoration from sticking on. Decorate the bottom first, next the sides; then only put the mould over ice. Now pour a little orange jelly lightly, not to injure the decoration, and let it get thick. When the orange jelly is frozen, thrust the mould deeper into the ice; then put a little more jelly to the height of the lower decoration on the sides; let the preparation be made firm again; mind, the jelly is never to come higher than the flowerets, till the bottom has been first made firm; then gradually ascend to the top. Cover and surround the mould with ice. When you wish to serve up, dip a towel into some hot water, and rub the mould all round. Ascertain that none of the jelly sticks to the sides before you meddle with the bottom of the mould; then rub the bottom with the hot towel, and turn the jelly neatly into a dish. Were it not for all these precautions, the two colours would melt and mix with one another. This jelly looks beautiful when well made.

N. B.—It is to be observed, that this jelly can only be made in winter time; for, during the summer season, it would melt, except made hard, then it would not be good; however, you may work it in a very cold place.

I shall not describe the great variety of jellies that can be decorated in this manner; it will be sufficient for learners to know, that when they are to decorate pine-apple jelly, they must give the same taste to the white jelly which is to be used for the decoration; the same must be done also for *noyau* and *maras-quino*. When you make white vanilla cream, use chocolate to decorate with, by making the first preparation as directed for Mosaic jelly. For lemon jelly, use lemon, and so on with any other sort of jelly.

No. 9.—*Pine-Apple Jelly.*

The pine-apple, although a very odoriferous fruit, is not very juicy. Clarify some sugar (see No. 6), take the rind of a pine-apple, and turn the best part equally. Let it be of the diameter of a crown-piece, but a little thicker. Boil it in the sugar, squeeze into the syrup the juice of a lemon or two, and put to it some isinglass ready clarified. Strain the whole through a bag, drain the pine-apples through a clean hair sieve; next put in the mould a little of the pine-apple jelly; and when there are about three-eighths of an inch deep at the bottom of the mould, put the mould on ice to freeze. When firm, lay slices of pine-apple symmetrically over the jelly. Mind that they are quite dry, and use a little jelly to make them stick together. When the jelly is frozen to a substance, put in a little more to freeze again; then fill the mould, and put some ice all round. If the pine-apple does not look well enough to be served in the jelly, send up the jelly by itself, but keep the slices of the fruit in sugar, as they will serve another day to make pine-apple fritters. This jelly appears very well with a Mosaic on the surface of the mould.

No. 10.—*Cherry Jelly.*

The best method of making this jelly consists in clarifying the sugar. (See No. 6.) When you have skimmed the sugar properly, and it boils, throw the cherries into it: take them off the fire; and when the decoction is cold, mix with it some cold clarified isinglass, squeeze three or four lemons into it, strain through a bag, and try the preparation. Next fill the earthen mould, and put it in ice. The author has already observed, that tin moulds would make these jellies turn of a dead blue colour.

No. 11.—*Jelly and Miroton of Peaches, à la Ude.*

Cut a dozen of peaches into halves, peel them gently, and boil them in a thin syrup, but do not boil them too long. If they are very fine, you may use them almost raw, but if common fruit, the syrup will improve the look of them. Break the stones, peel the kernels, and throw them into the hot syrup with the fruit. When the peaches have infused about an hour, you may use them for making jelly *en miroton*. which is done as follows: drain the peaches in a new sieve, take the syrup, and squeeze six lemons into it; put this through a jelly-bag, or through a pa-

per; when very clear, put some clarified isinglass
into it, and put some into a plain mould in ice.
When it is firm, dress the peaches over the jelly, and
put the kernels between, then stick all this together
with some jelly; when stiff, put some more jelly gently, let it freeze, and then fill the mould; put a great
quantity of ice round the mould, and some salt, as
this jelly is very liable to break; but it is one of the
most delicate that can possibly be made. When you
can procure peaches fine enough to appear in the
jelly, you may make it as directed, but by filtering
through the paper, and mixing afterwards with the
isinglass, you will obtain one of the best jellies possible.

No. 12.—*Calf's Foot Jelly.*

Although calf's foot jelly is seldom made alone,
it will be better to give the simple preparation, which
is as follows:—Bone the calf's feet first, put them
into warm water to disgorge all the blood, then boil
them in clear water, and skim till the water is quite
limpid. Then put the stew pan on a small stove,
and let it boil gently till the calf's feet are well done.
Drain the liquor through a double silk sieve; skim
the fat off with the most scrupulous attention, then
throw a large piece of sugar into the liquor. Six feet
make a large dish. Throw likewise into the jelly
the peel of four lemons, and also the juice; add to
this a stick of cinnamon, a few cloves, a little allspice,
and break four eggs whole, but very fresh, into the
mixture. Smell the eggs, one after another, for if
one of them should not be fresh and sweet, it would
spoil the whole jelly. Whip the jelly, but take care
the rod is not greasy. Lay the jelly on the fire, and
keep beating it till it begins to turn white, and to
bubble round the stew-pan. Then remove the stew-
pan from the fire, cover it, and lay some fire on the
cover. This fire is intended to preserve the strength
of the jelly, which otherwise (the steam dropping
from the lid) would become weak. When the jelly

has simmered for an hour on a very slow fire, strain it through a bag. It must be strained several times over to make it quite bright; then put it into the mould, and lay it on ice till it is frozen; send it up like all other jellies. It must be very clear and transparent.

No. 12.—*Madeira Wine Jelly.*

This jelly is made exactly in the same manner as the preceding one. When the jelly is nearly clarified, pour into the same stew-pan a bottle or two of Madeira. As the operation of clarifying takes away the strength of the wine, you must add half a bottle of brandy to it. You must observe that this jelly will keep for several days, and that accordingly what you have left, and what is sent down from table, will be sufficient to supply you with another *entremet* on another day. This is a common jelly, which cooks and *traiteurs* frequently serve; therefore, in order to avoid monotony, you must ornament it with another jelly, which you make as follows.

Take four spoonsful of the wine jelly, break the yolks of four eggs into a stew-pan, beat the eggs with the jelly, and lay it on the fire to thicken; then strain it through a sieve, lay it on ice, and use it for the same purpose; to decorate, as at No. 8.

N. B.—It will sometimes happen that the jellies made of calf's feet, will break, when you turn them upside down into a dish. To prevent this accident, throw in a pinch of isinglass when you are going to clarify the jelly. It gives it a greater substance. This jelly is a monotone, but the sagacity of the cook will in some respects alter this character, for instance, you give this jelly plain, sometimes with grapes in it, sometimes put it in a cylinder mould. When you have turned the jelly, you have some of the same in ice, take a stew-pan cover, chop some of the jelly very fine, and put it all round, sometimes in the middle, and try by your intelligence to supply the deficiency of the art whenever you can.

No. 14.—*Macedoine de Fruit.*

Wine jelly is undoubtedly the clearest, but when you intend to use it for *macedoine,* you should be particular in putting more syrup to it, as raw fruits require abundance of sugar; any fruit is good for *macedoine,* but peaches, apricots, apples, pines, &c. require to be boiled a little in clear syrup before they are used in the jelly. Other fruits, as strawberries, raspberries, grapes, currants, cherries, &c. are put in raw. Proceed as follows:

Have in the first place a good and clear wine jelly, prepared as directed at No. 13; then in summer-time use the fruit of the season; put first a little of the jelly in the mould, which must freeze; then arrange symmetrically a variety of fruits over the jelly, one strawberry, one grain of the grape, a little bit of greengage (fresh or preserved), and so on; then put some jelly to make them adhere together, when that bed is frozen, lay another row of fruit and jelly, till you have filled the mould to the top. Let the jelly freeze till dinner-time, then dip a cloth in hot water and rub the mould all over, turning it in the dish you intend to serve, and send it up. In winter you may likewise make a very handsome *macedoine* with pre-served fruit, as peaches, plumbs, greengages, cher-ries, apricots, pine-apples, &c., and even when you want all these, you may make a very good looking dish with pears and apples cut in different shapes, and coloured with carmine, cochineal, &c. some bits of pears *rosée,* and some yellow, some apples very white, a few bits of greengages, angelica, or cherries in brandy will give it a good appearance, and not prove of indifferent flavour.

To dye the fruit, you must boil it in a very light syrup; when you feel that the fruit is nearly done, you dilute a little *carmine* or *cochineal* in syrup, and put the fruit you mean to have of that colour into it. For the yellow use a little saffron dissolved in the syrup, let the fruit take the colour, then when you wish to make the *macedoine,* drain it very well, and put it symmetrically into the mould. A drop of syrup will tarnish the jelly, and the beauty of a *macedoine* is to be very clear.

FROMAGES Á LA GRACE, or FROMAGES BAVAROIS.

No. 1.—*Fromage d'Abricois.*

It will be necessary to premise, that there is but little difference in the manner of making *fromages*, they only vary in the taste; so that by recurring to this number, it will be impossible ever to commit a mistake.

If in the summer season, take, according to the size of them, eight or twelve ripe apricots; take away the peel and stones: throw the apricots into a mortar, and pound them with a little sugar. When well pounded, rub them through a tammy, and press upon the fruit with a new wooden spoon. Mix a little melted isinglass with this *purée.* Beat a pint of thick cream well, and mix it with the apricots also. Taste whether the cream is sweetened enough. Continue to whip it over ice, till you perceive that the isinglass is well melted and blended with the mixture; then put the *fromage* into a mould, round which you heap a large quantity of ice with salt. If you do not attend particularly to the stirring of it over ice, the apricot will fall to the bottom of the mould, so that when you turn the ice-cream upside down into the dish, it will appear of two colours, and the yellow part will be tough. In winter time take a pot of marmalade of apricots, and rub it into a *purée* through a hair-sieve, mix a little pounded sugar with it, and a little melted isinglass. Then as above, take a pint of thick cream, or more, according to the size of the mould, whip it well, mix it gently over ice with the fruit, and when they are well mixed, put them into the mould, and surround it with ice.

No. 2.—*Fromage of Strawberries.*

Take a pottle of strawberries, make a *purée* of them, put a sufficient quantity of sugar to sweeten it well, and add a little clarified isinglass. Next mix the whole with a pint of whipped cream, and proceed as directed above.

No. 3.—*Fromage of Raspberries.*

The same process as above. Make a *purée* of the raspberries, and whip the cream, &c. as above.

No. 4.—*Fromage of Pine-Apples.*

If you have any pine-apples left, you should mince them and make an infusion in a very little syrup, till they begin to be tender, then take them out of the sugar and pound them very fine in the mortar, add the juice of one lemon, and rub them through a tammy, with a little of the syrup, then whip your cream as before directed. Add the isinglass to it, mix all together, and put it in the mould as you do other cheeses.

No. 5.—*Fromage de Pêche, or Peach-Cheese.*

Proceed as above. Infuse the peaches in a little syrup, when they become tender, drain them; put the kernels in the mortar, which pound very fine; then put the peaches in the sieve; rub them through with the almonds of the peaches, and mix that with the cream as above.

No. 6.—*Fromage with Orange Flowers.*

In this case you must make an infusion. Boil half a pint of cream, into which throw a handful of orange flowers, and let the cream cool. When it is cold, and has acquired the taste of the flowers, strain it through a sieve, and mix it with another pint of thick cream; keep whipping it over ice till the mixture is made thick. Next take some melted isinglass, and mix it

well with some pounded sugar; put the whole with
the cream; keep stirring it over the ice till it acquires
a good substance; then fill the mould, and surround
it with ice.

N.B.—Fromages require but very little isinglass.
They must be very delicate indeed, but, above all,
extremely cold.

No. 7.—*Fromage à la Vanille.*

Here again you must make a decoction. Boil half
a pint of cream; and infuse two sticks of vanilla, cut
into halves; add a little salt and sugar. For the rest
proceed as above, No. 6.

*N.B.—*Vanilla that has served once, may serve a
second time, if you pound the sticks before they are
infused.

No. 8.—*Fromage au Marasquin.*

Whip a pint and a half of rich cream. When it is
quite thick, pour into it two or three glasses of *marasquino,* the juice of a lemon, and a little melted
isinglass. Next put the whole into a mould, and keep
stirring it over ice till the isinglass is well mixed, and
begins to freeze. Then proceed as above.

No. 9.—*Fromage au Chocolat.*

Proceed as above. Melt a quarter of a pound of chocolate that you have previously rasped or pounded; add
a little water to it; when melted, mix with it a little
isinglass and a little sugar; then mix that with whipped
cream, fill the mould and surround it with ice. Do
not neglect to whip it over ice, till you find that the
mixture begins to freeze, then put it into the mould,
and surround it with ice.

No. 10.—*Fromage au Café.*

See *Creams,* for the mode of infusing coffee; only
use one half of the cream for the infusion, which,
when cold, mix with the other half. Beat the whole
on ice, add isinglass, and then fill the mould, &c. &c.

Observation.—The *fromages Bavarois*, made of fruit, deserve the preference over those made with infusions. But in the winter season, for a grand dinner or supper, when a great variety is required, infusions may be recurred to; but in that case, use preserved fruit and sweetmeats of all kinds.

No. 11.—*Marbled Jellies.*

This method of making a jelly will answer the purpose of economy; as for instance, if you have a little orange jelly left, and should have served up on the preceding day a cream *à la Vénitienne*, keep this latter in a very cool place; cut it into unequal pieces, the same as the orange jelly; put the whole into a mould, and shake them together a little. When the pieces are well mixed, pour a little melted orange jelly into the mould; observe that it must be quite cold, or else the composition will become livid; if you pay proper attention, this jelly will be as good as it is pleasing to the eye.

No. 12.—*Marbled Cream au Café.*

When you have prepared the cream as directed above, have a little very brown *caramel* ready; take about half the cream, and add to it a little *caramel,* that it may be of a darker colour than the other half, but it must be of the same substance with respect to isinglass; then take a mould rubbed lightly over inside with oil, which you lean sideways, and put a little white cream into it; when that has acquired a good substance, throw in some of the brown cream, and so on alternately till the mould is quite full. Then cover the mould all over with ice. When you are ready to serve np, rub it with a towel dipped into hot water, the same as you do the *Mosaique.* (See *Jellies*, No. 8.)

No. 13. —*Marbled Cream, White Vanilla and Chocolate.*

Make both creams separately, as directed above. Try whether they are of the same substance, for if one should be thicker than the other, they would separate in the dish. Rub the mould lightly over with oil, give it a sloping direction, and pour a little vanilla cream into it; when that is frozen, turn the mould a little, and put in a little chocolate cream; let that freeze, and go on so alternately, till the mould is entirely full. Next cover the mould with ice. Use the same process for liberating the cream from the mould, as above.

The author closes here the list of creams and *fromages*, although their number is immense. He does not approve of using many odours for perfuming cream or jelly; rose-water, orange-flower water, jessamine-water, violet, tuberose, tea, and all the flowers in the world, may be used; but he does not admit those scents which are generally used for the toilette; if you choose, however, to give any other flavour, it is left to your own discretion.

HOT AND COLD PASTRY.

It will not be amiss to observe in this place, that notwithstanding the immense number of articles of pastry that may be made, you proceed nearly always on the same principle, and with the same paste. It rests with the intelligent practitioner to multiply the arrangements and forms: with regard to the taste, it will always be found to be a compound of butter, flour, sugar, &c. The various sweetmeats that serve for garnishing pastry, most essentially contribute to improve its appearance and savour. However, the puff-paste, which is sent up to table in above a hundred different forms, can be made in one single way only: it may, however, be more or less fine, and thicker or thinner. You may make it finer by using a great deal of butter, but then it has less substance. The author proposes to treat of the different kinds of paste. The baking of pastry requires particular attention. You must be well acquainted with the oven, to be enabled to send up nice pastry. The best prepared paste, if not properly baked, will be good for nothing. He recommends strict attention to these remarks; be also very punctual in observing the effects of the paste, and always use dry flour, as damp flour will spoil every thing.

No. 1.—*Pâte Brisée.*

It is impossible to point out the exact quantity of paste requisite for a pie, as that depends entirely on the size of it. Take two pounds of well sifted and dried flour, spread it on a dresser, make a large hole in the centre, into which put a pinch of salt, three eggs, yolks and whites together, a glass of water, and three-quarters of a pound of fresh butter. Work the butter with the flour till it begins to look like crumbs of bread, then mix the whole together, till it becomes quite malleable; if the paste is too firm, add a little water. Now work it well with your hands, and make it as firm as possible, for if it is not very firm, you will never be able to erect the circumference or flank works of a pie. The author has discovered a method, both easy and expeditious, of erecting these walls (for he will venture to call them so,) in such a manner as that they never tumble or shrink, as is too often the case under the management of many un-skilful pastry cooks.

Take a lump of paste, proportionate to the size of the pie you are to make; mould it in the shape of a sugar-loaf, put it upright on the table, then with the palm of your hand flatten the sides of it; always keep the middle high and upright; when you have equal-ized it all round, and it is quite smooth, squeeze the middle of the point at about half the height of it, and give it the shape of a hat; thus it is kept quite even, and this is executed with so much celerity, that you can make a dozen of them in an hour's time. Now, if you wish to make a cold pie, trim the middle of the paste and all round, with layers of bacon cut of an equal size; lay those layers double all over except on the border, that you may leave room to stick the cover or upper crust on. First put in some *farce* (see *Farce for Pies);* next having boned the game or poultry, season the middle well with salt, pepper, and allspice, and lard the most fleshy parts with slices of bacon highly seasoned; for it is to be observed, that pies taste very insipid, unless they are highly seasoned. Now open the bird by the back, spread it on the table, and put some of the *farce* over the inside: put plenty of salt, and close the bird, &c. to restore it to its former shape; lay it over the *farce.* If you dress more than one, mind that they are all equally filled with the *farce.* Should you wish to put in truffles, mince them, and pound them with the *farce,* and strew the pie equally with whole ones that have been well peeled, yet always as much towards the top as possible, that they may be seen at the opening of the pie. As wealthy individuals never eat any but the upper part of a pie, the author is induced to recommend the *timballe* in preference.

When the pie is quite full, cover it with bacon, the same as you do to trim the sides. Fill all the cavities with butter. Next spread with the roller a lump of paste, of a size somewhat larger than your pie. Use the brush all round. Mind that the top is quite level. Stick the top or cover well over the border, make a hole, like a chimney funnel, in the middle of this top or cover, and stick a piece of paste round it, made in the shape of a stick of sealing-wax. Now cut some blades or leaves of paste, which are to be made as hereafter directed. Place them close to each other round the aperture, without stopping it, and use a little water to make them stick. When you have done with the summit, pinch the bottom part, and the circumference of the upper part; decorate the sides or flanks to the best of your abilities. This, however, being only a matter of theory, it is impossible to enter into an explanation that would require volumes.

N. B.—The *feuilles* (blades, leaves) are made in the following shape ⬦. You must fold

down the point marked ‖, but not lay the leaves too
flat. Glaze the whole with an egg well beaten, and
next bake the pie in an oven that is not very hot.
Four hours are required to bake it: mind to watch its
baking, and if it should acquire too brown a colour,
cover it with paper.

No. 2.—*Cold Pie en Timballe.*

This sort of pie is preferable, in taste as well as in
appearance. The paste is made as under: choose a
stew-pan that will let the pie out easily when baked.
I mean a stew-pan that is not narrower at the opening than at the bottom; butter it well all round, and
spread enough of paste over the dresser with the
rolling-pin to fill the inside of it; then take a smaller
stew-pan, one that can go easily into the other, flour
it to prevent the paste from sticking to it, and put the
paste over the bottom of it. Keep it turned upside
down, then put the large stew-pan over the paste and
turn them both over together. Now take out the
small pan, and with your fingers stick the paste equally all round the large one, observing that you must
leave no air between the paste and the pan. Keep
the paste of an equal thickness. Next trim your
paste with slices of fat bacon, and then put in whatever you mean to make your pie of; whether poultry
or game. Put the breast downwards close to the
bacon, then squeeze some farce into all the cavities
to fill them up. Next put some veal all over the bird
or fowl, seasoning it very highly with salt, pepper,
spices, Cayenne, &c. &c. Then put a few slices of
ham, and fill up the pie, though not quite to the top,
with *farce;* cover the whole with slices of bacon; put
here and there a small bit of butter, and then turn
down the upper part of the paste all round the stew-
pan, laying it equally flat. Roll a bit of paste, the
same circumference as the stew-pan, about the thickness of a finger, rub the paste over with a brush dipped in water, and shut the pie with the round piece,
pressing hard with your hand every where, in order

to stick the two pastes together, then make an air-hole in your pie with the end of a knife, put it into a hottish oven, and when the top is sufficiently colour-ed, cover it with paper. Four hours are required to bake a large pie; a small one of course will take less time.

No. 3.—*To make cold or hot Pies, either of Fowl, or Game, either dressed or in Timballes.*

Timballes possess the peculiar advantage of never breaking in the oven, as the other pies often do, and, above all, the advantage of leaving the best part at the disposal of the eater.

The other way, the best part always remains at the bottom of the pie, and is generally lóst. As you leave the *timballe to cool* in the stew-pan, all the gravy runs downwards, and the fat remains at top. When you serve it, what was at the bottom is then at the top, and of course the best part comes out first.

For either pie or *timballe*, pick and clean properly your game or poultry, and singe them over the flame of the stove, then bone the birds, taking care to injure the skin as little as possible; then open them flat on the table, and season with plenty of salt, pepper, spi-ces, and Cayenne: cut some pieces of bacon (called *lar-dons*), about the thickness of your finger, and a pro-per length for larding; season them well also in the same way, and lard the inside of the birds with them; lard also some veal, as veal must always be used in pies. Pound some *farce* (See *Farce*, No. 15, page 106), with truffles, seasoning it highly; spread some of it over the flesh of the bird, and roll the bird into its original shape. Now proceed in all respects as di-rected above. If it is a *timballe*, put the bird first; and then the *farce* and veal, &c. If a raised pie, put the *farce* first over the bacon, then the veal, and the bird or fowl, as they must be always at the top. Ob-serve, that when you lard your veal and bird, the bacon must be put in symmetrically, so as to appear, when cut, like a draft-board.

Consommé for the inside of the Cold Pie.

Take all the bones and trimmings of the bird and veal, add to them a knuckle of veal, and a calf's foot, and put the whole into a stew-pan, with a bit of ham, an onion stuck with four cloves, a bunch of parsley and green onions, seasoned with thyme, bay-leaf, basil, and a bit of garlic; put with this a glass of white wine and a glass of water, cover the stew-pan hermetically, and set it on a slow fire. When the meat is sweated through, moisten it to the top with boiling water, and let it boil till the meat is done through. Season with salt and pepper, strain it through a silk sieve, and then reduce it almost to a glaze, to put into the pie when you take it out of the oven. Shake the pan to introduce the jelly every where.

No. 4.—Paste for Hot Raised Pies.

For a dish of *entrées*, take a pound of flour, half a pound of butter, three yolks of fresh eggs, and a pinch of salt. Sift the flour on the dresser, through a sieve that you keep for that purpose. Make a hole in the middle of the flour, put the butter, eggs and salt into it, with about a pint of clear water. Work this together in summer. In winter mix the butter first; in summer you may ice the butter, and use iced-water, that the paste may not be too soft. It is no easy matter to give directions in writing, for dressing the pie. After having made the paste with great care, make a ball, spread it on the dresser with the rolling-pin, then put it over a double buttered paper, and proceed to raise it all round, by pressing with your fingers, till you are able to form a round and deep shape, like the inside of a hat, then with two of your fingers press gently all round the bottom, to make a little projecting border; when you have done this equally, decorate it to the best of your ingenuity, line the inside with slices of fat bacon, and fill the pie with remnants of paste cut small, or with some chopped beef-suet; then put on a cover of paste, soldering it well with the border, having first rubbed it over with a brush dipped in water; after you have put on the ornaments, rub the paste lightly over with a brush dipped in *omelette* (called *dorure* or gilding,) and then bake the pie; when done, cut out the cover, empty well the inside, and use it for either pie or *soufflé.* You may sometimes use for these the paste made with hot water, which follows; but that paste is not eatable. It answers, however, just as well, for gentlemen rarely eat the crust.

No. 5.—*Hot Water Paste.*

Throw into an earthen pan as much flour as you want for your quantity of paste. Pour some boiling water into a stew-pan with a large lump of butter and some salt. Lay the whole on the corner of the fire till the butter is entirely melted. As you are to dilute the paste with boiling water, use a wooden spoon to beat it, but mind not to make it too soft: when you have beaten it well with the spoon first, remove it from the earthen pan, work it well on the dresser, and place it for a moment, covered in cloth, before the fire, that you may work it more easily. This paste may make either cold or hot pies, as directed above (See *Pâte Brisée*, page 385.) This paste does not taste so nice as the other, but you may work it with greater facility, and it is not liable to so many accidents.

TRUFFLES.

Be particular in smelling the truffles. Throw away those which have a musky smell; wash them well with a brush in cold water only: when very clean, pick out the larger to be served *à la servitie,* or *au vin de Champaign,* and peel the others very thin; cut them to be put into clarified butter with the *sauté* of either fowls or game; the trimmings are used to give flavour to different *consommés.* When they are used with large *entrées,* they are done with fowl or turkey, &c. in the *poële* or *braize.*

No. 1.—*Truffles, with Champaign Wine.*

After having selected the best truffles, trim a stew-pan with slices of bacon; put the truffles into that stew-pan, with a bunch of parsley and green onions, well seasoned;* moisten with a spoonful of good *consommé,* two glasses of Champaign, some salt and pepper, and if you have a good *poële* from fowls, put in some of it, fat and liquid together; set them to boil gently for one hour; let this cool in the stew-pan. When you wish to serve up, warm them again, and drain them in a very clean towel. Serve them up in a beautiful napkin, so perfectly white that it may contrast as strongly as possible with the black of the truffles.

No. 2.—*Truffles à l'Italienne.*

Wash and trim the truffles as above; cut them in slices about the size of a penny-piece; put them into a *sauté*-pan, with parsley and a little shalot chopped fine, some salt and pepper, and a little butter; put them on the fire, and stir them that they may fry equally; when they are done, which will be in about ten minutes, drain off some of the butter; then put a a little fresh butter, a spoonful of *Espagnole* sauce, the juice of one lemon, a little Cayenne pepper, and serve very hot. This is a relish.

Timballe for Macaroni.

The paste for a hot *timballe* should be a little more delicate than for a cold pie; put therefore more butter into it. Take a pound of flour, a little more than

---

* *Seasoned* means to put to it, thyme, bay-leaves, cloves, sweet basil, &c. &c.

half a pound of butter, two yolks of eggs, and a pinch of salt; work this with half a glass of water, making the paste as smooth as possible; proceed then as follows: butter a plain mould all over well, decorate the bottom a little and the sides, (by using some of the same paste, and adding some pounded sugar, the paste will take a browner colour, and will add to the appearance of the *timballes*,) spread the paste over a dresser, cut a piece of the size of the bottom of the mould (using the mould to measure with,) and cover the bottom of the mould and all the decorations without disturbing them; water the ornamented paste as above; then stick the other paste lightly over, and cut a bit of paste to put all round over the decorated parts; roll a little paste also to stick the whole together round the bottom; then fill the mould with beef-suet chopped fine, and make a cover to it of the same length; put this into the oven for an hour, and when done, empty it for use. It may be used for *macaroni, fricassée, blanquettes* of every kind, &c. &c.

Paste for Tourtes and Tarts.

Take a pound and a half of flour, a pound and a quarter of fresh butter, a large pinch of salt, four yolks of eggs, and half a glass of water. Mix this paste as lightly as possible, without handling it too much; spread it over the dresser with a rolling-pin, and then fold it in three, as you do puff-paste. Roll it out, and fold it up again. Do this four times running; this is what is called four-turned. Use this paste either for *tourte* of *entrées*, or pies of meat or fruit, or when it may be wanted.

Puff-paste.

Take the same quantity of butter as of flour, so that if you use two pounds of the one you must also use two pounds of the other, and so on. Weigh two pounds of very dry flour, and sift it; then lay it on the table, and make a very large hole in the middle; throw in a little pinch of salt, a few few small pieces of butter, and three yolks of eggs: use a little cold water to melt the salt; take water enough to make the paste of the same consistence as the butter. In winter time you must make the paste very firm, because then the butter is so. In summer time you must make the paste very soft on account of the butter being so. The reason why you are obliged to do so is, that if the paste were not made of the same substance as the butter, this latter, when you turn the paste, would break through. When you have worked lightly the flour, mould it into a large ball, which you flatten as quickly as possible; turn it in a spiral direction, and then flatten the middle. Lay butter on the table with a little water, handle it a little to extract the white liquid, and squeeze it in a clean towel, that no moisture may remain. Lay the ball of butter over the paste, flatten the butter with a cloth, then fold the paste over the butter all round, but in a square form, so as to wrap it well all over. Try whether the paste is firm enough to prevent the butter from breaking through it. Now powder a little flour over the table and the paste. Roll the paste as smooth as possible with the rolling-pin, as long as you can; fold it in three, and roll it over once again, taking care always to powder it over with a very little flour, to prevent its sticking to the table or to the rolling-pin. After having spread it well fold it again in three. Make two marks on the top with the rolling-pin, to remember that it has been rolled twice. Then put it into a *plafond* trimmed with a little flour, and place it on the ground to keep it cool, and leave it there for a little while. A moment after put the paste on the dresser, and proceed twice more as before; then let it rest again, and give it two turnings more, which will make six in all. Now give it a long shape, and fold it in two. You may then use it to make a *vol au vent*. When at the latter end, you fold the paste double only, and that is what is called half a turning; of course you are aware that the paste must have had six turnings and a half before you can make a *vol au vent*, and that you must keep the paste thicker than for other small articles of pastry. Cut the *vol au vent* of the size of the dish in which it is to be sent up, and immediately after put it into a *plafond:* brush it over with yolks of eggs, open it all round with the point of a knife, and put it into a very hot oven. Mind that puff-paste always requires the oven to be very hot. If you are not careful to keep the oven shut, the *vol au vent* will not rise properly. When it is well baked, and of a fine colour, and you are certain that it is done through, take it out of the oven, remove the middle, which serve as a cover, empty and throw away the paste of the middle which is not baked, and lay the *vol au vent* cleanly on some paper to extract the butter. When you are ready to serve up, dish the *vol au vent,* and fill it with what-ever you think proper.

With regard to small articles of pastry, spread more puff-paste, and cut it with cutters into different shapes; if intended for *entrées*, brush the paste over with the yolk of eggs, but do not glaze it with sugar. By glazing, is here meant, the sifting of fine pounded sugar over the pastry when baked and emptied, and using over it a red-hot salamander, or else putting it into a very hot oven for the sugar to melt and glaze. The best method of employing the paste will be found at the conclusion of the department devoted to puff-paste, but the immense variety of forms which you may give to this paste, will never alter its flavour, such varieties being only intended for the gratification of the eye; for this reason it is the author's intention merely to direct the reader's attention in this place to the dishes in most common use.

No. 1. — *Tourte à la Frenchipan.*

Spread on the pastry-table a bit of puff-paste trim-ming, about the size of the dish you intend to use, round, square, or oval, as it may happen; then cut a band of puff-paste long enough to turn all round the paste, and about an inch or two wide; moisten with the paste-brush all round the paste, and stick the puff all round the *tourte,* in the middle of which put the *frenchipan,* and bake it of a very good colour. When the paste is done, have some very fine pounded sugar in a silk sieve; sift some over the *tourte,* and pass the red salamander over it to glaze it of a good colour.

No. 2.—*Tourtes des Confitures (Peach, Plum, Apple, Apricot, or otherwise.)*

To make the above *tourte,* if it is with sweetmeat only, proceed as at No. 1; but if it is of peaches, apricots, or apples, you should boil the fruit first in a little syrup, then let them cool in the syrup, and when your paste is ready, drain the fruit through a sieve, and put it in the middle of the *tourte;* bake it as directed at No. 1, and reduce the syrup to pour on the *tourte* when you send it to the table. The *tourte* is a capital *entremet,* when well done.

No. 3.—*Flan des Pommes.*

If you would make a very good and eatable one, have first of all a mould, either in tin or copper-tin, which should be of the usual form of the dishes served for the *entremets;* make a paste as follows: put a pound of fine flour, sifted, on the paste table, make a hole in the middle, and break therein two whole eggs; add a small bit of buttter (say two ounces,) a little sugar, a very little salt, and a drop of water; mix these ingredients very quickly, and spread them on the table about the size of the mould. Butter the mould very well, and put in the paste, and fill the inside of the paste with some apple marmalade, well reduced, but not quite full. Put this in an oven of moderate heat; when the paste is sufficiently done to be taken out of the mould, put the *flan* again, in a baking dish, into the oven, to do the paste thoroughly. It would be better still if you were to bake the paste before you put the apple marmalade into it; when you have garnished first with apples, you cover the whole with some apricot marmalade, and put them again into the oven to finish. Sometimes you should glaze with sugar and the salamander.

No. 4.—*Flan de Pêche.*

Make the paste as above directed; and after having boiled the peaches in a little syrup, put them in the *flan;* when the paste is nearly done, reduce the syrup to pour over the fruit, but take care that the paste is well done. These *flans* are delightful when they are done to perfection. The crust is particularly delicious to eat with the fruit, when it is well done, before the fruit is added.

PASTRY FOR ENTREES.

No. 1.—*Vol au Vent.*

Vol au vent is to be made the same as puff-paste, only you must give in this instance six turns and a half; cut the *vol au vent* according to the shape of your dish, whether round, square, or oval; but it must be cut: *doré* as quick as possible; then mark the opening with the point of your knife, and bake it in a hot oven; when done, open the cover, take out all the crumb, and put it on a clean sheet of paper to drain the butter till dinner-time.

No. 2.—*Vol au Vent for Sultane.*

The same proceeding as above, only glaze this with sugar, as it is to serve for a sweet dish. The *sultane* is some sugar spined in a mould, to put over the aperture of the *vol au vent*, where you have put either apples, or cream, or plumbs, or apricots, &c. &c.

No. 3.—*Petits Patés of all sorts.*

Spread some puff-paste as directed above, about three-eighths of an inch thick; cut out twenty patties with a fluted cutter; rub a baking sheet over with a brush dipped in water, and put each of the patties on it at a distance from each other; *doré* them well, open a hole on the top of them with a small knife, then bake them quickly in the oven; when done, take them out; take off with dexterity the small bit of paste which you must keep for the cover; empty the crumb, put them on a clean sheet of paper, with the small cover on the side of them, and cover them also with paper till dinner-time.

For all other kinds of patties, it is the same process and the same paste; the variety consisting only in the size, and the flavour of the inside.

No..4.—*Small Timballes for all sorts of Entrées, or for Darioles à la Cream of every flavour.*

Butter eighteen *dariole* moulds well; spread some trimmings of puff-paste on the dresser; cut with a cutter a round of paste, large enough to fill the mould; have a bit of paste of the same form as the inside of the mould, but not so large; put the round piece over the latter, let it fall all round, and then introduce this into the mould; press equally every where with your finger, to keep the paste of the same thickness; cut off all the paste that is above the rim, fill the mould with trimmings of paste, and put on a false cover, to prevent the border of the paste from taking a bad colour. A dozen is always sufficient, except when the dishes are very large; bake them of a good colour: when done, empty all the inside, and garnish with whatever you think proper. For patties *au Jus*, fill the inside with *Godiveau*, and bake them with false covers: when done, take off the cover, and open them with a knife, to let in a spoonful of *Espagnole* sauce; then cover them with small covers made of puff-paste, and serve up very hot.

No. 5.—*Dariole à la Cream.*

Trim the mould as above, and put the following mixture into it: take a large spoonful of very dry flour; mix it well with an egg, five yolks, three

spoonsful of fine sugar, a small pinch of salt, eight
mouldsful of cream, two or thee macaroons ground
fine, and some lemon-peel or orange-flower: put a
small bit of butter into each mould, and fill them with
the above preparation; bake them on a baking-dish in
a pretty hot oven. When done, sprinkle a little sugar over them, take them out of the mould, and serve
up very hot. Twelve or fifteen for a dish.

No. 6.—*Ramequins à la Sefton.*

After you have made the pastry for the first and
second course, take the remains of the puff-paste, handle it lightly, spread it out on the dresser, and sprinkle over it some rasped Parmesan cheese; then fold
the paste in three, spread it again, and sprinkle more
cheese over it: give what we call two turns and a
half, and sprinkle it each time with the cheese: cut
about eighteen *ramequins* with a plain round cutter,
and put them into the oven when you send up the
second course; *doré* them the same as the *petits patés*,
and serve very hot on a napkin.

No. 7.—*Common Ramequins.*

Put into a small stew-pan a large glass of water, a
quarter of a pound of fresh butter, and a little salt; let
this boil; when the butter is melted, put to it two or
three spoonsful of fine dry sifted flour; stir with a
wooden spoon till the paste does not stick to the stew-
pan, then take it off the fire: break some eggs, one after
the other, and smell them, to see if they are sweet; mix
them with the paste, and continue adding till you see
the paste has acquired a good consistence; then put in
a spoonful of rasped Parmesan cheese, and a quarter
of a pound of Swiss cheese cut into small dice; mix
the whole gently to avoid breaking the cheese, and
dress the *ramequins* as you do the *petits choux; doré*
as usual, and bake them in a moderate oven, but do
not open the oven till they are nearly done, for that
will make them fall, and they never rise after.

No. 8.—*Cheesecakes.*

Put some curd from the dairy into the mortar, with a bit of very fresh butter, a little salt, a whole egg, and two yolks: rasp the peel of a lemon over some sugar, and put this also into the mortar; add four macaroons, and a bit of sugar: pound the whole together, and when very fine, take it out of the mortar; butter any quantity of tartlet moulds according to your company, spread some puff-paste over the dresser, cut with a round cutter as many pieces as you have moulds, and put a spoonful of the preparation to each; bake next in a pretty hot oven, and serve up very hot with powdered sugar. Sometimes you may glaze them with the salamander.

No. 9.—*French Cheesecakes.*

Take some of the *petit choux* paste, made with water; mix with it some *fromage à la cream*, that has been curdled cold, and then proceed for the rest as above.

PASTRY FOR ENTREMETS.

No. 1.—*Gateaux à la Polonoise.*

Spread about half a pound of puff-paste, to the size of half a sheet of foolscap paper, throw some flour lighty over the dresser, to prevent its sticking to it, and cut directly the paste into squares of two inches and a half: dip the paste brush into the *dorure;** and touch the four corners of the paste and the middle; turn each corner up to the middle, press them together with one finger, and brush them lightly over again with the *dorure;* put them into a very hot oven. You may have twenty-four for an *entremet;* but they must be small. When they are done, sift some pounded sugar over them, and glaze them very bright.

* *Dorure* is an egg beaten up, yolk and white together.

While they are hot, make a little hole in the middle
of the paste, and garnish with apricot or any other
marmalade.

No. 2.—*Puits d'Amour garnished with Jam.*

Spread some puff- paste as directed above, a foot
square, and three eighths of an inch thick. Have
a small cutter, cut about two dozen, brush a
plafond over with a little *dorure,* and put those small
pasties on it, pressing on each of them with your finger: then brush each of them over with the *dorure;*
open the little mark in the centre with a knife, and
bake them quickly in a hot oven. When done, glaze
as above, then take out the crumb in the middle, and
put the pasties on a clean sheet of paper, to draw off
the butter. Garnish with different coloured sweetmeats, as cherry and apricot jam.

No. 3.—*Petites Bouchées garnished.*

Spread some puff-paste as above, and cut it exactly
in the same form, but smaller; but instead of *dorure,*
use only the white of eggs lightly frothed. Pound
some treble-refined sugar very coarse, and sift it.
Spread the coarser part which remains in the sieve
over the pastry, and bake it directly; but the oven
must not be so hot as for the preceding article; push
in the little hollow in the centre, and garnish with
raspberry jam, or cherries.

No. 4.—*Lozenges garnished.*

Spread some paste as above, and cut it in the shape
of lozenges; open a small hole in the middle,
bake and glaze it as the preceding articles, and garnish the same with different coloured sweetmeats.

No. 5.—*Feuillantines Pralinées.*

Spread and cut some puff-paste as above, and brush
it over with white of egg; chop some Jordan almonds

very fine, mix them with some sugar, and spread them over the paste; bake them in an oven not too hot, and serve them without sweetmeats.

No. 6.—*Gateaux à la Manon.*

Spread some very thin puff-paste, on a buttered baking sheet; pour over it equally some apricot marmalade, put some *dorure* all round the edge, and lay over the sweetmeat another very thin paste, which you have rolled lightly round the rolling-pin; then put some *dorure* all over equally, mark with a knife on the surface some lines crossing each other, to cut it when done into long squares thus

; the marks on the squares are made with a knife as ornament, and to prevent bladders of air. Glaze as above, and separate the squares when cold.

No. 7.—*Croques en bouche.*

When you have some remnants of paste, handle them together, and spread it out with the rolling-pin very thin; roll the paste over the rolling-pin, and lay it on a buttered baking sheet; rub this over with white of egg. Spread some coarse sugar equally over it, mark it strongly through with some plain paste cutter, and bake it in a moderate oven. When done, take the shaped part to make the dish. You may cut them sometimes in plain rounds, and at other times hollow out the centre of the circle, making of it a strong ring called *lorgnettes.*

No. 8.—*Feuillantines garnished.*

Cut some puff-paste into pieces of the length of a finger, and about a third of an inch thick. Butter a baking dish, and lay the paste on it sideways, at a distance from each other; put them into the oven without *dorure.* Observe, that when the sides of the paste have spread and acquired consistence, you must glaze with fine sugar, and take them out when done. Then drain them of the butter, by putting them on a sheet of paper, and garnish lightly with sweetmeat.

No. 9.—*Petits Paniers, garnished with Jam.*

Spread some puff-paste on the dresser, about two-eighths of an inch thick, then cut with a cutter of

this shape ; put them into a baking dish,

and give them a good colour with the *dorure;* bake them in a very hot oven, and glaze with sugar; garnish the round part with cherries, and mark the lines on the side of the basket with currant-jelly cut into fillets. Eighteen for a dish.

No. 10.—*Petites Nattes, decorated.*

Spread some puff-paste about an eighth of an inch thick, cut out of it three ribbons, of the same length. Lay one on the dresser, and with your finger put a little *dorure* on the end of another, and stick it to the head of the first; then put the third in the middle by the same process, and plat them, beginning by the two outside ribbons; when platted, put again a little *dorure* to stick them together; *doré* them lightly, and bake them in a hot oven. Glaze with fine sugar, and when done, garnish between the twists with currant-jelly cut into fillets.

No. 11.—*Little Cockades garnished.*

Spread some puff-paste on the dresser, about a quarter of an inch thick, cut it with a large fluted round cutter, about the same as for patties; cut a hole in the middle with a small plain round cutter, then as quickly as possible with your finger turn the paste, so as to put the inside on the baking dish, and the outside above: put them at a great distance from each other on the baking dish, as the pastes spread sideways instead of rising; bake in a hot oven, and glaze of a good colour. When done, they represent exactly a cockade. Garnish with fillets of sweetmeat to form the plaits of the cockade.

No. 12.—*Apricot Cakes trellised.*

Spread some puff-paste over the dresser; trimmings will do for these cakes; spread it equally on a large buttered baking sheet, by using the rolling-pin as above. Spread some apricot marmalade over the paste equally, then cut some more paste long and narrow, roll it about the size of a strong cord, and arrange it crossways like a trellis over the marmalade; put *dorure* over the bars lightly, and lastly, bake in a moderately hot oven. When done, cut it into small oblong squares, and dress them on the dish one above the other.

As there is an immense variety of paste cutters, select your own forms; the paste is always the same. Decorate sometimes with almonds cut into different shapes, and sometimes with almonds coloured with green of spinach. It would be too tedious and minute to attempt even describing the various forms. The ingenuity of the practitioner will supply the ornaments which must always be made of sweetmeat.

BRIOCHE PASTE.

Take fifteen good fresh eggs, four pounds of very dry flour, and two pounds of fresh butter. Lay the flour on the table after you have sifted it. Divide it into four equal parts, take one of them to make the *levain;* make a hole in the centre, and use some yeast that has been well washed. What we call washing the yeast, is pouring some water over it, stirring it, and then letting it stand still. When all the dregs are at the bottom of the vessel, you throw away all the water that is on the top, and take about a large table-spoonful of the sediment which you put into the fourth part of the flour. Then take some hot water, pour it gently over the yeast, and mix the paste directly, in order to avail yourself of its strength. Do not make it too liquid; powder some flour in a little stew-pan, put the yeast paste* into the pan, make slight

* Yeast paste, is what we call *levain.*

slits over the paste: cover the pan, and lay it before the fire; a quarter of an hour after, see whether the yeast has risen; if it has swelled, dilute the *brioche* directly in the following manner:

Make a great hole in the remaining three fourths of the flour, put four small pinches of salt on as many different places, with a good pinch of sugar to correct the bitter taste of the yeast, and a litle water to melt the salt. Then take two pounds of butter, which you break into small pieces with your hand, and put in the middle of the flour: next break the eggs, and smell them successively to ascertain if they are good: mix the whole well together, and then *fraisez* the paste as follows; spread it lengthways on the edge of the table, then with the palms of both hands, press upon it, pushing it by degrees towards the middle of the table; when you have thus worked the whole of the paste, bring it back again towards the edge, and *fraisez* it a second time, again bring it near the edge of the table, and pour the yeast paste all over it; next divide the whole into small pieces, which you shift from one place to another; this operation is to mix the yeast with the paste properly. Now *fraisez* the paste well again twice, and gather the whole up together. Take a large sieve or an earthen pan, in which spread a towel, powder a little flour over the towel, put the paste on it, and cover it with the towel. In summer time remove the paste to a cool place, and in winter time to a warm one. Observe that the paste is better when made on the preceding day, and take care to break the paste several times before you use it; then cut it into equal pieces, and shape them with the palms of your hands; lay these on the less even size; shape off small balls which you turn also with your palms, brush them over with a beaten egg, then make a little hollow, put the small ball into it, brush twice over with the egg, and bake it in a hot oven. If you wish to make a large *brioche*, you must make a very large round well-buttered paper-case; and then mould your paste accordingly. Make a head the same as for the small one, and bake in a hot oven, but not so hot as is used for the small ones, for the larger the articles of the pastries are, the less must be the heat of the oven. The borders of the *brioche*, or pies, &c. would burn before the middle part could hardly be heated. When you perceive that the *brioche* has colour enough, if it should not be thoroughly baked, cover it with paper without losing sight of the colour. This same paste may serve to make all sorts of little *entremets*, such as

Les petites nattes en gateaux de Nanterre;

Les petits pains sucrés. The only difference is, that you must put some coarse sugar over these, and sometimes currants inside.

If you make them of different shapes, you give them different names, and by this means you make a multiplicity of *entremets;* however, you have already a sufficient number of them at your disposal, without introducing many sorts of *brioches*, as they are too nourishing after dinner; but they are very good for balls and routs.

It is easy to make a great number of different dishes with the *brioche* paste, by giving it different forms, and employing different means for the top; sometimes use the *dorure*, sometimes use white of egg, and sometimes coarse sugar spread over without colour; put paper over them to prevent them from taking too much colour. Sometimes you may use milk alone to colour it, sometimes the same paste.

When you have given several forms to the paste, and intend to give them different names, you may likewise change the flavour by using a little saffron dissolved in a glass of *malaga* and sugar: make some of one sort, with half of this paste, and with the remainder add a few black currants, and give to these a different form still; by these means you will obtain a multiplicity of cakes, having all the same original, but possessing different flavours, and different appearances.

Gateau de Compiegne.

The same paste as for *brioches;* only keep it more liquid with some hot milk. Put in a few stoned raisins and currants. This cake is made in a mould well trimmed with butter.

Baba.

Dilute this paste the same as the *brioche*. Take eight grains of saffron, which infuse in a little water, and then pour this water into the paste; add two glasses of Madeira, some currants, raisins, and a little sugar; then make the cakes as you do the *brioches*. You must butter the mould when you put them in; the oven must be moderately hot, as the *babas* must remain a long time in; after one hour you must look at them, and preserve the colour by putting some paper over them.

Brioches au Fromage.

Make this paste as for other *brioches*, only have some Swiss cheese, which you cut into dice, and throw into the paste while it is still liquid. Bake it as you would any other *brioche*.

NOUGAT.

For an *entremet*, cut in dice or in *filets* a pound of sweet almonds, and mix with them six or eight bitter almonds. Before you cut the almonds into dice they should be blanched, in order that the peel may come off. When they are cut equally, dry them in the oven, but keep them white; take three or four spoonsful of superfine pounded sugar, put it over a slow fire in a preserving-pan; when the sugar is melted without having used any water, throw the almonds in, but take care that they are quite dry. Stir the sugar with a clean wooden skewer. If you hear a noise when you throw them into the sugar, it is a sign that they are dry enough. Rub a mould slightly over inside with oil or butter, and lay some almonds in beds as thinly as possible; take an oiled lemon to press the almonds with: but be quick, otherwise the almonds will get cool, and then they can not be worked so thin. The *nougat* requires to be light, to be made to perfection. Sometimes you may make the *nougat* in a mould of the form of a vase, sometimes in small *dariole* moulds, according to your choice; it is always the same thing, but you may cut the almonds of different shapes. These *entremets* will give you at least six or eight varieties, when cut long and square; put them in the oven to soften them again, oil a broomstick and put it into the *nougat* to take the form of it, this you may call *gaufre la nougat*. Again, take some white almonds chopped very fine, and have a green of spinach made as directed in the sauces, then rub the almonds with the green to make them appear like *pistaches; (pistaches* are preferable, if at hand) but almonds are much cheaper and will answer as well; dry them very well, and make some sugar *au cassé*, which you will find explained hereafter. Dip the two extremities of the *nougat* but lightly in the sugar, and afterwards in the green almonds; put this over a clean paper in a dry place. You will find this *entremet* have a very good appearance and an excellent flavour. It may be made sometimes with white almonds, sometimes cut in lozenges and bordered with the green and white, &c.

Sometimes make a pound of almonds into *nougat*, oil a baking dish, and spread the *nougat* over it, oil the rolling pin, and flatten the *nougat* with it; if it will spread easy, put it in the oven again to make it soft; then cut it into small long squares, and keep it in a very dry place, to prevent the *nougat* from sticking to the fingers.

SWEET ENTREMETS AND HOT PASTRY

Dry Meringues.

It is to be observed, that *meringues*, to be well made, require the eggs to be fresh, and that you are not to break them till the very moment you are going to use them. Have some pounded sugar that is quite dry, break the white of the eggs into a clean and very deep pan, break them without loss of time,

till they are very firm, then take as many spoonsful
of sugar as you have whites, and beat them lightly
with the eggs till the whole is well mixed. Observe,
that you are to be very expeditious in making the
meringues, to prevent the sugar from melting in the
eggs. Have some boards thick enough to prevent
the bottom of the *meringues* from getting baked in
the oven. Cut slips of paper two inches broad, on
which place the *meringues* with a spoon; give them
the shape of an egg cut in half, and let them all be of
an equal size: sift some sugar over them, and blow off
the sugar that may have fallen on the paper; next lay
your slips of paper on a board, and bake them in an
oven moderately hot. As soon as they begin to colour remove them from the oven: take each slip of
paper by the two ends, and turn it gently on the table;
take off a little of the middle with a small spoon.
Spread some clean paper on the board, turn the
meringues upside down on that paper, and put them
into the oven, that the crumb or soft part may be
baked and acquire substance. When you have done
this, keep them in a dry place till wanted. When
you send them up to table, fill them with *crême à la
Chantilli,* or with something acid. Remember,
however, that you are not to use articles that are very
sweet, the *meringues* being sweet in themselves.
Mind that the spoon is to be filled with sugar to the
brim, for the sweeter the *meringues* are, the better
and crisper they are; but if, on the contrary, you do
not sugar enough, the *meringues* are tough. The
pink is sometimes made by adding a little carmine
diluted in some of the *apariel,* but the white ones
are preferable; if a clean sheet of paper is put into a
small stock-pot, and the *meringues* also put therein,
and well covered, they will keep for one or two
months as good and crisp as the first day: on which
account, if you have a vacancy for one dish, which
is wanted in haste, it will be found very advantageous
to have them made beforehand.

Meringues au Marasquin au Sucre Chaud.

For a pound of sugar take the whites of ten eggs,

and clarify the sugar as directed in its proper place.
Reduce it almost *au cassé*, then let it cool, while you
beat your eggs well; next put them with the sugar.
When the sugar begins to get cool, mix the eggs well
with it with a wooden spoon; then mix two spoonsful
of *marasquin* with the whole; dress the *meringues*
on some paper as above, and glaze with sugar sifted
over them, before you put them into the oven, which,
by the by, is not to be so hot as for other *meringues*.
As soon as the top gets a substance, take them from
the paper, stick two together, and put them into the
hot closet to dry. Leave the moist part in the middle. These *meringues* belong more particularly to
confectionary, as they are sweeter than any other.

Gimblettes Paste.

The *gimblettes* are introduced next to the *meringues*, because this kind of paste is made with the yolk
of eggs, whereas the whites only are used in making
the *meringues*. It is by his adherence to these principles of economy, that a good cook distinguishes
himself. For eight yolks take two ounces of butter,
half a pound of flour, a pinch of salt, one ounce of
sugar, and a little milk; work the paste with your
hand on the table; add to it a little rasped lemon-peel,
or a little orange-flower. Cut the paste into small
pieces, which roll up the size of your little finger,
and make rings with them: solder them with a little
dorure.* Next rub a baking sheet over with butter,
and lay the *gimblettes* on it. Mind that they are all
of an equal size. Brush them twice over with the
dorure, and bake them in an oven that is but very
moderately hot. This paste undergoes no change
while in the oven; let it get quite dry, for *gimblettes*
require to be made crisp. Sometimes you can twist
them to vary the form. This pastry is sometimes
given by the French ladies to their little dogs; it is
very delicate in flavour, when perfumed with orange-
flower, ranilla, lemon, or otherwise.

---

* Yolks of eggs well beaten.

Clarified Sugar.

Break the sugar in small pieces, weighing each about half a pound; put them into the stew-pan, with clear water, sufficient to dissolve this, add two or three drops of the whites of eggs (a trifle more if the sugar be very dirty), beat the water very well till you find it turn white, then pour it over the sugar, and put the stew-pan on the fire. Let the sugar boil before you skim away the dirt; pour a little more water over the syrup, then skim again, and when very clear, drain it through a clean silk sieve, and use when wanted. This sugar may be reduced so as to spin, but the surest way is to use treble refined sugar, broken small, and put it in a small preserving-pan with a very little clear water; put it over a sharp fire, keep the pan clean all round with a damp rubber, to prevent the sugar taking any colour; when you perceive that the sugar swells in a large globe, have some cold water in a glass; dip your finger very quickly into the water; then in the sugar, and again into the water; if the sugar that has adhered to your finger breaks very crisp, it is ready to spin, let it cool a little, and with a damp cloth wipe the side of the pan to cool the sugar, and prevent its taking too much colour. If you have a little apple-jelly at hand, put a tea-spoon full of it into the sugar: it will improve it wonderfully. This will warm again over a small fire, or at the mouth of the oven.

ROYAL PASTE, DITE AU CHOUX.

This paste is the basis of many sorts of pastry; it is used to make an infinite number of *entremets* of various forms, and of different denominations. The author will, in the first place, explain the manner of making it, and will next briefly enumerate its various appellations.

Take a stew-pan large enough to contain four pints of water; pour half a pint of water into it with a quarter of a pound or a little more of fresh butter, two ounces of sugar, a little salt, and the peel of a lemon;

let the whole boil till the butter is entirely melted.
Then take some very fine dry. flour, and shake it
through a sieve. Take the lemon-peel out with a
ladle, and throw a handful of flour into the preparation while boiling; pay attention, however, not to put
more flour than the liquor can soak up. Stir with a
wooden spoon till the paste can easily be detached
from the stew-pan, and then take it off the fire. Next
break an egg into this paste, and mix it well; then
break a second, which also mix; do not put more
eggs than the paste can absorb, but you must be careful not to make this preparation too liquid. It is almost certain, that about five or six eggs will be wanted for the above quantity; then form them *en choux,*
by which is meant, in the shape of a ball an inch in
circumference. As this paste swells very much, you
must *dress* it accordingly. Abroad, we use the tech-
nical word *coucher,* and we say *coucher les choux,
les biscuits,* &c. but in a foreign country we must as
much as possible adopt the expressions there in common use; I therefore say, *dress,* which is to put the
choux on a baking sheet, at an inch distance from
each other, in order that they may undergo a greater
effect in the oven. Brush them over as usual with
the *dorure,* to which has been added a little milk.
Put them into an oven moderately hot, but do not
open the oven till they are quite baked, otherwise
they would flatten, and all attempts to make them
rise again would be useless: next dry them. Sometimes you may glaze them; at other times you may
send them up without being glazed. To detach them
from the baking sheet, apply the sharp edge of your
knife, and take them off gently. Then make a small
opening on the side, into which put with a tea-spoon
such sweetmeats as you think proper, and send them
up dished *en buisson.*

N.B.—Be cautious to smell every egg before you
use it, for a bad one would spoil them all.

Les Petits Choux Pralinés.

The same paste as above, only when the *choux* are
dressed on the baking sheet and *doré,* sprinkle them

over with some sweet almonds chopped very fine, and mixed with a little pounded sugar. Next turn the sheet down, and powder again with the almonds; then bake and garnish with sweetmeats, as directed above.

Les Gimblettes à la d'Artois.

The same paste as above, with this only difference, that after having *dressed* the *choux* at greater distances, *dorez* them, by dipping your finger into the *dorure*, and then into the middle of each *choux*, pressing on the baking sheet. Turn your finger round a little to widen the hole; do this to every *choux*, and form a small crown; put them into a moderately hot oven, and do not open it till they are done. When they are baked enough, take some very fine pounded sugar, and throw it into a silk sieve. Shake the sieve gently over the *gimblettes*, and put them again into the oven for a moment to dry the sugar, next glaze of a fine colour with the salamander, and introduce sweetmeats, &c. Garnish as before.

Les Gimblettes Pralinés.

The same paste and method as above. Before you put them into the oven powder them over with chopped almonds, and bake them of a good colour: garnish the inside with sweetmeats.

Basket of Petits Choux à la Chantilli.

The same paste again, only in this case make the *choux* very small, rolling them on the paste-board with a little flour; then bake them like all others, but without glazing them. Next have some clarified sugar *au cassé*, stick the point of a small skewer into the *choux*, and dip them one after another into the sugar. Stick all the *choux* together round a buttered mould of the shape of a basket; stick them well together, especially about the top, for it is generally the upper part of the basket that is most liable to break. To make the handles, use the side of a stewpan of the same circumference as the height of the basket, and stick some of the *choux* close to each other to make the handles: next apply the handle to the basket, and stick it on. When ready to send up, pour some cream *à la Chantilli* into the basket, and then serve up. If you pay strict attention, this *entremet* will have a pleasing appearance.

N.B.—You can follow your own taste with regard to the shape you give to the *choux*, and vary the moulds accordingly, either made into baskets, round or oval, vases, &c. &c. Mind always to butter the moulds inside or outside; otherwise the sugar would stick, and the shape would not come out.

Crême à la Chantilli.

Have about a pint and a half of very good thick cream, put it into a cool place. When you want to garnish the pastry, or whatever you want to garnish, take a whip, as used in the kitchen, and whip the cream as quickly as possible. When sufficiently stiff, flavour it to your taste, and add very little sugar, as it will make the cream turn into water; sugar may be added at the table. This must be particularly attended to if you would have the *chantilli* look well, because if sugar is added, it will dissolve in the cream and spoil its appearance and flavour.

Pains à la Duchesse.

The same paste again, with this difference, that you must first make on the paste-board some round balls with the paste, and then roll them lightly as long as your finger; next lay them on the baking sheet, *dorez* them with milk only, and bake them either glazed or not, as you think proper: when done, open them at the bottom, and fill them with sweetmeats.—The number of forms that can be made with this paste is very considerable; but it is impracticable for the learner to undertake so many at once. If you make properly the articles you find here, your own understanding will soon lead you to improvement.

Choux en Biscuits, dits Gateaux à la d'Artois.

Take a pint of thin cream, which boil in a stew-pan large enough to contain four quarts, with a little salt, a little sugar, a pinch of orange-flower *praliné,* and two ounces of fresh butter. When the cream has boiled, skim off the orange-flower. Take some dry flour that has been sifted through a silk sieve, and throw a handful into the boiling cream. If the cream can absorb more, put a little more to dry on the fire, and keep stirring with the wooden spoon till the paste no longer sticks to it. Next take five very fresh eggs, break three of them whole, one after the other, and stir quick: then throw in the yolks only of the other two, but as that is not sufficient to moisten your paste properly, add as much thick cream to it as the paste can imbibe. Do not make this paste too liquid; *dress* the *choux* on a baking sheet, with a spoon; give them the shape of an egg, *dorez* them and put them into the oven. When they are baked, glaze them first with sugar; next use the salamander, and serve up hot.

Pain de la Méque.

The same paste as the above, with this addition only, when they are dressed on the baking dish, of some coarse sugar, and bake them as usual.

N.B.—This method is quite plain, but it can not be altered. You may sometimes stick two together with apricot marmalade between them.

Observation.—When you have succeeded so far as to make the *paté royale* well, it only requires a small share of abilities to produce an infinite variety of *entremets.* You may make a hole on the top, in the middle, and fill it with *créme patissiére* and put it into the oven again. Another time, if you wish to make rocks, or *croquantes,* you manage to frame the doors or apertures, by erecting small *choux* one above another, in the shape of an arch ; *pralinez* them with chopped almonds, made green with the green of spinach, and dried. You may also shape them into sheaves. Make these *choux* very small, but long; then cut the point of one side, and with the sugar *au cassé,* stick one against another round the dish, then stick another course close to the border of the dish, to strengthen the structure, so as to represent water-works. The *choux* are not to be of the same length in this case. With the point of a skewer put a little melted sugar all along the sticks, to stick them together properly. Fill the middle with frothed cream, which has been mixed with a little *marasquino*. If you should have a little sugar left, sprinkle it gently in a buttered mould to cover the cream, like a small *sultane*.

La Cascade à la Chantilli.

Make the *paté* or *choux* as directed at the *paté royale;* when the paste is made rather firm, put some on the pastry table; when you have spread some flour lightly, then roll this paste about eight inches in bulk, and put it in a baking dish, and *doré* with the eggs prepared for that purpose; make sufficient of this to stick round the dish which you mean to serve, let room, however, be left for another row not so long, to come precisely on the border of the inside; try if you have enough to shut close, as you must put cream in the middle. The *choux* should be close to one another; cut the points off one side; dip this in the sugar *au cassé*, then stick these on the dish, and go on all round; when they have all stuck in the dish, fasten them together, by dipping a skewer in the hot sugar, and dropping it between the sticks of paste; when they become solid, put the *chantilli au marasquin*, in the middle, and *spin* the remaining sugar in a little mould to cover the cream.

SAVOY BISCUITS, HOT.

Take a dozen fresh eggs, break them into a vessel, which is to be put into another containing some water nearly boiling. With these eggs mix a pound of superfine pounded sugar. Beat them well in the vessel which stands in the hot water. When you perceive that the eggs are no longer soft, put three quarters of a pound of flour into a silk sieve not very closely woven; mix the flour well with the eggs, which is done by shaking the sieve, then add about two spoonsful of orange-flour water. If you only use lemon, put in a spoonful of cold water. Rub a mould over with butter; powder some sugar round, fill that mould with the preparation, powder some sugar over it, and bake it in an oven moderately hot. Ascertain with a little skewer whether the middle part is sufficiently baked, before you take it out of the oven. If the biscuit is not very large, it will be done in three-quarters of an hour. Biscuits, like other pastries of a large size, require the oven not to be too hot, and therefore they must be kept in a longer time.

Savoy Biscuits, Cold.*

Take a little more than half a pound of very fine dry flour, one pound of very dry pounded sugar, and fourteen or fifteen eggs very fresh; if the eggs are large, fourteen are sufficient. Rasp over the sugar the peel of two lemons or oranges; put that sugar to dry; then have two vessels, one for the whites and one for the yolks; break the eggs one by one, and be particular in smelling them, as one bad one will spoil all; put the dry sugar with the yolks, and work them together with two new wooden spoons, put also the sugar of lemon; next whip the whites very firm, and to prevent them from turning, put a small pinch of calcined alum in powder; when the whites are very firm, take half to mix with the yolks; then put all together, and put the flour into a hair sieve, and sift it over the eggs; mix gently with the whip, then butter a mould, and powder it over with fine sugar; put the biscuit into the mould a little at a time, to prevent the bladders at the top; put some ashes on a baking-dish, and put the mould over this in the oven; the heat must be moderate; about one hour is requisite

---

* These biscuits are more delicate if made with the flour of potatoes: be careful to have the flour very dry, as this circumstance is of primary importance in the perfecting of this paste.

to bake this biscuit, and mind not to move it till it is quite done.

Biscuits in Cases.

Make some small paper cases, and use the same preparation as above. Do not fill the cases too much, and put some coarse sugar over them before you put them into the oven, which must not be too hot.

Biscuits à la Cuillière.

Take a silver spoon, and use the same paste as above. To dress Savoy biscuits, and biscuits à la Cuillière, you must glaze them with fine sugar, and bake them in a very temperate oven.

PASTE FOR TARTS.

Spread on the table two handsful of flour, two spoonsful of pounded sugar, a pinch of salt, an ounce of butter, and a little water to melt the salt. Make a hole in the middle of the flour; break into it two whole eggs besides the yolk of another; mix the paste well, and it will serve you for making tarts, tartlets, and for mounting *croquantes*. Increase the quantity of ingredients, according to the quantity of paste you may have occasion for. This paste is generally used to make the huge pieces; it can be made into all sorts of forms.

Apple Tart with Dry Paste.

Cut some apples in four quarters; peel, and put them into a baking tart dish, with a little lemon-peel; some white pounded or moist sugar; pour a drop of water into the bottom of the dish, and spread the paste, with the rolling-pin on the pastry table. Cut some of it very thin (as directed in the paste for tarts) and with the paste brush moisten it all round; roll the paste round the rolling-pin, and put it equally over the apple and the other paste. Press the paste all round with your finger to make it adhere. Take the dish in your left hand, and with a knife cut off, all round, the superfluity; then, with the back of the knife, make some marks all round the paste, about an inch distant from one another.

Crème Patissière, or Frangipane.

Put into a stew-pan the yolks of six fresh eggs, two spoonsful of fine dry flour, and mix them well with a wooden spoon; dilute this with a pint and a half of boiling cream, and a pinch of salt; turn this over the fire to do the paste. When it begins to boil, take it off the fire to mix it well; then put it on again for about twelve minutes. Melt a quarter of a pound of very fresh butter in a stew-pan, and when properly clarified, add it to the paste, and put the whole into a basin to cool. Next rasp upon a bit of sugar the peel of a lemon (put sugar according to your taste,) and add to it an ounce of bitter macaroons; if the paste is too thick, put to it a spoonful of cream; if too thin, the yolks of two eggs. This cream must take various flavours, as vanilla, orange, coffee, chocolate, &c. &c. but it is always the same cream. When you wish to make a very fine tartlet, mix with this cream some *fromage à la crème.* Put some trimmings of puff-paste into buttered tartlet moulds, and a spoonful of the cream over the paste, and a little star of paste over the middle: bake them in a pretty sharp oven. Glaze with fine sugar, and use the salamander, that the star may be well glazed. This sort of cream is used only for *tourtes,* tartlets, and *darioles.*

Almond Paste.

Take a pound of sweet almonds, blanch them in boiling water; take off the peel, and let them soak in cold water four hours; then pound them well in a mortar; add a little water, to prevent them from turning to oil, after they are very fine and quite in a paste, put in three-quarters of a pound of sugar well pounded, and mix all together in the mortar. If your paste is quite fine, take it out of the mortar, put it into a stew-pan over a slow fire, and stir it with a wooden spoon till it becomes white and dry; then put it again into the mortar, and mix with a little melted gum tragacanth, that has been strained through a towel: take care to keep it covered, to prevent it from drying. You may give what scent you please, as lemon, vanilla, rose, orange, &c. &c. If you use almond paste to make vases, or baskets, or tartlets, keep it always free from dust, spread it on a marble with a rolling-pin as thin as possible, and if you put it into a mould, butter the mould lightly, and give the paste the form of it. Bake in a moderate oven.

N.B. Almond paste should always be kept in a gallipot, covered with a damp towel, to prevent its drying.

Tartlets of Almond Paste.

Butter some tartlet moulds, and after having spread the paste on the dresser, cut it with a cutter to the size of the moulds: put a little sweetmeat in the middle, and a small rosette in the middle of that. Bake in a moderate oven.

Tartlets of Almond Paste with Strawberries.

Spread some almond paste over the pastry table, and cut the paste with a fluted cutter of the same size as other tartlets; butter slightly the moulds, and put them into a moderate oven. When the paste is done almost white, take them out of the mould, and garnish with currant jelly, raspberry, or apricot jam, &c. &c. As the sweetmeats do not go to the oven, they are always of a better colour and taste. In summer time, rub some strawberries through a hair sieve, mix what you have rubbed through with a little sugar and isinglass; put the mixture into ice, and when frozen put a little into each mould.

Tartlets of Jam.

Take some remnants of puff-paste, which spread on the table with the rolling-pin: have some tartlet moulds well buttered; cut some paste with the paste cutter, the same shape as the moulds, lay the paste in each of them, and put a tea-spoonful of aprico marmalade on the paste; then cover your mould with a little cover made as follows:

Take some *pate à l'eau chaude* (see page 390,) have a little board engraved with three little covers of different ornaments, have some coarse muslin, put to it a little fine powder, tie the muslin as if you were going to make a little bag of it, dust the board by shaking the little bag over it, to prevent the paste from sticking to it; lay some of the paste over an engraved part of the board, press with your thumb equally over the paste, then press with the flat side of your knife, and cut off the superfluity of the paste. Take the paste out of the mould with a little damp paste, and moisten the border of the tartlet; stick one of these little covers on each of the tartlets, and bake them without any *dorure;* but when done, glaze them with a little sugar, and use the salamander.

N.B.—You may also make some without covers, but those with covers look better, and the sweetmeats do not dry so much.

Gauffres à la Flamande.

Take a pound of fresh butter, a pound of fine dry flour, and six or seven eggs; first mix the eggs with the butter in a basin, put a little salt, then sift the flour over the eggs and butter, and add to it a spoonful of yeast. Next mix with the above a pint of double cream, work it well with your hand, and put the basin on the dresser till dinner-time. Grease the *Gauffre* mould with bacon fat for the first only, as the others will come out easily without any additional grease. When you serve up, sprinkle some fine sugar over them. If you put the sugar earlier, it will make them soft.

Gateau à la Madeleine.

Take the same weight of flour, sugar, butter, and eggs. In general, eight eggs are enough for an *entremet;* put a little salt and the rasped peel of a lemon; work this paste a little, till you have put all the butter into it. Melt a little butter in a stew-pan, and skim it well; pour a little into each mould, and then drain it, leaving, however, a drop at the bottom to facilitate the coming out of the *gateau.* Sift some ashes over a baking sheet, put the small moulds in it and then put paste into each of them, about half the depth, to give it room to rise. Bake them in a moderate oven. When done, turn them out on a clean sheet of paper, and put them again into the oven for a few minutes. By changing the form of the mould you produce a dish of a different appearance; and by occasionally emptying the inside with the point of a knife, and putting into the cavity either cream or sweetmeats, you make what is called *gateaux à la Madeleine farcies.* The more this paste is worked, the better and the finer will be the *gateau;* in general those sorts of paste require a good deal of labour.

Genévoise Paste.

The same proceeding as above, only add half a glass of brandy, about a quarter of a pound of sweet almonds well pounded, and a few bitter ones, blanched of course: when you have given the flavour you choose, as lemon, *cédrat,* or orange, spread the paste over a baking sheet, and level it equally with your knife; then put it into the oven. When done, use a cutter of what shape you please (as a round, or a star, or any other ornamental form), and cut out as many pieces as you can, and lay them on paper over a baking sheet, dry them in the oven, and let them be coloured on both sides. This paste can make a variety of dishes, differing both in form and colour; but the taste is the same, as sugar always prevails.

White Gimblettes of Genévoise.

Make the same paste as above, only when it is nearly done, take it out of the oven, and brush it over with white of egg, then after spreading over the egg some chopped almonds mixed with sugar, put it into the oven again. When done, take a round cutter, about two inches wide, and cut out as many as you can from the baking sheet; then take a smaller cutter, and cut a piece out of the middle, so as to produce a small wheel (this is what I call a *gimblette.*) Then dry them on paper in the oven, keeping them as white as possible. You may make a pretty casket in the middle, by sticking all the little round *génevoises* with sugar all over the mould, and filling the middle with a *crème à la Chantilly*, or *Caravoise*.

Rose, or Green Gimblettes of Genévoise.

The same as above, only dye the almonds with cochineal or green of spinach, after they have been blanched and chopped, and dried in the hot closet. Use them to diversify the colour; vary also the shape occasionally. You may cut the *genévoise* sometimes in long squares, sometimes in lozenges, sometimes let them remain in their natural yellow colour and border with chopped green almond, stuck with sugar *au cassés*.

Fruit Tart, English manner.

Spread some puff-paste over the table with a rolling-pin; cut a piece of the same size as the dish, and out of the trimmings cut some strips; brush the edge of the dish with *dorure*, and stick the strips on it; then put the fruit into the dish, with some sugar and a little water; roll the paste on the rolling-pin, and lay it over the fruit. Before you put the paste on, brush the strips with some *dorure*, to make it stick. When you have trimmed the dish all round, spread some white of egg over the tart, and sift some sugar over it: then dip the paste-brush into water, and shake it over the tart. Bake it properly, and serve up cold. Apples, however, are an exception, as they are better hot.

You must do all kinds of fruit in the same way: use sometimes the paste for tarts, page 417; but in that case, no strips are absolutely necessary.

THE END.

INDEX.

432